THE AMERICAN EXPRESS POCKET GUIDE TO

FLORENCE AND TUSCANY

Sheila Hale

SIMON AND SCHUSTER

NEW YORK

The Author

Born in New York, Sheila Hale has lived primarily in England and Italy since 1962. Formerly a staff writer for *Vogue*, she still works as a journalist, contributing regularly to several magazines including the *Telegraph Sunday Magazine* and *Harpers & Queen*, especially on the history and culture of northern Italy.

Contributor

Burton Anderson (Tuscan wines)

Acknowledgments

The author and publishers would like to thank the following for their invaluable help and advice: Burton Anderson, Professor Andreis of the Italian Institute of Culture, Lisa Beveridge, Julia Crosse, David Ekserdjian, Caroline Elam, Rosaria Falivene, Pamela Fiori, J. R. Hale, Italian State Tourist Department, Countess Aloisia Rucellai, Stella Rudolph.

Quotations

The author and publishers are grateful to those listed below for their kind permission to reprint the following extracts: Phaidon Press Ltd. (UK and US) for the quotations from *Piero della Francesca* by Sir Kenneth Clark (p127 and p177); Laurence Pollinger Ltd. and the Estate of the late Mrs Frieda Lawrence Ravagli (UK) and Viking Penguin Inc. (US) for the quotation from *Aaron's Rod* by D. H. Lawrence (p46).

Few travel books are without errors, and no guidebook can ever be completely up-to-date, for telephone numbers and opening hours change without warning, and hotels and restaurants come under new management, which can affect standards. While every effort has been made to ensure that all information is accurate at the time of going to press, the publishers will be glad to receive any corrections and suggestions for improvements, which can be incorporated in the next edition. Price information in this book is accurate at the time of going to press, but prices and currency exchange rates do fluctuate. Dollar amounts appearing in this book are at exchange rates in effect in mid-1982.

Editor David Arnold
Executive Editor Hal Robinson
Chief Sub-Editor Susan Chapman
Researcher Catherine Jackson
Editorial assistants Lynne Lynch, Sue McKinstry, Paddy Poynder

Art Editor Eric Drewery
Designer Sarah Jackson
Illustrators Jeremy Ford (David Lewis Artists), Illustra Design Ltd., Illustrated Arts

Editor-in-Chief Susannah Read
Executive Art Editor Douglas Wilson
Production Julian Deeming, Sarah Goodden
Consultant editors Ila Stanger, Maria Shaw (*Travel & Leisure*)

Edited and designed by
Mitchell Beazley International Limited
87–89 Shaftesbury Avenue
London W1V 7AD
© Mitchell Beazley Publishers 1983
All rights reserved including the right of reproduction in whole or in part in any form.
Published by Simon and Schuster
A Division of Gulf & Western Corporation
Simon & Schuster Building
Rockefeller Center
1230 Avenue of the Americas
New York, New York 10020

Library of Congress Cataloging in Publication Data.
Hale, Sheila.
The American Express pocket travel guide to Florence and Tuscany.
(The Simon and Schuster/American Express pocket travel guides)
Includes index.
1. Florence (Italy)—Description—1981—Guide-books. 2. Tuscany (Italy)—Description and travel—Guide-books. I. Title. II. Series.
DG732.H24 914.5′504928 82-3217
ISBN 0–671–45368–8   AACR2

Maps in 4-color by Clyde Surveys Ltd., Maidenhead, England.
Typeset by Vantage Photosetting Co. Ltd., Southampton, England.
Printed and bound in Hong Kong by Mandarin Offset International Ltd.

1983

Contents

How to use this book

The American Express Pocket Guide to Florence and Tuscany is an encyclopedia of travel information, organized in the sections listed on the previous page. There is also a comprehensive **index** and there are full-color **maps** at the end of the book.

For easy reference, all major sections (**Sights and places of interest**, **Hotels**, **Restaurants**) and other sections as far as possible are arranged alphabetically. For the organization of the book as a whole, see *Contents*. For places that do not have separate entries in *Sights and places of interest*, see the *Index*.

Abbreviations

As far as possible only standard abbreviations have been used. These include days of the week and months, points of the compass (N, S, E and W), San, Santa or Santo (S.) Santi or Santissima (SS.), Saint (St), C for century, and measurements.

Bold type

Bold type is used in running text primarily for emphasis, to draw attention to something of special interest or importance. It is also used in this way to pick out places – shops or minor museums, for instance – that do not have full entries of their own. In such cases it is usually followed in brackets by the address, telephone number, and details of opening times.

Cross-references

A special type has been used for cross-references. Whenever a place or section title is printed in sans serif italics (for example *Bargello* or *Basic information*) in the text, this indicates that you can turn to the appropriate heading in the book for further information. For added convenience, the running heads, printed at the top corner of the page, always correspond with these cross-references.

Cross-references always refer either to sections of the book – *Basic information*, *Culture, history and background*, *Planning* – or to individual entries in **Sights and places of interest**, such as *Accademia* or *Uffizi*. Ordinary italics are used to identify sub-sections. For instance: see *Calendar of events* in *Planning*.

How entries are organized

Belvedere *(Forte di Belvedere)* ▥
☎ 287055. Map **3**E4 ✠ Open Tues – Sun 8:30am – 1:30pm, exhibitions 9am – 8pm. Closed Mon. Main entrance from Via del Forte di S. Giorgio.

Crowning the hill of S. Giorgio is the ruthlessly practical Belvedere fortress surrounding its elegant shoe-box-shaped Mannerist palace, both built by Buontalenti in 1590 – 5 for Grand Duke Ferdinand I. The terraces are now used for modern **sculpture exhibitions** ▨ which are only occasionally worthy of a setting commanding some of the most magnificent views of Florence and the surrounding hills and valleys. At the top of the Costa di S. Giorgio is the S. Giorgio gate (c.1260), reduced to about half its original height, embellished with a fresco of the *Madonna and Saints* by Bicci di Lorenzo. The relief carving of St George is a copy of the original now in the *Signoria*.

Floors
To conform with local usage, "first floor" is used throughout the book to refer to the floor above the ground floor, "second floor" to the floor above that, and so on. The floor below the ground floor is the basement.

Map references
Each page of the color maps at the end of the book has a page number (2–16), and each map is divided into a grid of squares, which are identified vertically by letters (A, B, C, D, etc.) and horizontally by numbers (1, 2, 3, 4, etc.). A map reference identifies the page and square in which the street or place can be found – thus **Siena** is located in the square identified as Map **11G6**.

Price categories
Price categories are denoted by the symbols ☐ ❙☐ ❙❙☐ ❙❙❙❙ and ❙❙❙❙ which signify cheap, inexpensive, moderately priced, expensive and very expensive, respectively. In the cases of hotels and restaurants these correspond approximately with the following actual prices, which give a guideline at the time of printing. Although actual prices will inevitably increase, in most cases the relative price category – for example, expensive or cheap – will be likely to remain more or less the same.

Price categories	Corresponding to approximate prices	
	for **hotels** *double room with bath and breakfast; singles are not much cheaper*	for **restaurants** *meal for one with service, tax and house wine*
☐ cheap	under $30	under $8
❙☐ inexpensive	$30–45	$8–10
❙❙☐ moderate	$45–70	$10–20
❙❙❙❙ expensive	$70–145	$20–35
❙❙❙❙ very expensive	over $145	over $35

Bold blue type for entry headings.

Blue italics for address, practical information and symbols, encapsulating standard information and special recommendations. For list of symbols see p6.

Black text for description. Bold type used for emphasis. Sans serif italics used for cross-references to other entries.

Entries for hotels, restaurants, shops, etc. follow the same organization, and are usually printed across a narrow measure.
In hotels, symbols indicating special facilities appear at the end of the entry.

Villa Carlotta
Via Michele di Lando 3, 50125 Firenze ☎ *(055) 220530. Map 2E2* ❙❙☐ *❤ 28* 🛏 *28* 📧 *🚗 🚕* ═ *AE*
Location: Near Porta Romana and Boboli Gardens. On a quiet street lined with privately owned 19thC villas, this *pensione* has been modernized with a rather heavy hand but to a high standard of comfort. The proprietress is German, as are many of the guests.
🏠 ⬆ ♿ 🖂 ⬇ ⛱

5

Key to symbols

- ☎ Telephone
- ⓣ Telex
- ★ Not to be missed
- ☆ Worth a visit
- ✿ Good value (in its class)
- *i* Tourist information
- ⇋ Car parking
- Ⓗ Hotel
- ▬ Simple (hotel)
- ▥ Luxury (hotel)
- ▢ Cheap
- ▯▯ Inexpensive
- ▯▯▯ Moderately priced
- ▯▯▯▯ Expensive
- ▯▯▯▯ Very expensive
- ❧ Number of rooms
- ▭ Rooms with private bathroom
- ▤ Air conditioning
- ▱ Residential terms available
- Ⓐ American Express
- Ⓒ Carte Blanche
- Ⓓ Diners Club
- Ⓜ MasterCard
- Ⓥ Visa
- ▭ Secure garage
- ⇌ Own restaurant
- ▬ Meal obligatory
- ▭ Quiet hotel
- ⬍ Elevator
- ♿ Facilities for the disabled
- ▢ TV in each room
- ▱ Telephone in each room
- ▨ Dogs not allowed
- ✿ Garden on premises

- ⇶ Outstanding views
- ⇌ Swimming pool
- ⬆ Good beach nearby
- ♂ Tennis court(s)
- ✓ Golf course
- ⫘ Riding facilities
- ⤙ Fishing facilities
- ☷ Conference facilities
- Ⓡ Restaurant
- ⬆ Simple (restaurant)
- ⬆ Luxury (restaurant)
- ▭ À la carte available
- ▦ Set (fixed price) menu available
- ▬ Good for wines
- ⬆ Open-air dining available
- ▥ Building of architectural interest
- † Church or Cathedral
- ▣ Entrance free
- ▨ Entrance fee payable
- ▨ Entrance expensive
- ⤳ Photography not permitted
- ⫣ Guided tour available
- ⫦ Guided tour compulsory
- ▬ Cafeteria
- ✱ Special interest for children
- ⚑ Bar
- ◉ Disco
- ◨ Nightclub
- ✿ Casino/gambling
- ♫ Live music
- ⫩ Dancing
- ⇲ Revue

6

Before you go

Documents required

For citizens of the USA, EEC and British Commonwealth, a passport is the only document required for visits not exceeding three months. For longer visits, and for most other nationals, a visa must be obtained in advance in the country of departure. Vaccination certificates are not normally required, but if you are traveling from the Middle East, Far East, South America or Africa, you should check when buying your ticket.

To drive a car in Italy, you need an International Driving Permit, obtainable from the AAA. If you are bringing your car into the country, you must carry the vehicle registration document (logbook) and an insurance certificate or international green card.

Travel and medical insurance

It is advisable to travel with an insurance policy which covers loss of deposits paid to airlines, hotels, and tour operators, and the cost of dealing with emergency requirements, such as special tickets home and extra nights in a hotel, as well as a medical insurance policy.

The IAMAT (International Association for Medical Assistance to Travelers) has a list of English-speaking doctors who will call for a fee, as well as having member hospitals and clinics in Italy. Membership of IAMAT is free.

For information and a directory of doctors and hospitals that are members, write to: IAMAT, Suite 5620, 350 5th Ave., New York, NY 10001.

The nearest American hospital which accepts certain US medical insurance is in Rome. Always consult your own insurance company for advice when going abroad.

Money

The monetary unit is the lira (plural lire). There are coins for 50, 100, 200 and 500 lire, and notes for 500, 1,000, 2,000, 5,000, 10,000, 20,000, 50,000 and 100,000 lire. You may not take more than 200,000 lire in or out of the country without official clearance, but check this amount with your bank before you go. There are no restrictions on other currencies or travelers cheques taken into the country, but if you intend exporting more than 200,000 lire-worth of any currency you should complete form V2 at customs on entry.

Carry cash in small amounts only. Travelers cheques in all strong currencies may be cashed in Italian banks. Eurocheque holders can cash personal checks in most banks. Credit cards are not yet as widely recognized as in some other countries. The principal cards accepted in Florence are American Express, Diners Club, MasterCard, known as Eurocard, and Visa. (Carte Blanche is rarely found.) Outside Florence, you are usually expected to pay cash.

Customs

Any items clearly intended for personal or professional use may be brought into the country free of charge.

In the following list, the figures in brackets are the increased allowances for goods obtained duty and tax paid in the EEC. In all cases the allowances apply only to travelers over 17 years old.

Tobacco   If you are coming from an EEC country, you are

Basic information

allowed 300 cigarettes *or* 150 cigarillos *or* 75 cigars *or* 400g
tobacco. If you are coming from outside Europe, you are
allowed 400 cigarettes *or* 200 cigarillos *or* 100 cigars *or* 500g
tobacco; however, if you are coming from a non-EEC European
country, you are allowed half this amount.

Alcoholic drinks   1(1.5) liters spirits (over 22% alcohol by
volume) *or* 2(3) liters of alcoholic drinks of 22% alcohol or less;
plus 2(4) liters still wines.

Perfume   50g/60cc/2 fl oz (75g/90cc/3 fl oz).

Other goods   You may bring goods to the value of $500 ($200)
from the USA.

When returning, you can export up to 1,000,000 lire's worth
of goods. To export works of art, apply to the Export
Department of the Italian Ministry of Education.

Getting there

By air: The most convenient airport for all destinations in
Tuscany is Pisa. The small airport at Bologna also receives some
European flights. Unfortunately, Florence Airport is too small
to serve overseas aircraft. Passengers from outside Europe will
have to make a transfer stop or fly direct to one of the large
international airports at Milan or Rome. Pan Am, TWA and
Alitalia fly USA–Rome, and the two latter USA–Milan also.
Flight time to Rome from the eastern USA is about 8hr.

By train: The two main trans-European trains to Florence are
the Palatino from Paris (couchettes and sleeping cars only) and
the Italia Express from London stopping at Lille, Strasbourg,
Basel, Milan and Bologna. Both carry first- and second-class
passengers and reservation is obligatory.

By road: The highway (autostrada) connecting Rome-
Florence-Bologna-Milan is the A1. The A12 enters Tuscany
from the N along the coast from France via Genoa, and is linked
by the A11 from Lucca to Florence.

Climate

The weather in Florence is more variable than in most Italian
cities. The temperature ranges from a brisk average of
42°F(5.8°C) in Dec, Jan and Feb to a sticky 77°F(25°C) in late
July and Aug. It can rain at any time of the year but rarely for
prolonged periods in summer. The wettest months are Jan, late
Nov, Oct and Apr, in that order. Winters are much milder on
the Versilia than in Florence.

Clothes

Be sure to pack one comfortable pair of shoes for sightseeing. In
summertime light, loose clothing is essential for comfort. In
spring and autumn bring a sweater or light coat and umbrella.
In winter you will need full protection as it can become cold,
particularly at night.

Florentines are justly famous for their sense of fashion, but
their style is extremely understated. Informal day clothes will
take you virtually anywhere. Italian men do tend to wear ties on
most occasions, but there is no rule about wearing ties in
restaurants. Evening dress is rarely seen these days except in
private houses.

General delivery

Correspondence marked *Fermo Posta* plus the name of the town
and province will be held at the central post office. A small
charge is payable on collection; you must show your passport.

Getting around

From the airport to Florence
At Pisa incoming and departing flights are served by direct
buses to and from the terminal in Florence opposite the station;
the journey takes about 1hr. Taxis are available for the journey
but are expensive.

Public transport
Buses
City and inter-city buses are cheap and efficient. In Florence
the city lines, run by the ATAF bus company, are explained in
the Yellow Pages telephone directory. One ticket is good for up
to 70min of travel. For most buses, tickets must be purchased in
advance from bars or tobacconists, in the form of a *biglietto
semplice* (single ticket) or a *biglietto multiplo* (book of eleven
tickets). There are also new buses which accept exact change
only; these are marked by a hand holding a coin. There are two
main bus companies operating outside Florence.
LAZZI Piazza Stazione 4–6 ☎(055) 294178 (serves Tuscany
and Liguria)
SITA Via Sta Caterina da Siena 15 ☎(055) 211487/214721
(serves most parts of Italy)
Railroad services
The Florence station at Santa Maria Novella is one of the
busiest and best connected in central Italy. The information
office is open from 7am–10pm ☎(055) 278785. There are
stations at or near all the provincial capitals. Fares are quite
reasonable by European standards but they do vary according
to the speed and type of train. Trains are classified as follows.

Super-Rapido: Luxury first-class-only trains running
between the main Italian cities; a special supplement is charged
and seat reservations are obligatory. The Super-Rapido trains
stopping at Florence are the *Settebello* and *Ambrosiano* (Milan,
Bologna, Florence, Rome), and the *Vesuvio*, which continues to
Naples.

Rapido: Fast inter-city trains. Some carry only first-class
coaches; a supplementary charge is made. Seat reservations are
sometimes obligatory and for this too there is an extra charge.

Espresso: Long-distance express trains stopping only at main
stations and carrying both first- and second-class passengers.

Diritto: Trains stopping at most stations; both classes.

Locale: Trains stopping at all stations; both classes.
Taxis
Taxis do not usually respond to being hailed but it is worth
trying. There are stands in most of the main squares of
Florence, and taxis can always be called by telephone. For radio
taxis in Florence ☎4390 or 4798. Extra charges are made for
this service, also for each piece of luggage, for journeys made
between 10pm–7am, and on Sun and public holidays. The
driver is not required to take you outside the city limits; if he
does, the fare increases. It is customary to give the driver a
10% tip.

Getting around by car
Having a car in Tuscany is obviously a great advantage, but be
prepared to cope with Italian driving, which is notoriously
erratic.

International road signs are in use and vehicles drive on the
right; unless signposts indicate otherwise, cars must give way to

traffic coming from the right. It is obligatory to carry a warning triangle (which may be rented at the frontier), to be placed in emergency 55yd (50m) behind the stationary car.

The condition of the roads is variable. Tolls payable on the autostrada (highway) can be a considerable expense, but this is partly compensated for by the high standard of such roads, and the time that can be saved; other roads are, of course, not so consistently good.

Maximum speed limits are 50kph (32mph) in built-up areas, 110kph(70mph) on country roads and 140kph(85mph) on highways. Heavy, on-the-spot fines are strictly enforced for breaking these limits. Gasoline is expensive and visitors can no longer use coupons. Gas stations often close between noon–3pm and after 7pm.

Florence is served by highways in four directions. They are: the A1 running N to Bologna and SE to Rome via Arezzo and Chiusi; the Florence–Siena link which is due to be extended to Rome in the 1980s; and the A11 for Pistoia, Lucca, Pisa and the sea. The stretch of highway, A12, along the coast from Marina di Carrara to Livorno, will eventually be extended to Rome. For traffic information ☎(055) 577777.

It is wise to leave your car outside the historic center of the city you are visiting. Most cities are provided with attended parking lots for this purpose. Many centers are now zoned against traffic; where traffic is allowed it is directed through one-way systems that baffle even the natives.

Members of the AAA may join the ACI (Italian Automobile Club) at a reduced rate; membership entitles them to free assistance in the event of a breakdown.

Renting a car

The major international companies have branches in most cities and airports, and offer various reduced-rate schemes for cars booked in advance and paid for outside Italy. Companies can arrange to have a car waiting for you at your point of arrival. Cars rented from local agencies are often still somewhat cheaper, by up to 25%; these agencies can be traced through hotels or tourist offices.

Basic insurance is normally included in the rental rate with extra cover optional at fixed charges, and some companies require drivers to be over 21. Most firms require a deposit equivalent to the estimated total cost of rental. Value Added Tax (IVA) at 18% will be added to the final bill.

Mopeds

Mopeds can be rented in many towns if you have a driver's license. Ask at the *Azienda Autonoma* for a list of local companies.

Getting around on foot

If walking in Florence or other cities, pedestrians theoretically have precedence over vehicles at uncontrolled zebra crossings – but, in practice, it is safest to wait until there are a few people crossing at the same time.

See *Sports, leisure, ideas for children* for information on walking in the country.

Ferry services

Car and passenger ferries operate regularly between Elba and the mainland.

On-the-spot information

Public holidays
Jan 1; Easter Monday; Liberation Day, Apr 25; Labor Day
(*Festa del Lavoro*), May 1; Assumption of the Virgin
(*Ferragosto*), Aug 15; All Saints Day (*Ognissanti*), Nov 1;
Conception of the Virgin Mary (*Immacolata*), Dec 8; Dec 25
and 26. Shops, banks and offices close on these days. Feast days
in honor of local patron saints are not official bank holidays, but
many shops close in Florence on the Feast of St John the
Baptist, June 24.

Time zones
Italy is 6hr ahead of Eastern Standard Time, and from 7–9hr
ahead of the other time zones in the USA.

Banks and currency exchange
Banks are open Mon–Fri 8:30am–1:20pm, and closed on Sat,
Sun and national holidays. You will be required to show your
passport when cashing travelers cheques. Personal checks may
be cashed by Eurocheque cardholders. Most hotels cash
travelers cheques, but the rate is less favorable than at a bank.
Bureaus de change (*cambio*) are open during office hours.

Shopping and business hours
Shops are normally open 9am–1pm, 3:30 or 4–7 or 7:30pm.
Not all shops close Sun. In winter most shops in Florence close
on Mon morning, except for food stores, which close on Wed
afternoon. In summer some bigger shops close all day Sat, but
remain open on Mon morning.

Post and telephone services
Stamps may be bought from tobacconists (indicated by a 'T'
sign) and hotels as well as at the post office. The central post
office in Florence can be found at Via Pietrapiana 53–55.
   Mailboxes are red and marked *Poste* or *Lettere*; collections
may be erratic outside towns.
   Telegrams can be sent from post offices or over the
telephone; if writing in English it is safest to send the telegram
yourself from a post office.
   Public telephones, to be found in post offices, tobacconists,
bars and at some newsstands, are operated by *gettone* (tokens
obtained from tobacconists and bars but often used as currency)
which must be inserted when the caller answers. Each province
has its own code which must be used if ringing from outside that
province (see *A–Z* entries for codes); the Florence code is 055.
Long-distance calls can be dialed direct from boxes marked
Interurbano.

Public rest rooms
In Florence there are public rest rooms in the basement of the
Palazzo della Signoria, off the courtyard of the Pitti and in the
station. Otherwise, don't rely on them; they hardly exist. Most
of the larger bars have toilets which may be used in exchange for
the price of a coffee. *Signori* means 'men' and *Signore* 'women.'
Leave a tip.

Electric current
Electricity in most places is 220V AC. The standard two-
pronged plugs or adapters can be purchased in most countries.

Laws and regulations
Italy possesses one or two unusual bureaucratic laws. One of the

most important is registering with the police within three days of entering Italy, which then entitles you to stay in Italy for three months; if you are staying at a hotel this will be done for you. There is a strictly enforced requirement that passports should be produced when registering at hotels.

If you are driving do not leave the vehicle registration book or rental agreement in the car; if the car is stolen or towed away the police will not co-operate unless you can produce proof of your right to drive the car.

If you leave your bill behind in a restaurant the waiter may run after you into the street and press it into your hand. This is because a new law requires that each customer leave the premises with evidence that a taxable sum has been paid.

Topless sunbathing is illegal but is nevertheless common in many resorts; if you see topless Italian girls you can assume it is acceptable.

Customs and etiquette

When visiting churches, it is important to remember that they are not museums and it is offensive to interrupt services even in the cause of seeing a major masterpiece. Women may wear trousers but are expected to cover their shoulders.

Tuscans pride themselves on their egalitarian manners. In restaurants and hotels, a friendly handshake and even the clumsiest effort to speak Italian will often work wonders. Children are welcome even in the smartest restaurants; indeed they often get better service than adults.

At times, Italian friendliness can be rather a nuisance, particularly when directed towards women traveling on their own. A firm but courteous rebuff (*Va via, per favore*) is the most effective way of dealing with such attentions, which are generally just playful and rarely sinister.

Tipping

In a restaurant, if service is not included on the bill, leave 15%; if service is included, a small note per person is an adequate supplement. The usher who takes you to your seat in the cinema, theater or opera will expect a tip. If a sacristan or custodian does you any special favor, such as opening parts of a church or museum which are normally closed, you should be more generous. Porters, hairdressers and taxi drivers also expect small tips.

Disabled travelers

Unfortunately, Italian legislation regarding premises for the disabled is not enlightened. Many hotels are located in old buildings not equipped with elevators, but the Italian State Tourist Office (ISTO) publishes an *Annuario Alberghi D'Italia*, which marks suitable hotels for disabled visitors with the wheelchair symbol.

Some major galleries, like the *Uffizi*, are accessible to wheelchairs, but many are not. Remember that marble floors can be hazardous for crutches or calipers, and cobbled streets are not ideal for wheelchairs. Most restaurants are happy to accommodate wheelchairs with advance notice.

For further information and details of tour operators specializing in tours for the handicapped, write to the Travel Information Center, Moss Rehabilitation Hospital, 12th St. and Tabor Rd., Philadelphia, Penn. 19141, or to the Director of Education, Easter Seal Society for Crippled Children and Adults, 2023 W Ogden Ave., Chicago, Illinois 60612.

Local publications
The daily newspaper of Florence is *La Nazione*. The bimonthly magazine *Firenze Oggi/Florence Today*, available free from the *Azienda Autonoma* and many hotels, is written in both Italian and English and contains useful local information.

Addresses and telephone numbers

Tourist information
The *Azienda Autonoma di Turismo*, Via Tornabuoni 15, 50123 Firenze ☎(055) 216544/5, provides city maps and information about special events and opening times in the city. The *Ente Provinciale Turismo*, Via Manzoni 16, 50121 Firenze ☎(055) 678841/2/3, is responsible for providing information about the province of Florence. The other eight provincial capitals, Arezzo, Grosseto, Livorno, Lucca, Massa Carrara, Pisa, Pistoia and Siena, have their own tourist information boards.
Arezzo   Piazza Risorgimento 116 ☎(0575) 20839
Grosseto   Viale Monterosa 206 ☎(0564) 22534
Livorno   Piazza Cavour 6 ☎(0586) 33111
Lucca   Via Vittorio Veneto 40 ☎(0583) 46915
Massa Carrara   Piazza 2 Giugno 14 ☎(0585) 70894
Pisa   Piazza del Duomo ☎(050) 23535
Pistoia   Via 27 Aprile 13 ☎(0573) 21622
Siena   Via di Città 5 ☎(0577) 47051

Renting a cottage or villa
Agriturist, Via del Proconsolo 10, 50123 Firenze, provides information about old houses with character for rent or sale.

Airline companies
Alitalia   Lungarno Acciaioli 10–12, 50123 Firenze ☎(055) 263051/2/3. Reservations ☎(055) 2788.
Via Veneto 9/10, 50047 Prato ☎(0574) 29220/33220
British Airways   Via della Vigna Nuova 36–38, 50123 Firenze ☎(055) 218655
Pan Am   Lungarno Acciaioli 10, 50123 Firenze ☎(055) 282716
TWA   Piazza S. Trinita 1, 50123 Firenze ☎(055) 284691
    Florence's flight terminal is at Piazza Adua. International inquiries ☎(055) 214721; internal inquiries ☎(055) 296102.
Pisa Airport ☎(050) 25188

Automobile organizations
Automobile Club d'Italia (ACI)   Viale Amendola 36, Firenze ☎(055) 27841

Post offices
Central Post Office (Posta Centrale)   Via Pietrapiana 53–55, 50121 Firenze ☎(055) 212305; and at Via Pellicceria, 50123 Firenze ☎(055) 216122

Tour operators in Florence
American Express   c/o Universalturismo, Via Speziali 7, 50123 Firenze ☎(055) 217241
CIT   Via Cerretani 57–59, 50123 Firenze ☎(055) 294306
Wagons Lits/Cook   Piazza Strozzi 14–15, 50123 Firenze ☎(055) 218851

Basic information

Major libraries in Florence

Biblioteca Nazionale Centrale   Piazza Cavalleggeri 1,
☎(055) 287048
British Institute Library   Lungarno Guicciardini 9
☎(055) 263334
Vieusseux Library   Palazzo Strozzi, ☎(055) 215990

Major places of worship in Florence

St James's (American Episcopal Church)   Via Rucellai 9
☎(055) 294417
St Mark's (Church of England)   Via Maggio 16 ☎(055) 294764
Synagogue   Via L.C. Farini 4 ☎(055) 210763

Consulates

Austria   Via dei Servi 9, 50122 Firenze ☎(055) 215352
Belgium   Via dei Conti 4, 50123 Firenze ☎(055) 294276
Denmark   Via dei Servi 13, 50122 Firenze ☎(055) 211007
France   Piazza Sta Trinita 1, 50123 Firenze ☎(055) 213509
Netherlands   Via Cavour 81, 50129 Firenze ☎(055) 475249
Norway   Via Sassetti 4, 50123 Firenze ☎(055) 27621
Spain   Piazza di Salterelli 1, 50122 Firenze ☎(055) 212173
Sweden   Via della Scala 4, 50123 Firenze ☎(055) 296865
Switzerland   Via Tornabuoni 1, 50123 Firenze
☎(055) 216142
UK   Lungarno Corsini 2, 50123 Firenze ☎(055) 284133
USA   Lungarno Amerigo Vespucci 38, 50123 Firenze
☎(055) 298276

Australia, Canada, Germany, Greece, Ireland, Japan, New
Zealand and South Africa are countries not represented in
Florence; for help and information contact the consulate in
Rome.

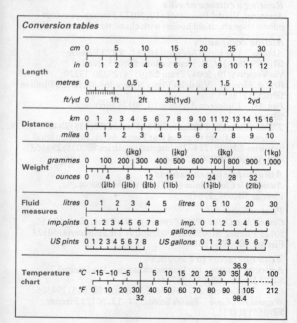

Emergency information

Emergency services

Police ⎫ ☎113.
Ambulance ⎬ You will be asked which service
Fire ⎭ you require.

Hospital casualty departments in Florence

Camerata Via Piazzola 68 ☎(055) 575807
San Giovanni di Dio Borgognissanti 20 ☎(055) 278751
Santa Maria Nuova-Careggi Ponte Nuovo ☎(055) 27741

Other medical emergencies

If your complaint does not warrant an ambulance,
telephone the *guardia medica* (doctor on call)
☎(055) 477891. A list of English-speaking doctors and
dentists is published in *Firenze Oggi*. The police can also be
telephoned on 4977.

Late-night pharmacies

Every *farmacia* (pharmacy) has the late-night roster of
druggists on call displayed in its window. This information
is also published in *La Nazione* or ☎110.

Automobile accidents

— Do not admit liability or incriminate yourself.
— Ask any witness(es) to stay and give a statement.
— Remember to use your warning triangle.
— Exchange names, addresses, car details and insurance
  companies' names and addresses with the other driver(s).
— Report the accident to your insurance company.

Car breakdowns

— Pull to the roadside.
— Put on flashing hazard warning lights and place warning
  triangle 50m(55yd) behind the car.
— ☎116 and tell the operator where you are, with plate
  number and type of car. The ACI will bring assistance.

Lost passport

If you lose your passport you should immediately report the
loss to the police and contact your consulate (see *Consulates
p14*) for emergency travel documents.

Lost travelers cheques

Contact the local police immediately. You must then
contact the issuing bank or company, or the address given by
them, and provide serial numbers and identification in order
to obtain replacements.

Lost property

If you lose anything it may be handed in at the lost property
office ☎(055) 216341. If you do not find it, report the loss
to the local police, as many insurance companies will not
recognize claims without a police report.

Emergency phrases

Help! *Aiuto!*
There has been an accident. *C'è stato un incidente.*
Where is the nearest telephone/hospital? *Dov'è il
telefono/l'ospedale più vicino?*
Call a doctor/ambulance. *Chiamate un
dottore/un'ambulanza.*
Call the police. *Chiamate la polizia.*

Tuscans in Tuscany

Tuscans quite properly regard themselves as the most civilized of Italians. They speak the purest Italian, their culture is the oldest in Italy, and they were responsible for creating the first Renaissance. They will also admit to being the least cosmopolitan of Italians and the most afflicted with *campanilismo*, the Italian word for provincialism which means, in the literal sense, excessive attachment to everything within sight of one's native bell tower.

Florence, the little city which helped to transform Western European civilization and which still possesses many of its supreme artistic achievements, is capital of a region which is predominantly rural. That harmonious trio, the vine, the olive and the cypress, climbs up to the walls of many Tuscan towns and villages and slips into the conversation of the most sophisticated city dwellers.

"They argue endlessly about *language*," observed the French writer Stendhal, who understood the Tuscan character better than most foreigners; "they argue no less about the price of various oils."

The Accademia della Crusca, the academic body which watches over the purity of the Italian language, sees its function in agricultural terms: it exists to sift the wheat from the chaff and its emblem is an agricultural flour sieve. Puccini was in all ways the prototypical Tuscan. His nights were spent composing for the great metropolitan opera houses of the world; but by day, as the guide will tell you if you visit his house at Torre del Lago, it was *la caccia* – the hunt!

Tuscans neither romanticize their countryside nor do they create artificial barriers between city and country. There is no Tuscan tradition of landscape painting or landscape gardening. If you come across an ornamental tree or herbaceous border in a suburban garden, the chances are that it was planted not by a native but by a homesick foreigner, probably English-born.

Two-thirds of mainland Tuscany is hilly, one-fifth mountainous, one-tenth plain. The cultivated land is extraordinarily productive thanks to naturally fertile soil and an abundance of both sunshine and rain. Farming in modern Tuscany is nevertheless not without its problems. Methods have changed drastically in the last 30yr: the white oxen which pulled the ploughs until 10yr ago have been replaced by machines in all but the most remote areas; the feudal *mezzadria* system by which the landowner gave a tenant farmer tools, seed and half the profit in exchange for labor died out in the 1960s and has not yet been satisfactorily replaced. The cost of agricultural labor today makes the wonderful Tuscan olive oil nearly as expensive as the liquid green-gold it resembles. In the industrialized vineyards beyond Pontassieve and above Siena disease-proof concrete vine supports have proliferated like tombstones. Elsewhere, wine growers, suffering the consequences of overproduction, have turned their fields over to easy crops, like tobacco and sunflowers.

Such changes are esthetically regrettable, but they have not fundamentally altered the appearance of a landscape which has been ordered over centuries by collaboration between man and nature. Tuscans have imposed their own character on their countryside: their methods are conservative, enlightened and motivated by a not unnatural desire to make a profit. The result is that the ecological balance remains relatively undisturbed and that Tuscany still looks, as Goethe noticed almost 200yr ago, the way Italy ought to look, and promotes a sense of well-being in most Northern Europeans.

The countryside still shelters a profusion of rare wild flowers, butterflies, birds and indigenous animals. The *macchia*, the dense Mediterranean scrub characteristic of the Tuscan coast, is now officially protected in designated areas, where it acts as a sanctuary for migrating birds, roebuck, deer, partridge and wild boar. In the wild mountains on the Umbrian border you may still sometimes hear the lethal moan of a wolf or the cough of the hoopoe. Some of the noble mountain forests of fir and beech have been maintained by monastic foundations for centuries. Elsewhere the woods are protected by their very utility. The chestnut trees which attain magnificent proportions on the lower mountain slopes produce chestnuts for flour; the beech trees which grow at high altitudes shed mast on which pigs are grazed; pine trees produce pine nuts; and the scented yellow *ginestra* is used to make brooms. In late summer and autumn the forest floor is a treasure trove of luscious mushrooms and white truffles.

Below the surface of this productive landscape is a wealth of minerals, mineral springs and building materials. The soil of Elba contains 150 different minerals and its iron mines produce much of Italy's total requirement. The hills which form a ridge running toward the coast from just below Siena are called the Colline Metallifere after the copper, zinc and lead they contain. Monte Amiata is one of the major sources of mercury in the world, and half a million tons of Carrara marble are quarried each year from the Apuan Alps. Then there are the colored marbles – red from the Maremma, dark green from Prato, yellow from the Montagnola hills W of Siena, which have supplied the festive dressing for many of the great Tuscan churches.

Tuscan towns are made out of the Tuscan countryside. No one town or village or city is like another because the shape, color and texture of each is determined by the contours and building materials of its particular site. Siena is built of burnt-Siena bricks from the clay hummocks to its SE, Cortona is a brown sandstone city, Volterra is honeyed limestone, and Florence is gray-brown *pietra forte* with its interior spaces often marked out by the soft, lead-colored *pietra serena* quarried from the Fiesolan hills.

The peace of mind that so many foreigners from industrialized countries find in Tuscany springs very largely from the fact that Tuscans are still in touch with their own blessed countryside – and with their own glorious past. Hard-working and inventive, they enjoy a higher standard of living than is to be found in many other parts of Italy. If you visit a vital, prosperous, well-kept town like Prato or Cortona, you will certainly not come away with the impression of a backward, dreamy people. But then watch young Tuscans – normally the least flamboyant of Italians – flag-waving perhaps or jousting or playing football in medieval or Renaissance costume on the occasion of their annual historic spectacle: they perform without a single trace of self-consciousness, and then they climb back into their jeans and go off to work at good jobs. None of these spectacles, least of all the Siena Palio, is performed primarily for the sake of tourists. Tuscans are at home within their region, past and present, and this means that they are enviably at ease within their own skins.

Time chart of Tuscan history

8th– 4thC BC	Area called Etruria after the Etruscans, the most ancient of the indigenous Italian tribes, skillful artisans and seafaring tradesmen.
6thC BC	Etruscan civilization reached from Po valley to Bay of Naples; federation of autonomous kingdoms or 'lucomonies' included Arezzo, Cortona, Chiusi, Fiesole, Populonia, Roselle, Vetulonia, Volterra.
351 BC	Etruria annexed by Rome.
3rd– 2ndC BC	Roman roads (the Aurelia, Clodia, Cassia and Flaminia) built across Etruria; Roman colonies included Ansedonia, Fiesole, Roselle and Volterra.
91 BC	Roman citizenship extended to Etruscans, whose cultural identity was gradually absorbed.
570 AD	Etruria occupied by the Lombards, from present-day Germany, whose deputies ruled from Lucca.
774 AD	Etruria annexed to Charlemagne's empire and administered, still from Lucca, by a succession of imperial margraves. The countryside was held by feudal landlords, lay and ecclesiastic; the Benedictine Abbadia S. Salvatore was the most powerful of the religious foundations.
11thC	First crusade opened trade with eastern markets and stimulated religious feeling; city life revived with formation of new class of merchants and artisans. Reforming religious orders founded at Vallombrosa and Camaldoli. Powerful warlords, such as the Guidi, Aldobrandeschi and Malaspina, still held large tracts of country in fee.
1115	Countess Matilda, the last of the Germanic margraves, died, leaving her lands to the Pope. With Papacy and Holy Roman Empire locked in conflict, the nascent Tuscan cities asserted their independence; experimental republican governments were administered from public buildings fortified against the unrepresented majority and jealous feudal landowners, with a magistrate or *podestà*, usually a foreigner, responsible for law and order. The most prosperous early communes were Arezzo, Florence, Pisa, Pistoia and Siena; a strong economy developed based on commerce, especially the cloth trade, and banking.
1125	Florence sacked Fiesole, the first, most violent conquest in gradual takeover of Tuscany.
1215	Tuscan participation in long-standing conflict between Pope and Emperor was sparked off by a feud between the Buondelmonti and Amadei clans, according to legend. In fact, the words 'Guelf' and 'Ghibelline,' for supporters of the Pope and Emperor respectively, were not used by chroniclers for several decades. By 1266 the Guelfs prevailed in Florence, with two main factions named the 'Blacks' and 'Whites.'
1293	The Ordinances of Justice consolidated the political power of the major guilds, excluding from government the feudal landlords.
1338	The chronicler Villani recorded Florence's population as 90,000. It was Europe's richest city. The Palazzo Vecchio, Duomo, and the churches of S. Maria

Novella and S. Croce had been built. Internal politics in the merchant oligarchy were chronically unstable. Dante's comparison of his native city to a sick woman tossing and turning in her bed, searching in any direction for rest and relief, still held.

1343   First of the Florentine bankruptcies after King Edward III of England defaulted on large debts. To reconcile civil factions, a foreigner, Walter of Brienne, Duke of Athens, was granted executive authority, but expelled within the year.

1348   The Black Death killed off more than one-third of the population of Tuscany.

1378   Armed uprising in Florence of the *ciompi*, the lowest-paid employees in the wool industry, seeking guild representation. After initial concessions, the result was a tightening of the merchant oligarchy.

1384   Arezzo fell to Florence which, although at war with Milan and Naples, continued its imperial expansion, gaining Montepulciano (1390), Pisa, the great prize (1406), Cortona (1411) and Livorno (1421). Chroniclers increasingly referred not to Tuscany but to the 'Florentine Empire.'

1434   After a brief exile, Cosimo de' Medici, from a rich business family, became unofficial leader of Florence, initiating a period of unprecedented stability, prosperity and achievement.

1469   Lorenzo the Magnificent, although only 20, was called upon to take charge of the city after the brief reign of Piero, Cosimo's son.

1478   Francesco and Girolamo Pazzi, encouraged by Pope Sixtus IV, made an ill-judged bid for power by plotting the assassination of Lorenzo and his brother Giuliano at High Mass in the Duomo. Giuliano was stabbed to death, Lorenzo escaped. The Pazzi family and its supporters were exiled or executed with the enthusiastic backing of the Florentine public. Sixtus served an interdict on Florence, and excommunicated Lorenzo.

1494   Charles VIII of France invaded Italy, took rebellious Pisa under his protection, and entered Florence. The Medici were expelled, and Florence governed according to a new, broader-based republican constitution supported by Savonarola, Dominican prior of S. Marco and a puritanical preacher.

1498   Savonarola hanged and then burned at the stake in the Piazza Signoria as a heretic, with the connivance of the Borgia Pope, Alexander VI.

1502   The democratic constitution proved an inefficient instrument at a time of unremitting war. After recapturing Pisa, Piero Soderini was elected head of government for life, and members of the old regime began to reappear in key offices.

1503   Leonardo and Michelangelo commissioned to fresco the walls of the council chamber of the republic with representation of past Florentine victories, but neither work has survived.

1512   The Medici were reinstated as leaders of Florence, and their control subsequently fortified by two Medici Popes, Giovanni as Pope Leo X, and Giuliano as Pope Clement VII.

1525	Accademia degli Intronati, the first of the modern literary academies, founded in Siena.
1527	As imperial mercenaries sacked Rome, Florence again expelled the Medici and reinvoked the Savonarolan republican constitution.
1530	Florence beseiged by imperial forces. Alessandro de' Medici installed as head of the defeated republic. The Signoria bell, symbol of republican government, was smashed in public.
1532	Alessandro created first Duke of Florence. First publication of Machiavelli's *The Prince*.
1537	Cosimo I, from a lateral branch of the Medici family, created Duke of Florence, after assassination of Alessandro. He ruled until 1574.
1559	Florentine conquest of Siena and its territories. The concept of Etruria was revived to emphasize the cultural and political unity of Cosimo's enlarged empire.
1563	The Accademia del Disegno, the first fine arts academy in Europe, founded with Cosimo I as patron.
1569	Cosimo I created Grand Duke of Tuscany by Pope Pius V. Of the six grand dukes who succeeded Cosimo, only his grandson, Ferdinand I (reigned 1587–1609), inherited his gift for leadership.
1582	The Accademia della Crusca, a scholarly body responsible for the purity of the Tuscan language, began work on a definitive Italian dictionary.
1589	Galileo demonstrated the first principles of dynamics at Pisa.
1593	The free port of Livorno, established by Cosimo I, was opened to all immigrants.
1610	Galileo discovered the satellites of Jupiter, the 'Medicean Planets,' and was made court mathematician to Cosimo II.
1737	Gian Gastone, the last of the Medici, died without an heir; the Tuscan grand duchy passed to the house of Lorraine, under whose enlightened rule Tuscany became known as a liberal oasis in a Europe otherwise suffering from despotic and inefficient governments. Administrative procedures and religious foundations were reformed and rationalized; agricultural improvements included draining swampy coastal plains and the Valdichiana.
1753	The Accademia dei Georgofili was founded and supported an agricultural economy.
1799– 1814	French occupation interrupted rule of House of Lorraine, now head of Austrian Empire.
1815	Restoration of Ferdinand III of Lorraine, who continued to implement progressive policies. The Congress of Vienna ceded Monte Argentario, Piombino and Elba to Tuscany. Lucca and Massa Carrara were still separate duchies.
1847	Lucca ceded to Tuscany.
1848	Uprisings spearheaded by middle-class radicals. Leopold II retired to Gaeta but was recalled in a year.
1860	Tuscany voted to be annexed to the united Italy emerging from the wars. The following year, a United Kingdom of Italy was officially proclaimed.
1865 –71	Florence capital of Italy. Part of the old city rebuilt as Piazza della Repubblica.

1944   German bombs destroy Por S. Maria, Ponte Santa
        Trinità and Borgo San Jacopo. Outside Florence the
        most severe war damage was inflicted on Grosseto,
        Livorno, Pisa and along the 'Gothic Line' from the
        Versilia through the Mugello into Romagna.
1966   Florence suffered its most severe flood in recorded
        history. The low-lying Santa Croce area was the worst
        affected. Some 1,000 paintings and 500 sculptures
        were damaged or destroyed.

The Renaissance

The first writer to popularize the idea that art was reborn in
central Italy shortly after 1300 was Giorgio Vasari in his *Lives*,
first published in 1550 at the end of the period he was
describing. According to Vasari's anthropomorphic
chronology, each art had its own life cycle: in painting Giotto
was the representative genius of vigorous youth, Masaccio of
early maturity, Michelangelo and Leonardo of perfected prime.
He contended that with these late Renaissance masters, art,
hitherto devoted to reproducing the appearance of the real
world, had triumphed over nature and become its own master.

It was not, however, until the publication of the French
historian Jules Michelet's *La Renaissance* in 1855 that the word
'renaissance' was applied not only to art but to an entire historic
period. Michelet was, in fact, describing 16thC France; but 5yr
later Jacob Burckhardt picked up the term and attached it to the
spirit of Italian history from 1300–1550. And there, dazzlingly
and maddeningly, it has stuck ever since.

The word is out of favor with modern historians. They argue
that all period labels are misleading because history is a
continuum, not a series of neatly packaged 'ages,' and that this
particular label is worse than most because it refers to the
activities of an unrepresentative elite minority.

A common reaction to all clinical historiography of the
Renaissance is rather like that experienced by the character in
E.M. Forster's novel *Where Angels Fear to Tread*. He was
forced to think of a dentist operating among the medieval
towers of a Tuscan hill town, and found it painful and
disgusting to accept "False teeth and laughing gas and the
tilting chair at a place which knew . . . . the Renaissance, all
fighting and beauty!" The Renaissance is a sensitive subject
because it contains the roots of our own civilization; yet we do
need the dentist-historians because it is also one of the most
complex of historic periods.

Fighting and beauty, yes, but also crises within
municipalities, wars between city-states, invasion from
without. Deference to the ideas and achievements of ancient
Rome and Greece set standards which stimulated every form of
thought and practical endeavor. Through the weight of
investment, the technique of business practice, and the
geographical reach of commerce, capitalism emerged in
something very like its modern form.

If to these developments we add transformation in the arts –
music and literature as well as painting, sculpture and
architecture – then we have a revolution. But a revolution
cannot last for 250yr. So we use a label: the Renaissance.
Modified, the label came to describe the outward flow from
Italy: the English Renaissance, the French Renaissance, and so
forth. Inwardly, however, the pulse rate had certainly been set
by Tuscany.

Tuscan architecture

Etruscan

Few non-mortuary buildings survive, but evidence suggests
Etruscan origins for the atrium, the central courtyard of the
Roman house, and a remarkable similarity between the
Etruscan villa type and that of 15thC Florentine palaces. The
Tuscan order was characterized by plain rounded columns and
capitals. Sections of city walls built with huge irregular blocks
remain at Volterra, Cortona and other Tuscan towns. Outside
the walls, rock-cut underground tombs were constructed.

See *Route 4* in *Planning*.

Roman

The Romans, superb engineers, developed the Tuscan arch as a
central structural element – Classical Orders were used mainly
for decoration. They were master town-planners, and the most
complete city remains are at Fiesole, Roselle and Cosa (now
called Ansedonia), one of the earliest and most extensive
colonies, still under excavation. Ruins of patrician villas can be
seen on Elba, Giannutri and near Porto Santo Stefano.

Romanesque *(11th–12thC)*

The most influential single building was the Duomo at Pisa,
with its tiers of open arcades, a mixture of Lombard and
oriental stylistic elements imitated in country churches and at

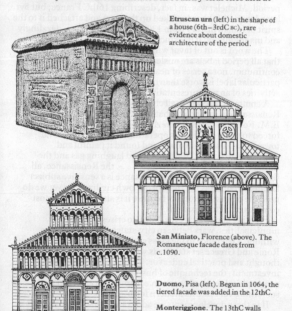

Etruscan urn (left) in the shape of
a house (6th–3rdC BC), rare
evidence about domestic
architecture of the period.

San Miniato, Florence (above). The
Romanesque facade dates from
c.1090.

Duomo, Pisa (left). Begun in 1064, the
tiered facade was added in the 12thC.

Monteriggione. The 13thC walls
(below) were built by the Sienese.

Carrara, Pistoia, Prato and Lucca. Florentine churches – the
Baptistry, Santi Apostoli, San Miniato – remained more strictly
within the Classical tradition; the Collegiata at Empoli marks
the western limit of the Florentine influence. The Benedictine
Abbey of Sant'Antimo, built in local alabaster but in a style
imported from northern Italy, is one of the most incandescently
lovely religious buildings in Italy.

Medieval towns bristled with defence towers; those of San
Gimignano and Monteriggioni are the best preserved.

Gothic (13th–14thC)

Gothic architecture was first introduced into Italy by the
French Cistercians who built San Galgano around 1218. A
native variation of the Burgundian model emerged first in
Florence with the preaching churches of Santa Maria Novella
and Santa Croce, and reached its noblest expression there with
Arnolfo di Cambio's Duomo. The two loveliest Gothic
structures in Florence are the Loggia dei Lanzi and the church
of Orsanmichele, also originally a loggia. Civic buildings
were conceived as fortresses: the Palazzo della Signoria at
Florence is the most imposing of these republican strongholds,
the Palazzo Pubblico at Siena the most graceful.

Renaissance (15thC)

The innovative genius of Brunelleschi (1377–1446) was
nourished first by Florentine Romanesque church architecture,

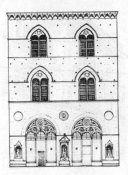

Palazzo Pubblico, Siena.
The most graceful Gothic
civic building in Tuscany,
built from 1297–1342.

Orsanmichele, Florence (above).
The church was built up from a
loggia, enclosed from 1380.

Loggia dei Lanzi, Piazza della
Signoria, Florence (right). Built
from 1376–82.

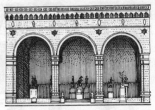

Innocenti loggia, Piazza SS
Annunziata, Florence (below).
Completed in 1426, an inaugural
building of the Renaissance.

later by Byzantine and Classical Roman engineering principles. His Innocenti loggia in Florence is the first building of the Renaissance, and his cupola of the city's Duomo its outstanding engineering achievement. Brunelleschi's genius reached its maturity in Florence with the Pazzi Chapel and Santo Spirito.

Of equal caliber but less influential in the Florence of his own day was the Genoese architect Leon Battista Alberti, whose Rucellai Palace and Chapel are elegant and scholarly restatements of Classical themes, and whose facade of S. M. Novella was later imitated all over Italy.

Michelozzo's Medici Palace in Florence remained the prototype for domestic building in Tuscany until the end of the century; there are fine Renaissance palaces at Pienza and Montepulciano. Perhaps the most magnificent of all Medici villas is Giuliano da Sangallo's symmetrical Poggio a Caiano, with its Classical arcaded basement.

High Renaissance and Mannerist (16thC)

The initiative passed to Rome. Michelangelo's first architectural works, the Laurentian Library and New Sacristy at Florence's San Lorenzo, were Papal commissions, built after he had worked for many years in Rome. His dynamic flouting of Classical order and constructional principles provided inspiration for the later Florentine Mannerist architects, Ammannati and Buontalenti.

Santa Maria Novella, Florence (above).

Rucellai Palace, Florence (above), built from the 1450s.

Medici Riccardi Palace, Florence (left), built from 1444–64.

Villa Medici, Poggio a Caiano (1480–85), Guiliano da Sangallo's adaptation of the antique Roman villa type.

24

The classicizing influence of the Roman High Renaissance style, founded by Bramante, is most evident in Antonio da Sangallo the Elder's domed church of San Biagio at Montepulciano, with a Greek cross plan.

Two 16thC Medici villas near Florence, Artimino and Petraia, were built by Buontalenti for Ferdinand I, and Giuliano di Baccio d'Agnolo's Palazzo Campana at Colle di Val d'Elsa shows Mannerist architecture at its most elegant.

Baroque and Neoclassical (17th–18thC)

The swirling theatricality of the Baroque was created in Rome, but Florence boasts some fine church facades: G. Silvani's San Gaetano is the most beautiful, and Ferdinando Ruggieri's San Firenze the largest and boldest. The master of Italian Baroque, Bernini, added the Chigi Chapel to the Duomo in Siena. Interesting palaces in Florence include the *trompe l'oeil* Cartelloni in Via S. Antonino, the Capponi in Via G. Capponi, and the Corsini on the Lungarno Corsini.

Modern (19th–20thC)

The seafront at Viareggio is lined with splendid Liberty-style hotels, and in Florence the Villino Broggi, Via Scipione Ammirato 99, is another delightful example of Liberty architecture. The 19thC cast-iron arcades of the Mercato Centrale show the use of new materials which culminated in the functionalist Florence Station and Nervi's Stadium.

Laurentian Library steps, San Lorenzo, Florence (left), by Michelangelo (1550s).

San Biagio, Montepulciano (above), designed by Antonio da Sangallo the elder, built 1518–45.

◀ **San Gaetano,** Florence (left), the best Baroque church facade in Florence, built in 1648.

Station, Florence (below). Designed by Nervi and built in 1935, the first functionalist station in Italy.

25

Tuscan sculpture

Etruscan

Etruscan sculpture was broadly Greek-based, but more vigorous and less rational in character. The finest examples in Tuscany are in the Florence Archeological Museum, but exceptional pieces do remain at Chiusi, Cortona and Volterra; and the museum at Grosseto is a beautifully organized introduction to the subject.

See *Route 4* in *Planning*.

Roman

Roman humanism led to a new emphasis on portraiture, and the Uffizi possesses one of the most distinguished collections of Roman busts in the world. The sarcophaghi in the Pisa Camposanto affected the new sculptural art created by the Pisani in the 13th–14thC, and Roman columns and capitals were often incorporated into Romanesque churches.

Romanesque

Romanesque figure sculpture developed relatively late in Tuscany. In Florence the work is mainly decorative, with Classical or Oriental motifs, as illustrated in San Miniato and the Baptistry.

Pisa emerged as the leading center in the late 12thC and produced the first named Tuscan sculptors: Gugliemo, whose ornate style is demonstrated in the decorations of the Pisa Duomo and Baptistry; and Bonanno, famous for the bronze doors of the Pisa Duomo. Followers of the Lombard Master Antelmi worked in Arezzo, the Casentino, Massa Marittima and Volterra. The wealth of Romanesque sculpture at Pistoia includes the more austere and highly individual work of Gruamonte.

The Pisani and the Gothic

Nicola Pisano and his son Giovanni (active 1258–1314) created a realistic and expressive figure style which looks modern even today. Their four famous pulpits in Tuscany are in the Pisa Duomo and the Siena Duomo and in the church of Sant'Andrea at Pistoia. Giovanni also carved the figures for the facade of the Siena Duomo which have now been removed to the Museo dell'Duomo, as well as a *Madonna* in the Pisa Duomo and a *Madonna and Child* in the Prato Duomo. They and their immediate successors, Andrea and Nino Pisano, and Tino da Camaiano, established Pisa and Siena as the most active centers, although Andrea is best known for the first doors of the Florence Baptistry. Tino's works are scattered, but well represented in the Duomos of Pisa and Siena and the Bardini Museum, Florence.

The exquisite relief carvings of another Sienese sculptor, Goro di Gregorio, on the tomb of St Cerbone in the Massa Marittima Duomo, demonstrate the continuing influence of illuminated manuscripts on Gothic sculpture despite the example of the Pisani. The most important Florentine Gothic sculptors were Andrea Orcagna, whose principal works are the relief carvings of the Orsanmichele Tabernacle in Florence, and Nanni di Banco, whose sinuous relief of the *Assumption* over the Porta della Mandorla of the Florence Duomo and the classical *Four Crowned Saints* on the facade of Orsanmichele point gently but firmly toward the dawning Renaissance.

15thC Renaissance

The richest collection of Renaissance sculpture is in the Florence Bargello, where, among many key pieces, are the

Donatello and Verrocchio *Davids*, and works by the Della
Robbias, Desiderio da Settignano, Antonio Pollaiuolo and
Antonio Rossellino, demonstrating the variety of
interpretations of the ideals and proportion of Classical
sculpture. The two best places in Florence to study the
evolution of Florentine sculpture from Gothic to Renaissance
are the exteriors of the Baptistry and Orsanmichele. Lorenzo
Ghiberti's first set of Baptistry doors, on the N, are still late
Gothic; the second set, on the E, are fully of the Renaissance.
Ghiberti is represented on the facade of Orsanmichele, as is the
transitional work of Nanni di Banco. Here, too, is Donatello's
St George predella (c.1418), the earliest known example of
realistic perspective applied to relief carving.

Donatello, who infused feeling and tension into Classical
forms, was the dominant genius of 15thC sculpture. To
appreciate his full range one must visit the Duomo Museum and
the churches of Santa Croce and San Lorenzo as well as the
Bargello.

The greatest master outside Florence was the Sienese Jacopo
della Quercia whose animated works in Siena include the
original carvings from the Fonte Gaia in the Palazzo Pubblico.

16thC Renaissance

The Florentine Michelangelo held that sculpture was the
highest art form, and his work in this medium has an
unprecedented expressive range. Important works at Florence
include his first carvings in the Casa Buonarroti and his last in
the Duomo Museum, as well as the *David* and *Slaves* in the
Accademia and the Medici Tombs in San Lorenzo.

Michelangelo's overpowering genius has caused his
contemporaries and Mannerist successors to be seen in an
unfair light in the eyes of posterity. A recently arranged room in
the Bargello is designed to show his influence on, as well as the
individual talents of, Andrea Sansovino, Vincenzo Rossi,
Vincenzo Danti, Giambologna and, most impressive,
Benvenuto Cellini. Outside Florence, the most exciting works
are Domenico Beccafumi's uncharacteristically restrained eight
bronze angels in the Siena Duomo.

Baroque and Rococo (17th–18thC)

The ivories in Florence's Argenti Museum express all the
inherent fantastication of the Baroque and Rococo spirit, and
Ferdinando Tacca's tomb sculptures in the San Lorenzo
Cappella dei Principi convey its authoritative courtliness.

The greatest Baroque sculpture was created and mostly
remains in Rome, although there are some Berninis in the
Bargello, Florence and the Siena Duomo. The Florentine
Pietro Tacca, sculptor to the grand dukes, produced a number
of notable works including the lovable and much-patted
Porcellino Fountain in the Florence Mercato Nuovo, and the
strange, wicked fountains in Santissima Annunziata. His four
Moors at Livorno are strenuous but empty of meaning. G.B.
Foggini, one of the most prolific Florentine Baroque artists,
both as sculptor and architect, is increasingly admired,
especially for his decorative stucco reliefs in the Carmine and
Santissima Annunziata.

19th–20thC

There is a revival of interest in early 19thC sculptor Lorenzo
Bartolini, whose work has a smoothly accomplished feel. There
are works by Marino Marini in his native Pistoia and at Florence
in the Alberto della Ragione Collection in the Piazza Signoria
and in the new Marini Museum next to the Rucellai Chapel.

Tuscan painting

Etruscan

The only Etruscan painted tombs now in Tuscany are in the
Florence Archeological Museum and at Chiusi.

The Byzantine Manner (12th–13thC)

Each center developed the so-called Byzantine Manner in its
own way, as one can see from the many painted crosses in
Tuscan churches. Panel paintings of other subjects are now
more usually in museums, although Bonaventura Berlinghieri's
St Francis has been left in San Francesco, Pescia. Other Tuscan
masters were Giunta Pisano and the St Martin Master,
represented at the Museo Nazionale at Pisa, Margarito
d'Arezzo, at the Galleria, Arezzo, and Guido da Siena, on show
at the Pinacoteca Nazionale, Siena.

Towards the end of the 13thC iconic stylization began to give
way to the more vigorous monumentality of Cimabue and the
Gothic grace and humanity of the Sienese master Duccio.
Cimabue's famous *Crucifixion* is in the S. Croce Museum,
Florence; he is also represented in the Uffizi and at
S. Domenico, Arezzo, and the mosaics he worked on are in the
Florence Baptistry and Pisa Duomo. Duccio is on show in his
hometown in the Museo dell'Opera Duomo and Pinacoteca
Nazionale, and at S. Francesco in Grosseto and the Uffizi.

Giottesque Realism and the International Gothic (14thC)

At the turn of the 13thC Giotto introduced a new kind of
painting, representing solid forms placed in three-dimensional
space and conveying the humanity of its subjects. His example
determined the course of Florentine painting through the High
Renaissance. His principal works in Florence are in the Bardi
and Peruzzi Chapels of S. Croce and in the Uffizi.

Two schools dominated Tuscan painting: Giottesque
Realism from Florence, and the International Gothic from
Siena. Giotto's successors include Taddeo Gaddi, Bernardo
Daddi, Giottino, Agnolo Gaddi and Spinello Aretino: they
refined his settings, but never quite matched his psychological
power. Two Florentine painters who rejected Giotto's example
and worked within the graceful but two-dimensional Gothic
tradition were Andrea Orcagna and Lorenzo Monaco. In
Florence 14thC painting is best represented in the churches of
S. Croce and S. M. Novella.

The great Tuscan interpreter of the International Gothic was
the Sienese master Simone Martini, whose major works are in
the Palazzo Pubblico and Pinacoteca Nazionale at Siena, the
Museo Nazionale in Pisa, and the Uffizi. Along with the Horne
Museum, Florence, these galleries also house works of the
Sienese Lorenzetti brothers, Pietro and Ambrogio, who
combined elements from both styles.

The Renaissance (15thC)

The astonishing story of Florentine *quattrocento* painting is best
told in the Uffizi, where portable works from the Medici
collections and Tuscan churches are arranged chronologically,
enabling one to follow the various innovations, preoccupations
and influences: perspective, light, anatomy, Neo-Platonic and
Christian symbolism, and the first contact with Flemish
Realism.

Fortunately, more masterpieces have remained outside this
didactic sanctuary than can be listed here. They include, in
Florence, the Carmine Masaccios, the Medici Palace Gozzoli
cycle, the S. Apollonia Castagnos, the S. Marco Angelicos, the

S.M. Novella Uccellos, and the Ghirlandaios in Ognissanti, S.M. Novella and S. Trinità.

The greatest masterpieces outside Florence are the Piero della Francescas at San Francesco, Arezzo, in the little church at Monterchi, and, at Sansepolcro, the *Misericordia* altarpiece and *Resurrection*. Filippo Lippi's outstanding works are the lovely frescoes in the Prato Duomo. The Museo Diocesano in Cortona possesses one major Angelico and a number of Signorellis. There are delightful narrative cycles at San Gimignano by Ghirlandaio in the Collegiata and Gozzoli in San Agostino.

High Renaissance and Mannerist (16thC)

Florence lost its artistic supremacy. The two greatest Tuscan geniuses, Michelangelo and Leonardo, left Tuscany after the first few years of the century. Only one painting by Michelangelo and three by Leonardo remain in Tuscany, all in the Uffizi, where there are also fine works by other 16thC masters including Andrea del Sarto and the early Mannerists.

The disturbing, highly intellectual style later called Mannerism was the last original Florentine contribution to mainstream Italian painting. The leading Tuscan Mannerist painters were Rosso Fiorentino, Pontormo, Bronzino, Salviati, Sodoma, Beccafumi.

The richest collection of 16thC paintings in Tuscany is at Florence in the Pitti's Palatine Gallery, where Cristoforo Allori's ravishing *Judith* sums up many of the achievements of the century, and where masters from other Italian centers compete for attention with Florentines, including Andrea del Sarto, Fra Bartolommeo, and the Mannerists.

At Arezzo, Vasari decorated his own house with allegorical frescoes which have a freshness and charm lacking in his official work. The great Pontormos outside Florence can be seen within a day. They are in S. Michele at Carmignano, at the Certosa Pinacoteca, Galluzzo, and at Poggio a Caiano. The Rossos are farther flung and are to be found at the Galleria, Arezzo, at S. Lorenzo, Sansepolcro; and one of his most stirring works, the *Deposition*, is housed in the Galleria Pittorica at Volterra.

Baroque and Rococo (17th–18thC)

The Baroque, like the Gothic, was a style Florentine artists never embraced wholeheartedly. The most splendid Baroque decorations are in the Pitti Palace, where the first rooms of the Palatine Gallery were frescoed by Pietro da Cortona, and in the ground-floor rooms of the Argenti Museum by A.M. Colonna and Giovanni da S. Giovanni.

The Florentine Rococo painters were not original but cannot be ignored. Their decorations, mainly frescoes, can be seen in many churches, notably San Firenze, the Badia and Ognissanti.

19th–20thC

The Pitti Gallery of Modern Art displays a vast collection of 19thC academic paintings. Several rooms there are devoted to the Tuscan school, known as the 'Macchiaioli' after their Impressionistic 'blotted' paintings, which reacted against the academic style. Also in Florence, the Alberto della Ragione Collection in the Piazza Signoria contains some interesting 20thC figurative pictures by Tuscan artists.

At Livorno, the Museo Civico possesses several works by Modigliani, who was born here, and by the Macchiaioli, for whom the town was a major center. The Futurist Gino Severini was born in Cortona, where a room in the Museo dell'Accademia Etrusca is devoted to his life and work.

Tuscany and literature

The great period of Tuscan literature began prodigiously, with three writers whose words have since been the chief shaping influence on the Italian language. Dante (1265–1321) was hounded out of his native Florence in 1302 into an exile during which he wrote the greatest work in the language, the *Divine Comedy*, a comprehensive vision of this and the next world. He signed himself "Dante Alighieri, a Florentine by birth but not by character," and his love-hate feelings for the beautiful city which ejected him are especially pungent in the first two parts of the poem, *Inferno* and *Purgatorio*. Spiritualized love is represented by the figure of Dante's Beatrice. Laura was the love of Italy's second greatest poet, Petrarch, born in Arezzo in 1304 to a father who had been exiled in the same purge as Dante. A good translation conveys the meticulous delicacy of his vastly influential love sonnets. His close friend Boccaccio, born in Certaldo in 1313, is the third of the 14thC Tuscan triumvirate. The hundred tales of his *Decameron* start with a description of Florence during the Black Death of 1348.

The traveler who has gone to Italy to study the tactile values of Giotto, or the corruption of the Papacy, may return remembering nothing but the blue sky and the men and women who live under it.

E. M. Forster, *A Room with a View* (1908)

The next burst of Tuscan vernacular literary talent came late in the 15thC with the subtle, polished poetry of Pulci, Poliziano and Lorenzo de' Medici; little has been worthily translated. Thereafter it was chiefly in prose that Tuscans of genius expressed themselves. Machiavelli's brief *The Prince* (1513) still retains the incandescence of its conviction that politics is not about morals but about getting things done, and the *Maxims* of his friend Guicciardini (1483–1540) conveys the realistic appraisal of human affairs Tuscans have prided themselves on ever since. *Storia d'Italia*, Guicciardini's account of the wars and crises of 1492–1534, has been called the most important work to have issued from an Italian mind.

The poems of Michelangelo, unusually troubled and ecstatic for the period, offer a balancing vision not only of his work but also of his times, as does the marvelously picaresque and direct self-revelation of Cellini's *Autobiography* (1558).

It was a scientist, Galileo (1564–1642), who was to be the last great writer of Tuscan prose. Since his *Dialogue Concerning the Two Chief World Systems* and *The Two New Sciences*, Tuscany has contributed little to the mainstream of Italian literature apart from two exceptional 20thC Florentine novels: Aldo Palazzeschi's *Sorelle Materassi* (1934), about genteel poverty in a Florentine suburb; and Vasco Pratolini's *Cronache di Poveri Amanti* (1947), a picture of working-class life in Santa Croce.

In the early 19thC Tuscany began to play a different literary role. Florence, the city which had exiled its own greatest geniuses, was now capital of a region which Shelley, in his famous letter to Medwin of 1820, described as the "paradise of exiles." Dostoevsky (1821–81) was one of these literary exiles, but mostly they were British or American, often taking refuge in Tuscany because the living was cheap, the climate healthy and the peace and order of its landscape and depth of its history cast a spell on the foreign imagination.

Many writers discovered in Tuscany their ideal working environment. Mark Twain, working on *Pudd'nhead Wilson* in Settignano in the 1890s, claimed he had written more in four months than he could in two years at home. Henry James pronounced the atmosphere of Florence better for mental concentration than Venice. D.H. Lawrence wrote *Lady Chatterley's Lover* (1928) sitting on the grass outside his villa at Scandicci, inspired, so his friends said, by contact with a sympathetic alien culture. Nathaniel Hawthorne, James Fenimore Cooper and Arnold Bennett all enjoyed productive visits to Florence.

Yet the many foreign poets and novelists who have attempted to write *about* Tuscany have generally failed. Elizabeth Barrett Browning's long verse polemics about the Risorgimento (1847–61) and George Eliot's novel *Romola* (1863) about Renaissance Florence are among the most ambitious and most unreadable efforts. William Dean Howells' *Indian Summer* (1886) is one of the more delightful of novels set in Tuscany; Anatole France's satire *Le Lys Rouge* (1894) is perhaps the sharpest and funniest; E.M. Forster's *Where Angels Fear to Tread* (1905) and *A Room with a View* (1908) are the ones which are still widely read.

Much of this fiction takes place within the foreign community, a large various group of cultivated aliens given to making crucial excursions into a landscape where the senses and intellects of the repressed Northern European may open and flower. Italians, when they appear at all, are often lazy opportunists or forces of nature. Stendhal (1783–1842) was unusual as a foreigner who really did want to understand how Tuscans of all classes lived and thought. The others, even those passionate 'Italophiles' the Brownings, didn't often meet real Italians, and their fictional treatments of Tuscany suffer from what Charles Greville, writing about Florentine society in 1830, described as "no foundation of natives."

The only novelist who turned the Florentine foreign community into the subject of truly great literature was Henry James (1843–1916). James did not wish to be regarded as one of the crowd of 'local' novelists, and disguised or sublimated his source material. Nevertheless, there is something of Florence in most of his Italian novels, and many of his characters are based in whole or part on Florentine acquaintances. *The Aspern Papers* is a notable example – although set in Venice, it was inspired by the story of Jane Clairmont, mother of Byron's daughter Allegra and stepsister of Mary Shelley, who spent her old age in voluntary exile in Florence in possession of many of Shelley's papers. James' concern with the experience of exile and the meeting of cultures gives us perhaps the truest impression of Florence as a paradise of exiles.

Reading list

In addition to books mentioned above, Giorgio Vasari's *Lives of the Painters, Sculptors and Architects* is still the essential basis of all the art history. For reference: Peter and Linda Murray's *A Dictionary of Art and Artists*; J.R. Hale's *A Concise Encyclopedia of the Italian Renaissance*; the Touring Club Italiano guides, *Firenze e Dintorni* and *Toscana*. J.R. Hale's *Florence and the Medici* is the clearest account of how and why the Medici took control; Harold Acton's *The Last Medici* closes the story. Judith Hook's *Siena* is a short account of the history and art. Mary McCarthy's *The Stones of Florence* is a vivid, personal essay. Also recommended: Iris Origo's *The Merchant of Prato*, on Renaissance commerce, *The World of San Bernardino*, on religious life, *War in Val d'Orcia*, on occupation and liberation.

Orientation map

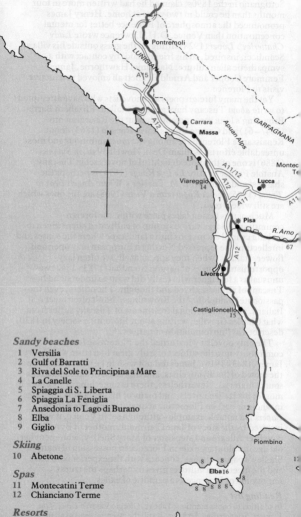

Sandy beaches

1 Versilia
2 Gulf of Barratti
3 Riva del Sole to Principina a Mare
4 La Canelle
5 Spiaggia di S. Liberta
6 Spiaggia La Feniglia
7 Ansedonia to Lago di Burano
8 Elba
9 Giglio

Skiing

10 Abetone

Spas

11 Montecatini Terme
12 Chianciano Terme

Resorts

13 Forte dei Marmi
14 Viareggio
15 Castiglioncello
16 Elba
17 Punta Ala
18 Castiglione della Pescaia
19 Monte Argentario
20 Giglio
21 Ansedonia
✳ Towns of major artistic/scenic interest

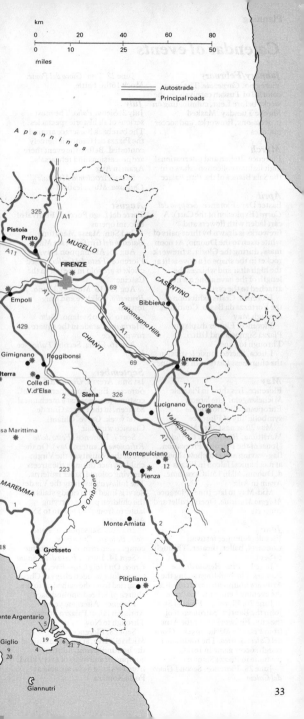

Calendar of events

January/February
Viareggio. *Carnevale*. The most colorful of Tuscan carnivals, in the weeks before Lent, culminating on Shrove Tuesday. Masked processions, fireworks, and soccer matches

March
Florence. Italian and international high fashion collections shown in the Sala Bianca of the Pitti Palace

April
Easter Day. Florence. *Scoppio del Carro* (Explosion of the Cart). A cart laden with flowers and fireworks is drawn by three pairs of white oxen to the Duomo. At noon mass, during the Gloria, a firework rocket in the shape of a dove is lit at the high altar and whizzes the length of the nave along a wire attached to the cart

Florence. Crafts exhibition at the Fortezza da Basso. Continues through May

Florence. Flower display in Piazza Signoria and Uffizi. Through to June

Lucca. Sacred music festival in the churches. Lasts until late June

May
Florence. Iris show in Piazzale Michelangelo. The largest European collection of the symbolic 'lily of Florence'

May 20 or next Sun. Massa Marittima. *Balestro del Girifalco* (Joust of the Falcon). Procession, flag-waving and crossbow shooting at mechanical falcon in Piazza d. Duomo, all in 15thC costume. Again in Aug

Mid-May to late June. Florence. *Maggio Musicale*. Opera, ballet and concerts

June
Fiesole. Summer festival. Concerts, ballet, theater. Through to Sept

June 17. Pisa. *Regata di San Ranieri*. The buildings facing the Arno are illuminated with torches the evening before the boat race

June 24. Florence. Feast of St John the Baptist, patron saint of the city. Fireworks over the Arno from Piazzale Michelangelo. *Gioco del Calcio Storico*. The traditional rough soccer game in 16thC costume in Piazza Signoria

June 28. Florence. Second *Gioco del Calcio*

June 28. Pisa. *Gioco del Ponte*. Mock 16thC battle

July
July 2. Siena. *Palio*. The most serious of all historic spectacles. The bareback horserace around the Piazza del Campo is fiercely contested. Before the event there are processions and rehearsals. Again in Aug

Siena. *Accademia Musicale Chigiana*. Music festival

August
Torre del Lago Puccini. Festival of Puccini operas

2nd Sun. Massa Marittima. *Balestro del Girifalco* (see May)

Aug 15, Assumption Day. Florence. *Festa del Grillo*. Caged crickets are sold in the fair in the Cascine

Aug 15–16. Montepulciano. *Il Bruscello*. Folklore and song festival

Porto Santo Stefano. *Palio Marinaro*. Parade in the square and rowing race

Aug 16. Siena. Second *Palio* (see July)

September
1st Sun. Arezzo. *Giostra del Saracino*. Eight horsemen in 13thC costume joust against a mechanical Saracen, in the Piazza Grande

1st week. Greve. Chianti Classico wine fair

Sept 7. Florence. *Festa delle Rificolone* (Lantern Day). On the eve of the Nativity of the Virgin children race through the streets carrying colored paper lanterns. The following evening the Via dei Servi is lined with candy stalls and the children parade carrying lanterns from the Duomo to SS. Annunziata

2nd Sun. Sansepolcro. *Palio della Balestra*. Crossbow competition in medieval costume

Sept 14. Lucca. *Festa della Santa Croce*. On Holy Cross Eve, a miraculous wooden effigy of Christ is carried from the cathedral to the church of S. Frediano and back

Florence. Alternate years. Antiques fair at Palazzo Strozzi. Through to Nov

Sept 28. Florence. On St Michael's Eve, at the beginning of the hunting season, hunting equipment and birds of every kind, from hawks to owls, are sold at Porta Romana

October
Prato. Season opens at Teatro Metastasio. The home company is one of the liveliest experimental theater groups in Italy. Until April

Florence. Winter fashion collections shown in Pitti

Mid-Oct. Impruneta. Agricultural fair of St Luke

Last Sun. Montalcino. *Sagra del Tordo.* Traditional shooting and eating of thrushes

November
Florence. Opening of main concert season at Teatro Comunale. Through to mid-Dec

December
Florence. Opening of opera season at Teatro Comunale. Through to mid-Jan

See also *Public holidays* in *Basic information.*

When and where to go

May and Sept are the ideal months to visit Florence; cool enough for vigorous sightseeing, summery enough for leisurely day trips into the hills. The countryside in May is radiant with wildflowers, scented with blossoms and young grasses. For the grand tourists of the 18th and 19thC, Sept was the start of the Florence season, and a very sensible time it still is, a little warmer and drier than May, and less crowded than Aug, which is in every way the most uncomfortable month.

In fact, those who do not wish to share their vacation with what seems like half the world should avoid Florence, a city ill-suited to mass tourism, in the week before and including Easter and from June through to the end of Aug. Overcrowding, as regular visitors know, can render the narrow medieval streets barely tolerable. However, if you must go in the high season, be sure to book a hotel in advance.

Whatever the season, the day will come when Florence seems too much: too much art, too much noise in the narrow streets, a stony maze from which one longs to escape. This is the day to go to Siena, gently dreaming on its landlocked hills, or to Lucca, proud and independent in its star of intact fortifications, the two most likeable provincial capitals.

Pisa should be visited for its churches and pictures as well as for the famous Duomo complex. There is pre-Renaissance sculpture in Pisa, Prato and Pistoia, and Renaissance churches in Prato and near Cortona and Montepulciano as fine and important as anything in Florence. The Renaissance paintings which stir the modern soul most profoundly are the Piero della Francescas in and near Arezzo.

Then there are the smaller hill towns, each with its own distinctive shape and character: San Gimignano still bristling with medieval watchtowers; windy Volterra; Romanesque-Gothic Massa Marittima; Pienza and Montepulciano like miniature Renaissance cities. In fact, there is hardly a town or village in Tuscany that is not worth visiting.

The Tuscan countryside is as elusive to the would-be categorizer as it is inspiring to native and visitor alike. Geographically there is no such thing as one Tuscany. Each of the valleys, mountains, plains and stretches of coast has its own beauty, and, as often as not, its own micro-climate. The best-laid plan for visiting Tuscany is the one that leaves room for spontaneous exploration and personal discovery.

Area planners and tours

Historically, Tuscany has been dominated by Florence since the late Middle Ages, but the region's constituent areas have in no way surrendered their individuality to their presiding sovereign. The names of these areas can often baffle foreigners because they have no administrative significance and no precisely defined geographical boundaries. For Tuscans they sum up everything, from the climate and landscape to the character of the native population and the local food and wine. Six of the most enticing are described here.

The Casentino The remote upper valley of the Arno, to the N of Arezzo, enclosed by wooded mountains. The magnificent specimen forests of beech, fir and chestnut, and the green pastures where white oxen can still occasionally be seen, are loveliest in spring and remain cool even in high summer. The monastic sanctuaries of Camaldoli and La Verna are good bases for walking, picnicking, and gathering wild strawberries and mushrooms. Hotels are few and simple.

The Chianti The heart of Tuscany and the landscape that matches many people's ideal of the way Italy ought to look. The area that originally gave its name to the wine has expanded over the centuries to include everywhere the wine is produced, which is now from a little to the N of Florence down to Siena. May is the best time, but in high summer, when Florence is hot and full of tourists and the Tuscan coast is crowded with Florentines, there is much to be said for basing a vacation on the Chianti. Alternatively, you could spend a long winter weekend riding or walking along the Etruscan roads which crest the hills, tasting and shopping for wine. The best of the hotels have character as well as swimming pools.

The Garfagnana The landscape of the upper valley of the fast-flowing Serchio and the valleys of its tributaries is one of the most fascinating in Tuscany for the variety of climate and vegetation. The chilly marble peaks of the Apuan Alps contrast with the lower slopes of the Apennines, wooded with magnificent chestnuts and luxuriant vegetation, and the mild, humid air of the lower altitudes. Lucca is just to the S, and Barga is the prettiest hill village.

The Maremma The word means coastal plain, but it is now most often associated with the province of Grosseto, including the coast known as the Costa d'Argenta (between Alberese and Ansedonia), the promontory of Monte Argentario and, inland, the foothills of Monte Amiata. The Etruscan-red soil is wonderfully fertile, producing vegetables, fruit, grain, flowers and vines in colorful abundance. The many Etruscan sites remind one that the Maremma was probably more densely populated in the pre-Christian era than it is now. The natives, physically tough and independent-minded, regard themselves as the wild westerners of Tuscany; the local cowboys, less often seen than they were, are known as *butteri*. Apart from the Etruscan and Roman sites, you should at least visit Massa Marittima, Pitigliano and the nature reserve of Monti dell'Uccellina. There are very few hotels except on the coast, but some excellent country restaurants.

The Mugello In the early Renaissance the river basin of the Sieve, the homeland of Giotto and the Medici, was considered to be the healthiest and most beautiful of the rural areas near the city of Florence. Protected by the Apennines to the N and well-watered by mountain springs, the climate of this lovely gentle green valley is more temperate than that of the Arno.

The Versilia This coastal strip in northern Tuscany boasts the region's longest uninterrupted stretch of white sandy beach, and has an even, balmy climate with mild winters and light rainfall. Forte dei Marmi is fashionable with Italians; Viareggio's prime is past, but it still has a certain decaying period charm. Some of the other resorts are squalid. There are a staggering 690 hotels, some excellent, and plenty of good fish restaurants.

Route 1: Pisa to Florence

Uninitiated visitors to Tuscany, automatically whisked from Pisa Airport to Florence, are often left with a dim impression of the intervening country, which does not reveal its treasures from the autostrada. Apart from three of the most artistically important Tuscan cities – Lucca, Pistoia and Prato – this slower, more interesting itinerary embraces Romanesque churches, Medici villas, radiant mountain landscapes, and some of the best restaurants in Tuscany. It is well worth the luxury of a rented car. Anyone unfamiliar with the highlights of the trip could allow two or three days. Otherwise, sections of the route could be followed as day excursions from Florence by taking the autostrada as far as Pisa, Lucca or Pistoia and then returning along the suggested roads.

Leave *Pisa* by the SS12 for *Lucca*, via S. Giuliano Terme and S. Maria del Giudice, where there are two Romanesque churches. From Lucca's Porta Elisa follow the SS435 for *Pescia*, turning off for the Romanesque church of S.Gennaro and for *Collodi*, on the left. After Pescia the road descends alongside River Pescia to *Montecatini Terme*. Heading now for *Pistoia*, one passes the remains of medieval fortifications at Serravalle. Take the *Empoli* road from Pistoia's Porta Leonardo da Vinci; it winds over Monte Albano, commanding ravishing views of the Arno valley as it approaches *Vinci* through woodland and olive groves. From Vinci, turn left on to the pretty *Carmignano* road which runs for 16km (10 miles) along the s flank of the Albano mountains through pine woods, olives and the vineyards which produce some of the finest Tuscan wines, and past the Romanesque church of S.Giusto. There is a tempting view of Florence from Carmignano, but don't miss the opportunity to visit the Etruscan tombs near Comeana, the village and Medici villa of *Artimino*, and another Medici villa at *Poggio a Caiano*, all within 10km (6 miles) of Carmignano. *Prato* is 8km (5 miles) N of Poggio a Caiano. Aiming now for Florence, eschew the autostrada and choose instead the Roman road along the base of the Calvana and Morello mountains, for *Sesto Fiorentino* and *Castello*.

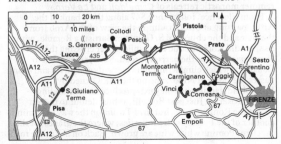

Route 2: The Chianti

In May, when the landscape of the Chianti is at its loveliest, this short journey into the heart of Tuscany is one of the essential pleasures of a Florentine holiday: all year round, it is a uniquely Tuscan delight. Blue signs point to the wine growers who will be happy to let you taste their produce and will sell wine, beautifully packaged, by the bottle or cellarful. Since there are some 250 producers in the Chianti Classico zone selling wine under their own labels, it can be difficult to select the best; see *Tuscan wines* for suggestions.

Visitors who want only one leisurely day's outing from Florence can simplify the itinerary by taking the Chiantigiana to Siena and returning to Florence on the SS2 or the autostrada. The whole circular tour can be made to fit into a busy day.

The starting point from Florence is Piazza F. Ferrucci. Take the 18thC wine road, the Strada Chiantigiana, SS222, the classic route into the Chianti which it bisects lengthwise. After Grassina the vista opens on to a hilly landscape punctuated by medieval towers. Shortly after passing the splendid Baroque Villa Ugolino, you are ushered by a large notice into the Chianti Classico wine zone. The road now descends to *Greve*. Just to the s, on the road for Lamole to the left, is the privately owned Renaissance Villa Vignamaggio, which appears in the background of an early drawing by Leonardo and where some romantics like to imagine the *Mona Lisa* was painted. At *Castellina* you can turn left on to SS429 into the historic center of the Chianti for Radda and *Gaiole*, and then approach *Siena* by the old Chiantigiana, SS408. Otherwise, continue s via Fonterutoli towards Siena, which you will enter close to the station. If you do not intend to visit Siena, turn right N of the city on to the SS2 for *Monteriggioni*, taking care to avoid the motorway entrance. After Monteriggioni, turn left for *Colle di Val d'Elsa, San Gimignano*, and *Certaldo*, each rising up one after another like medieval mirages. From Certaldo a sound but unspectacular road carries you NE across the Elsa and Pesa valleys for 23km (14 miles), past the castles of S.Maria Novella and Lucardo to *San Casciano*, at the NW limit of the Classico zone. Admirers of Machiavelli will want to rejoin the approach road to Florence by way of S.Andrea in Percussina (see *San Casciano*). After a stop at *Galluzo*, you re-enter *Florence* by the *Porta Romana*.

Route 3: Florence to Arezzo by the Pratomagno and Casentino

The drive to *Vallombrosa*, less than an hour from Florence, is a favorite Florentine family day outing. By allowing two days for this route to Arezzo you would have time also to visit the remoter monastic retreats of *Camaldoli* and *La Verna*.

From Florence, follow the SS67 along the N bank of the Arno, pausing at Sieci to admire the view of the Arno from the weir and the church of S. Giovanni Battista a Remole, with its splendid Romanesque campanile. After crossing the Sieve at *Pontassieve*, take the narrower road, SS70, signposted to Consuma, which climbs through vineyards and olives and soon passes the castle of Nipozzano on the left. Owned by the Frescobaldi family, its vineyards produce an outstanding Chianti Riserva. Just past Borselli, a short detour to the left passes the Romanesque church of Tosina on the way to Pomino, another of the Frescobaldi properties, where the grapes for the excellent Pomino white wine are grown. Back on SS70, the road

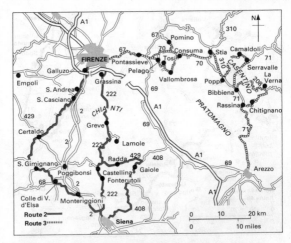

now climbs more steeply through beech, fir and pine woods towards Consuma. Just 1km (0.6 miles) before the village a right turn leads to *Vallombrosa*, secluded in its dense beechwood on the eastern slope of Monte Secchieta.

Those who wish to return to Florence may vary the route by returning to Pontassieve via Tosi and Pelago. Otherwise, return to the SS70 and turn right towards Poppi, crossing the Pratomagno range through the Consuma pass. Descending into the Casentino you can see Monte Falterona, where the Arno has its source, on the left, and ahead the castle of *Poppi*, like a transplanted Palazzo Vecchio. Fork left 10km (6 miles) after Consuma for the castle of Romena, the Romanesque church of Romena on a parallel road, and *Stia*. From there turn right onto the SS310 via Pratovecchio, where Paolo Uccello was born in 1397, and along the E bank of the Arno, past Campaldino, where Dante fought in the battle of 1289 against Arezzo, to *Poppi*. The road for the monastery and then the hermitage of Camaldoli is on the left just beyond Poppi. Then descend via Serravalle on to SS71 to *Bibbiena*, where a left turn onto the SS208 leads to the famous Franciscan sanctuary of *La Verna* high up in the mountains which separate the Arno and Tiber valleys. The road from La Verna via Chitignano, which rejoins the SS71 for Arezzo at Rassina, is rough in places but worth choosing for the views of the Pratomagno hills ahead as you descend. After Giovi, where the Arno curves away toward the W, you emerge from the Casentino into the suburbs of *Arezzo*.

Route 4: Tracking down the Etruscans

Traces of the elusive and intriguing Etruscans remain all over Tuscany. The tourist who enjoys walking or riding, or who takes shortcuts along unpaved byroads, will sometimes discover tombs and trails which are not necessarily signposted or identified. However, to appreciate the Etruscans' achievements in the arts and crafts one must also visit museums; some outstanding objects have been allowed to remain in the local museums on the following itineraries.

If you wish to test your interest in Etruscan sites before embarking on a longer journey, begin with *Fiesole*, Comeana

39

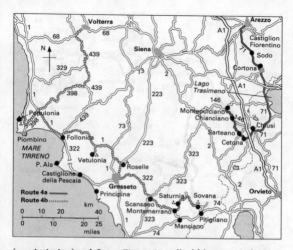

(see *Artimino*) and *Sesto Fiorentino*, all within easy reach of
Florence. Or, if you are making an excursion to San
Gimignano, go on to *Volterra*, a lovely drive only 27km (17
miles) to the SW. The two densest concentrations of the major
centers are in the Valdichiana and the Grosseto Maremma, most
conveniently visited separately.

a) The Etruscan sites of eastern Tuscany
In the pre-Christian era when the River Chiana was navigable,
the Etruscan cities of the Valdichiana were both prosperous and
artistically sophisticated thanks to fertile farmlands and trade
with other civilizations.

Start at *Arezzo*, the city Livy called the capital of the
Etruscan people. Then take the SS71 for *Cortona*, stopping just
to the N of the city for the tombs at Sodo. Have a look at the
extraordinary bronze lamp in the Etruscan Academy in Cortona
and, on the way S, visit the tomb near the station at Camucia.
The quickest way to *Chiusi*, which has one of the most
important Etruscan museums outside Florence, is by
autostrada. Alternatively, the SS71 loops round along the shore
of Lake Trasimeno. From Chiusi station, loop S and then NW to
visit the minor rural centers of Cetona, Sarteano, *Chianciano*
and *Montepulciano*, all of which preserve interesting Etruscan
fragments. Perugia and Orvieto, outside Tuscany, are nearby.

b) The Etruscan sites of southwestern Tuscany
This is a much longer journey, requiring about three days, and
it differs in that many of the major sites were abandoned by later
civilizations. The necropoli are often in dense woods or
cultivated fields, so wear stout shoes and be prepared to take the
car over unpaved roads.

Start at *Volterra*, allowing at least half a day for the walls,
gate, necropolis and the museum, with its 600 funerary urns and
miniature votive bronzes. After perhaps spending the night
here, *Populonia*, on the coast, is a 1½ hr drive to the SW, and
Vetulonia another hour farther on. The second night could be
spent on the coast at *Punta Ala*, *Castiglione della Pescaia* or
Principina a Mare. From Vetulonia continue along the Aurelia
(SS1) and turn left after 15km (9 miles) for *Roselle*, following

the signs *'ruderi'* for the access road. *Grosseto* is 10km (6 miles) to the S and worth visiting for the material excavated from Roselle, Vetulonia and other local Etruscan sites, featured in the Archeological Museum. Now travel inland by the SS322 via Scansano to Montemerano, where you turn left for *Saturnia*, and then *Sovana*; you might spend the third night in either. To complete a tour of the major sites, journey S into Lazio, for Vulci, Tarquinia, Cerveteri, and Veio.

Route 5: From Siena to the Valdichiana

This itinerary SE from Siena could be accomplished in one long day, but the variety and unfaltering beauty of the landscape of the *crete*, the Val d'Orcia and the Valdichiana, and the importance of the churches and hill towns, which include some of the finest examples of Renaissance architecture and town planning outside Florence, justify at least one overnight stop. Food and wine produced in this radiant countryside and served in the best of the restaurants is of exceptional quality.

One day Leaving Siena by the Porta Romana, the Via Cassia, SS2, follows the River Arbia through a strange, furrowed landscape of infertile clay hummocks known as the *crete*. After Buonconvento the Cassia begins to twist dramatically, and the view becomes more spacious with *Montalcino* and *Monte Amiata* visible on the right. From *San Quirico d'Orcia*, on its high plain overlooking the valleys of the Orcia and the Asso, take the SS146 which travels E to the Renaissance hill towns of *Pienza* and *Montepulciano*. The superb High Renaissance church of S. Biagio is on the left 2km (1.25 miles) before Montepulciano. Those who are returning to Siena should leave Montepulciano by the Porta al Prato, stopping briefly after 1km (0.6 miles) to admire the simple Mannerist facade of the church of S. Maria delle Grazie on the left, then proceeding N to Nottola, where you join the SS326 for Siena via Torrita di Siena and *Sinalunga*.

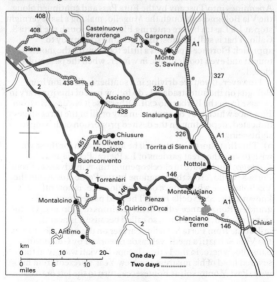

Two days Follow the route described on the previous page, and then make diversions to take in at least some if not all of the following excursions.
a) At Buonconvento turn left on the SS451 for *Monte Oliveto Maggiore*. Then continue for another 2km (1.25 miles) on the road for S.Giovanni d'Asso as far as lofty Chiusure, for the magnificent panorama of the moonlike landscape below. On the return drive to Buonconvento there are fine views of the *crete*, the Ombrone valley and *Monte Amiata*.
b) 10km (6 miles) s of Buonconvento, at Torrenieri, turn right for *Montalcino*. Then continue s into the Val d'Orcia for Sant'Antimo, set in an enchanted landscape of wheatfields, flickering olives and dark cypresses.
c) At *Montepulciano* turn right and follow the SS146 for *Chianciano Terme* ; the old city can be seen high on the left as one approaches the modern spa. *Chiusi* is 11km (7 miles) farther to the SE, by way of a beautiful undulating road running into the Valdichiana with the tributary of the River Chiana, the Astrone, with glimpses to the left of the lakes of Chiusi and Montepulciano.
d) Returning to Siena from Chiusi take the autostrada A1 as far as the Valdichiana exit for *Sinalunga*. Stay on the SS326 for 14km (9 miles), turning off for *Asciano*, and then returning to Siena on the SS438 through the *crete*, entering the city by the Porta Pispini.
e) Alternatively, leave the A1 at the Monte S.Savino exit, following the SS73 to *Monte S.Savino*, diverging briefly for *Gargonza* on the right, then for Castelnuovo Berardenga on the eastern edge of the Chianti near the source of the Ombrone. Return to Siena either by the SS326 or by the old Chiantigiana road, SS408.

Route 6: A day in the Mugello

In the days of the Grand Tour, travelers from the N crossed the Apennines into Tuscany by the Futa Pass and continued along the Via Bolognese through the Mugello, making a last overnight stop at La Lastra before entering Florence through the Porta S. Gallo. That is still the most dramatic and scenic way to approach Florence – perhaps a little too slow for the modern tourist and even too dramatic in winter, when the pass is often closed.

However, if you are driving in a southerly direction from Bologna on the autostrada A1, do follow part of this itinerary in reverse from the Barberino exit. Otherwise it is a day trip from Florence which may be enjoyed in any or all of the three stages indicated, depending on the desired proportion of driving to sightseeing.
a) This first short itinerary will be long enough for those who wish to visit the great gardens of La Pietra, Petraia and *Castello*; but be sure to check opening times in advance. From Porta S. Gallo, cross the Mugnone by the Ponte Rosso into the Via Bolognese which, once outside Florence, is now officially known as the SS65 della Futa. The road passes some of the grandest Renaissance villas in the environs of Florence. On the right, no. 120, is La Pietra, so called because it is near the old milestone from Porta S. Gallo. Farther on the right, no. 156, is the Villa Salviati, a medieval castle reworked by Giuliano da Sangallo, where, in the 17thC, Jacopo Salviati was given the severed head of his mistress as a New Year's present from his wife. Past Montorsoli at Fontesecca, turn to the left onto the

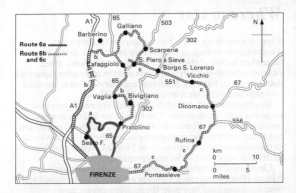

panoramic road of the Colli Alti (high hills), which twists for
15km (9 miles) along the slopes of Monte Morello, passing
Piazzale Leonardo da Vinci which commands magnificent
views of the Arno valley stretching out as far as the Chianti
Mountains, to *Sesto Fiorentino*, whence you could return to
Florence.
b) Complete only the first 6km (4 miles) of the Colli Alti, as far
as Piazzale Leonardo da Vinci. Returning to the SS65, continue
N past the park of the Villa Demidoff, adapted by Buontalenti
for Francesco de' Medici, but now demolished, to Pratolino.
For the convent of Monte Senario, a 13thC foundation
remade in the late 16thC and worth visiting for its lofty
situation, fork right from Pratolino. From Montesenario
descend into the basin of the Mugello valley via *Bivigliano*
rejoining the SS65 at Vaglia. Taking the left fork at the Novoli
crossroads, you pass on the left two of the earliest Medici villas,
both of which were once fortified castles made into hunting
lodges by Michelozzo for Cosimo il Vecchio: first Trebbio, now
only occasionally open to the public; then Cafaggiolo, now a
hospital, where Poliziano spent the rainy winter of 1478–9
instructing Lorenzo de' Medici's children. To return to
Florence rejoin the autostrada at Barberino. See also *Borgo San
Lorenzo*.
c) Otherwise, take another route and leave the SS65 N of
Cafaggiolo turning right across the Sieve for Galliano, looping
right for Sant' Agata and *Scarperia*, then following the SS503 s
toward San Piero a Sieve. Just before reaching San Piero a
Sieve, turn right for the medieval Franciscan monastery, Bosco
ai Frati, which was rebuilt in the Renaissance by Michelozzo,
where there is a wooden crucifix in the church attributed by
some scholars to Donatello. Take the SS551 from San Piero to
Borgo San Lorenzo. The landscape visible from the road along
this stretch is disfigured by industrial sprawl as far as Vicchio
and Vespignano, after which the road follows the broad curve of
the Sieve through gentle, cultivated country to Dicomano,
Rúfina, center of the smallest and choicest of the Chianti Putto
zones, and *Pontassieve*, where the Sieve joins the Arno. Turn
w on the SS67 for Florence. The road follows the N bank of the
Arno through the industrial vineyards which are controlled by
the Ruffino firm, and passes many interesting country churches
of which the most notable are S.Giovanni Battista a Remole at
Sieci and S.Andrea at Rovezzano situated on the outskirts of
Florence.

Where to stay

There is something in the Tuscan spirit which prevents
Tuscans from managing their luxury hotels with that perfected
flourish to be found elsewhere. There are, of course, good
expensive hotels in Florence, Siena and the more select spas and
coastal resorts, but their luxurious accommodation is too often
accompanied by soulless service and bland food.

More enjoyable and much better value are small, privately
owned or family-run hotels. You should book them in advance,
because they tend to have a loyal clientele, and because they are
not always to be found in obvious places – the only disadvantage
to traveling spontaneously in rural Tuscany. If it is growing
dark, look for a hotel at the nearest spa or resort.

Cleanliness is a virtue of Tuscan hotels, and the days when
Aldous Huxley described Tuscany as "under-bathroomed and
over-monumented" are past: the monuments are now
sometimes occupied by hotels, and have been bathroomed.
Standards and prices are firmly controlled by the Regional
Tourist Board: categories are deluxe and first- to fourth-class
for hotels, and P1 – P3 for *pensioni*. The distinction between
hotels and *pensioni*, which used to require full or half-board, has
broken down recently; while most Florentine *pensioni* have
dropped the meal requirement, resort hotels often insist on
residential terms.

Where to eat

There are two schools of thought about Tuscan food. One,
propounded by French advocates of the *nouvelle cuisine*,
maintains that the Tuscan emphasis on fresh ingredients simply
prepared is both healthy and delicious; and it is true that the two
words Tuscans most often use to describe good food are *genuino*
and *sano*, and that junk food is almost unobtainable. The
negative view, held by tourists who eat carelessly, is that a
perpetual diet of roast or grilled meat, white haricot beans,
chewy, unsalted bread and only one cheese, *pecorino*, can be
monotonous.

To enjoy Tuscan food at its best, one must follow certain
guidelines. There is virtually no such thing as a *grand* Tuscan
restaurant; fancy service, decor and prices can usually be taken
as a warning of indifferent, tastelessly elaborate food. The best
restaurants are generally outside cities, often in deeply rural
areas. Here you rarely see a menu. The specialities are not
predictable; the proprietor will tell you what has been prepared
that day, or you may simply be presented with a succession of
dishes.

The culinary glory of Tuscany is, in Elizabeth David's
words, "that remarkable *bistecca alla Fiorentina*, a vast steak,
grilled over a wood fire, which, tender and aromatic, is a dish
worth going some way to eat."

Pasta is usually available but is not a Tuscan speciality. The
farinaceous staple is bread, used to make the bread salad,
panzanella, and to thicken the excellent peasant soups which
vary by area. There are some 100 varieties of *pecorino*, which
changes character as it ages and absorbs the different flavors of
the leaves in which it is sometimes wrapped to mature. A
favorite summer antipasto is *pecorino* eaten with the new *fave*
(broad beans).

Florence (Firenze)

Map 2–7. 50100 Firenze. Population: 463,000 ***i*** *Via Tornabuoni 15* ☎ *(055) 216544/5. See Basic information.*

Florence is the most densely packed urban treasure house in Europe. If you were not detained by the profusion of artistic masterpieces it contains, you could walk across its historic center in half an hour. Only two of the sights recommended are beyond pleasant walking distance of the Piazza della Signoria. It is, then, a city which imposes no pattern on sightseeing, and one which can be explored according to the mood of the individual visitor.

To make the most of this freedom, however, you must adjust to the rhythm of the city, which rises early and closes down at midday for a long siesta. Churches close for three or sometimes four hours in the middle of the day, but they are often open from 7am and open again in the evening until 7pm or 8pm. Many museums are now open in the mornings only, closing usually at 2pm. Most remain closed all day Mon. Inevitably, in a city which possesses so much precious art that is fragile with age, there will always be some works that are withdrawn from the public gaze for restoration and some buildings that are temporarily closed. Although Florence does manage its museums and galleries more efficiently than many other Italian cities, strikes and lack of staff can occasionally lead to unexpected closings.

Postcards and catalogues are not sold in any Italian state museums but can be purchased from good bookshops and bookstalls.

Fortunately for the independent-minded visitor, mass tourism does not often penetrate beyond the Uffizi, Palatine Gallery, Bargello and Accademia, the four most visited sights in that order. The churches, chapels, painted refectories and small museums are usually peaceful even in high summer. Although no one will be able to take in all the city has to offer in one short visit – and it would be an exhausting waste of time to try – Florence does reveal its essential urban character to the visitor very quickly. Its narrow streets flanked by medieval and Renaissance palaces are, with very few exceptions, unspoiled as yet by modern intrusions. Since the last building boom under the Medici grand dukes, the fabric of Florence has suffered only four drastic changes.

The first happened in the mid 19thC when Florence disastrously prepared itself for its brief period as Italy's capital by demolishing its old walls and part of its center to make way for the Viale and the Piazza della Repubblica. The second was the destruction towards the end of World War II of Ponte Santa Trinità (subsequently reconstructed) and the areas to the N and s of the Ponte Vecchio. The third was the flood of 1966, the worst in the city's history. The fourth is the motor traffic which, since the early 1970s, has come to dominate Florence more cruelly than any of its hated tyrant-rulers, turning its beautiful squares into parking lots and roaring through its medieval streets.

Fortunately there is probably no other major city in the world from which escape is so easy and so delightful. Much of the lovely Tuscan countryside immediately outside Florence has been consciously and courageously defended from the worst ravages of modern development, and can be reached either on foot or by a short bus ride.

Sights and places of interest

So richly endowed with treasures is Florence that the use of
symbols denoting outstanding beauty or interest is inevitably
more selective and more personal than elsewhere. So much in
the city is worth seeing, so do yield to the temptation to wander
or linger anywhere; you will rarely be disappointed. A word of
warning: opening hours are altered with bewildering frequen-
cy. If there is something you especially want to see, check the
hours first with the *Azienda Autonoma* or tourist offices (see
Addresses and telephone numbers in *Basic information*).

Accademia *(Galleria dell'Accademia)* ★
Via Ricasoli 60 ☎ *214375. Map 3B4* ▨ ▨ *Open Tues–
Sat 9am–2pm, Sun and hols 9am–1pm. Closed Mon.*
In 1563, 70 leading Florentine artists founded the first
Academy of Art in Europe. The organizing members were
Vasari, Bronzino and Ammannati, and the president was
Cosimo I. Thus academic art, like so many modern institutions,
was a Florentine invention. First located at *Santissima
Annunziata*, the Accademia was moved to Via Ricasoli 66 in
1764. This building, with its spacious 14thC loggia, is now the
Florentine Art School and College.

The Accademia gallery nearby at no. 60 was founded in 1784
by Peter Leopold I, who donated a collection which was greatly
enriched by works brought here from the suppressed religious
orders in 1786 and 1808–10. Until World War I the Accademia
possessed an outstanding collection of early Tuscan
masterpieces, the best of which were transferred in 1913 to the
Uffizi. During the 1970s the display was reorganized and
enlarged in order to emphasize the link with the original
Academy of Art, and new rooms housing 18th and 19thC
academic paintings and sculptures, including hitherto
neglected works by Lorenzo Bartolini, were opened in 1982.

Meanwhile, most visitors will come here, as they have for
over a century, to gaze up at the *David* of Michelangelo.

Rm I, Sala del Colosso. Dominated by Giambologna's model
(c. 1582) for the *Rape of the Sabines* in the Loggia dei Lanzi (see
Signoria). On the walls are 16thC paintings by Fra
Bartolommeo, Perugino, Granacci, and others.

The *David* . . . . standing forward stripped and exposed and
eternally half-shrinking, half-wishing to expose himself, he is
the genius of Florence.

D. H. Lawrence, *Aaron's Rod* (1922)

Rm II, Salone di Michelangelo. Against the walls, which are
hung with magnificent 16thC tapestries, are four of
Michelangelo's unfinished *Slaves* (c. 1519–36) ★ first meant
for Pope Julius II's unrealized mausoleum in St Peter's in Rome
(the Louvre possesses two other slaves). The figures may
represent the liberal arts enslaved by the death of their patron,
Julius II. On the right wall are also the deeply expressive,
unfinished *St Matthew* (before 1505); and the Palestrina *Pietà*,
which Michelangelo possibly made while working on Julius II's
tomb and which was brought here in 1940 from the Church of
S. Rosalia di Palestrina in Rome. At the far end of the room,
Michelangelo's *David* (1501–4) ★ dwarfs and astonishes the
perpetual crowds. This tribune was specially built to receive the
David when it was brought here from the Signoria in 1873. The

statue was carved from a block of Carrara marble known as 'the giant', which had been spoiled by Agostino di Duccio and abandoned in the courtyard of the Opera del Duomo. The *David* established Michelangelo's reputation as the leading sculptor of his day, and has remained the most potent of all symbols of Florentine republicanism. But it has not always been admired: William Hazlitt, one of the many early 19thC travelers who were irritated by Michelangelo's style, described it as looking "like an awkward overgrown actor at one of our minor theaters, without his clothes."

The three Sale Fiorentine, entered from this room, are devoted to *quattrocento* Florentine pictures. Many are charming and instructive, like the cassone panel (1440–50) facing the entrance to the first room, which is a rich source of information about mid-*quattrocento* costume. Others, like Baldovinetti's *Trinità*, in the second room, are important but ruined.

Anthropological Museum *(Museo Nazionale di Antropologia ed Etnologia)* ⅧⅢ
Via del Proconsolo 12. Map 5C5. Open to guided parties on request.

Opened in 1869, this was the first anthropological museum in Italy. The collection is displayed on the ground floor of the Palazzo Nonfinito (see *Florence/Walk 2*) and is a fascinating documentation of ethnic custom and costume.

Antica Casa Fiorentina, Museo dell' The house
museum of Florence in the *Davanzati Palace*.

Arcetri and Pian dei Giullari
Map 7E4. Bus no. 38.

Florence may be hot and crowded, but half an hour's walk s from the Ponte Vecchio will lift you into the cool, high heart of Tuscany. At no.2 Pian dei Giullari is the **Astrophysical Observatory of Arcetri** with the first solar tower built in Europe (1872). Opposite the entrance is the Villa Capponi, with famous but private gardens. The **Torre del Gallo** is just to the E: this 19thC reconstruction was once owned by the antiquarian robber-baron Stefano Bardini (see *Bardini Museum*). In the adjacent **Villa la Gallina** are Antonio del Pollaiuolo's **frescoes of nude dancers**: persistent or specialist visitors have been known to gain access by appointment.

Pian dei Giullari takes its name from the minstrels who entertained Florentine patricians here from the 12thC. Galileo died in the **Villa il Gioiello** (no.42). On no.48 a plaque sentences to imprisonment anyone who dares to play any ball game within 200yd of the monastery of S. Matteo in Arcetri.

In the Via S. Margherita a Montici, at the Villa Ravà, no. 75, Francesco Guicciardini wrote his histories of Italy between 1537–40. Further on is the church of S. Margherita a Montici commanding stupendous views of the Arno and Ema valleys. Inside are two 14thC panels by the Master of St Cecilia.
(See also *Florence/Walk 4*.)

Archeological Museum *(Museo Archeologico)* ☆
Via della Colonna 38 ☎ *215270. Map 3B5* ◪ ✱ *Open Tues–Sat 9am–2pm, Sun and hols 9am–1pm. Closed Mon.*

To say that the Archeological Museum is of outstanding international importance may sound forbidding to the non-specialist. In fact, every visitor will find much here to delight the eye, stimulate the imagination and enrich further sightseeing in Florence and Tuscany. The Etruscan sculptures are an essential and fascinating grounding for those who intend to visit the sites; the Greek and Roman collections will deepen one's understanding of the Renaissance art they helped inspire.

Having suffered appalling damage from the 1966 flood, the museum still has an air of post-crisis impermanence. Many rooms are closed, others badly labeled, and all displays are subject to change, but the finest objects, of which only the highlights are mentioned here, have been brilliantly restored and are on public display.

Ground floor, Rm I. François Vase (c.570 BC), the earliest known Attic volute-krater, discovered in 1845 by Alexander François at Chiusi. Smashed by a member of staff of the museum into 638 pieces in 1900, the vase was restored in 1972.

Rm II. **Etruscan tomb sculpture** (6th–5thC BC), from Chianciano and Chiusi.

First floor. The **Egyptian Collection** is in Rms I–VIII to the left of the stairs. It consists mainly of objects discovered in 1828–9 during a Franco-Tuscan expedition directed by Ippolito Rossellini and Jean François Champollion. The prize piece is the large **chariot** in Rm VIII, found by Rossellini in a 14thC BC tomb at Thebes.

The **Etruscan, Greek and Roman Collection** is in the rooms to the right of the stairs and continues on the second floor.

Rm X. Etruscan tomb sculpture, including *Urn in the Shape of an Etruscan House* (6th–3rdC BC), no. 5539, from Chiusi, a rare piece of evidence about Etruscan architecture, worth bearing in mind when looking at 15thC Tuscan palaces. *Sarcophagus of the Fat Etruscan* (3rd–2ndC BC), no. 5482, from Chiusi, mentioned by Catullus.

Rm XIV. The greatest Etruscan bronzes, including: *Wounded Chimera* (15thC BC), discovered at Arezzo in 1553 (the two left legs were restored by Cellini); and *The Orator* (c.7th–2ndC BC), a funereal sculpture found near Trasimeno in 1566.

A small section of the ground floor, entered from Piazza SS. Annunziata, is reserved for special exhibitions. The garden and topographical display charting the evolution of Etruscan culture have been closed.

Argenti Museum   Collection of objets d'art in the *Pitti Palace*.

Badia Fiorentina ▥ ☆
Map 5C4.

The old Benedictine Abbey of Florence is the only church, besides the Baptistry and S. Miniato, mentioned by Dante, who tells us that he saw Beatrice at Mass here and that the bell tower of the Badia gave Florence the hours. According to Vasari, the abbey, founded in 978, was enlarged by Arnolfo di Cambio, c.1285. This 13thC building was reoriented and radically rebuilt in the 17thC, but the original apse can still be seen from the outside. The hexagonal Romanesque-Gothic **campanile** was completed in 1330.

The **interior** is best lit in the morning. The **portal** (1495) and **vestibule** leading to Via Dante Alighieri were designed by Benedetto da Rovezzano. The noble Baroque **ceiling** is by Matteo Segaloni, architect of the 17thC church. Immediately to the left of the entrance is Filippino Lippi's restless masterpiece, *St Bernard's Vision of the Madonna* (c.1485). Farther to the left is the **monument to Count Ugo**, benefactor of the 10thC foundation (1469–81), by Mino da Fiesole. To the right of the entrance, off the Renaissance Pandolfini Chapel, is the little chapel occupying the site of the church of S. Stefano, where Boccaccio delivered the first literary lecture, on the *Divine Comedy*. Among Baroque decorations elsewhere in the church is Ferretti's fresco over the presbytery of the *Martyrdom of St Stephen* (after 1734).

Oranges were cultivated in the center of the large 15thC cloister, designed by Bernardo Rossellino. The tombs date from the 13thC onwards. There is a nice view of the three towers of the Badia, *Bargello* and *Signoria* from the upper loggia.

Baptistry *(Battistero)* The city's oldest building, and once its cathedral. See *Duomo*.

Bardini Museum ▥
Piazza di Mozzi 1. Map **5***F5* ▥ ✝▥ *Open Mon–Tues, Thurs–Sat 9am–2pm, Sun and hols 8am–1pm. Closed Wed.*
Stefano Bardini (1836–1922) was the leading Italian art dealer of his day, and by 1883 he had amassed a fortune more than large enough to build this palace. He tore down a 13thC church to create the site and, like the American robber barons of the period, incorporated architectural members from older buildings.

The first-floor windows are framed with the altars from a church in Pistoia. The cool, spacious **interior** is embellished throughout with ceilings, door frames and chimney pieces from other earlier buildings. Bardini's taste was almost boundlessly eclectic, and the collection includes, on the ground floor, sculptures and architectural decorations from the Etruscan period to the Baroque.

On the second floor there are pictures, furniture, ceramics, tapestries, musical instruments, arms and armor. The Corsi Gallery is closed pending possible relocation.

Bargello, National Sculpture Museum *(Museo Nazionale)* ▥ ★
Via del Proconsolo. Map **5***C5* ▥ *Open Tues–Sat 9am–2pm, Sun and hols 9am–1pm. Closed Mon.*
There are a fair number of murderers in the National Sculpture Museum, of which the best known are Donatello's *David*, Verrocchio's *David*, Michelangelo's *Brutus* and Cellini's model for the *Perseus*. Thus Florentine Renaissance sculpture reflected the Florentine obsession with tyranny. It is an ironic coincidence that, during the turbulent period when these sculptures were created, the Bargello was the place where real murderers were tried and sentenced; and the message that crime doesn't pay even if committed in the name of freedom was advertised on the tower walls, frescoed with representations of the mutilated corpses of the condemned. The body of one of the Pazzi Conspirators was hung from a window, where Leonardo made a careful drawing of him, paying special attention to his clothes.

The Bargello was built around an earlier tower in 1255, 5yr after the establishment of the new Florentine Republic, as its first town hall or Palazzo del Podestà. In 1261 it became the official residence of the Chief Magistrate (*bargello*) and it was used also as a law court and prison. The Sculpture Museum, the most important in Italy, has been here since 1859, and was enriched in 1888 by the Carrand Collection of small bronzes, ivories, enamels, goldsmiths' work and ceramics.

The **courtyard** is the most picturesque part of the palace. Its loggia and staircase are 14thC. Among the sculptures are Ammannati's figures from the fountain in the Boboli gardens. To the right of the entrance is the new **sculpture gallery** ★ opened in 1975. Moving clockwise, you will encounter, most notably: Michelangelo's *Bacchus* (c.1497), his first large free standing sculpture, *Pitti Tondo* (c.1504) and *Brutus* (1540), which probably celebrates the assassination of Alessandro de' Medici; and Sansovino's *Bacchus*. There are also terra-cotta sketches of Michelangelo's works by his followers. Works by Cellini include the **four bronze statues** and the relief panel of *Perseus Liberating Andromeda*, now brought here for safekeeping from the Loggia dei Lanzi; also his model for the *Perseus* – he boasts in his autobiography that Cosimo I doubted that anyone had the skill to enlarge it. Of the *Narcissus*, he tells us that a defective block of marble dictated the form. His larger-than-life portrait bust of *Cosimo I* ★ was made in two parts, first in 1546 and again between 1555–57, for the fortress Cosimo built at Portoferraio. You cannot very well ignore Giambologna's enormous, violent *Victory of Florence over Pisa* (1570), or the splendid **bronze doors** by Vincenzo Danti.

Beyond the courtyard are 14thC sculptural fragments, of which the loveliest piece is Tino da Camaino's *Madonna and Child*.

First floor. The internal staircase leads to the Sala degli Avori with ivories from the Carrand Collection and, around the walls, 14th–15thC polychrome wooden *Madonnas*. Off the long Salone del Podestà, the law court frescoed during the brief reign of the Duke of Athens, is the frescoed Chapel of the Condemned with fine intarsiaed choir stalls (1493) and lectern (1490). On the other side of the Sala degli Avori are two rooms devoted to reliquaries and majolicas. Cross the **loggia**, with Giambologna's *Mercury* (c.1564) and bronze animals (c.1570), made for the Villa Medicea at Castello, to the **Salone del Consiglio Generale**. Notice especially on the walls: the terra-cotta *Madonnas* by Luca della Robbia and Michelozzo; on the far wall, Donatello's *St George* ★ (1416) from the facade of *Orsanmichele* (where the original predella remains) flanked by his busts of *Niccolò da Uzzano* and *Giovanni da Narni*; the two panels of *The Sacrifice of Isaac* by Brunelleschi and Ghiberti were competition entries for the second Baptistry doors.

Free standing sculptures. By Donatello: the *Marzocco* (1420), the heraldic lion of Florence, made for S. Maria Novella but moved in the 19thC to the Signoria where it is now replaced by a copy; and *Amore* (c.1430–40), described by Vasari as "dressed in rather bizarre fashion" – the modern word for it is camp. Compare the swaying elegance of Donatello's early marble *David* (1408) with the late bronze *David* (c.1430) ★ his most famous nubile boy and the first free standing nude of the Renaissance; the young, fragile and mystic *St John* shows a different aspect still of Donatello's complex artistic personality. Also, two sensitive busts by Desiderio da Settignano.

Second floor. At the top of the stairs is the Sala di Giovanni della Robbia where Giovanni Rustici's huge terra–cotta relief panel of *Christ and the Magdalen* demonstrates his superiority to Giovanni della Robbia. In front of the central window is Cellini's *Ganymede* and, opposite, Bernini's bust of *Constanza Bonarelli* ★ Off one end of the room is a display of arms and armor. Off the other, the Sala di Andrea della Robbia leads to the **Sala di Verrocchio**. In the center are Verrocchio's *David* (before 1476) ★ and Antonio Pollaiuolo's small bronze masterpiece *Hercules and Anteus*. Among the works displayed on the walls are, clockwise from the entrance: the marble bust of *Battista Sforza, Duchess of Urbino* (1474–7) by Francesco Laurana; Verrocchio's *Bust of a Woman* and *Madonna and Child* (c.1480); and the bust of *Piero Mellini* (1474) by Benedetto da Maiano. Portrait busts and relief carvings by Mino da Fiesole include the tondo of the *Madonna and Child* (1481). Across the Sala di Andrea della Robbia is the **Sala dei Bronzetti** ☆ containing the most important collection of bronzes in Italy. The magnificent 16thC chimneypiece is by Benedetto da Rovezzano.

Bellosguardo
Map 6D3. No bus connection.

Bellosguardo is one of the nearest of the hill villages s of Florence. You can walk it in half an hour either from *Porta Romana* or *San Frediano*, and will be rewarded for the steep climb by views as ravishing as the word *bellosguardo* (fine view) suggests. Via Bellosguardo forks to either side of the piazza. On the w side is the Villa Belvedere al Saracino (1502) by Baccio d'Agnolo, and farther along the Via San Carlo is the Torre Montauto, where Hawthorne stayed. On the E side of the piazza is the park of Villa Ombrellino, where Alice Keppel, Edward VII's last mistress, lived from 1925 to her death in 1947. Her daughter, Violet Trefusis, also died at the Ombrellino.

The best views are from the garden of the Villa di Bellosguardo, reached by a pretty little road running along the NE flank of the Ombrellino park.

In the piazza a plaque records the most famous of the numerous foreign visitors who have lived in and around Bellosguardo. Aldous Huxley's short story, *The Rest Cure*, is about a neurotic Englishwoman staying here.

Belvedere *(Forte di Belvedere)* 🏛
🕿 287055. *Map 3E4* 👁 *Open Tues – Sun 8 : 30am – 1 : 30pm, exhibitions 9am – 8pm. Closed Mon. Main entrance from Via del Forte di S. Giorgio.*

Crowning the hill of S. Giorgio is the ruthlessly practical Belvedere fortress surrounding its elegant shoe-box-shaped Mannerist palace, both built by Buontalenti in 1590–5 for Grand Duke Ferdinand I. The terraces are now used for modern **sculpture exhibitions** 🎨 which are only occasionally worthy of a setting commanding some of the most magnificent views of Florence and the surrounding hills and valleys. At the top of the Costa di S. Giorgio is the S. Giorgio gate (c.1260), reduced to about half its original height, embellished with a fresco of the *Madonna and Saints* by Bicci di Lorenzo. The relief carving of St George is a copy of the original now in the *Signoria*.

Two interesting buildings in the Costa di S. Giorgio are the splendid Baroque church of S. Giorgio, modernized by G.B. Foggini in 1707 and lately restored, with a boudoir-like oval ceiling frescoed by Alessandro Gherardini, and the house (no. 19) where Galileo was visited by Ferdinand I.

Boboli Gardens *(Giardino di Boboli)* ☆

☎226587. Map **4***F3* 🎫 ☕ ♣ *Open May–Aug 9am–6:30pm; Nov–Feb 9am–4:30pm; Sept–Oct and Mar–Apr 9am–5:30pm. Main gate to left of Pitti; others not always open.*

"The most important if not the most pleasing of Tuscan pleasure gardens . . . . because the Boboli is a court garden, and not designed for private use." Thus Edith Wharton explained the curiously lowering effect the Boboli can have on one's spirits. At certain seasons, when roses tumble through the somber plantations of holly and cypress or when Florence is gilded with slanting autumn light, the Boboli would be a fine place for a late-afternoon stroll. But as another American novelist, Mary McCarthy, has pointed out, this is just the time when the gates close.

Eleanor of Toledo ordered gardens to be laid out behind the Pitti as soon as she and Cosimo I took possession in 1549. The original designer was Triboli, who died before accomplishing the extraordinary technical feat of taming this wedge of steep quarry. Later alterations by Ammannati, Buontalenti and the Parigi gave the gardens their playful, grandiose complexity.

If you wander freely in the Boboli, the late Mannerist jokes will take you by surprise as they were intended to do. A more purposeful tour should include the following highlights:
1. Statue of *Pietro Barbino Riding a Tortoise*, Cosimo I's favorite dwarf immortalized by Valerio Cioli. **2. Buontalenti Grotto** (1583–88), a serious joke about nature; the casts of Michelangelo's prisoners replace the originals, now in the *Accademia*, which were installed here for a time in the 16thC. Giambologna's *Venus* is in the third recess, not always open. **3.** The **Kaffeehaus** (1776), for a drink and fine views. **4.** The **Amphitheater**, "One of the triumphs of Italian garden architecture" (Edith Wharton). Built from 1618 by the Parigi for spectacular grand-ducal entertainments. **5. Neptune Fountain** (1565) by Stoldo Lorenzi. **6. Porcelain Museum (Museo delle Porcellane)**, a small but choice collection of French, Italian, Viennese and German porcelains, formerly exhibited in the Argenti Museum, have now been installed in the airy Casino del Cavaliere. Panoramic views to the S from the terrace. **7. Cypress Alley (Viottolone)**, lined with statues of various periods, the most famous of which, towards the bottom, are the knowingly rustic 17thC groups of games. **8. The Isolotto** (1618) by A. Parigi. The shallow pool, the tall box hedges and the pots of oranges and entwined trees on the island provide cooling relief. Rising from the fountain is a copy of Giambologna's *Oceanus* (the original is in the *Bargello*).

(See also *Pitti Palace*.)

Botanical Garden and Museum *(Orto Botanico, Giardino dei Semplici)*

Via G. la Pira 4 ☎210755. Map **3***B4* 🎫 ♣ *Open Mon, Wed, Fri 9am–noon.*

In a stony city where most gardens are hidden behind high walls, this scholarly display of the vegetable heritage of Tuscany makes a refreshing change from art galleries and churches. It is also an excellent preparation for those who plan to visit rural Tuscany and would like to identify the native trees and flowers.

The Giardino dei Semplici, as it was originally called because its first function was the cultivation of medicinal plants, was founded in 1545 by Cosimo I. On the second floor of the Botanical Institute is a little museum founded in 1842.

Brancacci Chapel   A chapel in the *Carmine*, containing
Masaccio's influential frescoes.

Carmine *(Santa Maria del Carmine)* †
Piazza del Carmine. Map 2D2.

If Renaissance painting was born in Giotto's Arena Chapel at
Padua and reached its fullest maturity in Michelangelo's Sistine
Chapel, it was in the **Brancacci Chapel ★** of the Carmine (right
transept, best seen on a clear evening without electric light) that
it made its most innovative and lasting impact. Here, a century
after Giotto, the young Masaccio 'rivalled nature' and
revolutionized Western art. Most Renaissance painters, from
Fra Angelico to Raphael, studied these frescoes, but perhaps
none understood them as well as Michelangelo (whose nose was
broken by Pietro Torrigiano on the steps of the Carmine). Many
of the greatest 20thC artists continue to draw inspiration from
Masaccio's bold, rigorous, uncluttered technique.

The frescoes were begun around 1425 by Masolino, who was
joined a little later by his protégé Masaccio and so
influenced by the young genius that it is not always easy to
distinguish their work. The decoration of the chapel was
interrupted when they departed for Rome in 1428 and was
completed in 1485 by Filippino Lippi. The 18thC **ceiling** is by
Vincenzo Meucci and Carlo Sacconi.

There are seven sections by Masaccio. Facing the altar and
starting from the near left wall, the outstanding frescoes are the
first two in the upper tier: *Adam and Eve* ★ one of the most
tragic images in Christian art; and the *Tribute Money* ★ Once
you have seen these faces with their quick, watching eyes, you
will see them again and again in the streets of Florence. Below
the *Tribute Money* is Masaccio's last work in this chapel, *St Peter
Enthroned*; the left portion of this fresco was finished by
Filippino Lippi. On the altar wall, bottom left, is *St Peter Heals
with his Shadow*; top right, *St Peter Baptizes the Neophites*;
bottom right, *St Peter and St John Distribute Alms*. On the right
wall, upper tier, first section on the left, is found *St Peter Heals
the Lame Man*; the *Raising of Tabitha* on the right section of this
fresco is by Masolino. The Florentine houses in the center
background are thought to have been Masaccio's starting point.

The **Corsini Chapel** in the left transept was built in 1675–83
by P.F. Silvani. The splendid relief sculptures (1675–91) on
the walls and altar are by G.B. Foggini, and the cupola fresco of
the *Apotheosis of S. Andrea Corsini* (1682) by Luca Giordano.

The rest of the church is late 18thC, the original building
having been destroyed in 1771 by a fire which spared the
Brancacci and Corsini chapels. In a **museum** off the cloister are
a number of detached frescoes including fragments by Starnina.

Casa Buonarroti   Built by Michelangelo's family after the
artist's death, now the *Michelangelo Museum*.

Le Cascine
Map 6D3. Bus 17.

Surprisingly few tourists make use of Le Cascine, the shady
park which runs for 3km (1¾ miles) along the N bank of the Arno
W from Piazza Vittorio Veneto. Yet it is one of the few places in
the city where you can take the air undistracted by traffic and
artistic masterpieces; and the private tennis club and swimming
pool are open to foreign nonmembers.

Originally a dairy farm belonging to the Medici, the Cascine became the grand-ducal chase in the 17thC. Shelley composed his *Ode to the West Wind* while striding through the Cascine. Later in the 19thC the park was so full of fashionable carriages that Charles Lever described it as being to the world of society "what the Bourse is to the world of trade."

(See also *Florence/Shopping* for markets and *Sports, leisure, ideas for children*.)

Corridoio
Vasari's aerial link between the *Pitti Palace* and the *Uffizi*, offering superb views as it crosses the Arno.

Corsini Gallery 🏛
Palazzo Corsini, Lungarno Corsini 10. Map 4C2. Open on application only to groups and specialists. Entrance from Via de' Parione 11.

The most important private collection in Florence, with works by Signorelli, Pontormo, Raphael, Rigaud and other Italian and European artists of the 15th–18thC.

The palace (1648–56) which gives its name to this stretch of the lungarno is by Pier Francesco Silvani and Antonio Ferri.

Davanzati Palace and Antica Casa Fiorentina, Museo dell' *(Florentine House Museum)* 🏛 ☆
Piazza Davanzati, Via Porta Rossa ☎ 216518. Map 4D3. ▦ ✸ Open Tues–Sat 9am–2pm, Sun and hols 9am–1pm. Closed Mon.

The exterior of the Davanzati is the best-preserved of any mid-14thC palace in Florence. Inside, the House Museum offers a rare opportunity to explore an early palace interior and to learn about domestic life in 14th–16thC Florence. If George Eliot had known the Davanzati as it is today, *Romola* would have been a livelier novel. The house was built by the Davizzi family, who lived here for over a century before selling to the historian Bernardo Davanzati in 1578. The interior was badly mishandled in the 19thC after the suicide by defenestration of the last Davanzati, but was rescued and accurately restored by Elia Volpi just after the turn of this century.

Architecturally the building is midway between a medieval defence tower and a Renaissance palace. Apart from the 16thC roof loggia, a replacement of the original battlements, and the Davanzati coat of arms placed here in the 16thC, the facade looks very much like the one you can see in the Masolino-Masaccio fresco of the *Resurrection of Tabitha* in the *Carmine*.

The entrance loggia, initially used for important family celebrations, was converted into three wool shops by the end of the 15thC. The horizontal perches running across the windows were used, as shown in the Carmine fresco, for hanging out washing, or birdcages, and for festive drapes.

The interior is largely a reconstruction, and a very good one, by Volpi. The **courtyard staircase** is particularly worth noting as the only one of its type left in Florence. The well is an unusual luxury for a palace of this date; all five floors were served by a shaft carrying buckets of water by rope and pulley. Kitchens, as always in medieval palaces, are on the top floor. The sanitary arrangements include lavatories which you can see next to the bedrooms on the three upper floors. The house is unusual in having two *piani nobili*, on the second as well as the first floor.

Of the wall decorations, the most attractive and most complete is in the second-floor bedroom where a fresco cycle illustrates the medieval French poem *The Châtelaine of Vergi*.

Duomo ⏺ † ★

*Map **5**B4. Open 6:30am–noon, 2:30–7pm.*

Traffic swarms around the religious center of Florence, shaking the nerves of tourists and the very foundations of the cathedral. The Piazza del Duomo is the crossroads of the city's busiest streets, the headquarters of its ancient voluntary ambulance service (the *Misericordia*, an original Red Cross) and a magnet for the modern tourist industry; but it is no place for a meditative cup of coffee. To appreciate the grandeur and significance of the Duomo and its attendant buildings, you must first go away from it, glimpse its flagrant burst of color from the dark narrow city streets and take your coffee overlooking it from a rooftop or from the hills above, where you will see how disproportionately large the cathedral is in the small city.

The cathedral and its belfry suggested the grotesque similitude of a huge architectural zebra and its keeper – the former with a coating or skin, consisting of alternate stripes of black and white marble, the latter exhibiting, on its exterior, all the colours of the rainbow, all the chequers of a gigantic harlequin! Is there no mitigation of the penalty due to this gothic and tasteless idea?
James Johnson MD (1831)

The cathedral (Santa Maria del Fiore) clad in white marble from Carrara, green from Prato, and pink from the Maremma, could hardly be more of a contrast with the plain brown understated city around it. Like the two sides of the Florentine character: one is measured, conservative, puritanical; the other excessive, innovating, festive; and both are dominated by the great cranium-shaped intelligence of Brunelleschi's dome.

Arnolfo di Cambio was commissioned in 1296 to build a cathedral which would surpass anything produced by the ancient Romans and Greeks or by Florence's rivals the Pisans and Sienese. Work was interrupted by Arnolfo's death, began again in 1331, and after another pause resumed under the direction of Francesco Talenti from 1357–1364. The nave was completed in 1380, and the tribunes and the drum of the dome were finished by 1418.

The problem then was how to raise a dome over a space 42m (138ft) across and 55m (180ft) above the ground. No dome of this size had been built since antiquity, and various unlikely solutions were proposed before Brunelleschi, who had studied Classical building techniques in Rome, provided the answer. His dome, realized in 1436, was the supreme engineering feat of the Renaissance. The lantern was completed in 1461, after

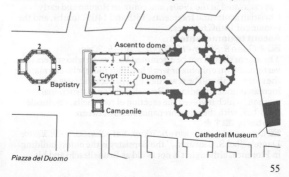

Piazza del Duomo

Brunelleschi's death; the gallery, on only one of the eight sides of the drum of the dome, was begun by Baccio d'Agnolo in 1506 but abandoned after Michelangelo called it "a cage for crickets."

The Neo-Gothic facade of the cathedral is a late 19thC interpretation of the original one. The apse is best viewed from the corner of Via Proconsolo and Via dell'Oriuolo. The S flank is the earliest section of the exterior, but the most beautiful of the doors, the **Porta della Mandorla**, is on the N nave. Above it is Nanni di Banco's lovely relief of the *Assumption of the Madonna* (1414–21).

The cathedral **interior**, the fourth largest in the world, is all the more imposing for the sparseness of detailed decoration. There are only a few major works of art to distract from the sense of echoing space. In the left aisle of the nave are the two famous monuments to *condottieri* (mercenary commanders), which have been cited as examples of Florentine meanness because they imitate marble in *trompe l'oeil* fresco. Both have long since been transferred to canvas: the first, **Monument to Niccolò da Tolentino** (1456) by Castagno; the second, **Monument to Sir John Hawkwood** (1436) by Uccello. Just before the crossing is an interesting panel painting of *Dante Explaining the Divine Comedy* (1465) by Domenico di Michelino.

Access to the vast octagonal **crossing** and the three polygonal tribunes of the apse will be barred until the 1990s while the dome is under restoration. Meanwhile, the question is whether the late 16thC frescoes of the *Last Judgement* on the interior dome by Vasari and F. Zuccari, now covered by netting, should be removed in order to reveal more clearly Brunelleschi's structure.

The noble octagonal marble **choir enclosure** (1555) beneath the dome is by Bandinelli, as is the high altar over which is a wooden **crucifix** (1495–7) by Benedetto da Maiano. The **bronze doors** to the New Sacristy are the only surviving work in this material designed by Luca della Robbia; they were cast by Michelozzo (1445–69). These doors were slammed on the Pazzi conspirators in 1478 after they had murdered Giuliano de' Medici, and Lorenzo de' Medici escaped through them. In the lunette above is a terra-cotta *Resurrection* (1444), also by Luca. Michelangelo's *Pietà* has been removed from the left tribune to the Cathedral Museum.

Crypt *(Santa Reparata)* ▥ †
▧ *Open 9:30am–12:30pm, 2:30–5:30pm.*
This crypt of the earlier cathedral, entered from the left aisle, was excavated in the 1960s, and contains Roman and early Christian sculptural fragments, 13th and 14thC tombs, and the remains of 14thC frescoes.

Ascent to dome lantern
▧ ✱ *Open 8:30am–12:30pm, 2:30–5:30pm.*
The ascent should not be attempted by anyone who suffers from vertigo, claustrophobia or weak legs, but those who can manage the steep climb will be rewarded by a panoramic view and an increased understanding of Brunelleschi's constructional method, which involved the erection of two shells, one inside the other, with these maintenance stairs between.

Baptistry ▥ † ★
▧ *Open Mon–Fri noon–5:30pm, Sat–Sun 9am–5:30pm.*
Dante's "bel S. Giovanni," the Baptistry is the oldest building in Florence, although it is not as old as Brunelleschi and his

contemporaries liked to believe. In the early 15thC it was
thought to have been the Roman temple of Mars, and it was a
deeper influence on Tuscan Renaissance architecture than any
real Classical building. Its date is still uncertain, but historians
agree that it is not earlier than the 4th–5thC AD, and that it was
probably built on the site of the old Roman praetorium. The
green and white marble cladding belongs to the 11th–13thC,
and the rectangular tribune was added in 1202. The Baptistry
was the cathedral of Florence for a century before the
completion of S. Reparata.

The gilded bronze Baptistry **doors** ★ chart the progress of
sculptural style from Gothic to the Renaissance.

The chronological order of the doors is: 1. **South gate**, from a
wax model prepared in 1330 by Andrea Pisano. The 20 highest
panels relate the story of John the Baptist; the eight below
depict the cardinal and theological virtues. The Renaissance
door surround is by Vittorio Ghiberti. Above the doors is the
Baptist and Salome (1571), by Vincenzo Danti. 2. **North gate**
(1403–24) by Lorenzo Ghiberti and assistants. These are the
doors resulting from the competition set in 1401. Brunelleschi's
losing entry and Ghiberti's winner can be seen in the *Bargello*.
The 20 highest panels illustrate scenes from the New
Testament; below are the four *Evangelists* and four *Church
Doctors*. Above the doors is *The Baptist between a Pharisee and a
Levite* (1506–11), by G.F. Rustici, with advice from Leonardo.
3. **East gate** (1425–52) by Lorenzo Ghiberti. Michelangelo
called these doors "the gates of paradise." They opened a new
artistic era when sculptural perspective replaced Gothic
stylization. The doors are divided into ten panels with Old
Testament scenes. The antique porphyry side columns were
presented to Florence by Pisa in 1117 in gratitude for help in the
conquest of the Balearic Islands. Above is the *Baptism of Christ*,
started by A. Sansovino in 1502, finished by V. Danti in 1564.

The exquisite Baptistry **interior** is more apparently Classical
than the exterior and incorporates Roman columns and
capitals. The 13thC mosaics in the vault—the *Last Judgment*,
the *Creation*, the *Story of Joseph* and the *Baptist*—have never
lost their magic despite five centuries of periodic restoration.
The 13thC tessellated marble **pavement** around the font,
representing the Zodiac, is unmatched in Florence, except by a
similar example in *San Miniato*. 14thC Pisan reliefs have been
applied to the 16thC font. To the right of the tribune is the **tomb
of Cardinal Baldassare Coscia** (1421–7), the schismatic Pope
John XXIII, by Donatello and Michelozzo.

Ascent of Campanile
◪ ✷ *Open 9am–noon, 2:30–5pm.*

The Campanile (1334–1359) ★ is known as 'Giotto's Tower'
although Giotto was responsible only for the first story. It was
carried on after his death by Andrea Pisano until 1348 and
completed by Francesco Talenti. The originals of the sculptural
decorations are in the Cathedral Museum. The climb up to the
bell tower is relatively easy and the views are spectacular.

Cathedral Museum *(Museo dell' Opera del Duomo)* ★
Piazza Duomo 9 ☎ *213229. Open Mon–Sat 9:30am–1pm,
3–5:30pm, Sun and hols 10am–1pm.*

The Cathedral Museum contains an accumulation of important
works transferred during the last century from the Duomo,
Baptistry and Campanile. The palace has been the
administrative headquarters of the Duomo since the early
15thC. Michelangelo carved the *David* in the courtyard.

Ground floor. Sculptures from the 14thC cathedral facade; 16thC drawings of the unfinished facade. In a new room is Brunelleschi's death mask, the wooden model for his dome made for the 1418 competition, and tools which were used for its construction. On the mezzanine is Michelangelo's *Pietà* (1550 – c.53) ★ here for the duration of the restoration of the cathedral dome. Perhaps his most tragic religious sculpture, it was made for what he planned would be his own tomb. Vasari says the head of Nicodemus is a self-portrait. Dissatisfied with his unfinished work, he broke it up and gave parts away. They were pieced together in the 18thC.

First floor. **Sala delle Cantorie**. Sit down and decide which of the two **choral galleries** ★ makes your heart sing more joyously. They were removed from the cathedral in the 17thC, stored away and forgotten until the 19thC. On the entrance wall is Luca della Robbia's (1431 – 8) with the original panels displayed below; opposite is Donatello's (1433 – 9). Underneath that is Donatello's stark, expressionistically penitent *Magdalen* (1435 – 55) ★ The 16 statues around the walls by Donatello and others are from the niches of the bell tower. The most startlingly realistic is Donatello's *Abakuk* (1434 – 6), known as 'Lo Zuccone' ('Big Head') which stands on the wall left of the entrance.

Sala delle Formelle ☆ The **relief panels** were brought here from the Campanile in the 1960s. The earliest are by Andrea Pisano, based on designs by Giotto. The series depicts man's spiritual progress by way of labor, art and the sacraments. "Read but once these inlaid jewels," wrote Ruskin, "and your hour's study will give you strength for all your life."

Sala dell'Altare. The **silver altar** from the Baptistry was begun in 1366, then labored over for a century by craftsmen and artists including Verrocchio and Antonio del Pollaiuolo.

English Cemetery *(Cimitero Protestante)*

*Piazzale Donatello. Map **3**B5 ▣ Open Mon–Sat, Apr–Sept 9am–noon, 3–6pm; Oct–Mar 9am–noon, 3–5pm; Sun and hols 9am–noon. Closed Jan 1, May 1, Aug 15. Ring for admission: tip expected.*

In this oval cemetery lie the remains of Protestants who died in Florence in the late 19thC. Many, like Elizabeth Barrett Browning, had come here from the chilly north to convalesce. Walter Savage Landor, Frances Trollope and Jean Vieusseux are among the famous foreigners buried here.

Firenze com'era Museum *(Topographical Museum of Florence as it was)*

*Via dell' Oriuolo 24. Map **5**C5 ▨ Open Mon–Wed, Fri–Sat 9am–2pm, Sun and hols 8am–1pm. Closed Thurs.*

The urban development of Florence from the 15th–19thC is traced in this fascinating museum with maps, topographical prints, plans, paintings, photographs. Among the maps of the 15thC city in the first room is an 18thC reproduction of the 1470 'Chain Map' (Carta della Catena); the original is in Berlin. In the following rooms the delightful lunettes painted by Giusto Utens for the Villa Artimino record the appearance of grand-ducal villas and gardens at the end of the 16thC; and 18thC Florence comes alive in Giuseppe Zocchi's prints of churches, palaces and villas. Finally, comes the shameful story of the destruction of the old center and the building of that monument to 19thC insensitivity, the Piazza della Repubblica.

Fortezza da Basso Ⅲ
Viale Filippo Strozzi. Map 2B3 🛱 ✲ *Open for crafts exhibitions only.*

The largest historical monument in Florence and the most signposted, the Fortezza da Basso is now a traffic island ringed by the Viale Filippo Strozzi. The fortress was built in 1534–5 for Alessandro de' Medici, the first Duke of Florence. Supported by Charles V, Alessandro's chief purpose was to cow the people of Florence into unquestioning obedience with a citadel, as one contemporary historian described it, "whereby the citizens lost all hope of ever living in freedom." The design is by Antonio Sangallo the Younger; the carved stones around the entrance depict the Medici emblem.

Within are a school, a restoration center, a barracks, and, since 1978, the **Crafts Exhibition and Merchandising Pavilion**, where some 30 exhibitions are held each year.

Foundling Hospital *(Spedale degli Innocenti)* One of the
inaugural buildings of the Renaissance. (See *Santissima Annunziata.*)

Fra Angelico Museum *(Museo dell' Angelico)*
Collection of Fra Angelico's work, now housed in *San Marco.*

Horne Museum Ⅲ
Via dei Benci 6. Map 5D5 🖾 *Open Mon, Wed, Fri 9am–1pm.*

The two enduring achievements of the English art historian Herbert Percy Horne (1864–1916) were his pioneering work on Botticelli, then a still undervalued artist, and the collection he installed in this palace where he lived during the last few years of his life.

The palace was built in 1489 for the Corsi family, and the architect was probably Cronaca, whose Guadagni palace in *Santo Spirito* it resembles. The Corsi were cloth merchants and the design of their palace answered the requirements of their trade: a large cellar for dyeing vats, a sunny gallery over the courtyard portico for drying wool. The stone capitals, carved in the workshop of Andrea Sansovino, are among the finest in Florence.

The **museum** contains no major masterpieces. Horne was not a rich man, but he collected at a time when a keen and educated eye could spot real bargains, and there are many small treasures throughout the museum. There are pictures by Daddi, Pietro Lorenzetti, Filippo Lippi, Beccafumi, Dosso Dossi, and others; Renaissance furniture and majolica; and the pre-industrial domestic utensils which were among Horne's special interests.

Innocenti Gallery *(Galleria dell' Istituto degli Innocenti)* A gallery in the Foundling Hospital in *Santissima Annunziata.*

Laurentian Library *(Biblioteca Medici-Laurenziana)*
Library designed by Michelangelo in *San Lorenzo*, epitomizing Mannerist architecture.

Medici Chapels *(Cappelle Medicee)* The Medici
commissioned some superb works of art for their own glorification in these famous chapels in *San Lorenzo.*

Medici Riccardi Palace 🏛 ★
Via Cavour ☎ 217601. Map **5***B4* 🔲 *Open Mon–Tues,
Thurs–Sat 9am–1pm, Sun and hols 9am–noon. Closed
Wed.*

The palace building boom in 15thC Florence was made possible
by the financial and fiscal policies of Cosimo il Vecchio, and his
palace, built between 1444–1464, was a prototype from which
Florentine palace architecture rarely departed until the 16thC.
The exterior of the palace is best seen from the corner of Via
Cavour.

According to one story, Brunelleschi made a model for the
Medici Palace which Cosimo rejected as being too elaborate.
Brunelleschi flew into a rage and either smashed the model or
sold it to Luca Pitti (see *Pitti Palace*). Certainly Cosimo would
not have wanted to build a family house that was too
ostentatious; he was, after all, the unofficial leader of a
supposedly republican government.

In the event it was Michelozzo, the loyal friend who had
accompanied Cosimo into exile, who built the Medici Palace, a
transitional mixture of medieval and Brunelleschian elements:
biforate windows as in the Palazzo Vecchio, arranged
symmetrically; graduated rustication, very heavy on the ground
floor, entirely smooth at the top; the first *all' antica* palace
cornice in Florence, but unsupported by architrave, frieze or
columns. The crenellated garden wall carries the design back,
with a jerk, into the Middle Ages. These walled side gardens
were attached to most new palaces in this area, but this is one of
the few to have survived.

The ground floor windows, enclosing what was originally a
loggia, were designed by Michelangelo, and are the first
appearance in Florence of the so-called 'kneeling windows'
which became such a common feature of 16thC palaces. The
proportions of the palace were radically altered when the
Riccardi, who bought it in 1659, added the seven northernmost
windows on the Via Cavour.

The interior, much altered over the centuries, now houses
the offices of the Prefecture. Vasari described the Medici Palace
as the first to be built for domestic convenience but, inevitably,
some of the great symbolic events of Florentine history took
place in these rooms. It was here that Lorenzo the Magnificent,
when only 21, accepted control of the government, "for in
Florence one lives ill in the presence of wealth without power."
Emperor Charles VIII was entertained here in 1494, and
Charles V of France in 1536.

Uccello's *Battle of San Romano* hung in Lorenzo's bedroom.
Donatello's *David* and *Judith* were both originally placed in the
courtyard. *Judith the Tyrant-Slayer* was taken away to the
Signoria after the Medici were expelled in 1494, and was
followed there 46yr later by Cosimo I the tyrant in person.
When Cosimo I moved out of the Medici's private palace and
into the Palazzo della Signoria, republican government in
Florence was irrevocably finished. Gradually, the old family
palace was stripped of many Medici-commissioned works of art
which are today among the greatest treasures of the city's
museums and galleries.

Benozzo Gozzoli Chapel *(Cappella di Benozzo Gozzoli)* ★
🔲 *Open Mon–Tues, Thurs–Sat 9am–noon, 3–5pm, Sun
and hols 9am–noon. Closed Wed.*

The **Benozzo Gozzoli Chapel** ★ retained its treasures.
Gozzoli's *Journey of the Magi* frescoes (1459), the artist's most

popular and imaginative works, were commissioned by Piero
de' Medici to commemorate his membership of the religious
confraternity of the *Three Magi*. Around the walls members of
the Medici family process on horseback through a fairytale
Tuscan landscape reminiscent of the Fiesolan hill of Vincigliata
(see *Tuscany/Fiesole*).

In the first floor **gallery**, reached by the second staircase on
the right of the courtyard, is one of the most exhilarating and
ridiculous sights in all Florence. It is Luca Giordano's ceiling
fresco, the *Apotheosis of the Medici* (1683), commissioned by the
Marchese Riccardi as a gesture of gratitude to the Medici whose
palace his family had lately bought.

Michelangelo Museum *(Casa Buonarroti)* ☆
Via Ghibellina 70 ☎ *287630. Map 5C5* ▨ *Open Wed–Mon
9am–1pm. Closed Tues.*

Michelangelo never actually lived here. The house was built on
a plot of land he bought for his nephew and was later partly
decorated in Michelangelo's honor by his grand-nephew
Michelangelo the Younger.

Ground floor. The drawings are reproductions; the originals
are sometimes shown on special occasions. The unfinished
Venus and *Prisoner* statues are probably not by Michelangelo.

First floor. In the room to the left of the stairs are the two
most interesting pieces in this museum. The *Madonna della
Scala* (1490–2), Michelangelo's earliest known work, is
extraordinarily prophetic in style, and like so many of his later
works it is unfinished. Poliziano suggested the subject for the
Battle of the Centaurs (1492), made while Michelangelo was
attached to the Medici household; the artist's preoccupation
with interlocking male figures began here. In the next room to
the left are architectural sketches and the **wooden model for
the facade of San Lorenzo** (1517), never carried out; the plain
architecture, typical of his early period, was meant to be a
setting for elaborate sculpture. Running along the left of the
courtyard is the gallery frescoed in homage to Michelangelo by
Baroque artists. In a room to the right of the stairs is the
wooden crucifix from S. Spirito, first attributed to
Michelangelo in 1962, although not all art historians agree on
this point. In the next room is a **large model of a river god**, the
only full-scale model by Michelangelo in existence.

Ognissanti ▥ †
*Piazza d'Ognissanti. Map 4C1. Refectory open 9am–noon,
2–4pm.*

The church of Ognissanti was founded in the late 13thC by the
Umiliati, the wool-weaving order who taught Florence the skill
which was to be the basis of its prosperity. The building was
made over completely in 1627 by the Franciscans. A complete
restoration was carried out after the 1966 flood. The facade
(1637) by Matteo Nigetti is one of the earliest appearances in
Florence of the Baroque style. The slender campanile, very like
that of *Santa Maria Novella* but simpler, is 13th–14thC.

The interior is decorated in best-boudoir 17th–18thC
Baroque. On the ceiling, *St Francis in Glory* (1770), frescoed by
Giuseppe Romei. Over the second altar on the right are the
restored remains of Dom. Ghirlandaio's fresco, the *Madonna of
Mercy Sheltering the Vespucci Family* (c.1472), which gives the
only authentic portrait of Simonetta Vespucci, whose funeral
was held in this church in 1476, and a probable portrait of

Amerigo Vespucci as a young boy. In the sacristy, entered from the left transept, is a large School-of-Giotto *Crucifixion*, a *Crucifixion* by Taddeo Gaddi, and a fresco of the *Resurrection* attributed to Agnolo Gaddi (its sinopia can be seen in the refectory).

The entrance to the **refectory museum** is to the left of the church and through the 15thC cloister. At the far end of the refectory is Dom. Ghirlandaio's fresco of the *Last Supper* (1480).

The two frescoes of saints in their studies, Ghirlandaio's *St Jerome* (1480) ★ on the left wall, and Botticelli's more mystic *St Augustine* (1480) ★ on the right wall, were originally in the choir of the church; the realistic detail of both was inspired by Flemish artist Jan van Eyck's *St Jerome in his Study*, which was owned by Lorenzo de' Medici.

Oltrarno

Although Florence is well served by bridges, any one of which is crossed in a minute, Florentines persist in referring to everything s of the Arno as the Oltrarno, or as the *Arno di là* (over there), as though it were still the suburb it used to be in the Middle Ages. The Oltrarno certainly has a very distinctive character, a far richer urban mix than you will find anywhere N of the Arno in that part of the city Florentines call the *Arno di quà* (over here). This is a working-class neighborhood, in which some of the oldest and wealthiest Florentine families have maintained palaces for centuries. Thus, some of the most fashionable restaurants and food shops are in and around San Jacopo, but you can just as easily choose your lunch from a market stall in Piazza *Santo Spirito* or eat with students and craftsmen in any one of many cheap family-run trattorias. You can buy chic boutique clothes or antiques, or you can have your old shoes repaired in a hole-in-the-wall workshop.

It was a place of refuge for early Christians, and even after the 14thC walls embraced the Oltrarno and it became the S. Spirito Quarter of the enlarged city, it remained a place favored by outsiders and subversives. The nobles took their last stand here in 1343; here the signal was given for the Ciompi Uprising. Luca Pitti, a leading opponent of the Medici, chose to build his palace on this, or rather 'that,' side of the Arno.

In the 16thC, after Cosimo I chose to make the *Pitti* the official ducal palace, the Oltrarno became the most fashionable address in Florence. Its most exclusive street, and still the most interesting for those who like palaces of the grand-ducal period, was Via Maggio, linked to the Via Tornabuoni by Ammannati's beautiful bridge of *Santa Trinità*.

(See also *Florence/Walk 3*.)

Orsanmichele ▥ † ★
Via dei Calzaiuoli. Map **5**C4.
Saloni, *Via Arte della Lana 1* ☎*294580* ⊙ *Open Mon–Sat 9am–2pm.*

The name Orsanmichele refers to an oratory, San Michele in Orto, which stood here in the 8thC. Later the site was occupied by a loggiaed grain market, famous for a miraculous image of the virgin painted on one of its pillars. This then burned down and was replaced by a grander loggia used as an oratory and as a trading centre by the guilds of Florence. This loggia, which is the basis of the present structure, was erected from 1337 by Francesco Talenti, Neri di Fioraventi and Benci di Cione.

From 1380 the loggia was enclosed by Simone Talenti and used exclusively for religious worship. The two upper stories were added as warehouses for emergency supplies of grain. The decoration of the church was supervised by the nearby Guelf organization which delegated responsibility for each of the outside niches to a guild. It is fortunate that this decorative program, planned from 1339, did not actually get under way until the early 15thC when Florentine sculpture, after a dullish period, leapt forward into the age of Donatello and Ghiberti.

Some original statues have been removed. Donatello's *St George*, made for the smiths and armorers guild, is now in the *Bargello*, and his *St Louis*, made for the Guelf organization, is in the *Santa Croce* Museum. However, more than enough remain to make the four facades of Orsanmichele the best place in Florence to study the evolution of Florentine freestanding sculpture.

E side (Via dei Calzaiuoli): Ghiberti's still Gothic *John the Baptist* (1414–16); Verrocchio's *Doubting Thomas* (1466–83) and above it the ceramic medallion by Luca della Robbia (1463). s side (Via dei Lamberti): Donatello's *St Mark* (1411–12); the *Madonna of the Rose*, attributed to Piero di Giovanni Tedesco. w side (Via dell' Arte della Lana): Ghiberti's *St Matthew* (1419–22) and *St Stephen* (1428); Nanni di Banco's Gothic *St Eligius* and classical *Four Crowned Saints*. N side (Via Orsanmichele): bronze copy of Donatello's marble *St George*, with the original predella of *St George and the Dragon* (1417), the first relief carving to achieve perspective illusion.

Interior. The odd but satisfying shape recalls the original secular function of the church. The pillars are frescoed with damaged and restored images of patron saints of the guilds. Orcagna's **tabernacle** (1348–59), one of the most beautiful Gothic aedicules in Italy, houses the miraculous image of the *Virgin* (1347), painted by Daddi to replace the earlier fresco destroyed by fire.

The upper stories of the church, the **Saloni di Orsanmichele**, are entered through the restored 14thC palace of the Arte della Lana (Wool Guild) across a connecting bridge. There are splendid views from these imposing rooms, restored in the 1960s.

Palatine Gallery Gallery in the *Pitti Palace* with an outstanding collection of 16thC Italian paintings.

Palazzo del Podestà Built as Florence's first town hall, the building now known as the *Bargello*.

Palazzo Vecchio See *Signoria*.

Pazzi Chapel Brunelleschi's chapel in the cloister of *Santa Croce*, which epitomizes the Early Renaissance.

Piazzale Michelangelo
Map 3E5.

Piazzale Michelangelo is the traditional orientation point for a holiday in Florence. The outlook over the city embraces some of the most celebrated and photographed views in the world. The **monument to Michelangelo** (1875) in the centre of the piazzale is dominated by one of the city's two reproductions of Michelangelo's *David* (the original is in the *Accademia*).

If you place yourself at the center of the balustrade facing the

Arno and above the tower of *San Niccolò*, you will see, looking left to right across Florence: the bell tower of the *Signoria*; the top of the tower of *Santa Maria Novella*; the *Badia* tower and immediately to its right the cupola of the *San Lorenzo* Cappella dei Principi; the white marble tower of the *Duomo*; Brunelleschi's dome; and, further right, the minaret-like tower of *Santa Croce*; the green dome of the Synagogue; and the concrete tower of Nervi's stadium complex. In the distance, left to right, are the hills and valleys of northern Tuscany: see *A–Z/Tuscany* for hills behind *Pistoia* and *Prato*; the tower of Petraia at *Sesto Fiorentino*; the three peaks of Monte Morello; *Fiesole*, with the hill of S. Francesco and the Mugnone valley to its left and Monte Céceri, Vincigliato, and *Settignano* to its right. Further right, on a clear spring day, you can see as far as *Vallombrosa* in the E. Back to Florence and moving to the far corner of the left balustrade and facing w, looking from the Arno southward, you can see: the dome of *San Frediano*, the tower of *Santo Spirito*, the silhouetted *Belvedere* and, dominating the view from the S, the Victorian crenellations of the restored Torre del Gallo on the hill of *Arcetri*.

A staircase to the right of the restaurant La Loggia (see *Florence/Restaurants*) leads to **San Salvatore al Monte**, begun in 1499 to a design by Cronaca.

Pitti Palace ▥ ★
Piazza Pitti ☎ 287096. Map **4**F2 ▥ *Tues–Sat 9am–2pm, Sun and hols 9am–1pm. Closed Mon.*

Luca Pitti's motive for erecting a building so unusually bold for mid-15thC Florence was partly a bid to outdo his political rival Cosimo de' Medici. When work began on the Pitti in the late 1450s, the more simply conceived *Medici Palace* was nearing completion. The design of the Pitti is traditionally, but without evidence, attributed to Brunelleschi, and it is possible that the plans carried out by Luca Fancelli could have been those Brunelleschi supposedly submitted to Cosimo who rejected them as too ostentatious.

Although the palace as left unfinished at Pitti's death in 1472 consisted of only the seven central bays of the present structure, both Machiavelli and Vasari commented on the unique size and splendor of the Pitti. Even now that the palace has been enlarged and altered, you can imagine the original impact of these lofty proportions dramatically clad like an Etruscan building in huge, rough-hewn stone blocks. Nevertheless, the Pitti Palace, only one room deep and carved into the steep slope of its own quarry, must have been an uncomfortable living space for Pitti's impoverished heirs.

In 1549 the Pittis sold their palace to Eleanor of Toledo, Cosimo I's wife, and in May of the following year the Medici entourage moved in. Five years later Vasari's **Corridoio** was thrown across the Arno to connect the old palace, the Palazzo Vecchio (see *Signoria*) with the new palace which was to be the grand-ducal and eventually royal residence for the next three centuries. Ammannati's extensions, the superb **courtyard ★** and the wings towards the Boboli Gardens, were carried out between 1558–70.

A lunette by Utens in *Firenze com'era Museum* shows how the Pitti looked at the end of the 16thC. The facade was enlarged to its present width in the early 17thC by G. and A. Parigi. The two front wings were added in the early 19thC after the return of the bland, good-natured Lorraine dukes (who entertained all foreigners at their palace regardless of social standing). Possession passed to the House of Savoy in 1860. Victor Emmanuel, who occupied the Pitti without much pleasure while Florence was briefly capital of Italy, installed his throne in a room which is now part of the State Apartments, overlooking the courtyard and the house, marked by a plaque, where the exiled Dostoevsky was writing *The Idiot*.

Palatine Gallery *(Galleria Palatina)* ★
■■ ✗ *Ticket also good for Argenti Museum.*

Try to allow the full morning for these two most important sections of the Pitti, the Palatine and Argenti. To reach the Palatine you must climb Ammannati's long, steep staircase to the first floor. The Palatine is famous for its great grand-ducal collection of 16thC paintings of which the supreme treasures are the Raphaels and Titians, mostly portraits; also of outstanding quality are the frescoes by Pietro da Cortona. The tiered arrangement, in keeping with the period of the rooms, is that of a 17thC princely collection; the works are thus placed for decorative effect and not, as in the Uffizi, according to date and school. Thanks to the splendid lighting, the good condition of the pictures and the impeccable taste and knowledge with which they are hung, it doesn't take long to accustom yourself to the lack of didactic guidance. Indeed, after the Palatine, the Uffizi seems dismayingly like a textbook.

From the vestibule you pass through two Neoclassical rooms to the Sala di Venere, where the gallery proper begins. On the ceiling, the bold **fresco allegory** (1641–2) ★ by Pietro da Cortona, which was commissioned by Ferdinand II and executed with the help of Ciro Ferri, begins with the *Ideal Prince Being Torn from the Arms of Venus*; the cycle continues through the next four rooms. In the center of the room is Canova's statue of *Venus*, sent to Florence by Napoleon as a replacement for the looted Uffizi *Venus de Medici*.

Paintings/Titian: *The Concert* (c.1510–13) ★ is an early work which passed as a Giorgione for 250yr after its purchase in 1654 by Cardinal Leopold; *Portrait of Julius II*, a contemporary copy of Raphael's original now in the National Gallery in London; *Portrait of Pietro Aretino* (1545) ★ who was the talented, roistering Venetian intellectual who thought so highly of this likeness that he presented it to Cosimo I; and *Portrait of a Lady, 'La Bella'* (1536) ★ with perhaps the same model as the *Uffizi Venus*. Of the two glowing landscapes by Rubens, *Peasants Returning from the Fields* (c.1637) ★ is the finer.

Sala di Apollo. On the ceiling (1647–60), *The Young Prince Converses with Apollo*, protector of the Arts and Sciences. Paintings: Guido Reni's late masterpiece *Cleopatra*; *Sacred Family and Deposition* by Andrea del Sarto; Rosso Fiorentino's *Madonna Enthroned with Saints* (1522), enlarged to its present size when it was bought from the church of S. Spirito. Titian: the intensely romantic *Portrait of a Man* (c.1540) ★ is known as 'The Englishman' because the subject may have been the Duke of Norfolk; and *The Magdalen* (c.1531) ★ is more ripe than repentant.

Sala di Marte. Ceiling (1645–7): the Medici arms surmounted by the grand-ducal crown dominate the composition. Paintings: Tintoretto's finest work in the gallery, *Portrait of Luigi Cornaro*; van Dyck's *Cardinal Bentivoglio* (c.1623), Papal Ambassador to Flanders and France; Titian's *Ippolito de' Medici* (1532), dressed as a grandee of Hungary and painted 3yr before he was poisoned at Gaeta; Rubens'

Consequences of War (1638) ✫ – Mars, escaped from the arms of
Venus, destroys Art, Charity and Scholarship; and Murillo's
sweet, lifelike *Madonna and Child*.

Sala di Giove, formerly the grand-ducal throne room.
Despite the fierce eponymous god, the frescoes (1643–6) in the
lunettes portray allegories of the secure peace Ferdinand II
tried to maintain in Tuscany. Paintings: Raphael's *Portrait of a
Woman, La Velata* (c.1516) ✫ – the virtuoso handling of the
sleeve contrasts with the purity of outline which was to
influence Ingres; P. Pollaiuolo's *St Jerome* (c.1450–70), a stark
anatomical analysis; Andrea del Sarto's graceful *St John the
Baptist as a Boy* (1523) ✫ which once belonged to Cosimo I and
hung in the Uffizi Tribuna – the background has been damaged
by early restoration; Fra Bartolommeo's monumental *St Mark*
(1514–16), and *Deposition* (c.1516) ✫ which was his last and
greatest work, left partly unfinished; and Perugino's *Madonna
Adoring the Christ Child*, known as the 'Madonna del Sacco'
after the bolster on which the child is seated.

The world is made up of earth, air, fire and water – but there is
another element – the Florentines.

Pope Boniface VIII (c.1300)

Sala di Saturno. The last of Pietro da Cortona's fresco
sequence (1663–5) was executed by Ciro Ferri. Raphael's
Madonna della Seggiola (of the chair) (c.1515) ✫ is now, as
always, the most popular picture in the Palatine. In the 19thC
the waiting list for permission to copy her was 5yr. The legend is
that the circular panel was taken from the end of a wine cask,
but the more plausible explanation for the tondo is Raphael's
wish to master a traditional Florentine compositional challenge.
Also by Raphael are portraits of *Agnolo* ✫ and of *Maddalena
Doni* (c.1505–6) ✫ which were painted a few years after their
marriage (an occasion celebrated also by Michelangelo's *Doni
Tondo* in the *Uffizi*). Leonardo's *Mona Lisa* suggested
Maddalena's pose. *Portrait of Cardinal Inghirami* (c.1515) ✫
– he was an important figure at the court of Leo X – and the
portrait reveals the character of the sitter as much through his
hands as face. The beauty of Perugino's *Deposition* (1495) ✫ has
been revealed by recent cleaning.

Sala dell'Iliade. Neo-Classical decorations. Paintings: Justus
Sustermans' *Portrait of Waldemar Christian, Prince of Denmark*
(c.1662), the artist's best-known work; Andrea del Sarto's
Assumption of The Virgin (c.1527), based on the similar, earlier
composition on the opposite wall; Artemisia Gentileschi's
dramatic *Judith*; Raphael's *Portrait of a Pregnant Woman, La
Gravida* (c.1504–8) ✫; and Velazquez' *Philip IV on Horseback*,
a studio work sent to Florence as a model for an equestrian
statue. In centre of room, *Charity* (1824) by L. Bartolini.

Sala dell' Educazione di Giove. Paintings: Caravaggio's
Sleeping Cupid (c.1608); and Cristofano Allori's *Judith* ✫ – one
of the most universally admired 17thC Florentine paintings for
its technical perfection and ravishing use of color.

Sala della Stufa. Formerly a bathroom, the **frescoes**
(1637–41) ✫ represent the Four Ages of Man and are among
Pietro da Cortona's minor masterpieces. Sala dei Bagno. An
early 19thC bathroom.

Sala di Ulisse. Paintings: Moroni's *Portrait of a Woman*,
intensely human; Raphael's *Madonna of the Impannata* (1514) –
the *impannate* are the waxpaper-paned windows in the

background; and Cigoli's expressive *Ecce Homo*.

Sala di Prometeo. Paintings: Filippo Lippi's *Madonna and Child* (c.1552), the quintessential Early Renaissance picture; Botticelli's *Portrait of a Woman*; D. Beccafumi's *Holy Family*. Off the Sala di Prometeo are four rooms decorated in the 1830s. Paintings include landscapes by C. von Poelenburg; Titian's portrait of *Tommaso Mosti* (1526); A. del Sarto's *Stories of Joseph* (1520–23); G. Schalken's *Girl with a Candle*; and fruit paintings by Rachele Ruysch.

Sala del Poccetti, named for the artist whose frescoes glorifying the House of Medici decorate the ceiling. Paintings: Rubens' *Portrait of a Woman*, probably Catherine Manners, Duchess of Buckingham; D. Fetti's two genre-like parables; F. Furini's exuberant *Hylas and the Nymphs*.

Volterrano Wing. Pictures by 17th and 18thC artists, notably Furini, Giovanni da S. Giovanni, Cigoli, Bilivert and Salvator Rosa. First room. Volterrano's *A Trick of the Parish Priest Arlotto* (c.1650) illustrates an anecdote about Arlotto, a jokester priest who lived in the Mugello in the 1440s. Last room. The most complete collection in existence of fruit paintings by 17thC Neapolitan woman artist Giovanna Garzoni.

Argenti Museum ☆
Entrance near left corner of courtyard 🚇 *Open Wed, Fri 9am–2pm, Sun 9am–1pm.*

Despite its name, this is not primarily a museum of silverware. The exquisite treasures bought or commissioned by the Medici and Lorraine dynasties which it contains form one of the richest displays of luxury craftsmanship in the world. There is no better place to follow the changing taste of Florence's rulers, from the sublime collection of Lorenzo's antique vases to the ridiculous, ingenious opulence that appealed in later centuries. The exhilarating Baroque frescoes of the ground floor apartments, used as reception rooms for important visitors by Ferdinand II, are rare in Florence for their sense of fun.

Sala di S. Giovanni. Frescoed by S. Giovanni (1634–36), Furini (1638–42) and others for the marriage of Ferdinand II and Victoria della Rovere, this room is one of the final, most exuberant tributes the Medici were to pay to Lorenzo the Magnificent.

Sala Buia. Lorenzo's collection of **antique vases** ★ is the glory of the museum. That a sensitive, discriminating poet-diplomat would have his initials carved on such objects shows the confidence of Renaissance man. Grotticina. Carved wooden relief by Grinling Gibbons given to Cosimo II by Charles II of England. The next three rooms are frescoed with stupendous illusionist architecture and historical or allegorical subjects by A.M. Colonna (1638–44). Sala degli Avori. Baroque ivory fantasies, some beautiful, some bizarre jokes.

First floor. Three rooms left of the stairs contain the silver treasure of the Archbishop of Salzburg, brought to Florence in 1815 by Ferdinand III. In the fourth are examples of the not altogether healthy grand-ducal interest in anthropology. Sala dei Cammei. A wonderful collection of cameos, with a *pietradura* mosaic of the Piazza Signoria (1598). Sala dei Gioielli. **Pietradura exvoto** (1617–24) of Cosimo II, a portrait in precious stones, the ultimate in grand-ducal decadence; and a fine collection of Baroque pearls and engraved classical gems mounted on rings.

Returning to the ground floor the exit is through the former grand-ducal bedroom.

Gallery of Modern Art (Galleria d'Arte Moderna)
🔳 *Tickets at the gallery entrance on second floor.*
In the 19thC when tourists, even more singlemindedly than
today, came to Florence to study the work of artists long dead,
this is what living Tuscan artists were producing: stuffy,
academic paintings, orgasmic nudes, and elaborate furniture.
Towards the end of the 19thC Italian painters reacted with their
own Impressionist movement. They are known as the
Macchiaioli, and their work is to be found in Rms
XXIII–XXVI, which also afford rare views of the Oltrarno and
the nave of *Santo Spirito*. The gallery has recently been
reorganized and houses some 2,000 works in its 30 rooms.

Appartamenti Monumentali. Occupying the right half of the
first floor and nowadays usually closed to the public, this
apartment, which includes the Savoy throne room, contains no
major work of art but is notable for some very fine late
Neo-Classical decoration. Most elegant are the oval Queen
Margherita's Dressing Room (late 18thC) and the Neo-Classical
Sala Bianca, where fashion shows now take place beneath
superb stuccowork by G. Albertolli (1776–80).

Meridiana Palace, Contini-Bonacossi Collection. Expected
to open to the public in 1984. Behind the right wing of the Pitti,
this sub-palace was the preferred residence of Victor Emmanuel.
It now houses a fine collection of Italian and Spanish paintings.

Coach Museum (Museo delle Berline). Although
advertised, the official word is that this is closed for some years.

Ponte Vecchio ★
Map **4D3**.
The Ponte Vecchio spans the Arno at its narrowest point and is
very likely the site of the Roman bridge which carried the N–S
traffic of the Via Cassia. The present structure dates from 1345,
when an earlier bridge was rebuilt so solidly that it has
withstood all subsequent floods. The jewelers of the Ponte
Vecchio were among the first to be notified of the impending
flood of 1966. Their stock was saved, but their shops and
Vasari's corridor, which crosses the river above the E side of the
bridge, were severely damaged. It has also survived the other
dangers. The oldest bridge in Florence was the only one spared
in August 1944, but the retreating German army blocked access
to it, mining Por S. Maria to the N and Borgo S. Jacopo to the S.

The Ponte Vecchio was the Sarajevo of medieval Italy. At its
N end, where an equestrian statue of Mars then stood,
Buondelmonte dei Buondelmonti was assassinated on the
Easter morning of 1215, and a smouldering personal vendetta
erupted into the Guelf-Ghibelline civil wars.

There have been shops on the Ponte Vecchio since the 13thC,
occupied first by tanners, then butchers, linen merchants,
greengrocers and blacksmiths. In 1593 Ferdinand I decided
that these "vile arts" were inappropriate to a passage linking the
two grand-ducal palaces. The shops were cleared and rented at
twice the price to 41 goldsmiths and eight jewelers. The present
tenants may not be able to trace their occupancy back that far,
but most have been here for many generations.

(See also *Florence/Shopping*.)

Porta Romana
Map **2E2**.
Porta Romana is the southernmost of the old city gates and one
of the modern city's busiest exits. Erected in 1326, the tower

has been cropped, but the doors are original, as is the 14thC fresco of the Madonna. A stretch of preserved walls runs N along Viale Petrarca to Piazza T. Tasso. To the s is the old Siena road and the new road to Poggio Imperiale and Impruneta. The Viale dei Colli Alti winds eastwards from Porta Romana to Piazza F. Ferrucci.

If the gate to the Boboli Gardens is closed, try the Annalena gate in Via Romana. Beyond this gate, in the villa in Via Colombaia, Florence Nightingale was born in 1820.

Rucellai Palace 𝕀𝕀𝕀 ★
Via della Vigna Nuova 18. Map 4C2. Only open to special group tours.

Probably the most beautiful and certainly the most carefully considered of all Florentine palaces, Alberti's Palazzo Rucellai was the first in Florence to conform to the Classical Orders. It was built in the 1450s for Giovanni Rucellai who, after an early retirement from business, devoted himself to scholarship.

Bernardo Rossellino supervised construction, the cost of which in labor alone must have been exorbitant. Alberti's complex and subtle design is chiseled on to a flat stone surface. If you look closely you can see where the stone blocks meet across the drawn rustication.

Contemporary documents leave many crucial questions about the Rucellai unanswered. Even the attribution to Alberti, although generally accepted on stylistic grounds, is undocumented. But examination of the stone work during the most recent restoration confirms the theory that Alberti's plan suggested only the five bays on the left (as you face the palace); the left door would thus have been the central and only entrance. It was very likely Giovanni Rucellai himself who supervised the extension of the module to the right, until he was interrupted by a financial crisis caused by the loss at sea of two ships. Along the entablature, Fortune's Sail, the Rucellai heraldic device, alternates with the Medici Diamond Ring: a reminder of the political alliance of the two families.

The Rucellai Loggia, opposite the palace, was probably made for the wedding celebrations of Giovanni's son to a grand-daughter of Cosimo il Vecchio. It belongs to the 1460s, and if the design was suggested by Alberti, the execution was oddly clumsy, as you can see from the inside (the Loggia is often used for art exhibitions). This was the last of the Florentine family loggias, which became impracticable due to the rising cost of land and therefore unfashionable. It could only have been built for a person as rich and as conservative as Giovanni Rucellai, who acquired over half a dozen properties to create the site.

Behind the left flank of the palace is the little church of San Pancrazio, long since deconsecrated and now housing sculptures left to the city by Marino Marini.

The adjacent **Rucellai Chapel ★** entered from the Via della Spada, is at last, after years under restoration, open to the public. Alberti designed this chapel, the first barrel-vaulted building in the city, in 1467 to house Giovanni Rucellai's funerary monument, the **Aedicule of the Church of the Holy Sepulcher**. An imitation in miniature of the original antique church in Jerusalem, this aedicule is Alberti's most fascinating work, and the one which epitomizes everything he stood for as an artist. Inside the aedicule is a damaged fresco of the *Resurrection* by Baldovinetti. The wall opposite the entrance separating the chapel from the church was built in the 19thC.

Santissima Annunziata 🏛 † ★
*Map 3*B4.

The **Via dei Servi**, which links SS. Annunziata to the Duomo, was built as a processional street between the two most important of the Florentine churches dedicated to the Virgin. It is named after the Servite Order, of which SS. Annunziata is the mother church. On the Feast of the Virgin's Nativity the Via dei Servi is lined with candy stalls and children carry paper lanterns from the Duomo to SS. Annunziata.

As you walk from the Duomo, notice among the 16thC palaces three on the left: the **Pucci** palace (entrance in Via de' Pucci), with an imposing but battered carved emblem of Leo X on the corner; the **Niccolini** palace (no. 15), built in 1550 to a design by Baccio d'Agnolo; and, on the corner of Piazza SS. Annunziata, the **Grifoni** (1557–63), one of the few brick palaces in Florence, built by Ammannati for one of Cosimo I's courtiers, and now the Riccardi Mannelli, used as the regional government headquarters.

Although Piazza SS. Annunziata is architecturally the most harmonious open space in Florence, the apparently unified design was achieved over a period of nearly two centuries. The square had assumed its present size by the 14thC, but the first attempt to regularize it was Brunelleschi's loggia of the **Innocenti Hospital** (1419–26) (**Spedale degli Innocenti**). The central arch of the church portico was built in the mid-15thC, probably by Antonio da Sangallo the Elder. Next, chronologically, came the **loggia of the Servite Confraternity** (1516–25), by Antonio da Sangallo the Younger and Baccio d'Agnolo, deliberately mimicking the Innocenti across the square. Finally, in the early 17thC, the church portico was extended into a loggia.

The equestrian **statue of Ferdinand I** in the center of the square is Giambologna's last work, finished in 1608 by his pupil P. Tacca. It is the subject of Browning's poem *The Statue and the Bust*. Also by Tacca are the two small, fantastic, poison-green **fountains** (1629).

The Spedale degli Innocenti was the first foundling hospital in the world, and Brunelleschi's **loggia ★** is the first building in Florence to apply new Classical ideas to the Tuscan Romanesque style. The original loggia consists of the central nine bays. Ten of the ceramic **tondos** of swaddled babies (c.1487) are by Andrea della Robbia; the two at either end, however, are imitations.

Innocenti Gallery *(Galleria dell' Instituto degli Innocenti)* 🏛 *Piazza SS. Annunziata 12* ☎ *284768. Map 5A5* ▨ *Open Tues–Sat: summer 9am–7pm; winter 9am–1pm; Sun and hols 9am–1pm. Closed Mon.*
This gallery on the first floor contains works by, among others, Luca della Robbia, Piero di Cosimo, and Domenico Ghirlandaio, including his *Adoration of the Magi* (1488).

The **Church ★** of SS. Annunziata was founded in 1234 by seven aristocratic families. It became an important shrine, visited by pilgrims from all over Europe, after it was dedicated in the 14thC to a miraculous image of the Virgin Annunciate. Michelozzo, who was the brother of the Servite Prior, rebuilt the church between 1444–81.

The central door under the portico leads to Michelozzo's atrium, known as the **Chiostro dei Voti** after the life-size wax effigies the pilgrims left of themselves. By the 17thC there were some 600 of these ex-votos in the church; all have disappeared.

The **frescoes** ✩ have recently been returned after restoration. Illumination is poor, so go in daytime, or use a flashlight. Right portico wall: the *Assumption* (1517) by Rosso Fiorentino; the *Visitation* (1516) by Pontormo. Right wall, far corner: the *Birth of the Virgin* (1514) by Andrea del Sarto. Nave wall: right of nave entrance, the *Arrival of the Magi* (1511) by Andrea del Sarto; left of nave entrance, *The Nativity* (1460–2) which is Baldovinetti's masterpiece, badly eroded by time and damp, but still showing one of the loveliest landscapes in Tuscan art. Left of the entrance from the portico and on the left wall: *Miracles of S. Filippo Benizzi* (1509–10), five of Andrea del Sarto's earliest frescoes.

The extravagantly stuccoed and gilded **nave** and side chapels, decorated in the 16th–19thC when SS. Annunziata was, as indeed it still is, the fashionable church of Florence, are in striking contrast to the strict harmony of the square. Immediately to the left of the nave entrance is the **tempietto** designed by Michelozzo for Piero di Cosimo to house the *Miraculous Image of the Virgin*, whose head is traditionally said to have been painted by an angel, but which has been repainted so often that it is now of no artistic importance. The *tempietto* bears an inscription which will interest students of the Florentine character that reads: 'the marble alone cost 4,000 florins'. Many of the nave chapels contain splendid Baroque and Neo-Classical decorations. One of the best is the first on the left, the **Feroni Chapel** (1692) by G.B. Foggini. Over the altar, in an ornate, twisting frame, is the *Vision of St Julian* (c.1455) ✩ by Castagno. The fresco was whitewashed 100yr after the artist's death as the result of an untrue story told by Vasari that Castagno had murdered Domenico Veneziano. In the second chapel on the left is Castagno's powerful fresco depicting the *Trinity* (1454–5) ★ In the right nave is B. Rossellino's *Monument to Orlando de' Medici* (1456); and to the right of the presbytery entrance, a marble *Pietà* by Bandinelli, who is buried here with his wife.

The **presbytery**, known as the Tribune or Rotonda, was begun by Michelozzo in 1451, finished by Manetti in 1477 according to advice given by Alberti, but much altered by the 18thC decorations. The chapel opposite the nave entrance was decorated by Giambologna for his own grave and those of other Flemish artists working in Florence; the frescoes are by Poccetti. In the next chapel to its left is a *Resurrection* (c.1550) by Bronzino.

The **Chiostro dei Morti** is entered from the left door under the facade portico. Over the door in the far right corner is one of Andrea del Sarto's most loved and famous works, the *Madonna del Sacco* (1525) ✩

Sant' Apollonia, Castagno Museum ▥ ★

Via XXVII Aprile 1 ☎ *287074. Map **3**B4. Open Tues–Sat: summer 9am–12:30pm, 3–6pm; winter 9am–12:30pm, 3–5pm; Sun and hols 9am–1pm. Closed Mon.*

Shortly after his return from Venice in 1444, Andrea del Castagno painted his *Last Supper* ★ for the nuns of S. Apollonia. The refectory of their former convent is now a museum centered round this fresco, which is probably the best-known and most influential of all *Last Suppers*, apart from Leonardo's in Milan. The scene is set in a fantastic marbled niche. Christ has not yet revealed the mystery of the sacrament. The sculptured peasant faces of the disciples are calm. On this side of the table the brooding figure of Judas prepares us for the announcement, "One of you shall betray me." Vasari said Castagno looked and behaved like a Judas, and there is certainly something sinister about much of his work.

Above the _Last Supper_, and of at least the same powerful quality, are his three _Scenes from the Passion_, tragically deteriorated. Their sinopie, uncovered when the frescoes were detached for restoration, are displayed on the opposite wall. Castagno's _Famous Men and Women_, painted for the Villa Pandolfini at Legnaia and once hung in this museum, are now stored in the _Uffizi_, where they will eventually be shown.

Santi Apostoli ▥ †
Map **4**D3.

Charlemagne did not found SS. Apostoli, as the inscription on the otherwise modest facade boasts, nevertheless, this beautiful little church in the center of medieval Florence is very old.

The portal is 16thC, probably by Benedetto da Rovezzano, but the **interior** ★ apart from the 15th–16thC side chapels, is the earliest on this side of the Arno except for the Baptistry (_Duomo_), with which it is roughly contemporary. Vasari confirms what will be obvious to anyone who knows the churches of _Santo Spirito_ and _San Lorenzo_ when he tells us that Brunelleschi was profoundly influenced by SS. Apostoli. Looking at the nave and aisles from the altar end, you might almost believe that Brunelleschi designed this interior. In the right aisle, second altar, is Vasari's _Immaculate Conception_ (1541), one of his best and most reproduced paintings, historically important as the most scholarly pictorial representation of a popular belief. At the top of the left aisle is a large terra-cotta tabernacle by Giovanni della Robbia which is of better quality than many of his works. Next to it is Benedetto da Rovezzano's **tomb of Oddo Altoviti** (1507), whose palace, also by Benedetto, stands on the S side of the square.

The tiny Piazza del Limbo takes its name from the unbaptized babies who were once buried here. To the left of the church is a relief of the _Madonna and Child_ by Benedetto da Maiano on the flank of the Rosselli del Turco palace, the facade of which, by Baccio d'Agnolo (1517), is in Borgo SS. Apostoli.

Santa Croce ★ ▥ †
Map **5**D4.

"Wait then for an entirely bright morning; rise with the sun, and go to Santa Croce, with a good opera-glass in your pocket."

If you are going to Santa Croce to study the numerous and instructive _trecento_ frescoes, you should follow Ruskin's advice. But do leave plenty of time. Ruskin scorned the Renaissance, but no modern tourist would want to rush in and out of the Pazzi Chapel and miss some of the finest Renaissance sculptures in Florence.

Santa Croce is not a particularly cheerful quarter. Before the 1966 flood, which caused terrible damage in this low-lying area, it was densely populated with working-class families and craftsmen's workshops. Many of these people have now moved elsewhere and the craftsmen have been replaced by the so-called leather factories which sell to tourists. But it is still a neighborhood which stretches one's sense of history. This was the center of the dyeing trade, one of the foundations of Florentine mercantile prosperity in the 14th–16thC. One of its main streets is still called Corsi dei Tintori, and some of the

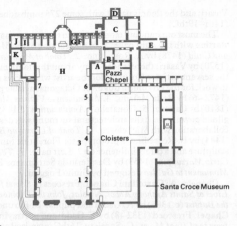

Santa Croce

palaces were built to accommodate the dyeing vats (see *Horne Museum*). The imagination is carried back much further by three streets which trace the semicircular outline of the Roman amphitheater immediately to the w of the Piazza S. Croce.

This great Franciscan preaching church was begun in 1294, possibly by Arnolfo di Cambio, "with Giotto at his side and Dante looking on," or so Ruskin liked to imagine. The Franciscans, as he says, wanted a church for "preaching, prayer, sacrifice, burial," not for "self-glorification or town-glorification." Be that as it may, consecration was delayed by a schism in the order until the 15thC, when the Renaissance artists who worked here were evidently indifferent to Franciscan ideals of self-abnegation.

Because Michelangelo and Galileo, among other great Italians, are buried here, S. Croce can be regarded as a kind of pantheon of Italian genius. 19thC romanticism found this idea irresistible and must take the blame for the hideous facade, which was paid for by an Englishman, as well as the unfortunate statue of Dante in the square and the minaret-like Gothic bell tower.

Apart from these anachronisms the square looks much as it did in the 16th and 17thC when football matches and other spectacles were staged here by the grand dukes. A disk, dated February 10, 1565 on the ground floor of the frescoed Palazzo dell' Antella (no. 21) marks the center line. The palace (1619), by Giulio Parigi, was frescoed in 20 days by 12 assistants of Giovanni da S. Giovanni. Less picturesque but architecturally more strenuous is the Serristori-Cocchi palace (no. 1, opposite the church) attributed to Baccio d'Agnolo.

During the period of puritanical hysteria induced by Savonarola, heretics were burned in this square, and book burnings continued until 1580. Earlier, in the prime years of the Medicean Republic, S. Croce was the setting for elaborate pageants in honor of Lorenzo the Magnificent's betrothal to Clarice Orsini and of Giuliano's love for Simonetta Vespucci.

The immense, barn-like **church interior ★** (see plan) is T-shaped: a broad nave crossed at the bottom by a straight row of 12 chapels. The nave side chapels were added in 1560 by

73

Vasari; and the floor is paved with some 276 tombstones (14th–19thC).

The most outstanding monuments in the nave are as follows, starting with the right nave: 1. Relief carving of the *Madonna and Child* (1478) by A. Rossellino. 2. *Tomb of Michelangelo* (1570) by Vasari; there is a sad irony about this tomb made by the servant-artist to Cosimo I for the artist who always refused to work for the tyrannical duke. 3. Octagonal marble **pulpit** (1472–6) by B. da Maiano. 4. *Monument to Vittorio Alfieri* (1810) by Canova. 5. Donatello's *Annunciation* (c.1435) ☆ in gilded *pietra serena*; the architectural surround was designed in collaboration with Michelozzo. 6. *Tomb of Leonardo Bruni* (1444) by B. Rossellino, a prototype for Florentine funerary sculpture and a direct influence on 7. Left nave: 7. *Tomb of Carlo Marsuppini* (1453) by Desiderio da Settignano. 8. 18thC *Monument to Galileo* designed by Giulio Foggini.

Chapels. **A. Castellani Chapel**. Frescoes of *Scenes from the Lives of Saints Anthony Abbot, Nicolas, John the Divine and John the Baptist* (c.1385) by A. Gaddi and pupils. **B. Baroncelli Chapel**. Frescoed (1332–8) by T. Gaddi and portraying *Scenes from the Life of Mary*. **C. Sacristy**. 16thC intarsiaed and inlaid bench chest. The beautiful *Crucifixion* on the right wall is by T. Gaddi. **D. Rinuccini Chapel**. Frescoes (c.1365) by Giovanni da Milano and the Master of the Rinuccini Chapel: right wall, *Scenes from the Life of Mary Magdalen*; and on the left wall, *Scenes from the Life of the Virgin*. Gothic wrought-iron gate (1373). **E. Novitiate Chapel** (1445) by Michelozzo, commissioned by Cosimo il Vecchio. On the altar, terra-cotta tabernacle of the *Madonna and Child with Angels and Saints* (c.1480) by Andrea della Robbia or a close follower. Galileo is buried in this chapel.

The two chapels to the right of the chancel, the Peruzzi (**F**.) and the Bardi (**G**.), were frescoed by Giotto at the height of his mature powers. An overwhelming influence on Masaccio and thus on the whole of *quattrocento* Florentine painting, they were covered with whitewash in the 18thC. Rediscovered in the 19thC they were subjected to heavy overpainting. These accretions have now been removed, and what you see is entirely by Giotto's hand. Enough is left to help you solve the puzzle but not quite enough to give instant esthetic pleasure. **F. Peruzzi Chapel** ☆ Frescoes (c.1326–30) on the right wall show *Scenes from the Life of St John the Divine*; on the left wall, *Scenes from the Life of St John the Baptist*. **G. Bardi Chapel** ☆ Ruskin compared this chapel to "a large, beautiful, colored Etruscan vase inverted over your heads like a diving-bell." Frescoes (c.1315–20) of *Scenes from the Life of St Francis*. Altarpiece on panel (c.1250–60) by the Master of the Bardi Chapel.

H. Chancel. Frescoes and stained glass (c.1380) of the *Legend of the True Cross* by A. Gaddi. The *Crucifix* over the altar is by the master of the Fogg Pietà. **I. Bardi di Vernio Chapel**. Frescoes (1335–8) show *Scenes from the Life of St Sylvester* by Maso di Banco. **J. Niccolini Chapel** (ask sacristan to open the gate). A remarkable anticipation of the 17thC Baroque style built in 1579–85 by Antonio Dossi. **K. Bardi Chapel**. The wooden **crucifix** by Donatello is supposed to be the one Brunelleschi criticized for looking like a peasant on a cross. To the right of the church is the entrance to the **cloisters**, the **Pazzi Chapel** and the **Santa Croce Museum**.

Brunelleschi planned the Pazzi Chapel around 1430. Building began in 1443, and the upper part of the facade was completed after his death. The **interior** ★ was more successful even than the *San Lorenzo* Old Sacristy, and probably sums up the modern ideal of the early Renaissance more completely than any other single monument in Florence; and there is no other place that has such a calming and restorative effect on the spirits. But it is not quite perfect. As you can see in the corners where fragmentary pilasters are awkwardly squeezed, Brunelleschi did not fully solve the mathematical problem he set himself here. The blue and white terra-cotta **tondos** of the *Apostles* in the chapel are by Luca della Robbia; the polychrome **tondos** of the *Evangelists* in the pendentives have been attributed to Brunelleschi.

Santa Croce Museum *(Museo Cimabue)* ☆
Piazza Santa Croce 16 ☎ *290369. Map* **5**D4 🚻 *Open summer 9am–12:30pm, 3–6:30pm; winter 8am–12:30pm, 3–5pm. Ticket also valid for Pazzi Chapel and Cloisters.*
The contents of the museum, especially the panel paintings, suffered gravely from the 1966 flood, but the two most important works are now on display in the refectory. On the right is Cimabue's *Crucifixion* ☆ which is one of the most tragic victims of the flood; on the left wall, Donatello's *St Louis of Toulouse* (1423) ☆ which was made for Orsanmichele and moved to the facade of S. Croce in 1463.

The **second cloister** is entered from the far right-hand corner of the first cloister, past a splendid **portal** by Benedetto da Maiano. Finished in 1453 by a close follower of Brunelleschi, this is one of the most beautiful cloisters in Florence.

San Felice 🏛
Map **4**E2.
This church, in its busy little triangular piazza a few steps from the Pitti, has an attractive Renaissance facade attributed to Michelozzo. The interior is calm, spacious and much restored with a good Giottesque crucifix over the right side door.

I heard last night a little child go singing.
'Neath Casa Guidi windows, by the church,
O bella libertà, O bella!
　　　　　Elizabeth Barrett Browning, *Casa Guidi Windows*

This may have been the first center for battered wives. In the Renaissance its Dominican nuns offered refuge to women who fled from their husbands. The Brownings lived at Casa Guidi (Piazza S. Felice 8) for 15yr until Elizabeth's death in 1861. A passionate supporter of the Risorgimento, Elizabeth's existence was marred by a loathing for her neighbor, Leopold II.

Santa Felicità 🏛
Map **4**E3.
There has been a church on this site for nearly 2,000yr, the first being a hiding place and burial ground for early Christians. In the Renaissance the Benedictine nuns of S. Felicita ran a successful quarry on their properties behind the church, but the building was much altered in the 16thC when it was used as a private chapel by the Medici dukes. In 1736 it was thoroughly remodeled by Ferdinand Ruggieri, who did not, however, disturb the facade portico built by Vasari in 1564 to support his aerial corridor, which passes through the church on its way from the Uffizi to the Pitti. Today the oldest monument in the square is the granite column erected in 1381.

Interior. To the right of the entrance is the Brunelleschian
Capponi Chapel decorated by Pontormo 1525–8 (light
switch behind a pilaster on the left). The *Deposition* ★ over the
altar is really a meditation on the beautiful, weightless body of
the dead Christ. It is probably Pontormo's most intensely felt
and emotionally affecting masterpiece – the figure in brown on
the right may be a self-portrait. On the right wall is his
Annunciation, revealed as another masterpiece by cleaning in
the 1960s. In the pendentives of the cupola are four **tondos of
the Evangelists** (the *St Mark* is by Bronzino). The grand-ducal
tribunes are on either side of the nave w of the transepts. The
charming choir (1610–20) is by Cigoli.

Around the corner from the square in Via Guicciardini is
Palazzo Guicciardini (no. 15), birthplace of the historian
Francesco Guicciardini and still occupied by his descendants.

San Firenze ▥ †
*Map **5**D5.*
The facade of S. Firenze, which unites three separate earlier
buildings, is the biggest and best 18thC Baroque spectacle in
Florence. On the left side is the **facade of the church of
S. Filippo Neri** designed by Ferdinando Ruggieri in 1715. The
central and right-hand section (1772–5), formerly the church
and convent of S. Apollinare, now the Tribunal, is by Zanobi
del Rosso. Opposite is the elegant **Gondi** palace (1490–1501) by
Giuliano da Sangallo. Ring for the porter to see the courtyard.

San Frediano
*Map **2**C2. Bus 13 to Piazza T. Tasso.*
The S. Frediano gate at the sw corner of the city was erected in
1332–4, and is the one through which Charles VIII entered
Florence from the old Pisa road in 1494. Filippino Lippi
painted the gate in the background of his Nerli altarpiece in
Santo Spirito. Nearby is the 17thC church of S. Frediano in
Castello, and on the lungarno end of its piazza is the handsome
granary made for Cosimo III.

You can climb to *Bellosguardo* from the gate in 30min.

San Gaetano ▥ †
*Via Tornabuoni. Map **4**C3. Rarely open except for
services.*
The best Baroque church facade in Florence, built by Gherardo
Silvani in 1648.

A plaque on the corner of Via de' Corsi and the Tornabuoni
commemorates the production in 1594 of the first opera *La
Dafne* by Jacopo Peri and Jacopo Corsi, the owner of the
original palace which has now been replaced.

San Lorenzo ★ ▥ †
*Map **4**B3.*
To build their parish church the Medici hired Brunelleschi for
the first and only time. Begun in 1419 on the site of a much older
church, S. Lorenzo was built, embellished and extended by
some of the greatest artists and most skillful craftsmen of the
15th–17thC. Most of this work was initiated, supervised and
paid for by the successive members of the Medici family who
are buried here.

Seen from its busy market square, S. Lorenzo is an
impressive if not harmonious complex. The taller of the two
domes at the chancel end covers the Cappella dei Principi; the

shallower cupola completes Michelangelo's New Sacristy. The bell tower is 18thC and the unexciting statue of Giovanni delle Bande Nere (1540) is by Bandinelli. Michelangelo's model for a proposed facade, commissioned in 1516 but judged unacceptable by his Medici patrons, can be seen in the *Casa Buonarroti*.

The **interior ★** is one of the most understatedly powerful in Italy, designed by Brunelleschi in 1420 but completed after his death by A. Manetti in 1460. The delay was caused by financial crises in the Medici banks, but it is evident that money was not stinted on the final construction. Even the *pietra serena* capitals and the arches which define the space were carved by leading sculptors of the day, including A. and M. Rossellino.

Highlights are as follows: 1. The *Marriage of the Virgin* (1523), an elegant and vivid picture by Rosso Fiorentino. 2. A fine and in its day influential **marble tabernacle** (c.1460) by Desiderio da Settignano. 3. and 4. **Bronze pulpits** by Donatello (c.1460), his last works, finished by pupils; the **Deposition panel** and **Resurrection panel** are by Donatello's own hand. 5. Bronzino's sadly faded fresco of the *Martyrdom of San Lorenzo* (1565–69). 6. Martelli Chapel. *The Annunciation* (c.1440) by Filippo Lippi, a masterpiece of perspective, clumsily restored.

The **Old Sacristy (Sagrestia Vecchia) ★** is entered from the left transept. Brunelleschi's early masterpiece (1421–8) was completed before the church itself; Vasari says Cosimo il Vecchio was present throughout the construction. This is one of the first mathematically conceived architectural spaces of the Renaissance: a perfect cube completed by a hemispherical umbrella dome. Donatello's **sculptural decorations**, carried out in the 1430s, consist of: the four polychrome medallions illustrating *Scenes from the Life of St John the Evangelist* in the pendentives; the four polychrome **tondos of the Evangelist** in the lunettes; and the **bronze doors** flanking the apse. Donatello was responsible for the architecture of the doors as well as the bronze relief panels: the right door is the *Door of the Martyrs*; the left is known as the *Door of the Apostles* despite its 20 figures. Left of the entrance is Verrocchio's elegant *Monument to Piero and Giovanni de' Medici* (1472).

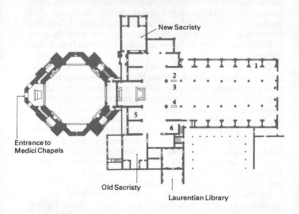

San Lorenzo

Laurentian Library *(Biblioteca Medici-Laurenziana)* Ⅲ ★
Piazza S. Lorenzo 🖼 �》 *Open Mon–Sat 9am–5pm.
Closed Sun and hols.*

This library was designed by Michelangelo in 1524–34, to
house the collection of classical and humanist manuscripts
founded by Cosimo il Vecchio, later removed to Rome by
Leo X and finally returned to Florence by Clement VII who
commissioned this building.

Vestibule. An early, dramatic, sophisticated break with the
rational, classical principles of 15thC Florentine architecture.
The staircase, which fills nearly the entire room, was left
unfinished by Michelangelo and completed in the 1550s by
Vasari and Ammannati.

Library. The comparatively simple rectangular space is in
deliberate contrast to the vestibule. The marble intarsia floor,
designed by Tribolo, repeats the ceiling's Medici motifs of the
ram's skull and the motto 'Semper'. Among the codices is the
Medici *Virgil*.

Medici Chapels *(Cappelle Medicee)* ★
🖼 *Open Tues–Sat 9am–7pm, Sun and hols 9am–1pm.
Closed Mon. Entrance from Piazza di Madonna degli
Aldobrandini.*

On the way to the chapels you pass through the lofty crypt
paved with tombstones of the Medici and Lorraine grand
dukes. The tomb of Cosimo il Vecchio is in the center. A
staircase on the right leads to the **Chapel of the Princes
(Cappella dei Principi)**. Designed by Don Giovanni de' Medici
and Buontalenti and built by Nigetti from 1602, this
portentous, claustrophobic grand-ducal shrine, clad entirely in
pietradura, is really a monument to Ferdinand I who ordered it.
It was the most expensive of all Medici building projects and the
one which posterity, until recently, was to judge as being in the
worst taste. The ground plan is based on that of the Baptistry
(*Duomo*). A room in the Opificio delle Pietre dure, Via degli
Alfani 78, is devoted to the design and construction of this
chapel.

The **New Sacristy (Sagrestia Nuova)** ★ was Michelangelo's
first realized architectural creation, begun in 1520 and left
unfinished, after interruptions, in 1534. It is an answer, half
respectful and half rebellious, to Brunelleschi's Old Sacristy.
Imitating the Old Sacristy, it makes a totally different
impression because, as Vasari tells us, Michelangelo would not
conform to the "measure, order and rule" that were the essence
of Brunelleschi's style. It was intended to be seen from behind
the altar.

Leo X and Clement VII, who paid for the New Sacristy, were
less concerned to glorify the two Medici dukes entombed here
than to strengthen the authority of these dukes' bastard heirs,
and the statues of the dukes in niches over their respective
tombs are, at the least, idealized portraits, if they are portraits at
all. The melancholy mood of the sculptures made between
1524–1533 probably expresses Michelangelo's despair at the
fall of the Florentine Republic. The catenary curve of the tomb
volutes was later copied exactly by Ammannati (who did some
restorative work on the New Sacristy) in the 1550s, for his
bridge at *Santa Trinità*. Michelangelo's original design
provided for a further pair of figures at the end of each tomb.

On the left is the **tomb of Lorenzo, Duke of Urbino**
(grandson of Lorenzo the Magnificent); the reclining figures
represent *Dawn* and *Dusk*. On the right is the **tomb of**

Giuliano, Duke of Nemours (Lorenzo the Magnificent's youngest son), with allegorical figures of *Day* and *Night*.

Lorenzo the Magnificent and his brother Giuliano are buried in the simple tomb opposite the altar. To confuse matters further, the Giuliano and the Lorenzo 'the Magnificent' (a common courtesy title in the 16thC) to whom Machiavelli successively dedicated *The Prince* are the dukes whose remains lie in Michelangelo's tombs and not the more famous 15thC Medici buried here in near anonymity. On this tomb is Michelangelo's deeply moving *Madonna and Child* (1521) which is flanked by *S. Cosma* by Montorsoli, and by *S. Damiano* by Raffaele da Montelupo.

In a room below, fresco drawings by Michelangelo and his pupils have recently been uncovered, and are often on display in the choir.

San Marco, Fra Angelico Museum *(Museo dell' Angelico)* ★
Piazza San Marco ☎ *210741. Map 3B4* ☒ *Open Tues–Sat 9am–2pm, Sun and hols 9am–1pm. Closed Mon.*

The **convent and cloisters** of S. Marco were Cosimo il Vecchio's greatest gift to Florence. Cosimo bought the site for the Dominican monks of Fiesole in 1436 and chose Michelozzo and Fra Angelico to build and decorate the new convent. Michelozzo's only work of genius was transmuted by Angelico into a supremely noble expression of balanced Christianity: sincere, compassionate, mystic, learned.

S. Marco witnessed one of the turning points in Florence's history. By the end of the 15thC Florentines had been swung off center into a hectic, puritanical religiosity incited by Savonarola, who became Prior of S. Marco in 1491. The Medici were expelled in 1494, and Jesus Christ was proclaimed King of Florence, with Savonarola acting as political leader. In 1498 the crowds who had wallowed in the demagogue's charisma turned against him. S. Marco was besieged, and Savonarola was captured, tried and burned at the stake in the Piazza Signoria.

In 1869 the suppressed convent of S. Marco became a museum honoring Fra Angelico. Today it is a nearly complete one-man show of his *oeuvre*. Most of his greatest panel paintings have been assembled here, brought in from churches, guilds, and other galleries including the *Uffizi*, which now retains only two Angelicos. During the 1980s new sections of the convent will be opened as a museum housing fragments salvaged from the old parts of the city demolished in the 1860s.

From the vestibule one enters Michelozzo's **Cloister of S. Antonino**. Most of the frescoes are 16thC, but some of the lunettes and the *Crucifixion with St Dominic* in the far left corner are by Angelico. To the right of the entrance is the **Ospizio dei Pellegrini** ★ which is the room where pilgrims were offered hospitality; it now houses 20 panel paintings by Angelico, well labeled as to date and provenance. The cult of Angelico as a naive painter stops here – if his spirit was still medieval, his technique was fully informed by the Early Renaissance. The outstanding works in this room are the *Deposition* (c.1435) from S. Trinità; the *Last Judgement* (c.1430) from S. Maria Nuova; the *Virgin Enthroned* (c.1433), painted for the linen drapers guild, the *Linaiuoli*; and the 35 *Scenes from the Life of Christ*, completed by Baldovinetti.

Across the courtyard, in the **Sala Capitolare** (the Chapter House), is Angelico's grand, mystic vision of the *Crucifixion* ★

(c.1442). Nearby in the cloister is the bell of S. Marco, the *Piagnona*, which gave the signal for the siege of the convent that led to the imprisonment of Savonarola. In the **refectory**, to the left of the stairs, is Dom. Ghirlandaio's clear, descriptive *Last Supper*, a variation on the one in the *Ognissanti* refectory.

First floor. The 44 **dormitory cells** ★ were frescoed by Angelico and assistants from 1439–45. At the top of the stairs is Angelico's justly famous *Annunciation*. If time is short, visit at least: cell 1. *Noli Me Tangere*; 3. *Annunciation*; 6. *Transfiguration*; 7. the *Crowning with Thorns*; and 9. the *Coronation of Mary*. The **library**, between cells 42 and 43, is Michelozzo's most inspired interior. This was the first public library in Europe, thanks to Cosimo il Vecchio, who donated the manuscripts. Cells 38 and 39 at the bottom of this corridor were reserved for Cosimo's retreats. Cell 11 was the prior's quarters, occupied by Savonarola, whose **portrait** by Fra Bartolommeo is in the vestibule, cell 12.

The adjacent church of S. Marco (1437–52) was built by Michelozzo, but subsequently updated by Giambologna in 1585, by P.F. Silvani in 1678 and by various 18thC decorators. In the center of the wooden ceiling is a canvas of the *Madonna in Glory* (1725) by G.A. Pucci. Poliziano and Pico della Mirandola are buried near the third altar on the left.

The administrative offices of the University of Florence, the various faculties of which are scattered all over the city, are on the E side of the square at no. 4, in the building where Cosimo I kept lions and which was later used as the grand-ducal stables.

Santa Maria Maddalena dei Pazzi † ☆
Borgo Pinti 58. Map 3C5. Open 9am–noon, 3–7pm.
Santa Maria Maddalena dei Pazzi was a Carmelite nun and member of the banking family who died in 1609 and was canonized in 1685. This church, originally built by Giuliano da Sangallo, was renamed and redesigned in her honor in 1628 by Luigi Arrigucci, who retained Giuliano's side chapels. The frescoes in the nave (1677) are by Jacopo Chiavistelli. The chancel was extended and richly decorated in the year of her canonization by P.F. Silvani, C. Ferri, P. Dandini, with two canvases by Luca Giordano. In the sacristy, off the bottom of the right aisle, is some good late Baroque stuccowork (1767).

The rest of the church complex is something of a box of surprises: frescoes by Poccetti in the Cappella del Giglio; an elegant **courtyard** (1492) by Giuliano da Sangallo, important as the first building project to carry out Alberti's instruction that arches must be supported on square pillars. But the compelling reason to visit S. Maria Maddalena dei Pazzi is in the old chapter room of the convent, where Perugino's **fresco of the Crucifixion** (1493–6) ☆ covers one wall. This lovely composition, set in a severe illusionist architectural frame, echoes the peace of the landscape bathed in early-morning light.

Nearby, at Borgo Pinti 68, is the large Panciatichi Ximenes palace, c.1499, built by Giuliano and Antonio de Sangallo as their own palace, and enlarged by Gherardo Silvani in 1620. Napoleon stayed here in June 1796.

Santa Maria Maggiore ▥ †
Via de' Cerretani. Map 4B3.
The interior is a pleasing mixture of 13thC Gothic reinterpreted by an early 20thC restoration, with 17th–18thC Baroque decoration. The side altars are by Gherardo Silvani with

frescoes and canvases by Giuseppe Pinzani, Pier Dandini, Volterrano, Onorio Marinari and Vincenzo Meucci.

The prize possession of the church is in the chapel to the left of the high altar. This 13thC polyptych of the *Madonna and Child* was attributed to Andrea di Cione by Berenson, but it is now thought to be by Coppo di Marcovaldo.

Santa Maria Novella ▥ † ★
Map 4B2.

Next to the station and only five minutes from the Duomo, S.M. Novella nevertheless seems remote from the rest of Florence, as indeed it was before the final ring of walls embraced the area and the Mugnone, which once flowed here through vineyards, was diverted N of the Fortezza da Basso. The feeling that you might almost be in a different city is emphasized by the only Florentine church facade completed in the 15thC and by the high proportion of comfortable but undistinguished 19thC buildings which fill gaps left in the 16thC when the population of Florence had not yet expanded as rapidly as expected. In the 19thC S.M. Novella was known as the 'Mecca of Foreigners.' Henry James, William Dean Howells, Emerson, Longfellow and Shelley were among the literary visitors who chose to stay just a little to one side of the inspiring but noisy city.

The church of S.M. Novella was built from 1246 by the Dominicans, successful protagonists at that time of a puritanical movement similar in its aims to the 16thC Reformation, and far stricter than the doctrine propounded by the Franciscans, whose rival preaching church was begun 48yr later at *Santa Croce*. The Dominicans had taken possession in 1221 of an old church which occupied the transept of the present building, and in 1245 the piazza was opened out to receive the crowds attracted by the Dominican preacher St Peter Martyr. The new church buildings, supervised by a succession of Dominican architects, were completed by 1360. A compromise between contemporary French and native Italian styles, S.M. Novella was the first Gothic church in Italy to break away from the imported Cistercian mold.

It was in S. Maria Novella that Boccaccio described the protagonists of the *Decameron*, talking of plague, and it was the fear and consequences of the plague of 1348 which occasioned

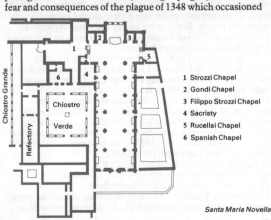

1 Strozzi Chapel
2 Gondi Chapel
3 Filippo Strozzi Chapel
4 Sacristy
5 Rucellai Chapel
6 Spanish Chapel

Chiostro Grande

Chiostro Verde

Refectory

Santa Maria Novella

the building of many of the chapels and cloisters. But there is no hint of these gloomy associations with dogmatism and death in Alberti's brilliant rationalization of the 14thC facade. Honoring the Gothic forms of the existing facade, and retaining the lower arcade and the round window, he raised it into a mathematically organized space containable within a perfect square. The volutes, an invention much copied by later architects, conceal the nave aisles. His **facade** ★ was begun in 1456. As you can see from the Rucellai device which sails across the center and from the inscription under the pediment, the patron was Giovanni Rucellai and the date of completion 1470. The two astronomical instruments were placed here in 1572.

The **interior** was updated in 1565–71 by Vasari, who deprived the nave of color and light by whitewashing frescoes and shortening the aisle windows to allow for his side chapels.

The **nave** appears longer than it is thanks to a trick of perspective played by the Gothic architects, who placed the supporting pillars at diminishing intervals. There are several distinguished monuments in the nave, but the outstanding work here is Masaccio's *Trinity* (c.1427) ★ with Mary and St John flanked by the donors, members of the Lenzi family. The central figures are set in an illusionist Holy Sepulcher, which may have been suggested by Brunelleschi, who designed the marble **pulpit** on the nearest pillar.

Left transept. The Strozzi Chapel occupies the raised presbytery of the original Romanesque church. The **altarpiece** (1354–7) shows *Christ giving the Keys to Peter and the Book of Knowledge to St Thomas*, by Orcagna. The frescoes (c.1351–7), by Nardo di Cione, have deteriorated: left wall, *Paradise*; altar wall, the *Last Judgement*, with Dante among the blessed; right wall, the *Inferno*. In the Sacristy is the *Crucifix* from the interior facade by Giotto. The Gondi Chapel, with striking **decorations in marble** (c.1503), by Giuliano da Sangallo, contains Brunelleschi's famous *Crucifix*, his only surviving wooden sculpture, made, according to Vasari, in answer to Donatello's *Crucifix* in *Santa Croce*, which Brunelleschi judged too crudely realistic. The chancel is decorated behind the high altar by Dom. Ghirlandaio with his most popular **frescoes** (1485–90) ★ which were commissioned by Giovanni Tornabuoni, Lorenzo de' Medici's uncle. Serious art historians used to dismiss this pretty narrative work as merely journalistic; Ruskin described them as not nice enough for nice people and not vulgar enough for vulgar people. But they are among the valuable pictorial documents we have of the period, and most modern visitors will be fascinated and charmed by them.

Right transept. The Filippo Strozzi Chapel is frescoed (c.1487–1502) by Filippino Lippi in a strange obsessive style steeped in Roman archeology and anticipating the Baroque: right wall, *Story of St Philip* ☆ and left wall, *Story of St John the Divine* ☆ Behind the altar is the **tomb of Filippo Strozzi** (1491–3) by Benedetto da Maiano. The Rucellai Chapel was raised in the 15thC. Duccio's Rucellai *Madonna*, now in the *Uffizi*, has been replaced at the altar by Nino Pisano's marble *Madonna and Child* (after 1348). In the pavement is Ghiberti's bronze **tomb of Leonardo Dati** (1425).

Cloisters (*Chiostri Monumentali*) ▥ † ★
▨ *Open Mon–Thurs, Sat 9am–2pm, Sun 8am–1pm. Closed Fri. Entrance to left of church facade.*
The **Chiostro Verde** (c.1350) is so named because of the green tint of Uccello's **frescoes of the Old Testament**, executed in

terra verde. They are detached and usually exhibited in the Refectory. Uccello's *Universal Deluge* (c.1445) ★ was restored in the 1950s and again after the most recent deluge of 1966. Although tragically deteriorated, it is recognizable as his masterpiece.

The **Spanish Chapel** (c.1350) ★ was an old chapter room of the convent, built by Jacopo Talenti, and used for worship in the 16thC by Eleanor of Toledo's Spanish courtiers. The monumental didactic **fresco cycle** (1365–7) by Andrea da Firenze and assistants is a schematic depiction of the Catholic way of life, which is determined by the scenes in the vault and over the altar. Left wall, theology, civilization and intellectual culture as revealed by St Thomas Aquinas; right wall, the practical way of life, with the church militant represented by an unrealized plan for the Duomo, the actual dome of which was of course not finished for another 80yr. Ruskin guessed, probably correctly, that the average tourist would spend 15min in the Spanish Chapel, studying "its vaulted book, the most noble piece of pictorial philosophy in Italy," whereas he had "taken five weeks to see the quarter of this picture."

In the piazza, the large obelisks, resting on bronze tortoises, mark the limits of the chariot race established here by Cosimo I in 1563. At the far end is the graceful, post-Brunelleschian **Loggia di S. Paolo** (1489–96), with a terra-cotta lunette over the doorway by Andrea della Robbia. In the Via della Scala is a perfectly preserved 17thC pharmacy (see *Florence/Shopping*). Immediately to the NW of the piazza is the central **station** (1935), the first functionalist terminal building in Italy. Although admired by many, a joke made by a rival architect has stuck to the station: "I can see the box the station came in," he said, "but where is the station?"

San Miniato ⅲ † ★

Map 3E5. Open 8am–12:30pm, 2–6:15pm. No visitors during services.

The sight of S. Miniato invariably makes people smile. A small, venerable green-and-white jewel, it stands above the city on the highest of the hills immediately to the SE. Apart from the Baptistry (*Duomo*) it is the oldest and most loved church in Florence.

According to a medieval legend, S. Miniato, persecuted by the Emperor Decius and decapitated in the amphitheater, carried his head across the river and up the hill to this place. The commemorative church was built in the 11thC. It was here that the miraculous *Crucifix*, now in *Santa Trinità*, spoke to S. Giovanni Gualberto who went on to found the reforming Benedictine order of Vallombrosa. After the last expulsion of the Medici in 1527 the hill was fortified by Michelangelo and used during the siege as a key defense post against the army of Charles V (see Vasari's fresco in the *Signoria*, Sala dei Cinquecento). Thirty years later the fortified church which had briefly been a symbol of Florentine love of freedom was occupied by the soldiers of the dictator Duke Cosimo I.

The facade dates from c.1090, except for the 13thC mosaic, restored in the 19thC when the Florentines loved S. Miniato perhaps a little too well, and the copper eagle over the pediment, emblem of the Guild of Calimala which administered the church, from 1288. The crenellated **Bishop's Palace** to the right was built in 1295 by Andrea dei Mozzi, Bishop of Florence, as a summer residence. During the 1529 siege Baccio d'Agnolo's squat bell tower, only just then completed, was shielded by mattresses against the Spanish cannonballs. The lovely Romanesque **interior ★** is marred only by the heavy hand of the 19thC restorer, who coated the stone column shafts with *scagliola* and brightened the polychrome ceiling. The smaller of the Corinthian capitals are Roman. The tapestry-like strip of **pavement**, inspired by Sicilian fabrics and one of the finest of its kind in Italy, is dated 1207 in the zodiac panel.

Nave. The giant St Christopher frescoed on the right wall is by an unknown 14thC artist. At the bottom of the nave is Michelozzo's **Crucifix Chapel** (1448). The glazed terra-cotta vault is by Luca della Robbia. Off the left nave the **Cardinal of Portugal's Chapel** (1461–6) **★** is a model of collaborative Renaissance art (ask the sacristan to open the gate). Commissioned by Alfonso V of Portugal to house the tomb of his nephew Cardinal James of Lusitania, who died in Florence in 1459, this exquisite chapel was built into the side of the basilica by A. Manetti. The **cardinal's tomb** on the right wall is by A. Rossellino. On the opposite wall, above the Bishop's throne, is Baldovinetti's *Annunciation*, on panel, carefully restored. The glazed terra-cotta **vault and tondos of the Holy Ghost and four Cardinal Virtues** are by Luca della Robbia. In the lunette facing the entrance are two *Angels in Flight*, frescoed by A. and P. del Pollaiuolo.

Sacristy (to the right of the raised presbytery). Frescoes by Spinello Aretino (1385–7) represent *Scenes from the Life of St Benedict*. Presbytery. The delightful marble **pulpit** (1209) is justly famous for its carving and intarsiaed fantasy animals. The 13thC mosaic in the apse was restored by Baldovonetti. Over the altar, left, is *S. Miniato* by Jacopo del Casentino. **Crypt.** The 36 columns are of various provenance. Frescoes in the vault show *Saints and Prophets* by Taddeo Gaddi.

Emerging from the church you can wander for a half-hour or so among the sweet, nostalgic 19thC and early 20thC tombs in the cemetery, planned in 1839 by Niccolò Matas. The whole church complex retains examples from nearly a thousand years of funerary tradition.

San Niccolò 🏛 †
Map 3D5.

The defense **tower of S. Niccolò** in Piazza Giuseppe Poggi was erected in 1324 and has been maintained at its original height by frequent restorations. The steps behind it lead up to *Piazzale Michelangelo*. To the SW, Via Belvedere runs along the old walls and the 16thC bastion to Porta S. Giorgio and the *Belvedere* fortress. Or you could walk W along Via S. Niccolò and Via dei Bardi, two of the best-preserved (and noisiest) medieval streets in Florence, to the *Ponte Vecchio*. The medieval road to *San Miniato* from Porta S. Miniato is the way described by Dante in *Purgatorio XII*, (l.100). Opposite Porta S. Miniato is the church of **S. Niccolò Sopr' Arno**, with a 15thC interior made over in the 16thC. A recent restoration had emphasized the difference in taste between the two centuries by uncovering the 15thC frescoes but leaving the 16thC tabernacle frames. Sinopias of the restored frescoes are also displayed.

San Salvi † ☆
Via S. Salvi 16. ☎ *677570. Map 7D5.*

The work of Andrea del Sarto, Browning's "faultless painter," can sometimes seem boringly academic to modern eyes. But his masterpiece in fresco, the *Last Supper* ☆ which was commissioned in 1519 for the refectory of the S. Salvi monastery, is one of the most sumptuous visual treats in Florence. This is the perfect normative High Renaissance painting, in a near-perfect state of preservation. Its beauty saved it during the siege of Florence, when workmen, instructed to tear down any building near the city which might be used by the enemy, refused to destroy this picture.

Closed to the public after the 1966 flood, the refectory was reopened in October 1981. The monastery is now an asylum. A visit to S. Salvi could be combined with a day in *Settignano* (see *A–Z/Tuscany*). On the way from the center, notice Nervi's admirable **Stadium** (1932).

Santo Spirito 🏛 † ★
Map 4E2.

When Florence was partitioned into four administrative sections in the 14thC, the city s of the Arno became the S. Spirito quarter. Piazza S. Spirito is still the heart of the *Oltrarno*; and it is the square connoisseurs of Florence often say they love most, the place where daily life seems least disturbed by tourists.

The most strikingly lovely of the palaces on the piazza is the **Guadagni** (1503–6) at no. 10, attributed to Baccio d'Agnolo and with a fine courtyard in the manner of Giuliano da Sangallo. In the palace next door, no. 9, is an elegant staircase leading to the Pensione Bardini.

The **church of S. Spirito** was built on the site of an earlier Augustinian monastery to a design by Brunelleschi. The foundation stone was laid in 1436 but the church was not completed until 1487, long after Brunelleschi's death. The delay was caused by financial difficulties, fire, and controversy over the interpretation of the master's design, which was fundamentally respected in the interior.

The modest voluted facade was applied in the 17thC. The slender bell tower (1503–17) is by Baccio d'Agnolo.

Brunelleschi's calm, rational **interior** ★ with its soaring forest of columns is spoiled only by the 17thC *baldacchino* in the chancel. The plan is a more subtle and complex variation on that of *San Lorenzo*. Around the perimeter are 40 semicircular chapels. Those in the transepts and apse give the clearest impression you can find in modern Florence of how 15thC religious art looked in its original context; some of the chapels have inevitably been altered, but more than enough have been left as they were to help you imagine the paintings you see in galleries back in their proper settings. Don't miss: right transept, Filippino Lippi's **Nerli altarpiece** (c.1490) ☆ and left transept, which is the most perfectly preserved part of the church, the **Corbinelli Chapel** (1492) – architecture and the sculptures by the young A. Sansovino. From the left nave, the door under the organ leads through a noble vaulted **vestibule** (1492–6), built by Cronaca to a design by Giuliano da Sangallo, into the octagonal **sacristy** (1489–92), also designed by Sangallo.

Refectory *(Cenacolo di Santo Spirito)*
Piazza S. Spirito 29 📷

This is the only part of the Gothic monastery to have survived the fire of 1471. The **frescoes**, badly damaged but of the greatest importance, were attributed by Ghiberti to Orcagna, an opinion not generally supported by modern scholarship.

Santo Stefano al Ponte ▥ †
Map 4D3.

The lower half of the facade and the attractive doorway are
13thC. The shoe of Buondelmonte dei Buondelmonti's horse is
supposed to have been hung here after his assassination (see
Ponte Vecchio).

The remarkable **interior** (1649–55) by Ferdinando Tacca is
unfortunately rarely open except for exhibitions. The raised
chancel is an imaginary reconstruction of a Roman theater.
Leading up to it is an extraordinary lasagna-like marble flight of
stairs (1574) by Buontalenti, formerly in Santa Trinità.

Santa Trinità ▥ † ★
Map 4D2.

Piazza S. Trinità is more a crossroads than a square. The central
column, from the Baths of Caracalla, given by Pius IV to
Cosimo I in commemoration of the victory of Montemurlo in
1537, doesn't really focus your attention, which is pulled to the
N along **Via Tornabuoni**. This is the fashionable shopping
street and the widest in Florence, built on the filled-in moat of
the 12thC city walls and now lined with 13th–16thC palaces.

Spanning the Arno to the S is Ammannati's **Ponte S. Trinità**
(1567–70) ★ which is the most graceful bridge in Europe.
Michelangelo advised on the design, and the curve of the
volutes is borrowed from his Medici tombs in *San Lorenzo*.
The bridge was destroyed by bombing in 1944 and rebuilt after
the war exactly as it had been before. One-sixth of the original
stone was retrieved from the Arno; the rest was supplied by the
quarries in the Boboli Gardens which were specially reopened.
The head of the *Primavera* statue was recovered only in 1961.

On the NE corner of the square (no. 1) is the **Palazzo Bartolini
Salimbeni**, now the French Consulate. The building was
finished in 1521 just after Raphael's Pandolfini palace (see
Florence/Walk 2), which greatly influenced Baccio d'Agnolo's
design for this, his most original palace. It was the first in
central Florence to adopt the Roman tabernacle windows, and
contemporary Florentines treated it as a huge joke, pinning
notices on the facade saying that it looked more like a church.
Baccio's reply is inscribed in Latin over the door: "It is easier to
carp than to imitate." Michelangelo thought the cornice made
the palace look like a man wearing a hat too big for his body.
The palace is also known as the *Per Non Dormire* after the
family motto inscribed over the windows. The courtyard is
decorated with elegant *sgraffiti*.

The first **church of S. Trinità** was built on this site by
S. Giovanni Gualberto, founder of the Vallombrosian Order, in
the late 11thC. The original Romanesque facade, depicted by
Dom. Ghirlandaio in the Sassetti Chapel inside the church, was
replaced by Buontalenti's uncharacteristically clumsy effort in
1594. The Gothic **interior** assumed its present appearance
beginning c.1250, when Nicola Pisano is supposed to have
begun the program of enlargement which continued
throughout the next century.

Right nave, fourth chapel. Compare Lorenzo Monaco's
pretty but heavily restored frescoes (c.1420–25) with his
altarpiece on the panel of the *Annunciation*; the predella panels
are especially fine. The gate is early 15thC.

Right transept. In the sacristy, the **tomb of Onofrio Strozzi**
(1421), to the left of the altar, is an early example of Renaissance
funerary sculpture. The second chapel to the right of the

chancel is the **Sassetti Chapel** ☆ frescoed by Dom. Ghirlandaio (1482–6) with *Scenes from the Life of St Francis* against a Florentine background: the Signoria, Piazza S. Trinità, the old Ponte S. Trinità. In the upper tier of the altar wall are portraits of, among other contemporary Florentines, *Francesco Sassetti*, who commissioned this chapel, *Lorenzo the Magnificent*, his adoring protégé *Poliziano* and his sons *Piero, Giovanni* and *Giuliano*. Over the altar is Ghirlandaio's *Adoration of the Shepherds* (1485), set in a Tuscan landscape. *Francesco Sassetti* and *Nera Corsi*, his wife, are portrayed on either side of the altar and are buried in the black marble **sarcophagi**, attributed to Giuliano da Sangallo, on the side walls.

Left transept, second chapel. On the left wall, the **tomb of Bishop Benozzo Federighi** (1455) ☆ is considered one of Luca della Robbia's masterworks for the intense humanity of the crucified Christ in the central panel and the finely modeled face of the bishop, a rare portrait by Luca. In the fifth chapel, the wooden statue of the *Magdalen* (c.1464), by Desiderio da Settignano and Benedetto da Maiano, invites comparison with Donatello's more tragic figure in the Cathedral Museum (see *Duomo*). In the third chapel is an *Annunciation* by Neri di Bicci, with a sweet, inept Adam and Eve, borrowed from Masaccio's Brancacci Chapel (see *Carmine*).

Lo Scalzo 血 † ☆
Via Cavour 69. Map 3B4.

The Brotherhood of St John was known as *lo Scalzo* because its members went barefoot in obedience to the rule of poverty.

In 1511 Andrea del Sarto, then 25, began to decorate their cloister in *terra verde* with scenes in austere *grisaille*, from the life of John the Baptist. He worked here on and off for a period of 12yr, developing the fresco technique which can also be admired in color at *Santissima Annunziata* and *San Salvi*.

The earliest of the Scalzo frescoes is the *Baptism of Christ*; the last to be painted was the *Birth of St John the Baptist*. Notice also especially the *Visitation* (1524), *Charity* (1520), and *Justice* (1515).

The frescoes, badly injured by damp, have been detached for restoration and replaced in their original positions.

Science Museum *(Museo di Storia della Scienza)* 血
Piazza dei Giudici 1 ☎ *293493. Map 3D4* ■ ✳ *Open Mon–Sat 10am–1pm, 2–4pm, Sun and hols 10am–1pm. Closed last Sun of every month.*

The medieval Castellani palace, which now houses the Science Museum, was at one time the seat of the Civil Tribune or Giudici di Ruota, which gave its name to the piazza from which one enters the museum.

For nearly three centuries after Florence had lost its artistic supremacy, the more intelligent members of the Medici-Lorraine grand-ducal families retained a passionate interest in all branches of science. In 1657 an Academy of Experiment, the Accademia del Cimento, was founded in the Pitti by Grand Duke Ferdinand II and his brother Cardinal Leopold, both pupils of Galileo. This is the historic nucleus of the museum, which is very large, carefully organized and clearly labeled. Printed guides are loaned to visitors on each floor.

Ground floor. An alchemist's laboratory; early scales, music boxes, bicycles, fire extinguishers, and more.

First floor. Rm IV is hardly large enough for the giant

armillary sphere made in 1593 for Ferdinand I by Antonio Santucci. The sphere demonstrates the theologically acceptable Ptolemaic theory in defiance of the sun-centered system evolved by Copernicus 50yr earlier. Rm V. In the case opposite the entrance is the lens with which Galileo discovered the four satellites of Jupiter, known as the Medici planets. Wonderfully delicate glass instruments from the Accademia del Cimento are displayed in the other two cases.

Second floor, opened in 1975. This floor was formerly the headquarters of the Accademia della Crusca, the scholarly body which sits in judgement on the purity of the Italian language. In Rm II is the **large burning lens** made for Cosimo III by Benedict Bregans of Dresden and later used by Sir Humphrey Davy and Michael Faraday to accomplish the combustion of a diamond. In Rm IV is the great lodestone (*Calamità*) given by Galileo to Ferdinand II. Rms V–VII. Anatomical wax models; 18thC surgical implements.

Third floor. Minerals and crystals collected in the 18thC.

Signoria
*Map **5**D4.*

People who dislike Florence often object most to this, its main square, with the asymmetrical fortress palace, the rows of statues symbolizing conflicting ideologies, and dull 19thC buildings. Lacking the gaiety and architectural unity of the central squares of Venice or Siena, the Piazza della Signoria will always appeal more to the historical imagination than to the sense of pleasure. The Signoria is still the political and commercial center of the city, as it has been for nearly seven centuries. The Palazzo Vecchio is still the city hall, and politicians still harangue the public from the *ringhiera*. Farmers still talk business outside the old commercial tribunal, now the agricultural center, in Via de' Gondi, and businessmen and bankers make deals over lunch at Cavallino. The only concessions to mass tourism are the postcard stalls, the high prices at the café Rivoire and the annual historic soccer game played in costume each year on June 24.

Embedded in the pavement of the square is a plaque marking the place where Savonarola was hanged and then burned on May 23, 1498. Those who honor his memory still lay flowers here.

Palazzo della Signoria (Palazzo Vecchio) **▥ ★**
Piazza Signoria **▧** *for upstairs rooms, open Mon–Fri 9am–7pm, Sun and hols 8am–1pm. Closed Mon.*

The foundation stone of the Palazzo della Signoria was laid in 1299. The design is traditionally attributed to Arnolfo di Cambio, but the building was not finished until at least a decade after his death. The Signoria was the cabinet of the new form of republican government established in 1293. Elected by the guilds, the Signori served for a period of only two months during which they lived virtually as prisoners inside the palace. The palace, like the constitution, was designed to prevent the government from being overtaken by extremists – subversive activity in the streets of such a small city could be easily searched out from the tall watchtower, where the great bell cast in 1322 tolled danger warnings and summoned the populace to 'parliaments,' or general assemblies.

The irregular shape of the palace and the off-center position of its tower were not, as is often thought, the result of Gothic whim. The trapezoidal plan derives from the reluctance of the then Guelf Government to build on land previously owned by a Ghibelline family. The tower was thriftily erected on the foundations of an earlier family tower close to the church of S. Piero Scheraggio, incorporated into the *Uffizi* in the 16thC. But the original entrance, on the N flank of the palace, was originally placed symmetrically. This side, facing Via de' Gondi, was extended in the late 15thC when the Sala Consiglio Maggiore was built over the customs hall.

The W side, facing the piazza, looks very much as it did in the 14thC, except for the mezzanine windows enlarged by Michelozzo and the absence of the 14thC *ringhiera*, or tribune, which was destroyed in the early 19thC. Almost nothing, however, remains of the original interior, which was remodeled from the mid-15thC to the late 16thC according to the needs of violently shifting styles of government, from the Medici-controled republic to the revivals of true republicanism in 1494–1512 and 1527–30, to the hereditary duchy finally established in 1537.

A key date to remember when visiting the palace is 1540, when Cosimo I took the unprecedented step of moving his household from the ancestral *Medici Palace* to the Signoria, which was converted into a ducal palace by his court architect Battista del Tasso. Ten years earlier, in 1530, Duke Alessandro de' Medici had signaled the irrevocable end of parliamentary government by ordering the great bell of the Signoria to be smashed publicly in the piazza. Ten years later, in 1550, Cosimo was persuaded by his wife Eleanor of Toledo to change the official ducal residence to the *Pitti*. The Signoria palace was henceforth known as the Palazzo Vecchio (the Old Palace). Vasari, who succeeded Battista as court architect in 1555, was instructed to labor on until his death in 1574, covering the walls of the old palace with carefully programed frescoes glorifying the achievements, ancestors, virtues and mythological counterparts of Cosimo I. Since few modern visitors share this single-minded adoration of Cosimo I, a tour of the palace can be a dispiriting experience. A brief visit, however, should include the following sights.

The two gilded lions and Christ's emblem were placed over the **entrance** in 1528, but an inscription of the same date, inspired by Savonarola's teachings, which originally read 'Jesus Christ, King of Florence Elected by Popular Decree,' was replaced with the present words by order of Cosimo I. The **courtyard** was remodeled by Michelozzo in the middle of the

15thC. Stuccowork and frescoes of views of Austrian cities were added under Vasari for the wedding of Francesco de' Medici to Joanna of Austria in 1565. The porphyry **fountain** replaced the original well in c.1555; the original of Verrocchio's bronze putto, made in the previous century for the Medici villa at Careggi, is now upstairs in the Cancelleria.

State Apartments *(Quartieri Monumentali)* ▄▄
Vasari's **staircase** (1560–3) leads to the **Salone dei Cinquecento** (1495–6), known also as the Sala del Consiglio Maggiore, originally built by Cronaca to house the enlarged representative government of the penultimate republic, but later modified and decorated under Vasari's direction. It is the largest room of its kind in existence and one of the most unpleasant, not square, and lined by Vasari's frantic frescoes commemorating the Florentine victories over Pisa and Siena; the fresco program relates to Cosimo I, seen in glory on the ceiling. Some of the statues, especially Vincenzo de' Rossi's *Hercules and Diomedes*, provide welcome comic relief. But the only beautiful thing in the room is Michelangelo's *Victory* ✩ which was made for the tomb of Julius II some time between 1506–34 and presented to Cosimo I by the sculptor's nephew. Off this room is the windowless **Studiolo of Francesco I** ✩ which is a treasure-trove of late Mannerist art, built as a retreat for Cosimo's solitary, gloomy son, who kept his most precious small possessions in the cabinets, which were decorated from 1569–73 by more than 30 artists according to an allegorical system dictated by Vincenzo Borghini to Vasari. Each wall represents one of the elements, earth, air, fire and water.

From the Sala di Leo X (1556–62), rebuilt and decorated by Vasari and others, a staircase leads to the Sala degli Elementi on the second floor. The Terrazza di Saturno, to the left of the stairs, commands a wonderful view to the SE. To the right of the stairs are the **private apartments of Eleanor of Toledo**. The **chapel** (1540–5) ✩ is frescoed by Bronzino.

At the end of the long Salotta di Eleanora, where the detached fresco of the *Expulsion of the Duke of Athens* (c.1343) shows the palace as it was in the 14thC., is the **Sala dei Gigli** (1476–80) ✩ by Benedetto da Maiano, one of the few beautiful rooms in the palace, with **frescoes** (1481–5) by Dom. and Dav. Ghirlandaio. The intarsiaed **doors**, with carved marble surround, and the figure of the *Baptist* (1476–81) above are by B. and G. da Maiano. Off this room in the small **Cancelleria** is the original of Verrocchio's bronze **putto** (1476) from the courtyard fountain, and the famous 16thC *Portrait of Machiavelli*, attributed to Santi di Tito; also the original relief carving of *St George and the Dragon* (c.1270) from the Porta S. Giorgio.

The Sala dell' Udienza, entered from the Sala dei Gigli through the intarsiaed doors, was also built by B. da Maiano; the figure of *Justice* (1476–8) over the door is by the two Maiano. The **frescoes** (1550–60) are by Cecchino Salviati at his best. Donatello's *Judith and Holofernes* (c.1456–60) ✩ which was made as a fountain for the courtyard of the Medici Palace and dragged to the Piazza Signoria after the expulsion of the Medici in 1494 as a symbol of the new republic was brought inside from the piazza in 1980.

Returning through the Sala dei Gigli, the stairs lead up, past the euphemistically named **Alberghettino** where Cosimo il Vecchio and Savonarola were imprisoned, to the **tower** ★ which commands what is probably the best view of all. Down this flight of stairs is the **Mezzanine**, where pictures and sculptures left to the city in 1934 by the American Charles Loeser (Collezione Loeser) are displayed in three rooms. The treasures of the collection are Bronzino's *Portrait of Laura Battiferri* ☆ who was Ammannati's poetess wife, and a marble *Angel* by Tino da Camaiano.

In the piazza, the row of statues, which runs from the northern part of the square parallel with the facade of the palace, was deliberately aligned in the 16thC to point in perspective diminution towards the *Uffizi*.

From N to S they are: 1. Giambologna's equestrian statue of *Cosimo I* (1594). 2. Ammannati's *Neptune Fountain* (1563–75), a reference to Cosimo's maritime victories – the embarrassed figure of Neptune, 'Il Biancone,' the 'White Giant,' caused a 16thC critic to coin the rhyme, "*Ammannato, Ammannato, che bel marmo ha rovinato,*" ("What beautiful marble you have ruined"). The nymphs and satyrs, which Ammannati came to regret as provocation of sinful thoughts when he fell under the influence of the Counter-Reformation, were made with the collaboration of Giambologna and other younger artists. 3. Copy of Donatello's *Marzocco* on an elegant 15thC base; the original is in the *Bargello*. 4. Copy of Michelangelo's *David*; the original was moved to the *Accademia* in 1873. 5. Bandinelli's infelicitous *Hercules and Cacus* (1553); Hercules was another of Cosimo's symbols. Flanking the entrance to the palace are two marble herms by Vincenzo de' Rossi and Bandinelli.

The **Loggia dei Lanzi** (1376–82) ★ as it has been called since the 16thC when Cosimo I's Swiss Lancers stood on guard here, was built for important public ceremonies by Benci Di Cione and Simone di Francesco Talenti, probably to a design by Orcagna. Michelangelo once advised that the arcaded module should be repeated all round the perimeter of the piazza, a plan which would certainly have saved the square esthetically. The present arrangement of the statues was settled on in the 19thC.

At front, left to right: 6. Cellini's *Perseus* (1545–54) ★ the casting of which is described in detail in his autobiography; the originals of the relief panels and small statues round the base are now in the *Bargello*. 7. Two lions flanking the stairs; the one on the right-hand side is Classical, the other is a 16thC copy. 8. Giambologna's *Rape of the Sabines* (1583).

Middle row, left to right: 9. *Rape of Polixena* (1866) by Pio Fedi. 10. *Ajax (or Menelaus) Supporting the Body of Patroclus*, Roman copy of a 4thC BC Greek original. 11. Giambologna's *Hercules Fighting the Centaur Nessus* (1599).

Against the back wall are six Roman statues of matrons or empresses. On the NE side of the square is the three-bay **Uguccioni** palace (c.1550); the design is thought to have been sent from Rome by Michelangelo. From the balcony, a bust of Cosimo I looks out at the statue of himself on horseback.

Raccolta d'Arte Moderna Alberto della Ragione
Piazza Signoria 5 🚌 *Open Mon, Wed–Sat 9am–2pm, Sun and hols 8am–1pm. Closed Tues.*
This collection of modern art, given to the city by the Genoese Alberto della Ragione, has been installed on two floors of the Casa di Risparmio, and provides a comprehensive overview of the mainstream figurative, landscape and still-life traditions in Italian painting from the 1930s to 1960s. Sculptures by Marini, Manzù, and others; paintings by, among others, De Pisis, Mafai, Morandi. Of local interest are the views of and from Via S. Leonardo (see *Florence/Walk 4*) by Ottone Rosai.

Stibbert *(Museo Stibbert)*
Via Stibbert 26 ☎ *475731. Map 7C4* 🏛 🖼 🚻 🛊 *Open Thurs–Tues 9am–1pm. Closed Wed. Guided tours on the hour.*

The Villa Stibbert is a house worthy of Citizen Kane. The private museum Frederick Stibbert created here in the late 19thC is not quite as large as Hearst's Californian monster mansion, but it is scarcely less amazing. Of Italian-Scottish parentage, Stibbert was an obsessive collector of everything – from buttons to arms and armor. The armor collection, one of the most important in the world, is displayed on model phalanxes which you can imagine marching against one another through the innumerable, vast, gloomy rooms.

Nearby in the Via Bolognese is the **Villa La Pietra**, with one of the most beautiful Italian gardens in Tuscany, re-created at the turn of this century by an Englishman, open to guided parties by arrangement.

Strozzi Palace 🏛 ☆
Map 7D5 👁 *Opening hours vary according to exhibitions.*

Of the 100 or so palaces built in 15thC Florence the Strozzi was the largest. Filippo Strozzi acquired over a dozen properties to create his site, and the building took 44yr, from 1489 to 1536. Strozzi watched his palace being built from his small house, to the left (facing the palace from the piazza), which he built as temporary accommodation. The design of the Strozzi is based on G. da Sangallo's wooden model (see Piccolo Museo), but Cronaca, who supervised the building, made significant alterations; and it is he who added the massive cornice, a reproduction of an ancient Roman cornice.

The palace is faced on three sides with huge blocks of *pietra forte*, supplied by four quarries including two in the *Boboli*. Apart from this sheer quantity of stone and the scrupulously Classical cornice, the exterior, which still conforms to the type of the *Medici Palace*, was not architecturally innovative. The fine **lamp brackets** by Niccolò Grosso on the corners flanking the main entrance are rare surviving examples of Renaissance ironwork. The interior is the first of the Renaissance to be made completely symmetrical.

Piccolo Museo di Palazzo Strozzi
👁 *Open Mon, Wed, Fri 4–7pm. It is usually possible to gain admittance outside these hours by applying to the Vieusseux Office.*

On the left side of Cronaca's splendid interior courtyard is the entrance to this small museum, which explains how the Strozzi was built, and where you can see the differences between G. da Sangallo's original model and the actual palace.

Vieusseux Library *(Gabinetto Vieusseux)*
👁 *Open Tues–Fri 9:15am–12:45pm, 3:15–6:45pm, Sat 9:15am–12:45pm. Closed Sun, Mon.*

At the right of the courtyard, this lending library has always been a favorite meeting place for literary resident foreigners, especially in pre-Risorgimento Florence when it was a center of liberal activity. Any member of the public can borrow for a nominal fee. About a third of the collection is in English.

The first floor rooms of the palace are used for temporary exhibitions.

Topographical Museum   A pictorial history of the city's growth, known as *Firenze com'era*.

Uffizi 🏛 ★

Piazzale degli Uffizi 6 ☎ *218341. Map* **5**D4 ▰ 𝒳 ▱ *Open Tues–Sat 9am–7pm, Sun and hols 9am–1pm. Closed Mon.*

The painters of 15thC Florence trained in one another's workshops and watched each other's progress with jealous eyes, each sparking off the other's genius and contributing to a chain of innovative masterpieces which is one of the wonders of western civilization. The world's largest and finest collection of paintings from this period is found in Rms 7–15 of the Uffizi. First-time visitors on a very tight schedule are advised to take the elevator straight to the picture galleries on the second floor and explore these rooms first. But there is, of course, a great deal more. Nearly all of some 1,700 works of art displayed here are outstanding.

The building, which parades in solemn double file from the Piazza della Signoria to the Arno, was designed by Vasari in 1560 as a suite of offices for Cosimo I; hence the name Uffizi, which means offices, and the official mood of the handsome architecture. Buontalenti carried on the project after Vasari's death, continuing to make modifications and additions until 1586. In 1581 Francesco I had the upper loggias glazed and made into a museum, where he could escape from the duties of state.

The remains of the Zecca, where the famous florin was minted, were incorporated into the fabric of the building and explain the absence of colonnades at the base of the W wing where it joins the Loggia dei Lanzi. The former church, S. Piero Scheraggio, was absorbed into the N end of the opposite wing; the gloomy statues in niches are the work of 19thC hacks.

In 1743 the Uffizi and its contents were bequeathed to the people of Florence by the Palatine Electress Anna Maria Lodovica, widow of the last Medici grand duke, Gian Gastone. The enlightened Lorraine dynasty continued to add to the extraordinary collection assembled by the Medici over the previous 300yr. In this century the threat of vandalism, theft and damp has driven more and more masterpieces out of the churches and into this relatively soulless sanctuary. Florentines complain about the Uffizi with some justification. It is too crowded, with an attendance of almost 1.5 million in 1980, the highest of any Italian gallery. But the worst of the coach tours can be avoided by visiting the gallery in the late afternoon. Too many sections are subject to unannounced and prolonged closure; and too many paintings are stored for lack of space, a problem which has led to the State Archives being moved to new headquarters in Piazza Beccaria.

The following selective tour of the galleries will take at least 3hr and will be much more enjoyable if divided into two or more visits.

Do remember that this is not only a picture gallery. The superb Classical statues lining the stairs and corridors were regarded as the chief glories of the Uffizi until hardly more than 100yr ago (nobody looked at Botticelli with much interest until the 1880s). Shelley visited the Uffizi every day during his stay in Florence, but took notes only on the sculptures, and Gibbon toured the gallery 12 times before looking at a picture.

The elevator is for the picture galleries only. Opposite, at the end of the corridor, is a fresco of the *Annunciation* (1481) by Botticelli, damaged but still recognizable as one of his best works. Vasari's great staircase leads to the first floor.

Exhibitions from the **prints and drawings collection**, which is
otherwise closed to the general public, are frequently held in
rooms to the left and are highly recommended. The staircase
carries on to the picture galleries.

East corridor. The finest of the 16thC tapestries lining the
corridor are the *Months of the Year*, woven in the Medici
factories, and the Flemish-made *Festivities at the Court of
Catherine de' Medici and Henry III*. The collection is arranged in
chronological order through the gallery's two wings. The
Florentine pictures are deliberately displayed in order to
illustrate the impact made by one master upon another, from
Giotto through to Michelangelo and the early Mannerists.

Rm 1. Antique carvings.

Rm 2. Three huge **altarpieces of the Maestà ★** offer a unique
opportunity to examine the roots of Florentine and Sienese
painting as they were to flower over the next 200yr. On the
right, Cimabue's severe and massive image (c.1280) marks the
epitome of the Byzantine Middle Ages. On the left, Duccio's
composition (c.1285) is similar, but notice the lighter
construction of the throne, the more human relationship
between Madonna and Child, and the treatment of the
Madonna's hem, a virtuoso passage that anticipates the linear
style of Simone Martini and Botticelli. In the center, Giotto's
less-cluttered altarpiece (c.1310) achieves a new sense of
realistic space by the use of *chiaroscuro*, and the placing of the
angels' heads at varying angles.

Rm 3. In the second quarter of the *trecento*, Duccio's
successors brought Sienese Gothic painting to a peak of
sophistication from which it thereafter declined. In Simone
Martini's *Annunciation* (1333) ★ the exquisite, poetic vision
and fluttering line are in marked contrast to Giotto's measured
abstraction. The saints are by Simone's brother-in-law Lippo
Memmi. Pietro Lorenzetti's altarpiece *Scenes from the Life of the
Blessed Humility* (1341) is more interesting for the charming
small panels than for the prosaic central figure. Ambrogio
Lorenzetti's *Story of St Nicholas* (c.1330) was painted in
Florence, but the last panel, in which St Nicholas obtains
miraculous supplies of grain for the starving population of
Myra, is poetic and detailed in a way that Florentine painting
rarely was.

Rm 4. The painters of the Florentine *trecento* worked more
successfully in fresco (see *Santa Croce*, *Santa Maria Novella*)
than on panel, and they are not especially well represented in

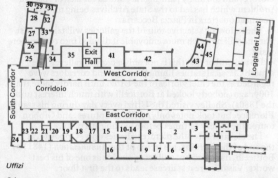

Uffizi

the Uffizi. Here one can see the work of Bernardo Daddi,
Taddeo Gaddi, Giottino and Orcagna.

Rms 5 and 6. In the early *quattrocento*, nearly 100yr later than
Siena and the rest of Europe, Florence produced its only great
Gothic painter, Lorenzo Monaco, whose *Coronation of the
Virgin* (1413) dominates the room. But his *Adoration of the
Magi* (c.1420) is a far more contemplative, less elaborate
picture than the visiting Gentile da Fabriano's contemporary
treatment of the same subject on the far wall. Gentile's fairytale
extravaganza *Adoration* ★ brings the International Gothic in
this gallery to a resounding climax. Credit for the delightful *Life
of the Anchorites in the Thebaid*, now attributed to Gherardo
Starnina and dated c.1400–10, has in the past been given to
artists as disparate as Pietro Lorenzetti, Fra Angelico and
Uccello. This is by no means the naïve work it appears at first.
The little figures are executed in the naturalistic manner of
Giotto, and the sky, for the first time in this gallery and perhaps
in the Renaissance, is blue not gold.

Rm 7. The earliest pictures in this important room are by
artists whose full genius is better appreciated elsewhere in
Florence. Masaccio and Masolino are represented here by a
Virgin and Child with St Anne (1424). Fra Angelico's one-man
show is in the Monastery of *San Marco*, where you can compare
this *Coronation of the Virgin* (1430) with a later fresco on the
same subject. There are only two other pictures by Domenico
Veneziano in Florence, neither currently on view (there are
only 12 in the world). This *Sacra Conversazione* (1445–8) ★ is
one of the supreme achievements of the Early Renaissance
master of light. Its limpid colors and precisely described
architecture give it the atmosphere of a perfect silence.
Domenico must have been deeply affected by the even greater
genius of his pupil Piero della Francesca, whose diptych of
Federico da Montefeltro and Battista Sforza (c.1460) ★ was
painted in Urbino. The **triumphs** on the reverses represent four
cardinal virtues for Duke Frederico and four theological virtues
for his duchess. The deep backgrounds evoke Piero's native
landscape near Arezzo. Piero wrote a treatise about perspective,
the new science which fascinated Paolo Uccello to the point of
near insanity. This obsession is the real subject of the *Battle of
San Romano* (1456) ★ which was painted 26yr after the event
and hung in a room in the Medici palace. Two flanking panels
were sold in the late 18thC and are now in the Louvre and the
London National Gallery. The Uffizi piece is the least
impressive of the three because of its inferior condition and
relatively confusing composition.

Rm 8. Filippo Lippi, a disciple of Masaccio, was much
imitated in his own time. The latest and loveliest of the Uffizi
Filippos is the *Madonna with Angels* (c.1465) ★ which scholars
take as evidence of Botticelli's apprenticeship to the older
master. For Filippo's major achievement in Tuscany, see *Prato*
(in *A–Z/Tuscany*). Filippo's Sienese contemporary Vecchietta
is represented by a *Madonna Enthroned* (1457). Notice also
Baldovinetti's appealing works.

Rm 9. The Pollaiuolo brothers, Antonio and Piero, were
sculptors, engravers and goldsmiths as well as painters. Piero is
usually judged the less talented, mainly on the evidence of these
Six Virtues (1469), ordered by the Merchants' Tribunal. The
seventh, *Strength*, was Botticelli's first public commission. The
virtues do indeed seem crude and static when compared to
Antonio's tiny but vividly dramatic panels of *The Feats of*

Hercules in the case between the windows. Antonio's interest in anatomy drove him to undertake human dissections. He was, above all, one of the most gifted draftsmen of the Renaissance, an innovator in the use of line to convey muscular action. In the same case are two exhilarating scenes from the grisly _Story of Judith_, by the young Botticelli when he was still under the influence of Pollaiuolo.

Rms 10–14. The great Medici Botticellis hang in this room, recently converted into one large area. The design of the room and the gray lighting are controversial. Botticelli was the greatest linear painter before Matisse, and the powerful melodic line and lyrical nostalgia of his art can touch the heart even of those who have no wish to analyze his technique or his meaning. Of all the complex intellectual programs he realized for his humanist patrons, the _Primavera_ (c.1480) ★ painted for an adolescent cousin of Lorenzo de' Medici, is the most arcane – it is also the most popular. Here, then, is one possible gloss. In comes the Wind God Zephyr from the right. At his touch, flowers grow from the lips of the nymph Chloris, and she becomes Flora, Goddess of Spring. Spring is the season of love, but the figure of Venus at the center of the composition warns us with a gesture toward the three graces that love is not so simple. The graces represent three of the many forms love can take: the love of beauty, the love that cherishes, and the love that lusts (the position of the raised hands refers to sexual intercourse). Cupid remains blindfolded until the correct balance has been decided. Mercury points to heaven where the only perfect solution is to be found.

The _Birth of Venus_ (c.1485) ★ was commissioned as a companion piece to the _Primavera_ after Botticelli's return from Rome. The _Adoration of the Magi_ (c.1475) ✪ is one of a series of _Adorations_ from the 1470s; others are in Washington and London. This one is of special interest because members of the Medici family appear among the adoring Magi. Lorenzo de' Medici is at the left foreground, Botticelli himself is in yellow on the extreme right. The _Man with a Medallion of Cosimo il Vecchio_ (c.1475–80) may be another self-portrait. The _Madonna of the Magnificat_ (c.1482) ✪ is perhaps the loveliest of his religious paintings, and all the more so now that it has been cleaned; its elaborate curving design has been compared to a section cut through a rose. The _Calumny of Apelles_ (c.1495–1500) is one of the few late Botticellis in the Uffizi. The frenzied, dazzlingly stylized execution reflects the political and moral earnestness that afflicted many sensitive Florentines at the end of the century under the influence of Savonarola.

Set out from the walls on a screen is a large _Adoration of the Shepherds_ known as the _Portinari Altarpiece_ (c.1475) ✪ by the Flemish master Hugo van der Goes. Commissioned in Bruges by a Medici bank agent, Tommaso Portinari, this marvelous feat of naturalistic painting had a profound effect on all artists who saw it after its arrival in Florence in 1488. Behind it is another Flemish work, Roger van der Weyden's _Entombment of Christ_ (c.1450), painted in Florence. Dom. Ghirlandaio and Filippino Lippi were particularly influenced by the van der Goes and are represented in this section of the room by _Adorations_. For Ghirlandaio and Filippino see _Santa Maria Novella_ and _Santa Trinità_.

Rm 15. There is no complete or completely accepted Leonardo in the Uffizi, but no other gallery possesses such fascinating evidence of his early development. His earliest known piece of work, done when he was still in his teens working in Verrocchio's studio, is the profiled angel in the *Baptism of Christ* (begun c.1470). Vasari tells us that Verrocchio, recognizing that this angel was beyond his own very considerable capabilities, abandoned the painting. Vasari does not mention the *Annunciation* (c.1475) ☆ and its attribution has been debated by opposing teams of distinguished art historians since it was brought into the gallery in 1867. The unfinished *Adoration of the Magi* (1481) ☆ is really a drawing rather than a painting, the preparatory scaffolding Leonardo left behind when he moved to Milan in 1482. To appreciate how startlingly ahead of its time this conception was you need only to compare it with Lorenzo di Credi's small *Annunciation* (1485), a faultlessly graceful piece typical of its period. Piero di Cosimo's *Perseus Liberating Andromeda* (1515–20) and *Immaculate Conception* (c.1505–10) show this idiosyncratic artist more at home with the mythological subject. Also, Signorelli's *Crucifixion with Mary Magdalen* and the Umbrian Perugino's *Christ in the Garden of Olives*.

All Florentine work of the finest kind . . . is absolutely pure Etruscan, merely changing its subjects, and representing the Virgin instead of Athena, and Christ instead of Jupiter.

John Ruskin, *Mornings in Florence*

Rm 18. The Tribune ★ was designed in 1584 by Buontalenti as an inner temple of the arts and restored in 1970 to something like its original appearance. When Zoffany painted the Tribune in 1775 for Queen Charlotte of England, this windowless octagonal room was one of the high points of the Grand Tour. The best works of art in the gallery were displayed here, but nothing in Florence had such drawing power as the *Medici Venus* ☆ A Roman copy of a Praxitelean figure of the 4thC BC, it was brought into this inner sanctum in the 17thC by Cosimo III, who is said to have feared that she might corrupt the morals of art students in Rome. For nearly 200yr she remained a potent sex symbol for educated Europeans, inducing a cultural-erotic trance which men struggled to describe in prose and poetry. Engravings, drawings and reproductions of all sizes flooded across the Alps. Louis XIV had her copied in bronze. She was the only statue in Florence called to Paris by Napoleon. In the puritanical 19thC, a plaster cast in Philadelphia was kept under lock and key. Nathaniel Hawthorne found himself panting as he approached her along the Uffizi corridors. We cannot easily share such raptures today; but it is as well to be reminded of the vagaries of taste when in an art gallery. Among the many fine 16thC portraits in the Tribune are Vasari's *Lorenzo de' Medici* (painted 60yr after his death); Bronzino's *Lucrezia* and *Bartolomeo Panciatichi* (he is the quintessential Florentine, dry, wary, arrogant); and *Eleanor of Toledo with her Son Giovanni I*.

Rm 17. Entrance (from the Tribune only) is often barred. The Room of the Hermaphrodite takes its name from a Hellenistic copy (2ndC BC) of an extraordinarily sensual bisexual figure. Here hang two superb Mantegnas ☆ the *Adoration* and *Madonna of the Stonecutters* (both c.1489).

Rm 19. Signorelli's *Holy Family* (c.1491) anticipates Michelangelo's *Doni Tondo* in Rm 25. By Perugino, *Madonna and Child with Saints* (1493) and the fine portrait of *Francesco delle Opere* (1494), a Florentine craftsman.

Rm 20. Dürer's _Portrait of the Artist's Father_ (1490) and _Adoration of the Magi_ (1504). Lucas Cranach's _Adam_ and _Eve_ (1528) face Dürer's _Adam_ and _Eve_.

Rm 21. Giovanni Bellini's _Sacred Allegory_ (c.1490) ✩

Rm 22. Holbein's almost tactlessly faithful _Portrait of Sir Richard Southwell_ (1536); Altdorfer's _Martyrdom_ and _Departure of St Florian_ (c.1525).

Rm 23. Correggio's _Rest on the Flight into Egypt._ The Roman portrait busts of boys in this and the previous room are of the kind that influenced the facial types of the boys portrayed by Luca della Robbia and Donatello.

South corridor. Fine views and Classical sculptures.

West corridor. This section of the gallery originally housed workshops and laboratories. The 16thC conception of 'art' embraced the crafts and sciences. Among the tapestries, note particularly the _Passion of Christ_ series, woven in Florence, and the Flemish _Scenes from the Life of Jacob._

Rm 25. The _Holy Family_, known as the _Doni Tondo_ (1504) ★ is the only picture in Florence by Michelangelo apart from the drawings in the _Casa Buonarroti_ and the recently discovered drawings at _San Lorenzo._ It was commissioned by Angelo Doni on the occasion of his marriage to Maddalena Strozzi during the period when the artist was in Florence working on the _David._ In opposition to Leonardo, Michelangelo held that sculpture was the supreme art, and this tondo aspires to three dimensions. The Classical past, represented by a frieze of nudes in the upper half, is linked to the new Christian era by the figure of John the Baptist. With its emphasis on gesture and deliberately shocking colors, this was a key picture for the 16thC Mannerists. The inventors of Mannerism, Pontormo (Rm 27) and Rosso Fiorentino, whose astonishing _Moses Defending the Daughters of Jethro_ (1523–4) ✩ hangs next to the _Doni Tondo_, were both deeply neurotic – agoraphobic, morbid and asocial and, until recently, ignored or despised by critics. But the gratuitous violence of Rosso's _Moses_ (the text from _Exodus_ says nothing about all this wrenching and pounding) and its cynicism (the daughter with one breast exposed is the quintessential silly woman) seem appropriate to our own tense age. The upper right-hand corner could have been painted in this century.

Rm 26. For Andrea del Sarto see also _Pitti, San Salvi, Scalzo_. _Madonna of the Harpies_ (1517) ✩ is a masterpiece of his early maturity. Raphael's _Virgin of the Goldfinch_ (1506) shows the influence of his first contact with Florentine artists; his penetrating, scholarly portrait of the first Medici Pope _Leo X with Cardinals Giulio de' Medici and Luigi de' Rossi_ (c.1519) ✩ is one of his finest late works.

Rm 27. Pontormo began his career as one of Andrea del Sarto's many satellites, but by the time he painted the _Supper at Emmaus_ (1525), he had discovered other models; in this case it was a woodcut by Dürer. His masterpieces are elsewhere in and near Florence: see _Santa Felicità_ in _Florence_; _Carmignano, Galluzo, Poggio a Caiano_ in _A–Z/Tuscany._

Rm 28. Titian's euphemistically entitled _Venus of Urbino_ (1538) ★ is not a Venus but a pinup, one of the most intimate, alluring female nudes ever painted. Visitors to Florence have been falling in love with her since she arrived in 1631 as part of the inheritance of Vittoria delle Rovere. For Byron she was '_the_ Venus.' Other fine Titians include _Flora_ (c.1515), _A Knight of Malta_ (c.1518), and portraits of _Eleanora_ and _Francesco Maria della Rovere_, Duke and Duchess of Urbino (1537).

Rm 29. Parmigianino was the leading central Italian Mannerist. The striking, intricate *Virgin of the Long Neck* ☆ left unfinished at his death in 1540, is his best-known work.

Returning to the corridor via Rm 34 (Veronese and Moroni), the entrance to Vasari's **Corridoio** ★ is immediately right. Tours of it must be guided, and they are booked in advance at the ticket office; but, although restored and officially reopened in 1973, it is all too rarely open. Vasari built this long covered passage for Cosimo I in 1565. It links the Uffizi to the Pitti, crossing the Arno with the Ponte Vecchio and passing through the church of Santa Felicità. The views are nearly as magnificent as the pictures, the most celebrated of which are the series of self-portraits.

Rm 35. Tintoretto's *Leda* (1570); Federico Barocci's *Madonna of the People* (1575–9).

Rm 41. Rubens and Van Dyck.

Rm 42. The large collection of 20thC self-portraits is out of place in this fine Neo-Classical room, which has housed the 4thC Roman sculptures of *Niobe and her Children* ☆ since 1790.

Rm 43. Caravaggio's *Sacrifice of Isaac* (c.1590), *Bacchus* (c.1589), and *Medusa* (after 1590). Also, Claude Lorraine's *Seascape* (1677).

Rm 44. Three portraits by Rembrandt, including one of his greatest self-portraits, *Self-Portrait as an Old Man* (c.1664) ☆

Rm 45. 18thC French, Venetian and Spanish paintings by Nattier, Chardin, G. B. Tiepolo, Canaletto, Guardi and Goya.

At the end of this corridor are rest rooms and a pleasant bar, which opens on to a terrace over the Loggia dei Lanzi.

Exit hall (formerly Rms 34–40). The famous *Wild Boar* is a Roman copy of a 3rdC BC Hellenistic original and was the model for Pietro Tacca's *Porcellino Fountain* in the Mercato Nuovo. The exit staircase is by Buontalenti.

Zoological Museum, 'La Specola'
Via Romana 17 ☎ *222451. Map 4F2* 🖼 ✚ *Open Tues 9am–12:30pm, Sun 9am–noon. Anatomical rooms Sat 3–6pm.*

The Torrigiani palace which houses the Zoological Institute is known as 'La Specola,' after the astrological observatory set up here in 1775 by Grand Duke Peter Leopold.

The museum, on the second floor, is divided into two sections. The Zoological Museum consists of a collection of specimens arranged in order of organic complexity from mollusks to mammals, including hunting trophies donated by Victor Emmanuel and ending with a small selection of wax models of human and animal anatomy.

The full collection of some 600 **anatomical wax models** ☆ is displayed in the next rooms. They are among the most extraordinary objects in Florence, and remind you just how deep are the roots of the Florentine fascination with human anatomy. The Renaissance artist P. Pollaiuolo dissected corpses in order to improve his understanding of how the human body works. Here, from 1775–1814, an artist, Clemente Susini, and a physiologist, Felice Fontana, collaborated to make these tinted wax reproductions of every part of the human body. The famous *Embryonic Twins* and models of reproductive organs are in a room off Corridor 31.

Next door are the *Plague Victims* by the late 17thC Sicilian Gaetano Zumbo. The custodian will usually open these rooms on request.

Walks in Florence

The compact city of Florence can only be truly appreciated on foot. The first two walks, which cover different areas of the city center, share a common plan (on opposite page).

Walk 1/Getting to know Florence

On your first evening in Florence, an after-dinner stroll in the center, taking in the *Uffizi*, *Signoria* and *Duomo*, will make you at home in the dense cluster of the city's historic nucleus. Florence is at its best, its most beautiful, after dark when the charabancs have departed and the floodlighting touches even the most familiar monuments with fresh magic.

Start at Piazza *Santa Trinità* in order to enjoy the floodlit view of *San Miniato* and the *Belvedere* from Ponte S. Trinità and to admire the recently installed lighting of the **Via Tornabuoni**. If you can resist window shopping, plunge into medieval Florence along Via delle Terme, named for the Roman baths which occupied this site, to the 14thC **Palazzo di Parte Guelfa** on the left. Turn right opposite it under Chiasso delle Misure and left into Borgo *Santi Apostoli*, crossing Por S. Maria into Via Lambertesca, which brings you past Buontalenti's bizarre **Porta delle Suppliche** into Piazzale degli *Uffizi*. A left turn leads straight into Piazza *Signoria*. Turn right around the N corner of the Palazzo Vecchio into Via dei Gondi and Piazza *San Firenze*, where the towers of the *Badia* and *Bargello* rise with dignity beyond the Baroque extravaganza of the S. Firenze facade. Take the Via del Proconsolo, turning left after *Badia* into Via Dante Alighieri. The Casa di Dante is a 19thC fiction made believable by the night lighting. Opposite is the Castegna tower, all that remains of the earliest seat of communal government. Turn right into Via S. Margherita, left at the Corso and immediately right into Via dello Studio, where you will be rewarded with one of those astonishingly sudden views of Brunelleschi's Dome, as though it had arrived from outer space. The cathedral complex – campanile, Baptistry, *Duomo* – reveals itself as you turn left along its S side. Third left is Via de' Calzaiuoli, which brings you past *Orsanmichele* back into the *Signoria*.

Walk 2/A palace walk

This is a walk devoted entirely to those domestic buildings which Italians rather grandly call palaces. It can be divided into three separate walks if you want to go slowly and thoroughly. It will take you, in roughly chronological order, past many of the most important Florentine palaces built for the merchants and bankers of the 14th–16thC.

Florentines, being the least pretentious and most ironically humorous of Italians, will often refer in conversation to a hut as a palazzo and a palazzo as a little house – which doesn't in the least mean that they are not proud of their palaces. A surprising number are still lived in by descendants of their first owners; most are used – as flats, restaurants, shops, offices – your hotel might be in a palace. If you are not with a large party is always worth ringing the bell and asking to see the courtyard; that is the kind of independently motivated interest Florentines respect. The palaces built in Florence during the 15thC boom provided a model for the rest of Italy. In 15thC Tuscany there was no significant advance on the basic Florentine type except in *Pienza (A–Z/Tuscany)*. Nevertheless, there are certain

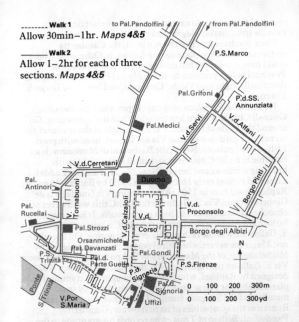

practical or decorative additions to Florentine palaces which
you encounter less often outside the city.

The stone benches, or *muriccioli*, which run along the base of
so many palaces were a government-imposed condition of
building permission. If you decide to rest and gossip on one of
these public benches, you will be exercising a civic right dear to
the republican hearts of Renaissance Florentines. Machiavelli
was shocked to find no *muriccioli* in Venice.

The projecting upper stories supported on brackets known as
sporti were a device to grab more living space in a crowded city.
Legislation against them generally failed.

The black-and-white decoration, or *sgraffiti*, on facades and
in courtyards originated in the 15thC and was carried on
through the 19thC. Two good 15thC examples not encountered
on this walk are the **Coverelli** palace in Via dei Coverelli and the
Lanfredini palace on Lungarno Guicciardini. The 16thC
master of *sgraffiti* was Poccetti.

I. Start in the morning at the *Davanzati*, the best-preserved
14thC merchant's house in Florence. Next, to see what had
happened to palace architecture a century later, cross the
bottom of the Tornabuoni onto Via del Parione; the first right
and an immediate left into Via del Purgatorio, brings you into
the little piazza facing Alberti's *Rucellai Palace*. Take the Via
della Vigna Nuova back to the Tornabuoni, across which you
see the *Strozzi*, later, larger and less refined than the Rucellai.
Down the Tornabuoni to Piazza *Santa Trinità*. On its NE corner
is the early 16thC **Bartolini Salimbeni**, the Roman-style palace
Florentines thought looked more like a church. Now look up
the **Via Tornabuoni** for a minute before strolling up it. The
palaces are 13th–16thC. At the top, partly closing the vista, is
the **Antinori** palace, built in the 1460s by the Boni family, who

received permission to extend their site onto public land to provide this suitably elegant finish to the Tornabuoni.

Once you have reached the Antinori, the **Cantinetta** restaurant is an ideal place to stop for lunch. Otherwise, you could have a delicious but expensive snack at **Giacosa** or **Procacci** before pressing on to the Medici Palace by way of Via Rondinelli, right into Via de' Cerretani, and left along Borgo S. Lorenzo.

II. The *Medici Palace* reopens at 3pm when the **Benozzo Gozzoli Chapel** is often less crowded than in the morning. Go around the S side of the palace and turn right at the corner of the crenellated garden wall onto **Via de' Ginori**, lined with good 13th–16thC palaces. No. 9, the **Barbolani di Montauto**, is an example of a 15thC palace modernized in the 16thC with kneeling windows and herms. Nos. 17–21, **Palazzo Taddei**, is a fine and typical early 16thC palace (1503) by Baccio d'Agnolo; Raphael lived here in 1505. After crossing Via Guelfa, Via de' Ginori becomes **Via S. Gallo**. In the 16thC this was a street of churches, monasteries and high garden walls. It has a rather forlorn atmosphere now, but in the 18thC a carriage ride to the S. Gallo gate was the fashionable evening outing. On the left, no. 25a, is the severely beautiful portal, possibly designed by Michelangelo, of the **Monastery of S. Apollonia**. Farther along Via S. Gallo on the right, no.74 is the **Pandolfini** palace (1520), designed by Raphael, who evidently thought the asymmetrical plan suitable for a large suburban site, and built by two members of the Sangallo family. The style of the palace is as Roman as the sympathies of its first owner, Gianozzo Pandolfini, Bishop of Troia, who records his gratitude to the Medici Popes for their help in acquiring the property in the inscription under the magnificent cornice. If you turn right at the corner of the Pandolfini and right again into Via Cavour, you will soon come, on the left, to no. 57, the **Casino di S. Marco** (1574), built on the site of the Medici sculpture gardens by Buontalenti in his most bizarre, satirical vein. Francesco I had his alchemical laboratories here. The Casino is now the Court of Appeals but, more to the point, if you happen to be thirsty there is a little bar off the inner courtyard to the left.

Turn right out of the Casino, left into **Piazza S. Marco**, pausing only to admire the cathedral dome rising spectacularly on your right, and take Via Cesare Battisti into the northern corner of Piazza *Santissima Annunziata*. The rose-brick palace on the corner of Via dei Servi, a cavalier exception to the arcaded harmony of the square, is Ammannati's **Grifoni** palace. Its main entrance is on **Via dei Servi**, lined with grand-ducal palaces. Notice especially two on the right: no. 15, the **Niccolini** (1550), designed by Baccio d'Agnolo with 19thC *sgraffiti*; and on Via Pucci, the **Pucci** palace, ancestral home of the fashion designer, with a fine emblem of Leo X on this corner. Via dei Servi finishes at the *Duomo*.

III. Alternatively, on leaving the Piazza *Santissima Annunziata*, take the first left off Via dei Servi into **Via degli Alfani**. On the right is a 1930s restoration of Brunelleschi's once-important *Rotonda di S. Maria degli Agnoli*. No. 48, on the left, is the **Giugni** palace (c.1577), one of Ammannati's best buildings. The courtyard, usually open, is remarkable for the alarming use of detached Classical elements. The Tuscan order was employed as a patriotic reference to the newly unified grand-ducal Tuscany. Notice the beautiful 16thC wooden gate. Farther along, two simpler palaces on the left, nos. 34 and 32,

are also by Ammannati. The green dome you see ahead belongs
to the synagogue. On the next right is **Borgo Pinti**, which boasts
14th–16thC palaces. At no.26, the house with the bust of
Cosimo I over the door, Giambologna lived and died and Pietro
Tacca founded an academy.

At the bottom, as you pass under the Volta di S. Piero – bar
on the left serves rough wine and good ham sandwiches – you
are crossing the second circle of walls into the 12thC city. Now
turn right onto **Borgo degli Albizi**, a street rich in good 16thC
palaces. No.18 is the **Altoviti**, known as Palazzo dei Visacci
after the herm portraits of famous Florentines. Avoid the
restaurant inside. No.26 is palazzo **Matteucci Ramirez di
Montalvi**, built by Ammannati for a favorite of Cosimo I whose
emblem as Duke of Siena is over the door; remains of *sgraffiti* by
Poccetti. No.28, the **Vitali** palace, is also by Ammannati.
Opposite the Vitali, in the lobby of the cinema specialising in
pornographic films, are the remains of a 15thC courtyard. On
the corner of Via del Proconsolo is the **Nonfinito** palace, now
housing the Institute of Anthropology, begun in 1593 by
Buontalenti for Alessandro Strozzi but left unfinished. A left
turn onto Via del Proconsolo will bring you into Piazza *San
Firenze*, where Giuliano da Sangallo's exemplary **Gondi** palace
(1490–1520) is on your right opposite the S. Firenze facade. If
you are in luck and have energy enough left to ring the bell (at
no. 2), you will be admitted into one of the most beautiful
courtyards in Florence. You are now a minute's walk from the
Signoria and have earned a good dinner. If you choose to dine at
Cavallino, you will be looking out over the most famous
Florentine palace of all.

Walk 3/The Oltrarno

Allow 2hr. *Maps* **4**&**5**

This zigzag route through the *Oltrarno* will take you to its three
important churches and past many of its most interesting palace
facades. A conveniently delicious beginning to the afternoon
would be lunch at **Celestino**, but there are plenty of other
restaurants to choose from on the Oltrarno. Start off at about
3pm, when the churches begin to reopen, from Piazza *Santa
Felicità*. The Medici dukes went home to the Pitti from this
church by way of Vasari's aerial corridor, but you must make do
with the Via Guicciardini, where the Machiavelli family once
lived opposite the Guicciardini palace (no.15). Passing the *Pitti*
on your left, turn sharp right at Piazza *San
Felice* onto **Via Maggio**, so called because it was and still is the
widest (*maggiore*) street on the Oltrarno. Palaces are

14th–17thC, but most of the earlier ones were modernized in
the grand-ducal period when Via Maggio was the best address
in Florence. No. 26 is **Bianca Cappello's house**, remodelled in
1570–4 by Buontalenti for the Venetian mistress and future
wife of Francesco I, who paid the bill. The Cappello emblem is
over the rusticated doorway; _sgraffiti_ are by Poccetti. At the
bottom of Via Maggio, turn left onto Via S. Spirito. On the right
corner of Via dei Coverelli is **Palazzo Coverelli**, with good
restored _sgraffiti_. Turn left onto Via dei Coverelli, bearing left
around the apse and side of the church of _Santo Spirito_.
Imagine what the exterior would have looked like if
Brunelleschi's unique plan had been carried out; he intended
the 40 curved backs of the interior chapels to be expressed on
the outside. Crossing Piazza S. Spirito, turn right at its sw
corner onto Via S. Agostino. Where it crosses Via de' Serragli
there is, on the right, a tabernacle (1427) by Lorenzo di Bicci.
Turn left onto Via de' Serragli and first right onto Via dell'
Ardiglione, which soon bends to the right along the side of a
pretty walled garden; from its gate there is a picturesque view of
the apse of the _Carmine_ church. This is one of those rare
Florentine streets where the bustle and noise of the city never
seem to penetrate; it might have been this peaceful when
Filippo Lippi was born in 1406 at no.30. A left turn onto Via S.
Monaca brings you to the church entrance. If it is now early
evening, Masaccio's frescoes might be lit by the setting sun.

Walk 4/To Arcetri and Pian dei Giullari

Allow 2hr. Maps **6&7**

The Tuscan countryside is only about 10min by foot from the
Ponte Vecchio. Take the narrow Costa di S. Giorgio from
behind the church of _Santa Felicità_, past the _Belvedere_ and
onto **Via di S. Leonardo**, the most entrancing street in the
environs of Florence, lined with old villas and walled gardens.
Jasmine, wisteria and roses clamber in season through the olive-
and cypresstrees. On the left is the 11thC S. Leonardo in
Arcetri, its facade an early 20thC reconstruction. Ottone Rosai
lived at no. 49; his paintings of Via di S. Leonardo can be seen
in the Alberto della Ragione collection (_Signoria_). A plaque
marks the house on the corner of Viale Galileo where
Tchaikovsky lived in 1878, "his music nourished by the soft
hills of Tuscany." After crossing the Viale, bear left onto Via V.
Vivani, left again onto Via del Pian dei Giullari. As you climb,
the view to the right, overlooking the Astrophysical
Observatory, becomes more and more wild and spectacular. At
Pian dei Giullari (see _Arcetri_) you could stop for lunch or dinner
at **Omero**, or continue walking along Via S. Margherita toward
Ponte a Ema and Antella.

Staying in Florence

Florence is well supplied with hotels and *pensioni* of every style and category, but there are still not enough to accommodate everyone who wishes to visit the small city in the peak tourist season or during major exhibitions and trade fairs. From Easter to late Sept it is wise to book rooms as far in advance as possible. If you must find a hotel at the last minute, try the reservations center at the station. There are also three cooperative booking services: **Coopal** (*Via S. Lucia 8/12* ☎ *(055)* 219531); **Florence Promhotels** (*Borgognissanti 138* ☎ *(055)* 211160); **Toscana Hotels** (*Via S. Lucia 8/12* ☎ *(055)* 216695). The Ente Provinciale per il Turismo publishes annually a full list of all hotels and *pensioni* in the city and province.

The distinction between hotels and *pensioni* is no longer clear-cut. Most *pensioni* in the city have abandoned the obligation to have meals in their dining rooms; some no longer serve meals at all, and are therefore not, strictly speaking, boarding houses. Even the most sophisticated, central and comfortable *pensioni* charge considerably less than hotels for an equivalent room and bath. But what they do not offer – and you do not pay for – are the services executives may require, such as hall porters, full switchboards, telexes.

The general standard of cleanliness and basic efficiency in both hotels and *pensioni* is high, although service, even in luxury hotels, is not what it was. If you are sensitive to noise, resist the temptation to take a room overlooking a busy street or square; the Lungarno in the center is especially noisy. Ask for a room on the courtyard or garden, or choose a hotel on the edge of the center. Distances given refer to walking time.

Florence hotels and pensioni

Hotels

Aprile ▮▢
Augustus ▮▮▮
Baglioni ▮▮▮▮
Balestri ▮▮▢
Berchielli ▮▮▢
Continental ▮▮▢
Croce di Malta ▮▮▮▮
David ▮▢
De La Ville ▮▮▮▮
Excelsior ▮▮▮▮ ▥
Helvetia-Bristol ▮▮▮▢
Kraft ▮▮▢
Liana ▮▢
Lungarno ▮▮▮▮
Plaza Lucchesi ▮▮▮▮
Porta Rossa ▮▢
Principe ▮▢
Regency ▮▮▮▮
Royal ▮▢
Savoy ▮▮▮▮ ▥

Villa Belvedere ▮▮▢
Villa Cora ▮▮▮▮ ▥
Villa Medici ▮▮▮▮ ▥

Pensioni

Adria ▮▢
Annalena ▮▢
Bartolini ▮▢ ▰
Cestelli ▢
Costantini ▢ ▰
Hermitage ▮▮▢
Monna Lisa ▮▢
Morandi ▮▢ ▰
Pendini ▮▢
Pitti Palace ▮▮▢
Residenza ▮▮▢
Rigatti ▮▮▢
Silla ▮▢
Splendor ▢ ▰
Tornabuoni-Beacci ▮▮▢
Villa Carlotta ▮▮▢

Adria
Piazza Frescobaldi 4, 50125 Firenze ☎ *(055) 215029. Map 4D2* ▢ ✎ 10 ▭ 6 ➬ ▥ ⇌ *Closed Aug.*
Location: *Oltrarno, near Ponte S. Trinità.* A nice, old-fashioned *pensione* on the Arno which would suit those traveling alone.
⬍ ⚲ ⪤

Annalena
Via Romana 34, 50125 Firenze ☎ *(055) 222402. Map 4F2* ▮▢ ✎ 20 ▭ 16. *Closed May.*
Location: *Opposite the Boboli Gardens.* A comfortably furnished *pensione* on the first floor of a 15thC palace overlooking the largest private rear garden in Florence.
⬡

105

Aprile
Via della Scala 6, 50123 Firenze
☎ (055) 216237. Map **4***B2* ▯□
🗪 *32* ➖ *26* ➡ AE ⓪ VISA
Location: Near the station. The Via
della Scala is not the most
salubrious street in Florence, but it
has its surprises, including this
friendly and unpretentious little
private hotel in a 15thC Medici
palace. Some rooms, especially on
the top floor, have charm.
‡ 🗁 🕭 🌥

Augustus
Vicolo dell'Oro 5, 50123 Firenze
☎ (055) 283054 ⓣ570110. Map
4D3 ▥ 🗪 *67* ➖ *67* ▤ ➡ AE
⓪ VISA
Location: Near Ponte Vecchio. The
Augustus was opened in 1970 by
the excellent Penguin chain in a
large new building protected from
the hurly-burly of central Florence
by its own tiny square just behind
the Arno. Decor is soothingly
modern in shades of cool beige with
recessed lighting and thick carpets.
Some rooms have balconies.
🖂‡ ⅙ ▢ 🗁 🌥 ◁≡ ⅄

Grand Hotel Baglioni
*Piazza Unità Italiana 6, 50123
Firenze* ☎ (055) 218441
ⓣ570225. Map **4***B2* ▥ 🗪 *195*
➖ *195* ▤ 🖾 ➡ AE CB ⓪
⓪ VISA
Location: Opposite the station. An
enormous, efficient, well-staffed
hotel, ideal for executives.
‡ ⅙ ▢ 🗁 🌥 *on roof* 🎖 ⅄

Balestri
*Piazza Mentana 7, 50122
Firenze* ☎ (055) 214743. Map
5E4 ▥ 🗪 *49* ➖ *45* ▤ ➡ AE
⓪ ⓪ VISA *Closed Dec–Feb.*
*Location: On the Arno 5min E of
Ponte Vecchio.* A 19thC hotel which
has been for four generations in the
same family, whose style of
management is nevertheless more
enthusiastic than practiced. The
location is superb.
‡ ◁≡

Bartolini ◼
*Lungarno Guicciardini 1, 50125
Firenze* ☎ (055) 296452. Map
4D2 ▯□ 🗪 *16* ➡ ➡
*Location: Oltrarno, near Ponte S.
Trinità.* To stay at the Bartolini is
the traditional initiation rite of
young, Spartan Anglo-American
scholars. Others who are
undaunted by two flights of steep,
ill-lit stairs have been known to
conquer the heart of the eccentric
proprietress, but she won't take

you in if she doesn't like you.
There is a view of the Arno, but not
the one E. M. Forster described in
his novel *A Room with a View.*
🌥 ◁≡

Berchielli
*Lungarno Acciaioli 14, 50123
Firenze* ☎ (055) 211530. Map
4D3 ▯□ 🗪 *78* ➖ *28* ▤ AE ⓪
*Location: On the Arno near Ponte
Vecchio.* This fine old hotel has
recently changed management.
The bedrooms are enormous, but
those facing the Arno are very
noisy. Substantial extra charge for
private bathroom.
‡ 🗁

Cestelli ◼
*Via Borgo SS Apostoli 25,
50123 Firenze* ☎ (055) 214213.
Map *4D3* □ 🗪 *6* ▯ *1*.
Location: Near Via Tornabuoni.
Tiny and immaculate *pensione* in
the medieval heart of the city.

Continental
*Lungarno Acciaioli 2, 50123
Firenze* ☎ (055) 282392
ⓣ57110. Map *4D3* ▯□ 🗪 *63* ➖
59 ➡ AE ⓪ VISA
Location: Near Ponte Vecchio. An
efficient hotel in a new building
incorporating the 13thC Torre
Guelfa dei Consorti. The best
rooms are in the tower – others are
neat and functional but noisy.
‡ 🗁 🌥 *on roof* ◁≡ ⅄

Costantini ◼
*Via de' Calzaiuoli 13, 50122
Firenze* ☎ (055) 215128. Map
5C4 □ 🗪 *11* ➡ ➡
Location: Near the Duomo. Very
basic, but clean and cheerful.

Croce di Malta
Via della Scala 6, 50123 Firenze
☎ (055) 282600 ⓣ570540. Map
4B2 ▯□ 🗪 *100* ➖ *100* ▤ 🖾
➡ ➡ AE
Location: Near the station. The
extraordinary Space Age-
Renaissance decor may not be to
everyone's taste, but the luxurious
duplex apartments overlooking the
garden are in a calmer style and the
attic bedrooms are delightful.
‡ □ 🗁 🌥 ⇌ 🎖 ⅄

David
*Viale Michelangelo 1, 50125
Firenze* ☎ (055) 6811696/7.
Map *7D4* ▯□ 🗪 *26* ➖ *18* ▤
➡ AE CB ⓪ ⓪ VISA
*Location: Oltrarno, 15min E of
Ponte Vecchio.* A pleasant, privately

owned hotel conveniently placed for the Firenze-Sud autostrada junction. Secluded in its own tree-shaded garden and nicely decorated in an unfussy, country-hotel style.
🏨 ‡ 📷 🦢 ❧

De La Ville

Piazza Antinori 1, 50123 Firenze 🕿 *(055) 261805/8* 🕭 *570518. Map* **4C3** 🔲 🗪 *75* 🛏 *73* ▦
🏨 🍴 ⇌ *AE* 🕓
Location: N end of Via Tornabuoni. A modern (1961) hotel next to the Palazzo Antinori. The building is soundproofed and furnished with creamy, comfortable good taste.
🏨 ‡ 📷

Excelsior 🏨

Piazza Ognissanti 3, 50100 Firenze 🕿 *(055) 294301* 🕭 *570022. Map* **4C1** 🔲 🗪 *217* 🛏 *205* ▦ 🏨 🍴 ⇌ *AE* *CB* 🕓 🕓 *VISA*
Location: 10min W of Ponte Vecchio. The grand old hotel of Florence retains all the solid, spacious luxury of the 1920s – but not, alas, the stylish service. Red marbled pillars, wooden ceilings, polished furniture; every comfort from thick pastel carpets to enormous bathrooms. (See **Il Cestello** under *Florence/Restaurants*.)
‡ ⅋ 📷 ⪜ ♟ ♈

Helvetia-Bristol

Via dei Pescioni 2, 50123 Firenze 🕿 *(055) 287814. Map* **4C3** 🔲 🗪 *60* 🛏 *60* 🚗 *AE* 🕓 🕓 *VISA*
Location: Off N end of Via Tornabuoni. A genteel, late 19thC hotel facing the Strozzi palace. The same family, of Swiss origin, has run it since 1895.
‡ 📷

Hermitage

Vicolo Marzio 1, Piazza del Pesce, 50122 Firenze 🕿 *(055) 287216. Map* **4D3** 🔲 🗪 *17* 🛏 *12* 🏨 🗪
Location: Near Ponte Vecchio. A comfortable, modern *pensione.* The dining room and roof garden look out over tiled roofs onto the historic center.
🏨 ‡ 📷 🦢 ❧ *on roof* ⪜

Kraft

Via Solferino 2, 50123 Firenze 🕿 *(055) 284273* 🕭 *58523. Map* **2C2** 🔲 🗪 *65* 🛏 *65* ▦ 🏨 ⇌ *AE* *CB* 🕓 🕓 🕓 *VISA*
Location: Near Le Cascine. An extremely well-managed hotel in a

relatively peaceful part of the city, owned by the son of the great Swiss hotelier. Stronger on efficiency than charm. Forgettable food.
🏨 ‡ ⅋ 🦢 ❧ ⪜ ≈ *on roof.*

Liana

Via Alfieri 18, 50121 Firenze 🕿 *(055) 587608. Map* **3C5** 🔲 🗪 *20* 🛏 *12* 🗪
Location: 15min E of Duomo. A pleasant villa in a quiet street, on the edge of the center which housed the British Embassy from 1864–70. All the immaculately clean rooms face onto the big garden, planted with mature trees.
🏨 ❧

Lungarno

Borgo San Jacopo 14, 50125 Firenze 🕿 *(055) 264211* 🕭 *570110. Map* **4D3** 🔲 🗪 *71* 🛏 *71* ▦ 🚗 *AE* *CB* 🕓 🕓 *VISA*
Location: Oltrarno, near Ponte Vecchio. A modern hotel (1968) which hangs over the Arno and, at the back, has been wrapped round the 13thC Torre Marsili. The most attractive rooms are the 14 overlooking the Arno and the 13 within the tower. The proprietor's collection of 20thC art is distributed throughout the hotel.
‡ ☐ 📷 ⪜

Monna Lisa

Borgo Pinti 27, 50121 Firenze 🕿 *(055) 214041. Map* **3C5** 🔲 🗪 *21* 🛏 *19* *AE* *VISA*
Location: 5min E of Duomo. The Renaissance Neri Palace, part of which dates from the 14thC, retains the atmosphere of a proudly maintained private palace. Polished Tuscan brick floors and antique furniture, original vaulted wooden or frescoed ceilings, and an elegant *pietra serena* staircase. By contrast with the reception rooms, many of the bedrooms are disappointing, especially the singles, which are cramped and sometimes overheated. Eighteen rooms overlook the pretty garden or courtyard; others are noisy.
🏨 📷 ❧

Morandi 🏨

Piazza SS. Annunziata 3, 50122 Firenze 🕿 *(055) 272687. Map* **5A5** 🔲 🗪 *26* 🛏 *4* *AE* *CB* 🕓 🕓 *VISA Closed Dec–Feb.*
Location: 5min NE of Duomo. A decent, basic *pensione* behind Antonio da Sangallo the Elder's Loggia of the Servite Order. The ten front rooms look across the busy piazza at the Innocenti loggia;

the back rooms are quieter and
cooler in summer.
‡ 🖼 ◄€

Pendini
Via Strozzi 2, 50123 Firenze
☎ _(055) 211170_ ⊕_571580. Map_
_4C3_ ⫴ ▭ ☎ _37_ ▭ _22_ 🍴 🚃 AE
⊕ ⊕ VISA

Location: Piazza della Repubblica.
Busy, carefully managed and dead
central pensione, with big,
comfortably furnished rooms.
‡ 🖼

Pitti Palace
Via Barbadori 2, 50125 Firenze
☎ _(055) 282257. Map 4E3_ ⫴
☎ _25_ ▭ _14_ 🍴 🚃 AE VISA

Location: Oltrarno, near Ponte
Vecchio. A modern pensione run
with efficiency and charm by an
American. There is a pretty roof
terrace and a good restaurant.
Interior rooms are quieter.
‡ 🖼 ☘ _on roof_ ◄€

Plaza Lucchesi
Lungarno Zecca Vecchia 38,
50122 Firenze ☎ _(055) 264141_
⊕_570302. Map 3D5_ ⫴ ☎ _100_
▭ _100_ ▦ 🍴 🚃 AE ⊕ VISA

Location: On the Arno near S.
Croce. Once a large pensione, this is
now an efficient hotel retaining
traces of its former character. The
views from the front rooms are
spectacular, but so is the noise.
‡ 🖼 ◄€

Porta Rossa
Via Porta Rossa 19, 50100
Firenze ☎ _(055) 287551. Map_
_4D3_ ⫴ ☎ _83_ ▭ _60_ AE CB ⊕
⊕ VISA

Location: Off s end of Via
Tornabuoni. The Palazzo
Torrigiani was a hotel as early as
the 14thC, but the present
establishment dates from the
19thC. It is now faintly seedy but
with a venerable charm that still
appeals, especially to French and
English travelers. The bedrooms
are huge and will accommodate as
many as six beds each – groups
welcome.
‡ 🖼 ◄€

Principe
Lungarno Amerigo Vespucci
34, 50123 Firenze
☎ _(055) 284848. Map 4C1_ ⫴
☎ _21_ ▭ _21_ ▦ 🍴 🚃 AE CB
⊕ ⊕ VISA

Location: On the Arno near
Ognissanti. An elegant and
comfortable small hotel on a
relatively quiet stretch of the

Lungarno. Some bedrooms have
retained old brocade wall hangings
and marble bathrooms. A loyal
American clientele appreciates the
efficiency and character.
🖾 ‡ 🖼 ☘

Regency
Piazza M. d'Azeglio 3, 50121
Firenze ☎ _(055) 587655_
⊕_571058. Map 3C5_ ⫴ ☎ _31_
▭ _31_ 🍴 🚃 AE CB ⊕
⊕ VISA

Location: 15min E of Duomo. This
chic and comfortable small hotel in
its tranquil treelined square might
have been imported direct from
Paris. The building dates from the
period when Florence was capital
of Italy; its mid-19thC grandeur
has been enlivened with bold,
sophisticated decorative schemes.
The bedrooms are in dazzling but
well-judged color combinations.
See Florence/Restaurants.
🖾 ▢ 🖼 ☘

Residenza
Via Tornabuoni 8, 50123
Firenze ☎ _(055) 284197_
⊕_570215. Map 4C3_ ⫴ ☎ _25_
▭ _18_ 🍴 🚃

Location: Next to Strozzi palace. A
pensione on the top floors of a
Renaissance palace. The top floor
rooms are nicest, having been
renovated; some have balconies.
‡ 🖼 ☘ _on roof_ ◄€

Rigatti
Lungarno Generale Diaz 2,
50122 Firenze ☎ _(055) 213022._
Map 5E4 ⫴ ☎ _28_ ▭ _15_ 🚃
🖾

Location: On the Arno near the
Uffizi and S. Croce. This pensione
enjoys a superb position on the top
two floors of the Palazzo Alberti,
with spacious, uncluttered rooms,
an elegant drawing room hung with
old brocade and an outstanding
view from the little terrace. The
five rooms overlooking the garden
are especially quiet; there is also a
roof garden for sunbathing in
summer. Food is wholesome and
varied, and during the months
when the dining room is closed
(Nov, Dec, Mar) an arrangement
can be made with a nearby
trattoria.
🖾 ☘ _on roof_ ◄€

Royal
Via delle Ruote 50–54, 50129
Firenze ☎ _(055) 483287. Map_
_3B4_ ⫴ ☎ _30_ ▭ _30_ ▦ 🚃 AE
⊕ VISA

Location: 10min N of Duomo. A

convenient base for excursions to
the N and W, or for any traveler who
requires absolute peace and quiet.
The handsome 19thC palace
overlooks its own gardens, but the
interior decor is depressing.
◨‡🖻🌱

Savoy 🏨
*Piazza della Repubblica 7,
50100 Firenze* ☎ *(055) 283313*
📞*570220. Map 5C4* ⅢⅢ 📞 101
🛏 101 ▦ ☎ 🏠 ⇄ AE ◐ ⬤
VISA
*Location: In the heart of the historic
center.* The most central, if not the
most fashionable, of the grand old
Florentine hotels. Service is
efficient but rather impersonal.
‡🕭◻🖻🐦

Silla
Via dei Renai 5, 50125 Firenze
☎ *(055) 284810. Map 5F5* ⅢⅢ
📞 34 🛏 26 AE
*Location: Oltrarno, near Ponte alle
Grazie.* An airy, spacious *pensione*
which is especially attractive in
summer. There is a large terrace,
and the view across the Arno is
fringed by trees in the little park.
‡🖻🌱🍸

Splendor 🏠
Via S. Gallo 30, 50129 Firenze
☎ *(055) 483427. Map 3B4* ◻
📞 30 🛏 20.
*Location: Near S. Marco, 10min N
of Duomo.* Simple and good-
natured *pensione* with big,
adequately comfortable rooms and
a pretty rose-clad terrace
overlooking San Marco.
◨🌱

Tornabuoni-Beacci
*Via Tornabuoni 3, 50123
Firenze* ☎ *(055) 212645. Map
4C3* ⅢⅢ 📞 30 🛏 24 ▦ 🏠 ⇄
🏠 AE ◐ VISA
Location: N end of Via Tornabuoni.
Alinari prints, faded chintzes and
rubber plants in big pots give a
dignified old-fashioned feel to this
well-known *pensione* on the top
three floors of the 14thC Palazzo
Minerbetti. Regulars include
writers, fashion buyers, actors and
ministers of state, mostly from
English-speaking countries, who
are grateful for the homely but
unintrusive atmosphere and
comfortable rooms (the good
reading lights are an unaccustomed
luxury in Florence). Meals are
served in your room if you wish,
and there is a roof terrace for
breakfast and drinks.
‡🖻🌱🍸

Villa Belvedere
*Via Benedetto Castelli 3, 50124
Firenze* ☎ *(055) 222501. Map
7E4* ⅢⅢ 📞 27 🛏 27 ▦ 🏠 🏠
⇄
*Location: Poggio Imperiale, 3km (2
miles) S.* Just the hotel for a peaceful
family holiday, in a reconstructed
Medici villa overlooking Florence.
◨‡🖻🌱 ⬩≈ ᣕ 🍸

Villa Carlotta
*Via Michele di Lando 3, 50125
Firenze* ☎ *(055) 220530. Map
2E2* ⅢⅢ 📞 28 🛏 28 ▦ 🏠 🏠
⇄ AE
*Location: Near Porta Romana and
Boboli Gardens.* On a quiet street
lined with privately owned 19thC
villas, this *pensione* has been
modernized with a rather heavy
hand but to a high standard of
comfort. The proprietress is
German, as are many of the guests.
◨‡🕭🖻🌱🍸

Villa Cora 🏨
*Viale Machiavelli 18, 50125
Firenze* ☎ *(055) 2298451
📞570604. Map 2E3* ⅢⅢ 📞 56
🛏 56 ▦ 🏠 ⇄ AE VISA
Location: Near Boboli Gardens. A
sumptuous Neoclassical villa set in
a large private park and retaining
its extravagant mid-19thC Rococo
decorative features: elaborate
fireplaces, gilded stucco, frescoed
ceilings, Venetian-glass
chandeliers. The Cora would still
suit the Princess Eugenia, who
stayed here in 1876, but is
nowadays often enjoyed by
expensively packaged tourists and
businessmen. A car service ferries
guests into Florence, or you can
stroll through the Boboli Gardens
to the Pitti in 20min. A restaurant
with piano bar, the Taverna
Machiavelli, is next door.
◨‡🕭🖻🌱 ⬩≈ ᣕ

Villa Medici 🏨
Via Il Prato 42, 50123 Firenze
☎ *(055) 261331* 📞570178, Map
6D3* ⅢⅢ 📞 108 🛏 108 ▦ 🏠
⇄ AE ◐ ⬤
Location: Near Le Cascine. The
frontage is that of an 18thC Corsini
villa; the rest was built in 1960 to a
standard and in a style that would
suit James Bond. In the
immaculate apartments, decorated
in somber chintzes and dark wood,
international businessmen and art
dealers conclude deals in private.
Most of the rooms have balconies
and overlook the gardens.
◨‡🕭◻🖻🌱 ⬩≈ ᣕ
ᣕ

Eating in Florence

Florentines are as stubbornly conservative about food as about most important matters. It is true that some restaurants cater deliberately to tourists; it is also true that the best-known restaurants can drop their standards overnight if the proprietor changes. But the ordinary, everyday Florentine trattoria has altered little over the centuries.

At its best, a Florentine meal has its roots in the Tuscan countryside. It will be centered round roast, grilled or boiled meat, preceded by *crostini* or thick peasant soup and followed, perhaps, by *castagnaccio*, a flat tart made of chestnut flour. Fresh fish is a rarity; spaghetti and pizza are available but considered tourists' fodder.

Despite galloping inflation of Italian food prices, it is still possible to eat very reasonably in Florence. Some of the most popular restaurants – **Anita**, **Coco Lezzone**, **La Maremma da Giuliano**, **Sostanza** – keep their prices down by encouraging a fast turnover (no lingering over coffee) and concentrating on food rather than comfort. If you are on a restricted budget, try the students' trattorias in Via Palazzuolo, the craftsmen's trattorias in the Santo Spirito quarter, or those patronized by the vendors from the Mercato Centrale, the main food market N of San Lorenzo. *Tavole calde*, which serve hot food at counters, are also good value.

If, at the other end of the price scale, you intend to have just one truly memorable meal, the first choice on all counts – food, wine, ambience – must be the **Enoteca Pinchiorri**. Otherwise, some of the most enjoyable of the expensive restaurants are **Da Noi**, **Le Fonticine** and the dining rooms of the **Excelsior** and **Regency** hotels.

See also *Where to eat* in *Planning*.

Restaurants classified by area

The center of Florence is a small, dense area – you will probably always be within walking distance of most of it.

Arcetri
Omero ▥▢

Duomo
Al Campidoglio ▥▢
Mossacce ▢ ❧
Regency ▦

Ognissanti
Il Cestello ▦
13 Gobbi ▥▢
Harry's Bar ▦
Osteria I Rosso ▥▢
Il Profeta ▥▢
Sostanza ▢ ❧

Pitti
Alfredo sul Arno ▥▢
Il Barone ▥▢
Celestino ▥▢
Mamma Gina ▥▢

Santa Croce
I Che C'e C'e ▥▢
Dino ▥▢
Enoteca Pinchiorri ▦
Il Fagioli ▢
La Maremma da Giuliano ▥▢
Da Noi ▦

Santa Maria Novella
Le Fonticine ▦

Otello ▦
Sabatini ▦

San Miniato
La Loggia ▥▢

Santo Spirito
Cammillo ▦
Cantinone del Gallo Nero ▢
Carmine ▥▢ ❧

Santa Trinità/Via Tornabuoni
La Bussola ▥▢
Cantinetta Antinori ▥▢
Coco Lezzone ▥▢
Doney ▥▢
Silvio ▥▢

Signoria/Uffizi
Acqua al 2 ▢ ❧
Anita ▢ ❧
Antico Fattore ▥▢
Buca dell'Orafo ▥▢
Il Cavallino ▥▢
Mario da Ganino ▥▢
Paoli ▥▢
Pasquini ▥▢

Outskirts
Il Cigno ▦

110

Acqua al 2 ♣

10/19/90

Via dell' Acqua 2 (near the Bargello) ☎ *(055) 284170. Map 5D5* ☐ ☐ 🍽 *Closed lunch, Mon, Aug.*

A cozy, crowded little restaurant much appreciated by young night-owls. It serves only the outside courses of a meal, and the idea is to try several different sorts of the antipasti, pastas and desserts.

Alfredo sul Arno

Via dei Bardi 46 (Oltrarno, near Ponte Vecchio)
☎ *(055) 283808. Map 5E4* ▥
☐ 🍴 🍽 ▤ AE ⊙ ⊙ VISA
Closed Sun.

As the most central of the few restaurants in Florence which have terraces on the Arno, Alfredo is irresistible to tourists; but not many return for the sake of the food.

Anita ♣

Via del Parlascio 2 (near S. Firenze) ☎ *(055) 218698. Map 5D5* ☐ ☐ *Closed Wed eve, Sun, Aug.*

Unfortunately for the regulars, who include picture restorers from the Uffizi and foreign scholars working at the nearby Biblioteca Nazionale, the word has spread that Anita gives top value for money, and it is now more crowded than ever. Good honest Tuscan food is served at communal tables with unceremonious but cheerful efficiency. *Specialty: Spaghetti alla fiacheraia (with chilis).*

Antico Fattore

Via Lambertesca 1/3 (near Uffizi) ☎ *(055) 261215. Map 5D4* ▥ ☐ *Closed Sun, Mon (winter), Sat (summer), Aug.*

This was once the rendezvous of such distinguished Italian artists and writers as Montale and De Chirico, and it still has a slightly high-minded atmosphere. The new proprietor continues to serve genuine Tuscan peasant food of the kind which, as he says, "kept the poor healthy for five hundred years before the age of mass production." Tables are mostly communal and service slipshod.

Il Barone

Via Romana 123 (near Porta Romana) ☎ *(055) 220585. Map 7D4* ▥ ☐ 🍴 *Closed lunch, Sun.*

An attractive, intimate restaurant run with a welcome touch of exoticism by the Colombian proprietress who was educated in North America and is now married to a Florentine. There is a romantic garden behind. The menu is international, often changes, and not every new experiment succeeds. *Specialties: Carpaccio, fondue bourguignonne, cheesecake.*

Buca dell' Orafo

Via dei Girolami 28 (near Ponte Vecchio) ☎ *(055) 25619. Map 4D3* ▥ ☐ *Closed Sun, Mon, Aug.*

Popular trattoria in the cellars of the old Goldsmith's Hall offering a limited selection of typical Florentine dishes. *Specialty: Bistecca alla fiorentina.*

La Bussola

Via Porta Rossa 58 (off Via Tornabuoni) ☎ *(055) 293376. Map 4D3* ▥ ☐ AE VISA *Closed Mon.*

A late-night restaurant in the historic center which serves light one-course meals like pizzas and salads, and is later on adorned by resting ladies of the night from the Via Tornabuoni.

Cammillo *George Coulter*

Borgo S. Jacopo 57 (Oltrarno, near Ponte Vecchio)
☎ *(055) 212427. Map 4D3* ▥
☐ AE VISA *Closed Thurs, Jan 1–15, Aug 1–15.*

A rather impersonal trattoria which has nevertheless remained a great favorite with Americans. The menu is unnecessarily long, especially as there is only one really compelling item. *Specialty: Scampi al curry.*

Al Campidoglio

Via Campidoglio 8 (near Piazza Repubblica) ☎ *(055) 287770. Map 4C3* ▥ ☐ AE ⊙ ⊙ VISA *Closed Thurs, three weeks in Aug.*

A large, immaculate, old-fashioned restaurant with a balanced menu.

Cantinetta Antinori

Piazza Antinori 3 (N end of Via Tornabuoni) ☎ *(055) 292234. Map 4C3* ▥ ☐ 🍴 🍴 🍴 *Closed Sat eve (May–July, Sept), Thurs eve (Aug, Oct–Apr).*

In an elegant room off the central courtyard of the 15thC Antinori palace, this chic, crowded restaurant serves products from the Antinori estates which you can have as a quick snack at the bar or build into a full dinner. Wines, oil, bread and cheese are all excellent.

10/18/90
near White boar

Cantinone del Gallo Nero
Via Santo Spirito 6 (near S. Spirito) ☎ *(055) 218898. Map 4D2* ☐ ☐ ☰ *Closed Mon, Aug.*

Wine bar with a lively and discriminating young clientele in the brick-vaulted cellars of a 15thC palace. Light Tuscan dishes and an excellent selection of Chianti Classico wines. *Specialties: Crostini, soups.*

Carmine ✿
Piazza del Carmine 18 (near S. Spirito) ☎ *(055) 218601. Map 2D3–4* ☐☐☐ ☐☐ ☐ *Closed Sun.*

A rough, reliable old favorite which is especially pleasant in summer with tables in the piazza.

Il Cavallino
Via Delle Farine 6 (Piazza Signoria) ☎ *(055) 215818. Map 5D4* ☐☐☐ ☐☐ ☐ ☐ [AE] [VISA] *Closed Wed, Aug 1–24.*

Don't be suspicious of the star location – it might have turned Cavallino into a tourist trap, but hasn't. This is the sort of restaurant Florentines treat as a second home. Whether you dine alone with a book or with a large party of friends the service is quick and courteous and the food pleasant.

Celestino
Piazza S. Felicità 4 (Oltrarno, near Ponte Vecchio) ☎ *(055) 296574. Map 4E3* ☐☐☐ ☐ *Closed Sun, Aug.*

A small, fashionable, noisy trattoria run with polished professionalism by three former members of the **Sabatini** staff. *Specialties: Fonduta alla piemontese (autumn and winter), cieche (Jan, Feb), scampi alla pescatora.*

Il Cestello dell' Hotel Excelsior
Piazza Ognissanti 3 ☎ *(055) 294301. Map 4C1* ☐ ☐ [AE] [CB] ☐ ☐ [VISA]

Hotel restaurants in Tuscany are usually best avoided, but the restaurant of the Excelsior is, as one might hope, an exception. The panorama from the roof terrace is spectacular. Tuscan and 'international' dishes are expertly prepared and pastas are unusually well done.

I Che C'e C'e
Via dei Magalotti 11 (near S. Croce) ☎ *(055) 262867. Map 5D5* ☐☐☐ ☐ *Closed Mon, July.*

A friendly little restaurant not often discovered by tourists, which serves original, piquant food. *Specialty: Riso alle rose.*

Il Cigno
23 Via Varlango (5km (3 miles) w of centre) ☎ *(055) 666794. Map 6C2* ☐☐☐ ☐ ☐ *Closed Mon, Tues, Aug.*

A trattoria on the Arno which serves hearty Tuscan food on a shaded terrace.

Coco Lezzone
Via Parioncino 26 (near Via Tornabuoni) ☎ *(055) 287178. Map 4C3* ☐☐☐ ☐ *Closed Sun, Aug.*

A minuscule, white-tiled trattoria which looks like a public rest room and is always crammed with chic Florentines packed elbow to elbow on long benches at communal tables. The attraction is the uncompromisingly high quality of the ingredients, especially the meat. *Specialties: Pappa al pomodoro, fagioli al fiasco, castagnaccio.*

Dino
Via Ghibellina 51 (near S. Croce) ☎ *(055) 241452. Map 5C5* ☐☐☐ ☐ ☐ ☐ ☐ ☐ [VISA] *Closed Sun eve, Mon, mid-July to mid-Aug.*

The menu of this coolly handsome 'enogastronomico' is designed to accompany the Italian wines from the well-stocked cellar. The cheese board is always excellent. *Specialties: Risotto alla Renza, filetto di maiale al cartoccio.*

Doney
Via Tornabuoni 46 ☎ *(055) 214308/48. Map 4C3* ☐☐☐ ☐ [AE] ☐ [VISA] *Closed Mon, Aug.*

The place settings were acquired in 1825 from the grand-ducal household, and the complicated 'continental' style of the food reflects the same period. For a while the standard sagged under the weight of its own operatic pretensions, but a new chef has improved matters. The bar also serves afternoon tea. *Specialties: Vichyssoise, filetto Strogonoff, petti di pollo alla Doney.*

Enoteca Pinchiorri
Via Ghibellina 87 (near S. Croce) ☎ *(055) 242757/77. Map 5C5* ☐☐☐ ☐ ☰ ☐ *Closed Sun, Mon lunch, Aug.*

This is the only restaurant in Florence which deserves to be judged by the highest European standards. The proprietor, Giorgio Pinchiorri, has built up an outstanding cellar stocked with some 70,000 bottles of the finest Italian and French wines. His French wife, a native of Nice, is a culinary poetess and perfectionist who has created a light, subtle and original cuisine by marrying the best French and Italian traditions. The attentive service and the calmly elegant environment they have created on the ground floor of the 15thC Ciofi-Iacometti Palace encourages guests to take their pleasure seriously and at leisure. There are no specialties, as such, because everything is very special indeed. There is a *menu de degustazione* of seven courses, and if you allow the waiter to fill your glasses with the appropriate wine for each course, you will be able to sample the glories of the cellar without committing yourself to full bottles.

Il Fagioli

Corso Tintori 47 (near S. Croce) ☎ *(055) 244285. Map 5E5* ▯
▭ *Closed Sat, Sun, Aug.*
This straightforward Tuscan trattoria is a less distinguished, but more comfortable, spin-off from **Coco Lezzone**.

Le Fonticine

Via Nazionale 79 (near the station) ☎ *(055) 282106. Map 4A3* ▥ ▭ *Closed Sat, Aug.*
The excellence of the cuisine, and especially the pasta, must be partly explained by the Emilian origins of the proprietress. Popular with visiting business executives.
Specialties: Frito di cervella e carciofi, portafogli alla bolognese, crema al marscapone.

13 Gobbi

Via del Porcellana 9 (off Borgognissanti) ☎ *(055) 298769. Map 4B2* ▥
▭ ▮ *Closed Sun, Mon, three weeks in Aug.*
Hungarian or Tuscan specialties accompanied by good draft beer or Chianti and gently eccentric piano music. *Specialties: Malfatti di spinacci, zuppa di cipolle, gulyas all'Ungherese, piatto di legno.*

Harry's Bar

Lungarno Vespucci 22 (near Ognissanti) ☎ *(055) 296700. Map 4C1* ▥ ▭ ▤ ▮ *Closed Sun, mid-Dec to mid-Jan.*
Modeled on the original Harry's Bar in Venice, but with no business connection, this is a haven for English-speaking visitors. Attentive bilingual service, a good selection of American cocktails, and an adequate, short menu which hardly ever changes, although the *bresaola di vitello* is a delicious variation.

La Loggia

1 Piazzale Michelangelo (near S. Miniato) ☎ *(055) 287037. Map 3E5* ▥ ▭ ▰ ▮ ▮ ▮
Closed Wed, two weeks in Aug.
The spectacular view over the city from the spacious 19thC *palazzina del caffè* makes this an ideal venue for a first meal in Florence. The food is better than it was but still rather anonymous and the service can be hectic. Reservation essential for restaurant, especially for Sun lunch. Also a café.

Mamma Gina

Borgo S. Jacopo 37 (Oltrarno near Ponte Vecchio) ☎ *(055) 296009. Map 4D3* ▥
▭ ▰ ▮ *Closed Sun, Aug.*
Once a beloved trattoria known for the culinary inventiveness of its proprietress, now a kind of circus stage-managed by professionals from **Sabatini**. Gasp at the way the illusion is created that this is unusually good, or at least typically Florentine, cooking! But it is time to liven up the act with something more original than the sauce trick, whereby the same sauce actually reappears over and over again on apparently different dishes.

La Maremma da Giuliano

Via Verdi 16 (near S. Croce) ☎ *(055) 218615. Map 5D5* ▯
▭ ▮ *Closed Tues, Wed, Aug.*
This family-run trattoria is often uncomfortably crowded for the good reason that almost everything on the long menu is delicious. *Specialty: Crostini di fegatini e prosciutto di cinghiale.*

Mario da Ganino

Piazza dei Cimatori 4 (near Piazza Signoria) ☎ *(055) 214125. Map 5C4* ▥
▭ ▮ *Closed Sun, Aug.*
A first-class restaurant masquerading as a humble *fiaschetteria* (wine shop). The proprietor is notorious for his disagreeable manners, but nobody denies that he is a genius in the kitchen. *Specialties: Penne al pomodoro, fritto misto, segato di carciofi.*

Mossacce ✿
*Via del Proconsolo 55 (between
Duomo and Bargello)*
☎ *(055) 294361. Map* **5** *C5* ⬛
⬜ *Closed Sat Eve, Sun, Aug.*
Always full of students and local
office workers. Seating is
uncomfortable and opening
courses are dull, but all the meat
dishes are excellent and represent
exceptional value. ***Specialty:
Arista o vitello al forno.***

Da Noi
Via Fiesolana 46 (near S. Croce)
☎ *(055) 242917. Map* **3** *C5* ⬛
⬜ 🚤 🏠 ⊞ *Closed Mon, Tues
lunch, Aug.*
The most interesting of the new
(1980) restaurants is owned by
Bruno Tramontana and his
Swedish partner Sabina Bush, who
worked previously at the **Enoteca
Pinchiorri.** Their culinary style is a
similar blend of Italian and new
French. Only five tables and one
sitting for each meal, so it is
essential to make reservations
several days in advance.

Omero
Via Pian dei Giullari 11 (Arcetri)
☎ *(055) 220053. Map* **7** *E4* ⬛
⬜ *Closed Tues, Aug.*
Such a sympathetic rustic
environment in such a splendid
location above the city cannot be
entirely spoiled by routine, lack-
luster food and service which one
encounters too often here.

Osteria I Rosso
Borgognissanti 1 (Ognissanti)
☎ *(055) 284897. Map* **4** *C2* ⬛
⬜ ⟨VISA⟩ *Closed Sun, Mon lunch,
three weeks in Aug.*
Small, central basement trattoria
serving good, clean Tuscan
country food. Reservations are
essential.

Otello
*Via degli Orti Oricellari 28 (near
the station)* ☎ *(055) 215819.
Map* **2** *C3* ⬛ ⬜ ⊞ ⟨AE⟩ ⟨CB⟩ ⓐ
ⓞ ⟨VISA⟩ *Closed Tues.*
A large, bright, welcoming
restaurant more appreciated by
foreigners than locals, who rightly
judge that the prices are over the
top. Service is sympathetic – it is
the kind of place where a woman
can happily eat alone. The menu is
basically Tuscan, with variations,
or you can choose from trolleys
laden with antipasti, salads, roast
and boiled meats. House wine and
good oil from the proprietor's
country estate.

Paoli
*Via Tavolini 12 (near
Orsanmichele)*
☎ *(055) 216215. Map* **5** *C4* ⬛
⬜ ⟨AE⟩ ⓐ ⓞ ⟨VISA⟩ *Closed Tues,
late June to early July.*
The environment is so spectacular
that one scarcely minds the drearily
inoffensive food. Have an omelet
and admire the imitation-Gothic
frescoes, polished mahogany
benches, wrought-iron
lampbrackets – all (apart from the
Anigoni canvas and a bust of
President Wilson) redolent of the
early 19thC when Paoli was
founded in the beautiful
storerooms of a 14thC palace.

Pasquini
*Via Val di Lamona 2 (near
Mercato Nuovo)*
☎ *(055) 218995. Map* **5** *D4* ⬛
⬜ *Closed Sat eve, Sun.*
A sympathetic and sensible little
trattoria offering traditional
Tuscan food. ***Specialties: Penne
alla grecque, penne di russo.***

Il Profeta
Borgognissanti 93 (Ognissanti)
☎ *(055) 212265. Map* **4** *C1* ⬛
⬜ ⊞ ⟨AE⟩ ⟨VISA⟩ *Closed Sun, Aug.*
Soothingly understated one-room
restaurant run as a cooperative by
former members of the **Sabatini**
and **Harry's Bar** staff. A classical
menu is varied by specialties of the
day. ***Specialties: Crostini, lasagne
al pesto, baccalà.***

Regency
*Piazza Massimo d'Azeglio 3 (E
of Duomo)* ☎ *(055) 587655.
Map* **3** *C5* ⬛ ⬜ ⟨AE⟩ ⟨CB⟩ ⓐ ⓞ
⟨VISA⟩
The Regency and the **Excelsior** are
the only hotels in Florence with
restaurants worth visiting for their
own sakes. This intimate paneled
dining room is a delight, and the
short menu fulfills its promises.

Sabatini
*Via Panzani 41/43 (near the
station)* ☎ *(055) 282802. Map*
4 *B3* ⬛ ⬜ ⟨AE⟩ ⓐ ⓞ ⟨VISA⟩
Closed Mon, two weeks in July.
To say of another establishment
that it is managed by former
employees of Sabatini is a
guarantee of professional
management. Sabatini itself is no
longer the most famous and
fashionable restaurant in Florence,
but it retains its pleasant
environment, and one often eats
better here than its critics suggest.
Specialty: Risotto ai funghi.

114

Silvio
Via del Parione 74 (near Via Tornabuoni) ☎ *(055) 214005. Map 4C2* ▮▯ ▢ *Closed Sun, late June to mid-July.*
An unprepossessing exterior has so far protected this attractively rustic restaurant from the rush of attention it deserves. One of the few Florentine restaurants which serves really fresh fish (on Tues and Thurs).

Sostanza ♣
Via del Porcellana 25 (near Ognissanti) ☎ *(055) 212691. Map 4C2* ▢ ▭ *Closed Sun, Aug.*
One of the oldest and best-known workingmen's trattorias in Florence, in one white-tiled room with a clattering kitchen at the end. Tables are shared, service harassed but cheerful. *Specialty: Bistecca alla fiorentina.*

Bars, cafés and ice cream shops

The bar is the nerve center of Italian daily life. If you need a telephone, a bus ticket, a rest room or simply want to ask directions, look for the nearest bar, which will never be far away. In an Italian bar anyone can drink anything at any time of day. Ordinary coffee (*caffè normale*) is a short, potent espresso; if you like it weaker, ask for *caffè lungo*. *Macchiato* is with a dash of milk, *corretto* is laced with brandy. The coffee is almost unfailingly excellent and a *cappuccino* with a sweet roll makes a better and cheaper breakfast than you will find in any hotel. Many larger bars also sell pastries, sandwiches, ice cream, groceries, even light meals. If you sit down the price doubles.

Open-air cafés are not characteristic of Florence. Most of the best-known cafés give onto the Piazza della Repubblica.

Ice cream, as always in Italy, is light and wholesome, made with milk and eggs in an endless variety of flavors.

Doney
Via Tornabuoni 46
☎ *(055) 214309/48. Map 4C3. Open 11:30am – 3:30pm, 5 – 11:30pm. Closed Mon, Aug.*
In the 19th to early 20thC, Doney's café was the fashionable rendezvous of the Florentine aristocracy and literary foreigners. The young have now moved to **Giacosa**, but this is still an elegant venue for tea or an aperitif.

Donnini
Piazza della Repubblica 15
☎ *(055) 211862. Map 4C3. Open Tues – Sun summer 6am – 1pm, winter 6am – 11pm. Closed Mon.*
Delectable hot sandwiches, pastries and the best ice cream in this piazza.

Giacosa
Via Tornabuoni 83
☎ *(055) 296226. Map 4C3. Open 7am – 11pm. Closed Mon.*
This is where the young elite meet for coffee and buy their pastries, *marrons glacés* and hand-made chocolates. The *cappuccino* is the best in town, and there are also sandwiches and hot snacks. The

Negroni was invented here in the 1920s by Count Camillo Negroni.

Giubbe Rosse
Piazza della Repubblica 13 – 14
☎ *(055) 212280. Map 4C3. Open 8am – 2:30am. Closed Thurs.*
Opened in 1888 as a beer hall, Giubbe Rosse – so called because the waiters then wore red jackets – became the meeting place of intellectuals. Now it is a useful bar-restaurant specializing in American breakfasts.

Perché Non
Via Tavolini 19 ☎ *(055) 298969. Map 5C4. Open 8am – 9pm.*
Outstanding ice creams, sorbets and *semi-freddi* made exclusively for Perché Non; in summer there are at least 30 varieties.

Procacci
Via Tornabuoni 64
☎ *(055) 211656. Map 4C3. Open 8am – 1pm, 4 – 11pm. Closed Mon.*
As a treat, pamper your taste buds with a plate of Procacci's exquisite truffle rolls. The bar serves cold drinks only.

Rivoire
Piazza Signoria 5
☎ *(055) 214412. Map 5D4. Open
8am–midnight. Closed Mon.*
Not the exclusive tearoom it once
was, but the hot chocolate is
superb, and the view of the Palazzo
Vecchio justifies the high prices.

Robiglio
Via dei Servi 112
☎ *(055) 212784. Map 5B5. And
Via dei Tosinghi 11*
☎ *(055) 215013. Map 5C4. Open
8am–midnight. Closed Mon.*
A large and luscious selection of
pastries. Specialties include *Saint-*

Honorés, millefeuilles, meringues
and *torta rustica.*

Vivoli
Via Isola delle Stinche 7
☎ *(055) 292334. Map 5D5. Open
8am–midnight, Sun
10am–1:30pm, 4pm–midnight.
Closed Mon.*
Don't be deceived by the humble
premises – Vivoli is one of the great
Italian ice cream makers. Some two
dozen flavors as well as open
sandwiches, pastries and coffee.
The only *gelateria* in Florence
which will satisfy the true
connoisseur of ice cream.

Nightlife

Florence enjoys a livelier nightlife than many small Italian
cities, thanks partly to its large student population.

Discos and piano bars
The largest and most popular discos are **Space Electronic** (*Via
Palazzuolo* ☎ *(055) 293082*) and **Yab Yum** (*Via Sassetti 5*
☎ *(055) 282018*). Smaller discos and piano bars include: **Full
Up** (*Via della Vigna Vecchia 21* ☎ *(055) 293006*); **Jackie O'**
(*Via Erta Canina 24* ☎ *(055) 216146*); and **Oberon** (*Via Erta
Canina 12* ☎ *(055) 216516*).

   You can hear good jazz at **Bebop** (*Via dei Servi*
☎ *(055) 263004*); **La Rosa** (*Via S. Zanobi 88* ☎ *(055) 433445*);
and **Salt Peanuts** (*Piazza S. Maria Novella* ☎ *(055) 293376*).

Late-night restaurants
The best ones are **Acqua al 2** and **La Bussola** (see
Florence/Restaurants) and **Giubbe Rosse** (see
Florence/Bars, cafés and ice cream shops).

Movie theaters
The **Cinema Astro** (*Piazza San Simone* ☎ *(055) 222388*) shows
English language films every evening except Mon.

Music and theater
The *Maggio Musicale*, a festival of concerts, recitals, opera and
ballet, is held in various venues throughout the city during
May–July. Information and tickets from **Teatro Comunale**.

Teatro Comunale
Corso Italia 16 ☎ *(055) 216253. Map 6D3. Box office open Mon–Sat
9am–noon, 3–6pm, Sun 9am–noon.*
The main concert season is Oct–Nov, and the opera season normally
lasts from mid-Dec to mid-Jan. If you want to take a score with you to the
opera, it can be bought at **R. Mauri** (*Via del Corso* ☎ *(055) 283052*).

Teatro della Pergola
Via della Pergola 32 ☎ *(055) 262690. Map 5B6.*
The principal legitimate theater. Plays are in performance all year round
except during the *Maggio Musicale*, when the theater is given over to
music.

Shopping

When shopping in Florence bear in mind the Florentine character, which is unique in Italy and is as remarkable a legacy of the
Renaissance as any church or monument. At all social and
economic levels Florentines share a profound respect for two
skills: craftsmanship and business, the activities which made
Florence the richest city in 15thC Europe. They are a reasoning
but also reasonable people with clever hands, quick wits,
laconic manners and a disdain for the cheap and showy. It is a
compact, sophisticated city where good craftsmen still abound.

Shopping hours
Normally 9am–1pm, 3:30pm–7pm, with slight variations.
Most shops close on Mon mornings, but open all day Sat, except
for food stores which close on Wed. In summer some of the
bigger shops close all day Sat but open Mon.
    Most large shops will send your purchases abroad if you wish.
Otherwise, there is a useful parcel-wrapping service near the
post office in Vicolo dei Cavallari.

Where to shop
The Via Tornabuoni is the Fifth Avenue of Florence. Most of
the grandest shops are in this area, near the Duomo, Piazza
della Repubblica, Ognissanti, along the Lungarno, and across
the Arno around Borgo San Jacopo.

How to shop
The business-like Florentines understand comparative
shopping and bargaining. An aggressive manner will get you
nowhere, but even in big, established shops you can try asking
for a discount (*sconto* or *gentilezza*) if you buy more than one
item. (See clothing sizes table on p212.)

What to buy
The best buys are anything made locally of leather, silk and
straw (bags, hats and novelties). You can still buy the service of
craftsmen in Florence, which is one of the few cities left in
Western Europe where making and repairing of anything is
done quickly and skillfully. Bookbinding, picture framing and
reproduction antiques are Florentine specialties.

Antiques, auctions and reproductions
Many of the established antique shops are in Borgognissanti,
Via dei Fossi and Via Maggio. Auctions are held in autumn and
spring, the two leading houses being **Sotheby Parke Bernet**
(*Via Gino Capponi 26* ☎ *(055) 571410*) and **Casa d'Aste Pitti**
(*Via Maggio 15* ☎ *(055) 296382*). An important antiques fair is
held every 2yr in the Strozzi palace.

Fallani Best
Borgognissanti 15 ☎ *(055) 214986. Map 4C1.*
The top Italian dealer in Art Nouveau and Art Deco.

Ugo Camiciotti
Via S. Spirito 9 ☎ *(055) 212137. Map 4D2.*
French Second Empire clocks and mirrors, signed and dated.

Giovanni Pratesi
Via Maggio 13 ☎ *(055) 296568. Map 4E2* AE ◇ ⬡ VISA
A new and respected young dealer with a more eclectic stock of
paintings, sculpture and furniture.

Florentine craftsmen are highly skilled in every branch of restoration, and many a Florentine-made reproduction has been innocently passed by experts and honest dealers.

Manetti e Masini
Via Bronzino 125
☎ (055) 700445. Map **6**D3.
Began as restorers of antique majolica, and soon found they could produce exact copies. They sell charming fabrications of 18thC plates, tureens, vases and ceramic stoves, and repair china.

Raffaello Romanelli
Lungarno Acciaioli 72–78
☎ (055) 296047 AE ① ⓒ VISA
The firm has been making life-size copies of the most famous

sculptures since 1860; it will also make period fireplaces, tabletops and chess sets.

Zecchi
Via dello Studio 19
☎ (055) 211470. Map **5**C4 AE
CB VISA
Zecchi stocks a full range of restorers' and artists' materials, many not available elsewhere in Europe. You can buy _lapis lazuli_ from Afghanistan, pure gold leaf, powdered pigments for frescoes, natural gums and resins.

Beauty

The apparently casual chic for which Florentine women are noted is not quite as natural as it looks. They pay scrupulous attention to their hair and skin.

Antica Farmacia di San Marco
Via Cavour 146
☎ (055) 210604. Map **5**B4.
This beautiful pharmacy, with its vaulted frescoed ceilings and rows of majolica jars, was founded in the 15thC by the Dominican monks of San Marco. Their specifics include an anti-hysteric, which might come in handy if you are visiting Florence in Aug. Excellent rose water and eaux de cologne.

Dante
Lungarno Corsini 36
☎ (055) 294893. Map **4**D2.
The favorite hairdresser of the American community.

Mario e Laura
Via del Sole 21 ☎ (055) 294300.
Map **4**C2.
A charming married couple who, as well as being skilled and efficient hairdressers, will tell you everything that's going on in Florence.

Mario di Via Della Vigna
Via della Vigna Nuova 22
☎ (055) 294813.
Hairdressers to glamorous and busy women, including the Pitti fashion show models. The salon

offers a range of beauty treatments, and there is a well-stocked perfumery.

**Officina Profumo-
Farmaceutica di Santa Maria
Novella**
Via della Scala 16
☎ (055) 216276. Map **4**B2.
A perfectly preserved grand-ducal pharmacy which sells superb hand-made soaps, creams, lotions for every skin type and a delectable _pot pourri_. Everything is made to original 17thC formulae. Service is notoriously grudging.

Profumeria Aline
Via Calzaiuoli 53
☎ (055) 215269. Map **4**C4.
The largest selection of cosmetics and perfumes in town, carrying the concessions for ranges such as Clinique and Lauder.

Profumeria Inglese
Via Tornabuoni 97
☎ (055) 263748. Map **4**C3.
Founded by an Englishman in 1843. The mahogany shelves are well-stocked with cosmetics, soaps and perfumes, but the medicines have been moved down the Via to the Farmacia Inglese.

Books and prints

Florence has been catering to the needs of bookish foreigners for centuries, and foreign-language books are generally available. There are also a number of internationally renowned specialist bookstores.

Alinari
Via Strozzi 19 ☎ *(055) 213081.*
Map 4C3 AE ⊙ ⊙ VISA
The Alinari family began
photographing Florence and
worthy Florentines in 1852. Copies
of their early sepia photos are still
available, along with prints,
engravings, cards and calendars.

BM
Borgognissanti 4
☎ *(055) 294575. Map 4C1.*
A useful shop selling books in
English and Italian on Florentine
culture and history, as well as
maps, guidebooks, fiction and
children's books.

Centro Di
Piazza dei Mozzi 1
☎ *(055) 213212. Map 5E5* ⊙
One of the most important serious
art bookshops and publishers in
Italy, hidden away in a basement.
The fine catalogues the firm
produces for major European
exhibitions are on sale.

Paperback Exchange
Via Fiesolana 31
☎ *(055) 213054. Map 3C5.*
Over 10,000 English language
titles in stock, mostly popular
fiction. A recycling system gives
you 25–40% of the original price of
your old paperbacks toward any
you buy at 75% of the cover price.

Porcellino
Piazza del Mercato Nuovo 6–8
☎ *(055) 212535. Map 5D4* ⊙
VISA
The first self-service bookshop in
Florence and the place to look for
the catalogues and guides which
are maddeningly not sold in
museums and galleries.

Seeber
Via Tornabuoni 68
☎ *(055) 215697. Map 4C3* AE
CB ⊙ ⊙ VISA
Founded in 1865 to serve the
foreign community and now one of
the largest and best-known general
bookshops.

Book endpapers and binding
Italy was the home of printing and all the crafts of book
production. Book-binders selling hand-printed or marbled
endpapers – by the sheet or applied to anything from jewel cases
to desk sets – have proliferated in the last 10yr; but the prices
may put their ends beyond your means.

Bottega Artigiana del Libro
Lungarno Corsini 38–40
☎ *(055) 263488. Map 4D2.*
The newest and so far the cheapest
source of endpapers.

Gianni e Figlio
Piazza Pitti 37 ☎ *(055) 212621.*
Map 4E2.
This delectable little shop opposite

the Pitti, founded in 1856, is the
grandfather of all the paper shops.

Il Papiro
Via Cavour 55 ☎ *(055) 215262.*
Map 5B4 AE CB ⊙ ⊙ VISA
The most enterprising of the paper
shops specializes in marbled papers
made here. (*Branches at Piazza
Duomo 24 and Via degli Alfani 12.*)

Clothes
Florence is no longer the center of the Italian ready-to-wear
industry. The fashion news – and money – is now made in
Milan. But Florentine women continue to dress, as they always
have, with an impeccable chic that is never flamboyant but
often striking. It is a look that depends on quality: the finest
printed cotton jersey or silks, smooth gaberdines and, of
course, beautiful Florentine leather accessories – these are the
kind of clothes you will see in abundant, if not inexpensive,
supply.
   Some of the best-known non-Florentine designers have
outlets in and off the Via Tornabuoni, which is where you will
find **Giorgio Armani**, **Yves St-Laurent**, **Roberta di
Camerino**, and **Valentino**. Other fashion streets are Via de'
Cerretani, Via Roma, and Via Calimala; for younger, trendier
clothes, look across the Arno in Via Guicciardini and Borgo San
Jacopo. See also *Leather p121.*

Neuber

Via Strozzi 32 ☎ *(055) 215763.*
Map 4C3 AE ⊕ VISA

Clothing for men, women and
children, all of very good quality
and mostly bearing the labels of
foreign houses, including Hermès,
for which Neuber is the exclusive
outlet. There are lots of English
tweeds and cashmeres and a good
selection of ties, shirts and scarves.

Principe

Via Strozzi 21/29
☎ *(055) 216821. Map 4C3* AE
CB ⊕ ⊙ VISA

One of a high-class Tuscan chain –
the others are in Forte dei Marmi,
Livorno and Pisa – selling well-
styled, conservative men's,
women's, children's and babies'
clothes at all prices.

Pucci

Via dei Pucci 6 ☎ *(055) 283061.*
Map 5B4 AE

The Marquese Emilio Pucci began
designing skiing and resort clothes
in the late 1940s; soon his printed,
signed silk shifts and evening
pajamas were an international
status symbol. The Pucci materials
and colors are still ravishing and
are seen at their best in the *atelier*
on the first floor of the Marquese's
ancestral palace. (*A boutique is at
Via Ricasoli 20.*)

Valditevere

Lungarno Soderini 1
☎ *(055) 282707. Map 2C2* AE
⊕ ⊙ VISA

An exclusive boutique which sells
reticently classical clothes made
from its own beautiful materials.

Jewelry

Brunelleschi, Verrocchio, the Pollaiuolo brothers, Cellini,
Ghiberti – some of the greatest Florentine artists trained as
goldsmiths. It has been said that the Florentines may have
inherited their gift for metalwork from the Etruscans. The
shops on the Ponte Vecchio have been occupied by jewelers and
goldsmiths since 1593.

Gherardi

Ponte Vecchio 8
☎ *(055) 287211. Map 4D3* AE
CB ⊕ ⊙ VISA

Known in Florence as the 'official
coral keeper,' Gherardi's prices are
about twice what you would pay in
Naples, the source of most Italian
coral, but the quality and design
are superb. He also specializes in
cultured pearls, jade, turquoise,
tortoise-shell and cameos.

Manelli

Ponte Vecchio 14
☎ *(055) 213759. Map 4D3* AE
CB ⊕ ⊙ VISA

The Manelli family has been
dealing in semiprecious and hard
stones for four generations. They
can be bought loose or they will
string them into a necklace in half
an hour or make earrings in a
week.

Melli

Ponte Vecchio 44–46
☎ *(055) 211413. Map 4D3* AE
⊕ VISA

A rarified collection of antique
jewelry, antique porcelains, silver
and small objets d'art.

Piccini

Ponte Vecchio 23
☎ *(055) 294768. Map 4D3* AE
CB ⊕ ⊙ VISA

Jewelers to the jet set, although the
Concorde crowd may find the
designs slightly dated and the
prices too high-flown. They also
sell antique jewelry and silver, and
will re-set your heirlooms. A family
firm since 1895.

Rajola

Ponte Vecchio 24
☎ *(055) 215335. Map 4D3* AE
CB ⊕ ⊙ VISA

Very chic enamel work and pieces
set with colored stones.

Settepassi

Ponte Vecchio 28
☎ *(055) 215506. Map 4D3* AE
⊕ VISA

The oldest and one of the grandest
Italian jewelers specializing in
precious stones and oriental pearls
set to match the incomes and tastes
of the wealthiest Italian families,
and to adorn crowned heads of
Europe. They also sell antique
and modern silver.

Tozzi

Ponte Vecchio 19
☎ *(055) 283507. Map 4D3* AE
CB ⊕ ⊙ VISA

A beguiling stock of delicate
objects – coral charms, gold-mesh
purses, Baroque pearls – some old,
some modern, some real bargains if
you know your own taste.

Leather

Leather is to Florence what glass is to Venice; that is to say there is altogether too much of it, and very little of what is most prominently on display bears the slightest relation to the unrivalled workmanship of the great artisans who are still active, and whose creations are found in the shops below.

If you want to see how it's done, visit the **Leather School** (*Piazza Santa Croce 16* ☎ *(055) 282034*).

Alessandrini
Via Vacchereccia 17
☎ *(055) 216088. Map 4C3* AE
© VISA
The Florence outlet for the desirable soft leather handbags manufactured by the Tuscan firm Enny; up to 20% cheaper here.

Beltrami
Via Calzaiuoli 31
☎ *(055) 214030. Map 5C4*
AE CB © VISA
Top quality, up-to-the-minute men's and women's shoes, accessories and clothes. Service is tirelessly agreeable. (*Branches at nos. 44 and 101*).

Cellerini
Via del Sole 9 ☎ *(055) 282533.
Map 4C2* AE CB VISA
Silvano Cellerini is the most skilled and stylish independent artisan in making leather, lizard and crocodile handbags in the city. He and his wife and five assistants produce only enough stock for this shop; nothing is sold abroad.

Ferragamo
Via Tornabuoni 16
☎ *(055) 292123. Map 4C3* AE
CB © VISA
Salvatore Ferragamo was the first of the internationally renowned Italian shoemakers. He started in Hollywood in 1914, and bought this palace in the Tornabuoni in 1936. The business now has branches all over the world and makes clothes, ties and scarves as well as handbags – all in the master's mould of controlled quality and unfaltering stylishness.

Gucci
Via Tornabuoni 73
☎ *(055) 287251. Map 4C3* AE
© VISA
Although you can buy some of the most beautifully made and expensive leather goods in the world here, there are also relatively inexpensive small presents such as key cases and purses. The Gucci stock is almost identical worldwide, but prices in the home stores are up to 40% lower.

Lucie
Via del Parione 12
☎ *(055) 294826. Map 4C2* AE
© VISA
Sensible ladies' shoes made to measure in 15 days at prices which compete with ready-to-wear.

Raspini
Via Romana 25–29
☎ *(055) 213077. Map 4F2* AE
CB © VISA
Raspini is one of the glamorous names in Florentine leatherware, but unlike **Ferragamo** and **Gucci** it has no outlets abroad – only licensed imitators. The shoes, bags and leather coats – all for men *and* women – are stunning. So are the clothes by top Italian designers. So are the prices, and if you are in a mousey mood you may get catty service. (*Branches at Via Martelli 5–7 and Via Por S. Maria 72.*)

Linens and lingerie

Loretta Caponi
Borgognissanti 12
☎ *(055) 213668. Map 4C1* AE
© VISA
The dreamily girlish nightdresses hand-embroidered exclusively for Loretta Caponi are among the prettiest – and the most expensive – things you will see in Florence.

Industrie Feminile Italiane
Lungarno Corsini 34
☎ *(055) 284761. Map 4D2* AE
CB © VISA

Founded as a cooperative in 1901, this shop sells a vast selection of hand-embroidered table linen, sheets, towels, handkerchiefs and baby clothes. The ladies will also embroider trousseaux.

Tosco Tessile
Via del Corso ☎ *(055) 213780.
Map 5C4* AE © VISA
Every kind of household linen from inexpensive towels and pillowcases in cheerful colors to exquisite sheets and table cloths.

121

Street markets

Mercato delle Cascine
Map **6**D3. Open Tues 7am–1pm
This weekly market in the Cascine
park is like a huge department
store laid out under the poplars
along the Arno.

Mercato Centrale
Maps **4**&**5**A3–4. Open Mon–Sat
7am–1pm, 4–7:30pm.
Immediately N of Piazza S.
Lorenzo, this impressive 19thC
cast-iron food market is the central
outlet, wholesale and retail, for
fresh meat, fish and vegetables,
and cheeses, oils and countless
other foods.

Mercato Nuovo
Map **4**D3. Open daily
9am–5pm.
The famous straw market, also
known as the Porcellino. As well as
straw there are leather goods,
ceramics, linens, and other hand-
made goods.

Mercato delle Piante
Piazza della Repubblica. Map
4C3. Open Thurs 7am–1pm.
A weekly flower market held under
the loggia of the central post office.

Mercato delle Pulci
Piazza dei Ciompi. Map **3**C5.
Open Tues–Sat 8am–1pm,
3:30–7pm.
The flea market of Florence sells
picturesque junk at irritatingly
jacked-up prices, but is good for
ex-votos and old postcards.

Mercato di San Lorenzo
Maps **4**&**5**B3–4. Open daily
8am–8pm.
The biggest and most popular of
the street markets sprawls all
around the church of S. Lorenzo
and into the adjacent streets. Best
shoe bargains in town are to be
found on the Borgo S. Lorenzo
side, where sandals and espadrilles
are half the shop price.

Textiles and trim
Florence still manufactures some of the most gorgeous
furnishing fabrics in the world. It is an industry which dates
back to the Middle Ages.

Antico Setificio Fiorentino
Via della Vigna Nuova 97
☎ (055) 282700. Map **4**C2.
Silk furnishing fabrics – taffetas,
damasks, brocades, velvets, satins,
borders, fringes and *passementerie*
– will be made to order (minimum
30m/yds) in any color or style.
The factory across the Arno (Via
Bartolini 4 ☎ (055) 282700) may
be visited by appointment –
telephone in advance.

Lisio Tessuti d'Arte
Via dei Fossi 45
☎ (055) 212430. Map **4**C2.
This astonishing firm was founded
in 1906 by a master weaver who
was inspired to reproduce the
finest antique woven silk fabrics.
Of the many designs taken from
Old Master paintings, the
Primavera brocade is the most

popular. Lisio has made hangings
for the Sistine Chapel, costumes
for the Palio and for historic films,
and his creations are exhibited in
textile museums throughout the
world. The most elaborate designs
are produced at the rate of only a
few inches a day and prices, not
surprisingly, are high, but you
could follow the example of
Florentine women who buy just
enough for an evening skirt or
dress.

Silvi
Via dei Tavolini 5
☎ (055) 213104. Map **5**C4.
One of the most chic of the many
Florentine trim shops, selling a
dazzling choice of braid, bindings,
passementerie, curtain ties and
fringing. Everything is made by
hand and of natural fabrics.

Toys

Bianca Benedetti
Via della Riva 20
☎ (055) 666589. Map **5**C5.
A doll's hospital where dolls are
lovingly made whole again by
craftsmen who have cared for them
as they passed from one careless
generation to another.

Dreoni Giocattoli
Via Cavour 31–33
☎ (055) 216611. Map **5**A5 [AE]
[CB] [DC] [MC] [VISA]
Florence's largest toy shop. A
wide-ranging stock and an
especially good selection of model-
making kits.

Tuscany A – Z

The joy of Tuscany is that almost any corner of its beautiful and varied landscape is likely to harbor some natural or man-made treasure. Within this A – Z section, text and symbols describe highlight attractions. More cursory listings note additional sights and reliable but unremarkable hotels and restaurants.

Abbadia San Salvatore

Map 9I7. 143km (89 miles) s of Florence, 75km (47 miles) s of Siena. 53021. Siena. Population: 8,232 i Via Mentana 97
☎ *(0577) 778608.*
This dour little industrial town near the summit of *Monte Amiata* has grown up around the medieval abbey of San Salvatore. Skiing and climbing nearby. The medieval center is near Piazza XX Settembre.

Sights and places of interest

Abbazia di San Salvatore †
The abbey, founded in 743, became the richest and most powerful center of Benedictine feudalism in Central Italy. All that remains is the 11thC church, adapted in the late 16thC and, below, the 8thC crypt supported by 36 columns with wonderful capitals.

Borgo Medioevale (*Old Town*)
A rare and fascinating example of a Gothic-Renaissance mountain village which is almost completely intact.

Ⓡ Near the summit of *Monte Amiata*, 14km (9 miles) w at Pianello, **Sella** (☎ *(0577) 789747* ⅢⅢ *open July – Sept 15, Dec 15 – Apr 15*) is a mountain refuge popular with Sun skiers; some rooms.

Abetone

Map 15C4. 90km (56 miles) NW of Florence. 51021. Pistoia. Population: 859 i Piazza delle Piramidi Abetone
☎ *(0573) 60001.*
In the mountains above *Pistoia* near the Tuscan-Emilian border, Abetone is one of the oldest established ski resorts in the Apennines, with the most difficult and best-equipped runs in Tuscany. There is also a short summer season for walkers and climbers. Fir trees grow in the protected **forest of Abetone**. Nearby resorts include Cutigliano and San Marcello.

Ⓗ There are some 35 hotels which maintains adequate but not luxurious standards. Two of the most comfortable are: **Abetone e Piramidi** (☎ *(0573) 60005* ⅢⅢ); and the **Piccolo Bellavista** (☎ *(0573) 60029* ⅢⅢ *to* ⅢⅢ), both open July – Aug and Dec – Apr.

Ⓡ Outside Abetone: **Da Bizzino** (*Via Secchio 70* ☎ *(0573) 60195* ⅢⅢ) is worth the 10min drive for fresh-picked mountain mushrooms, fresh pasta and apple tarts; at Cutigliano, 12km (7½ miles) to the SE, is **Da Fagiolino** (*Via Carega 1* ☎ *(0573) 68014* ⅢⅢ *closed Tues, Oct*).

Anghiari

Map 13F8. 105km (65 miles) SE of Florence, 28km (17 miles) NE of Arezzo. 52031. Pistoia. Population: 6,052.
This walled hill village in the upper Tiber valley gave its name to the battle nearby in 1440 between Florence and Milan.

Sights and places of interest
In the 18thC church of **Santa Maria delle Grazie** is a *Last Supper* (1531) by G. A. Sogliani. The Renaissance **Palazzo Taglieschi** (*Piazza Mameli 16; ring for entrance*) houses a museum of local art and customs.

☑ **Castello di Sorci** ✿
Monterbone, 4km (2½ miles) on Arezzo road ☎ *(0575) 78288* ☐
▣ ▣ *Closed Tues.*
Overlooking the lovely green Sovara valley. There is no fuss and no
choice: five hearty, wholesome courses and as much wine as you can
drink at an astonishingly low fixed price. See also *Caprese Michelangelo*.

Ansedonia

*Map 8J5. 186km (115 miles) sw of Florence, 45km (28 miles)
s of Grosseto. 58016. Grosseto. Population: 316.*

The rocky promontory on the s coast of Tuscany was the site of
the Roman city of Cosa, founded in 273 BC. Excavations have
produced evidence of a large and flourishing commercial and
agricultural colony, and in 1980 an important 1stC BC villa and
its attendant farm buildings were uncovered nearby at Sette
Finestre. In recent years Ansedonia has been developed with
vacation villas.

Sights and places of interest
Ruins of Cosa
Entrance through Porta Romana.
After passing through the best-preserved of the gates, the Roman main
street leads to the Forum. Nearby, a recently excavated private house
and garden have been partially reconstructed; the domestic objects and
decorations can be seen in the small **museum/restoration center** built by
the American Academy (☑ *open Tues–Sun 9am–2:30pm*). Above is the
walled Acropolis and, at the highest point, the Capitolium, from which
there are splendid views.
    Below, on the beach beyond the Roman port, which has long since
silted up, is the so-called **Tagliata Etrusca**, a canal cut by the Romans
between their port and the Lake of Burano.

Nearby sights
Lake of Burano
Capalbio Scalo ☎ *(0564) 898829* ☑ *Open Mon–Wed, Fri during
Sept–May 10am to midafternoon. Closed May–Aug.*
A bird sanctuary since 1968.

☑ **Il Pescatore** (*Via della Tagliata 13* ☎ *(0564) 881201* ☐ *to* ▮▮
closed Tues), near the Tagliata; **Pitorsino** (*on SS Aurelia near Orbetello
Scalo* ☎ *(0564) 862179* ▮▮ *to* ▮▮▮ *closed Wed (except July–Aug), mid-Jan
to Feb*). See also *Capalbio, Orbetello, Port'Ercole, Porto Santo Stefano.*

Arezzo ★

*Map 12F7. 81km (50 miles) se of Florence. 52100. Arezzo.
Population: 92,087* **i** *Piazza Risorgimento 116*
☎ *(0575) 20839.*

Arezzo today is a busy, prosperous, provincial town at the
center of the rich farming country of the Valdichiana and
Valdarno. Its factories manufacture agricultural equipment,
women's fashions, leather goods and costume jewelry; its
streets buzz with new, imported motorcycles driven by stylish
young Aretines with good jobs and a long, proud ancestry
stretching back to the Etruscans.
    Etruscan Arezzo was one of the most powerful and
sophisticated cities of the federation. Later, under the Romans,
it became a key stronghold thanks to its strategic location
commanding all the passes of the central Apennines. Aretine
craftsmen were famous throughout the Roman world for their
metalwork and ceramics. As an independent republic from the
late Middle Ages its sympathies were predominantly
Ghibelline, and it was in the Guelf-Ghibelline Battle of
Campaldino in 1289 that Arezzo suffered its first defeat by the
Guelf Florentines. The republic recovered in the early 14thC

under the leadership of Bishop Guido Tarlati, when the
Duomo, Palazzo del Comune, the Pieve and the church of San
Domenico were built, but finally surrendered to Florence in
1384. Petrarch, Spinello Aretino, Pietro Aretino and Vasari
were all born in Arezzo; and it was a leading Aretine family, the
Bacci, who were responsible for what is unquestionably one of
the most inspired commissions in the history of Renaissance
patronage: Piero della Francesca's frescoes in the church of San
Francesco.

Events: An antique market is held in the Piazza Grande, the
main square, on the first Sun of every month; the stalls do
business from noon on the previous day.

The annual historic spectacle is the Joust of the Saracen
(*Giostra del Saracino*), which takes place in the Piazza Grande
on the first Sun of Sept.

An international choral festival in June attracts competitors
from all over the world.

Sights and places of interest
Casa di Giorgio Vasari ▥ ☆
Via XX Settembre 55 🅿️ *Open Tues–Sat 9am–2pm, Sun, hols
9am–1pm.*
Vasari lovingly supervised the building of his own house (1540–48), a
delightful example of Mannerist domestic architecture. He also executed
the frescoes, the most ingenuous and charming of all his creations.

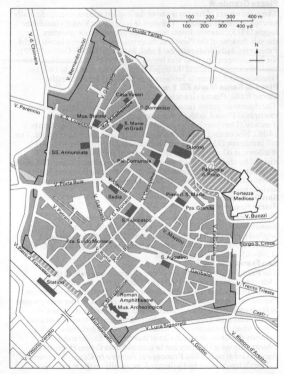

Duomo †

The imposing 13th–14thC cathedral of Arezzo has an early 20thC facade, a 19thC campanile and, on the right flank, an attractive 14thC portico. The interior is illuminated by high stained-glass windows by Guillaume de Marcillat of which the finest is the *Expulsion from the Temple* at the bottom of the right aisle. The 14thC tomb of *S. Donato* in the apse is a collaborative work by Sienese, Florentine and local artists. At the bottom of the left aisle is Piero della Francesca's oddly stiff *Magdalen* (after 1466), his only surviving work in Arezzo apart from the frescoes in San Francesco. To its left is the magnificent tomb of *Bishop Guido Tarlati* (1330) by Agostino di Giovanni and Agnolo di Ventura, possibly to a design by Giotto. In the sacristy, entered from the left aisle, is a striking and strongly personal detached fresco of *St Jerome* by Bartolomeo della Gatta. The late-18thC Chapel of the Madonna of Comfort contains fine terra-cottas by the Della Robbias.

Museo Archeologico Mecenate

Via Margaritone 10 🖭 *Open Tues–Sat 9am–2pm, Sun, hols 9am–1pm.*

The loggia of the 16thC monastery which now houses the Archeological Museum is built round a curve of the 1stC BC Roman amphitheater. The famous **coralline vases** ☆ glazed according to a technique invented by Aretine craftsmen in the 1stC BC and later much copied, are in Rm. VII.

Museo Statale d'Arte Medioevale e Moderna ⅢⅢ

Via S. Lorentino 8 🖭 *Hours as Museo Archeologico.*

Attractively arranged on three floors of the 15thC **Bruni-Ciocchi Palace**, which has a fine courtyard possibly designed by B. Rossellino. There are important paintings by local artists, notably Margaritone d'Arezzo, Parri di Spinello, Spinello Aretino, Bartolomeo della Gatta; and, in Rms. VI–VIII, a fine **collection of majolicas** (13th–18thC).

Piazza Grande ★

The main square of Arezzo is one of the liveliest and most architecturally heterogeneous in Tuscany. The NE side is closed by Vasari's handsome **loggia** (1573); its store-fronts retain their original stone counters. On the w is the apse of the Pieve and the extraordinary layered facade of the **Palazzetto della Fraternità dei Laici**; its ground floor is Gothic (1377), the Renaissance first floor was begun after 1434 by B. Rossellino, who made the sculptures, and the upper loggia was completed in 1460 by Giuliano and Algozzo da Settignano, who added the balustrade.

Pieve di Santa Maria ⅢⅢ † ★

Corso Italia, Piazza Grande.

The rigorously ornate **facade** of this parish church is the outstanding example of Pisan-Lucchese Romanesque architecture in eastern Tuscany. The church was erected between the mid-12thC and early 14thC. Notice the fine relief carvings (1216) over the central portal. The tall campanile (1330) is the emblem of Arezzo; pierced by 40 bifore windows, it is known locally as 'the tower of 100 holes.' The nave is divided by clustered columns supporting early Gothic arches. The oldest part of the church is the raised presbytery where Pietro Lorenzetti's polyptych of the *Madonna and Saints* hung over the high altar until withdrawn in 1979.

San Domenico †

Piazza Fossombroni.

Built between 1275 and the early 1300s, San Domenico has a Romanesque portal and a Gothic campanile – which retains two of its original bells. The interior is like a giant scrapbook of fragmented frescoes (15th–16thC). Over the high altar is a moving painted *Crucifix* (1260–65) by the young Cimabue.

San Francesco ⅢⅢ †

The Franciscan basilica in the center of Arezzo was built in the 13th–14thC in the simple Umbrian-Tuscan style; the campanile is 15thC. In the choir is one of the major artistic masterpieces of Europe: Piero della Francesca's noble, compelling **frescoes** ★ that were painted in the middle of his career; the subject is the *Legend of the True Cross*. The legend links man's original sin to his redemption by tracing a series of events whereby the tree from which Adam ate the forbidden fruit becomes the Cross on which Christ is crucified. Earlier painted interpretations of the subject can be seen in *Santa Croce/Florence* by Agnolo Gaddi and in **San Franceso** at *Volterra* by Cenni di Francesco.

Piero's frescoes are badly decayed, especially on the w wall, and it takes time to adjust one's eyes to the complex dimensions of the scheme and the bare patches of plaster left by the latest restoration. Binoculars can be rented in the church shop. The tonality of the right wall is cooler, and the quality of the painting is higher; it was painted without assistance, probably from 1452–59, before Piero's visit to Rome. The series is thought to have been finished on the left wall after his return, with a good deal of assistance. The narrative unfolds as follows.

Right wall, apex: In the right section of the frame Adam announces his impending death; in the left section, the dead Adam is surrounded by his children and Seth plants a branch of the tree in his father's mouth. **Central band, left section:** The tree, grown so large that even Solomon cannot use it for his palace, has been made into a bridge over the River Siloam; the Queen of Sheba instinctively recognizes its sacred origins and kneels at the bridge. **Right section:** The Queen of Sheba is received by Solomon and predicts to him that a man will be nailed to the tree and the Jews will thereby be disgraced.

Right window wall, center: The beam is buried by Solomon's order; the scene deliberately prefigures the Carrying of the Cross. **Bottom:** Constantine is asleep in his tent on the eve of battle; an angel announces that he will be victorious if he fights for the sign of the Cross. **Right wall, lowest band:** The victory of Constantine over Maxentius.

Left window, middle section: Judas is tortured and reveals the whereabouts of the Cross.

Piero had the power of creating forms which immediately satisfy us by their completeness; forms which reconcile the mathematical laws of proportion with the stress and tension of growth, forms which combine the resilience of a tree trunk with the precision of a pre-dynastic jar.

Sir Kenneth Clark, *Piero della Francesca*

Left wall, central band, left section: The Empress Helena discovers the Cross; in the background a view of Arezzo represents Jerusalem. **Right section:** Judas proves the Cross by raising a man from the dead; the church in the background recalls the architectural style of Piero's friend and fellow mathematician, Alberti. **Lowest band:** 30yr after the discovery of the Cross, the Persian King Chosroes has stolen it from Jerusalem; he is defeated in battle by Heraclius, Emperor of the East. **Apex:** Heraclius returns the Cross to Jerusalem.

The other frescoes in the chapel are outside the main narrative. The most important is the *Annunciation*, on the lowest section of the left window wall, probably painted in 1466 after Piero's visit to Urbino. The prophet to the right of the window's apex is by Piero, the one on the left by an assistant. Returning to the nave, notice in the third chapel on the left the superb late 13thC *Crucifix of St Francis*, and in the second chapel the Pieroesque frescoes of the *Miracles of St Anthony of Padua* by Lorentino d'Arezzo. The glass of the rose window (1524) of the interior facade is by G. de Marcillat.

Other sights

Other points of interest in Arezzo include the Palazzo Comunale; the Fortezza Medicea, which commands splendid views; the churches of S. Maria in Gradi, SS. Annunziata, S. Agostino, and the Badia; and 1.5km (1 mile) to the s of the Piazza della Repubblica, the church of S. Maria delle Grazie, with a graceful portico by B. da Maiano. In summer it is pleasant to picnic in the Passeggio del Prato, the public gardens.

H R Continentale

Piazza Guido Monaco 7, 52100 Arezzo ☎ *(0575) 20251* **IIII** 🛏 *80* 🛏 *80* 🍽 ▦ *AE* ◉ ⓒ *VISA* *Restaurant closed Fri, July.*

Modern, comfortable and central. The local businessmen's favorite and the most reliable kitchen in Arezzo.

✦ 🗌 ♨

R Al Principe

Giovi, 8km (5 miles) to N ☎ *(0575) 362046* **IIII** *to* **IIII** ▭ 🚗 *Closed Mon, Aug.*

Cool and elegant, with a garden shaded by a huge chestnut tree.

⊞ ⊞ Alternatives are: **Cecco** (*Corso Italia 215* ☎ *(0575) 20986* ⅢⅠ *to* ⅢⅠⅠ *closed Mon, Aug)*; or **Il Torrino** (*Madonna del Torrino, 8km (5 miles)* SE *on Sansepolcro road* ☎ *(0575) 357915* ⅢⅠ *to* ⅢⅠⅠ *closed Tues*).

Shopping

A little shop with no name (*Piazza Grande 10*) is crammed with attractive rustic linens and woolen sweaters made locally.

Artimino

Map **15***E5. 22km (14 miles)* W *of Florence. 50042. Firenze. Population: 260.*
An old walled village in a wine-producing zone.

Sights and places of interest
Artimino, Villa dell' Ⅲ ☆
🖭 ⊟ *Open Wed 8am–noon, 2–5pm.*
This smiling Mannerist villa, known as the 'Villa of the Hundred Chimneys,' was built by Buontalenti as a hunting lodge for Ferdinand I. The rooms are decorated with good *pietra serena* fireplaces and frescoes attributed to Poccetti and Passignano. The estate has a shop and small restaurant where its own wines are available (see *Tuscan wines*).
San Leonardo Ⅲ †
This well-preserved Romanesque church was allegedly founded by Countess Matilda in 1107. It was constructed with Etruscan fragments from the nearby necropolis of Pian di Rosello.

Nearby sights

There are two Etruscan tombs near Comeana, 3km (2 miles) N, where signs point to the **Tomba dei Boschetti** (7thC BC) and the monumental **Tomba di Montefortini** (*ring for custodian*).

⊞ **Da Delfina**
Via della Chiesa ☎ *(055) 8718074* ⅢⅠ *to* ⅢⅠⅠ 🖵 ➘ 🕿 ◛ *Closed Mon eve, Tues, Aug.*
A pleasant restaurant which serves rich country food, specializing in game and the excellent Artimino wines. Reservations essential.

Asciano

Map **12***G6. 91km (57 miles)* SE *of Florence, 20km (12½ miles)* SE *of Siena. 53042. Siena. Population: 5,897.*
A walled medieval hill village in the upper Ombrone valley. The Corso Matteotti is lined with interesting old houses.

Sights and places of interest
Museo d'Arte Sacra
Piazza Sant'Agata 🖭 *Open daily 9am–noon, 2–5pm.*
Left of the Travertine Collegiata di Sant'Agata (11thC but much restored) is this notable collection of 14th–15thC Sienese School painting and sculpture. Of special interest are the **polyptych** by the young Matteo di Giovanni; *St Michael and the Dragon* by A. Lorenzetti; *Nativity of the Virgin* by the Master of the Osservanza; *Madonna* by Barna; and two graceful wooden statues of the *Annunciation* by Francesco di Valdambrino.
Museo Etrusco
Corso Matteotti 🖭 *Open daily 9am–noon, 2–5pm.*
In the former church of S. Bernardino, this museum houses material from the Etruscan necropolis of Poggiopinci, 5km (3 miles) E of Asciano.

Bagni di Lucca

Map **15***D4. 101km (63 miles)* NW *of Florence, 27km (16 miles)* N *of Lucca. 55021. Lucca. Population: 7,991* **i** *Via Umberto I 101* ☎ *(0583) 87946/87245 (May–Oct).*
The healing properties of the sulfurous and saline waters at the Baths of Lucca were recognized from the 13thC, but a

foreigner, Napoleon's sister Elisa Baciocchi, gave Bagni di Lucca its Empire tone. Mrs Trollope was scarcely exaggerating when she wrote "Bagni di Lucca belongs, like so much else in Italy, exclusively to foreigners"; the list of distinguished foreign literary visitors includes Montaigne, Heine, Lamartine, Shelley, Byron, Landor, the Brownings and Ouida.

A little seedy now and certainly not fashionable, Bagni di Lucca is nevertheless an inexpensive place to take the waters or merely to savor the somewhat claustrophobic atmosphere created by the mild, humid climate, the mature plane trees, and the weight of nostalgia for the vanished Victorian presence. Those who enjoy hill-climbing will share the pleasure Shelley took in scaling the steep chestnut-clad slopes.

In the Piazza del Bagno is a charming early-19thC bathhouse, now abandoned and crumbling. Just above is the **Palazzo Bonvisi**, where Shelley and Byron stayed and which Montaigne described. The **English Cemetery**, across the River Lima and reached by a bridge behind the Circolo dei Forestieri, is overgrown and untended.

Ⓗ **Bridge** (*Ponte a Serraglia, 3km (2 miles)* w ☎ *(0583) 97147* ▮▯).

Ⓡ **Circolo dei Forestieri** (*Piazza Varraud* ☎ *(0583) 86038* ▮▮▯ to ▮▮▮▮) is a big, sedate restaurant overlooking the Lima.

Bagno a Ripoli
*Map **12**E6. 7km (4 miles)* SE *of Florence. 50012. Firenze. Bus no. 33. Population: 25,139.*
This suburb of Florence was named after the remains of a Roman bath discovered in the 17thC. There is pretty hill country above and the 14thC church of S. Pietro a Ripoli.

Ⓗ **Villa La Massa**
50010 Candeli, Firenze ☎ *(055) 630051* ▮▮▮▮ ❧ 40 ▭ 40 ▤ ▭
▭ ⇌
A 16thC villa on the Arno, now a nicely furnished and well-run hotel.
▭ ▣ ⚓ ⟨⟨ ≈⚑ ♨

Ⓡ **Centanni**
Via Centanni 7 ☎ *(055) 630122* ▮▮▯ ⬜ ⛲ ▤ ▭ *Closed Sun and Aug.*
In an entrancing location, especially on a hot summer evening.

Ⓡ Also charmingly situated: **Donnini** (*Via Rimaggio* ☎ *(055) 630076* ▮▯ to ▮▮▯ *closed Sat eve, Sun, Aug*).

Barga
*Map **14**D3. 111km (70 miles)* NW *of Florence, 37km (23 miles)* N *of Lucca. 55051. Lucca. Population: 10,952* ⓘ *Piazza Angelio* ☎ *(0583) 73499.*
The prettiest hill town in the Garfagnana stands above an active industrial new town.
   Event: An opera festival takes place in summer.

Duomo †
The rectangular, buttermilk-colored Duomo, rebuilt from the 9thC, contains an extraordinarily well-preserved late 12thC **pulpit**, sculpted with all the serious charm of the period with scenes from the *Lives of Christ and Mary*. In the apse is a wooden statue of *St Christopher*. In the chapel to the right are attractive unglazed Robbianesque terra-cottas.
   The **loggetta of the Podestà**, to the left of the Duomo, preserves a rare set of 15thC official measures.

Bibbiena

Map 12E7. 59km (37 miles) SE of Florence, 32km (20 miles) N of Arezzo. 52011. Arezzo. Population: 10,716 i Via Cappucci ☎ (0575) 93098.

The chief town of the Casentino, the remote upper valley of the Arno enclosed by wooded mountains. The great monasteries of *Camaldoli* and *La Verna* are reached by road from Bibbiena. The 16thC Dovizi Palace stands opposite the 15thC church of San Lorenzo. Off the La Verna road is the Renaissance church of Santa Maria del Sasso, with interesting paintings inside.

H R **Amorosi Bei**
Via Dovizi 18, 52011 Bibbiena, Arezzo ☎ (0575) 593046 ◫ □ ⊇ 20 ▭ 12 ▱ 📷 *Restaurant closed Wed; last orders 7:30pm.*
This old inn has a solemn turn-of-the-century atmosphere.

Bivigliano

Map 12D6. 18km (11 miles) N of Florence. 50030. Firenze. Population: 620 i Via delle Scuole 4.

A summer resort on the W slope of Monte Senario.
High above the town is the Convent of Monte Senario, the mother house of the Servite Order, founded in the 13thC. The buildings date mostly from the late 16thC. Stupendous views of the Arno and Sieve valleys.

Nearby sight
9km (5½ miles) S is the 15thC Servite **Convent of La Maddalena**, with frescoes by Fra Bartolommeo.

H **Giotto Park** (☎ *(055) 406608* ◫ to ◫◫ *closed Nov–Mar except Christmas*).

R In the town, **La Giulia** (*Via Roma 2* ☎ *(055) 406607* ◫ to ◫◫ *closed Fri*). **Dino** (*Via Faetina 329* ☎ *(055) 580932* ◫ to ◫◫ *closed Wed*), a cheerful country inn with rooms, 5km (3 miles) S at the Olmo crossroads near La Maddalena.

Borgo San Lorenzo

Map 12D6. 29km (18 miles) NE of Florence. 50032. Firenze. Population: 14,724.

The principal center of the Mugello, this town, now an industrial center, was destroyed by an earthquake in 1919.

Nearby sights
3km (2 miles) N, approached by a fine avenue of cypresses, is the church of **S. Giovanni Maggiore**, with an 11thC campanile and, inside, a rare Romanesque intarsiaed ambo.
5.5km (3½ miles) w is **S. Piero a Sieve**, where the parish church contains a terra-cotta font in the style of Luca della Robbia; above is Buontalenti's S. Martino fortress.
7km (4 miles) SE is **Vespignano**, birthplace of Giotto. The house designated as Giotto's is N of the road. Farther along is **Vicchio**, where Fra Angelico was born and where Benvenuto Cellini took refuge from 1559–71 in the house next to the Oratory in Corso del Popolo.

R **Da Felicina** (*S. Piero a Sieve* ☎ *(055) 848016* ◫ *closed Sat*).
Farther N are two useful restaurants near the autostrada exit at Barberino di Mugello: **La Capannina** (*Viale Don Minzoni 88, Carallino Mugello* ☎ *(055) 8420078* ◫ *closed Tues*); and **Settimo Gualtieri** (☎ *(055) 641051* ◫◫ *closed Wed*).

Camaldoli

Map 12E7. 71km (44 miles) SE of Florence, 46km (28 miles) N of Arezzo. 52010. Arezzo. Population: 50.

Camaldoli, mother house of a reforming Order of the
Benedictines founded in the early 11thC by St Romuald, stands
isolated high in the Apennines above the Casentino. Its
buildings are mostly of the 17th–18thC, and of little interest
apart from the 16thC **pharmacy**.

Eremo
🖼 *Open 9–11am, 3:30–6pm.*

2.5km (1½ miles) above the monastery, at 1,104m (335ft), is the **eremo**
(hermitage) where the medieval monks lived in absolute isolation in the
midst of their magnificent **forest**. The delightful Baroque church of Il
Salvatore and the 20 monastic cells, including the one occupied by St
Romuald, may be visited.

There are two modest inns near the monastery, and fine walking.

Ⓡ **Il Cedro**
Moggiona, 5km (3 miles) s on the Poppi road ☎ *(0575) 5680* ▮▯
▱ *Closed Mon during Oct–May.*
A serious and popular small restaurant overlooking the mountains.
Specialties: Sformati, tortelli di patate, polenta con funghi.

Capalbio
Map **8***J6. 182km (113 miles) sw of Florence, 18km (11 miles)*
NE of Ansedonia. 58011. Grosseto. Population: 3,950.
This walled medieval village is near the large **Maremma
hunting reserve**, open to the public in season (*inquiries to
Riserva Turistica di Caccia dell'Ente Provinciale per il Turismo,
Castello Collacchioni* ☎ *(0564) 896024*). Walk around the 14thC
ramparts and through the old unspoiled streets.

Restaurants
Capalbio is well endowed with attractive, aromatic restaurants
which serve hunters' food, especially wild boar and roebuck
cooked in unusually appetizing ways. Most light open fires in
the winter and spread onto terraces in summer.

Da Maria (*Via Comunale 1* ☎ *(0564) 896014* ▮▯ *closed Tues except Aug*);
La Torre ☎ *(0564) 896070* ▮▯ *closed Wed*); near the hunting reserve,
5km (3 miles) NW, **Al Fontanile dei Caprai** ☎ *(0564) 89216* ▮▯ ⊕
closed Mon, lunch during July–Aug).

Caprese Michelangelo
Map **13***F8. 123km (76 miles) SE of Florence, 45km (28 miles)*
NE of Arezzo. 52033. Arezzo. Population: 1,799.
An agricultural hill village where Michelangelo was born on
Mar 6, 1475, while his father was the Florentine magistrate
(*podestà*). The magistrate's house, the Casa del Podestà, is
opposite the entrance to the restored 14thC **Castello**.

Ⓗ Ⓡ **Fonte della Galletta** (*6km (4 miles) to w* ☎ *(0575) 793925* ▮▯ *to*
▮▮▯ *closed Oct–Apr, restaurant closed Wed*).

Ⓡ **Il Cerro** (☎ *(0575) 793923* ▮▯ *to* ▮▮▯).

Carmignano
Map **15***E5. 22km (14 miles) w of Florence. 50042. Firenze.*
Population: 7,691.
This little town is surrounded by vineyards which produce the
venerable Carmignano wines (see *Tuscan wines*).

San Michele †
In this Gothic parish church hangs Pontormo's *Visitation* ★ one of his
greatest and best-known masterpieces.

Ⓡ See *Artimino, Poggio a Caiano*.

Carrara

Map **14***D2. 126km (80 miles)* NW *of Florence, 55km (34 miles)* N *of Pisa. 54033. Massa-Carrara. Population: 70,213*
i Piazza 2 Giugno 14 ☎ *(0585) 70668.*

To reach the Duomo in what remains of the old center of Carrara, one must penetrate a vast modern boomtown still thriving on the quarries which have yielded their famous marble for over 2,000yr and are today one of the major world sources, producing 500,000 tons a year.

Sights and places of interest
Duomo 🏛 † ☆

An especially ornate version of the Pisan-Lucchese style. The lower facade and lovely portal date from the 12thC, and the Gothic upper story, with its rose window, as elaborately carved as an ivory Indian box, was added in the 14thC. The simple, elegant interior contains a 14thC *Virgin Annunciate* and *Angel* in the Gothic style.

Piazza Alberica boasts some fine Baroque palaces including Pietro Tacca's birthplace. In Piazza C. Battisti is the Neoclassical **Teatro degli Animosi** (1840), admired by Dickens and other 19thC travelers.

Mostra Nazionale Marmi e Macchine

Viale XX Settembre 🅿 ✳ *Open Mon, Thurs, Sun 10am–1pm, Sat 10am–1pm, 4–7pm.*

A permanent exhibition demonstrating techniques of marble quarrying, cutting and carving. The **quarries** themselves, 7km (4 miles) to the E, at Colonnata and Fantiscritti, will admit visitors.

Ⓡ **Soldiani** (*Via Mazzini 11* ☎ *(0585) 71459* ▥ *closed Mon and Aug 1–22*) is cool and pleasant; 7km (4 miles) toward Marina di Carrara at Avenza is **Il Muraglione** (*Via Fivizzano 13* ☎ *(0585) 58771* ▥ *to* ▥ *closed Wed*), an old country inn.

Cascina

Map **14***E4. 75km (47 miles)* SW *of Florence, 17km (10 miles)* SE *of Pisa. 56021. Pisa. Population: 34,701.*

In this center of furniture manufacture is the 12thC **Pieve di Santa Maria**, a remarkably well-preserved example of the Pisan Romanesque style. The 14thC Oratory of San Giovanni is frescoed (1398) inside by Martino di Bartolomeo.

Nearby sights

Vicopisano, 6km (4 miles) to the NE, retains picturesque 14thC fortifications restored by Brunelleschi.

9km (5½ miles) to the NW is Calci, with a fine 11thC Pisan-Romanesque **Pieve**. Nearby on the Montemagno road is the **Certosa di Pisa** (🅿 🛉 *open May–Oct Tues–Sat 9:30–11:30am, 3–6pm, Nov–Apr 10am–noon, 2–5pm*), a splendid complex of 17th–18thC Baroque buildings.

Castellina in Chianti

Map **12***F6. 50km (31 miles)* S *of Florence, 21km (13 miles)* N *of Siena. 53011. Siena. Population: 2,843.*

This small town was the first seat of the medieval Chianti League and one of the original centers of the Chianti Classico winegrowing zone. The medieval **Rocca** was extended by the Florentines in 1400; Etruscan remains include the 4thC BC tomb of Montecalvario, and a well.

Ⓗ **Tenuta di Ricavo**
53011 Castellina in Chianti, Siena ☎ *(0577) 740221* ▥ 🐾 24
🛏 24 🚗 �»🏠 *Closed Nov–Mar.*

Location: 4km (2½ miles) S, *on San Donato road.* An isolated medieval farming village transformed into an excellent Swiss-managed hotel.
🏮 🍴 ⚓ 🎣

H **Villa Casalecchi**
53011 Castellina in Chianti, Siena ☎ *(0577) 740240* ◫ *to* ◫◫
◑ 14 ▭ 14 ▬ ▣ ⇒ AE ⦿ VISA *Closed Nov–Mar.*
Location: 1km s, on Siena road. Enfolded in a pine forest in the hills.
▱ ❄ ⫷ ≈

R **La Torre**
Piazza Umberto ☎ *(0577) 740236* ◫ ▱ ▬ ▬ *Closed Fri, Sept.*
A generous choice of perfected rustic dishes.

Castello

*Map **6**B3. 6km (3½ miles) nw of Florence. 50019. Firenze. Bus
no. 14 to Caregqi from Florence Duomo or station.*

Here, at the base of Monte Morello, are three important Medici
villas within pleasant walking distance of one another. Two
more Medici villas, **Trebbio** and **Cafaggiolo**, are a short drive
up the Via Bolognese (see *Route 6* in *Planning*), and *Artimino*
and *Poggio a Caiano* are to the w. See *Sesto Fiorentino*.

Sights and places of interest
Villa Medicea della Petraia ◫◫ ☆
▣ ▦ *Open Tues–Sun summer 9am–6:30pm; winter 9am–4:30pm.*
The old castle, of which the adapted central tower remains, was rebuilt
from c.1575–90 by Buontalenti for Cardinal Ferdinand de' Medici. In
the courtyard, glassed over by Victor Emmanuel, who used it as a
ballroom, is a pleasing fresco cycle by Volterrano glorifying the Medici.
On the upper terrace of the garden is an elegant marble **fountain** by
Tribolo dominated by Giambologna's bronze *Venus*. There is a
magnificent park to the e of the villa.
Villa Medicea di Careggi ◫◫
Viale G. Pieraccini ▣ ▦ ▦ *The villa is now a nurses' home; to
visit, apply to the hospital of Santa Maria Nuova in Florence.*
Careggi was one of the earliest villas used by the Medici for rest and
study. The old castellated house was modified for Cosimo il Vecchio by
Michelozzo, who added the loggiaed wing to the left in the 1430s.
Cosimo, his son Piero and his grandson Lorenzo the Magnificent all died
here. The villa was burned and looted after the expulsion of the Medici,
and restored in the 16thC by Pontormo and Bronzino.
Villa Medicea di Castello ◫◫◫ ☆
▣ *Garden only open daily 9am–6:30pm or sunset.*
Castello belonged to Lorenzo di Pierfrancesco de' Medici; Cosimo I was
brought up here and hired Tribolo in 1537 to redesign the well-preserved
gardens ★ which were completed in 1592 by Buontalenti, who rebuilt
the villa. The **fountain** of *Hercules and Anteus*, with statues by
Ammannati, was designed by Tribolo. The **grotto**, with fountains and
wonderful exotic animals, is by Giambologna. The colossal bronze
half-figure known as *January* in the terraced park is by Ammannati.

H **Villa le Rondini**
Via Bolognese Vecchia 224, 50019 Castello, Firenze
☎ *(055) 400081* ◫ *to* ◫◫ ◑ 35 ▭ 35 ▬ ▣ ⇒ AE VISA
A peaceful hotel in a 16thC villa on the hill of Monterinaldi.
▱ ▨ ❄ ⫷ ≈ ⸾

R **Lo Strettoio**
Serpiolle ☎ *(055) 453247* ◫ ▱ ⊜ *Closed Sun, Mon, Aug.*
Honest home cooking in an old mill. Reservations essential.

Castiglion Fiorentino

*Map **12**G7. 100km (62 miles) se of Florence, 17km (10½
miles) s of Arezzo. 52043. Arezzo. Population: 11,164*
i Corso Italia 111.

This walled market town, one of the most important in the
Valdichiana, slopes down a hill above the Arezzo–Cortona
road.

Sights and places of interest

The graceful 16thC **Loggia del Vasari** in the central Piazza del Municipio frames a fine view, and from the **castle keep** above it one can see over the Valdichiana as far as *Monte Amiata*.

Palazzo Comunale/Pinacoteca
Piazza del Municipio 🖾 🎟 *Open Mon–Sat 9am–noon, Thurs, Sat also 4–6pm, Sun 10:30–11:30am.*

The most notable works in the gallery include a cheering 15thC reliquary bust of *St Ursula* as a shy, happy girl, made in the Rhineland; a 13thC Umbrian painted crucifix; and paintings by Bartolomeo della Gatta.

There are also paintings by Bartolomeo della Gatta in the **Collegiata** and, in the adjoining **Pieve**, a *Deposition* (1438) by Signorelli. The late 13thC church of **S. Francesco** possesses a *St Francis* (1280–90) by Margaritone d'Arezzo.

Nearby sights

On a hilltop 4km (2½ miles) s is the imposing 13thC **Castello di Montecchio Vesponi** (*not open to the public*), given by the Florentines to the English *condottiere* Sir John Hawkwood.

Shopping

Matteo Capitini (*Via Roma* 🕿 *(0575) 65559* ■□ *to* ■■■). Fine hand-made ceramics.

Castiglione della Pescaia

Map **10**/*4. 162km (101 miles) s of Florence, 22km (14 miles) w of Grosseto. 58043. Grosseto. Population: 8,376*
i *Piazza Garibaldi 6* 🕿 *(0564) 933678.*

The main coastal resort of the Maremma is also a busy fishing village, and private and professional craft moor in the lively harbor at the mouth of the River Bruna. Above is the 14th–15thC **Rocca Aragonese** defending the original medieval village, now overgentrified. To the s stretch sand beaches.

Hotels

The hotels on the harbor are noisy and charmless. Instead try **Gli Archi** (*Via Montebello 28* 🕿 *(0564) 933083* ■□), a modest pensione in the center; or, outside the village at Poggiodoro, **David** (🕿 *(0564) 933867* ■□ *to* ■■■).

Riva del Sole ▥
58043 Castiglione della Pescaia, Grosseto 🕿 *(0564) 933625*
■■■ ☜ *176* ▭ *176* ▦ ⇌ ➠ 🄰🄴 🄲🄳 � *Closed Oct–Mar.*
A large, modern hotel in a new resort 3km (1¾ miles) up the coast.
🕭 ▱ ☑ ⚓ ⇌ ℃ ℘ ✓ ♨ ⛱ 🎿

Roccamare
Loc. Roccamare, 58043 Castiglione della Pescaia, Grosseto
🕿 *(0564) 941124* ◉ *500286* ■□ *to* ■■■ ☜ *51* ▭ *51* ▦ ▱ ⇌
🄰🄴 🄵 🄲🄳 � *Closed Nov–May.*
A complex of bungalows, just beyond Riva del Sole.
☒ ▱ ▱ ⚓ ℃ ℘ ♨

ⓡ **Da Romolo**
Via della Libertà 10 🕿 *(0564) 933533* ■□ □ *Closed Tues, Oct.*
The best of the fish restaurants. *Specialty: Spaghetti con frutti di mare.*

ⓡ Alternatives are: **Il Gambero** (*Via Ansedonia* 🕿 *(0564) 933735* ■□); **Grottino** (*Corso Liberta* 🕿 *(0564) 933970* □).

Certaldo

Map **11**F5. *40km (25 miles) sw of Florence, 40km (25 miles) nw of Siena. 50052. Firenze. Population: 15,899.*

Certaldo Alto, the fortified red-brick village where Boccaccio spent much of his life and died in 1375, stands above a modern suburb in the valley of the Elsa. The village was rebuilt in the 15thC and restored, a little too crisply, in the 19thC and again after World War II.

Sights and places of interest

Casa del Boccaccio
Via Boccaccio 18 🔲 *Ring next door as signposted for entry.*
A postwar reconstruction of a house which possibly belonged to Boccaccio's family.

Palazzo Pretorio
Piazzetta del Vicariato 🚘 *Open 9.00–12.30, 13.30–18.00.*
Rebuilt in the 15thC, this palace has a pretty courtyard with *quattrocento* frescoes by P. F. Fiorentino and, in the adjacent chapel, fresco fragments by Gozzoli and Giusto d'Andrea.

SS Michele e Jacopo ✝
Boccaccio's tomb was removed in 1783 by those who disapproved of his work. The modern tomb carries his own epitaph and his portrait bust (1503) by G. F. Rustici.

🅷 🆁 **Il Castello** (*Via della Rena 6* ☎ *(0571) 668250* 🔳) is a simple hotel with a cool brick terrace.

🆁 **Osteria del Vicario** (*Piazzetta Vicariato* ☎ *(0571) 668228* 🔳 to 🔳🔳 *closed Wed*) has an arcaded terrace.

Chianciano Terme

Map 9H7. 120km (75 miles) SE of Florence, 85km (53 miles) SE of Siena. 53042. Siena. Population: 7,294 ℹ *Azienda Autonoma di Cura, Piazza Indipendenza* ☎ *(0578) 63167.*
If you are driving from *Chiusi* you will see two Chiancianos: the old hill town and, below it, the modern spa, one of the most important in Italy. The curative powers of the waters have been valued since the Roman age. There are various types of water for internal consumption or bathing.

A lovely rural road to the S leads to Sarteano, after 7.5km (5 miles), and Cetona, 14km (9 miles), two Etruscan villages.

🅷 There are some 200 hotels and boardinghouses of all categories during the season (April 16–Nov 15): **Capitol** (*Viale della Liberta 42* ☎ *(0578) 64681* 🔳 to 🔳🔳); **Fortuna** (*Via della Valle 76* ☎ *(0578) 64661* 🔳🔳); **Macerina** (*Via Macerina 27* ☎ *(0578) 64241* 🔳 to 🔳🔳); **Michelangelo** (*Via delle Piane 146* ☎ *(0578) 64004* 🔳🔳 to 🔳🔳); **Park** (*Via Roncacci 30* ☎ *(0578) 63603* 🔳); **Raffaello** (*Via dei Monti* ☎ *(0578) 64633* 🔳🔳); **Sole** (*Via della Rosa 40* ☎ *(0578) 60194* 🔳🔳); **Taormina** (*Via Roncacci 12* ☎ *(0578) 63808* 🔳).

🆁 **La Casanova**
Strada della Vittoria 10 ☎ *(0578) 60449* 🔳🔳 🔲 ➤ 🏠 ➤ *Closed Nov–Feb, Mon during Mar-May, Oct.*
Set invitingly in a wooded park, this elegant restaurant offers Tuscan cooking with inventive touches.

Chiusi

Map 9H7. 126km (79 miles) SE of Florence, 67km (42 miles) S of Arezzo. 53043. Siena. Population: 9,108 ℹ *Via Petrarca 4* ☎ *(0578) 20003.*
The Etruscan city of Camars, one of the greatest of the lucomonies, is best known to classical scholars and readers of Macaulay's *Horatius* for its king, Lars Porsena, who attacked Rome in 508 BC. Today Camars lies buried around and under the little town of Chiusi, whose street plan is that of Clusium, the Roman military colony it became in 296 BC.

Sights and places of interest

Duomo ✝

Beneath the campanile of the Romanesque cathedral, constructed from building fragments of the two earlier civilizations, is a large **cistern**, possibly 1stC BC. To visit, apply to the Museo Etrusco.

Museo Nazionale Etrusco ★

Piazza del Duomo ⊡ Open Tues–Sat 8:30am–2pm, Sun, hols 9am–1pm.

One of the outstanding Etruscan museums in Italy. The material, excavated from the vast necropolis surrounding the city, notably demonstrates the influence of Greece, Mesopotamia, Egypt and Rome on this sophisticated and receptive culture. There is a superb and varied collection of cinerary urns and sarcophagi, of which the most famous is the sarcophagus depicting the battle of the Gauls with a **portrait of Lars Sentinates** on the cover. Also noteworthy are specimens of the heavy black *bucchero* ware, imitating metal, which was made only in Chiusi, and an unusually fine collection of Attic vases.

Necropoli Etrusca

Visits only with guides from the Museo Etrusco.

The most notable Etruscan tombs are: To the N, along the Via delle Tombe Etrusche: the c.3rd–4th BC Tomba della Pellegrina, with fine sarcophagi; the 5thC BC **Tomba della Scimmia** (Monkey Tomb), which retains rare wall paintings; and the Tomba del Granduca, with cinerary urns. To the E: the 5thC BC **Tomba Bonci Casuccini**, with its original door and frescoes of games; and the 1stC BC Tomba delle Tassinaie.

[H] [R] **Il Patriarca** ✤

Querce al Pino, 53043 Chiusi ☎ (0578) 27007 ▮▮ 22 ▭ 22 ▭ ▭ VISA Restaurant closed Wed.

The most pleasant of a cluster of hotels serving the autostrada exit.

[R] **La Fattoria**

2.5km (1½ miles) to the N, on shore of Lake Chiusi. With rooms ☎ (0578) 21407 ▮▮ to ▮▮▮ Closed Mon, Jan–Feb.

The tiled floors and beamed ceilings give a farmhouse atmosphere.

Colle di Val d'Elsa

*Map **11**F5. 49km (30 miles) S of Florence, 25km (15 miles) NW of Siena. 53034. Siena. Population: 15,618 **i** Piazza Arnolfo di Cambio 5 ☎ (0577) 921692.*

There is an impressive view of this two-tiered town from the *Monteriggioni* road. The upper town has conserved its medieval street plan and some fine architecture.

Colle di Val d'Elsa has been a manufacturing center of fine crystal glass from the mid-14thC. Fiercely contested between Siena and Florence in the 13thC, the town became part of the Florentine dominion in 1333. The architect and sculptor Arnolfo di Cambio was born here in 1232.

Sights and places of interest

Colle Bassa

The lower town is also known as il Piano, and its hub is the lively Piazza Arnolfo di Cambio. Nearby in Via dei Fossi is the church of **S. Agostino** with an unfinished 13thC facade and beautiful 16thC interior designed by Antonio da Sangallo the Elder.

Colle Alta ☆

The upper town and the remains of its 12thC–13thC fortifications are strung along the ridge of the hill. Notice the frescoed palace facades on Via XX Settembre and other streets. The **Porta Nuova**, leading to the Volterra road at the end of Via Gracco del Secco, is a fine piece of late 15thC military architecture, probably by Giuliano da Sangallo. The medieval village is reached by a bridge from which there are fine views; straddling the ravine is the splendid unfinished Mannerist **Palazzo Campana** (1539) by Giuliano di Baccio d'Agnolo.

The **Via del Castello** opens into the Piazza del Duomo where the 14thC Palazzo Pretorio houses the **Antiquarium Etrusco** (⊠ 🎫 *open Tues–Sat 10am–noon, 4–7pm*), displaying material excavated from a necropolis near Monteriggioni. Inside the Baroque **Duomo** (1619) is a bronze *Crucifix* over the high altar attributed to Giambologna and a bronze lectern by P. Tacca. The **Palazzo Vescovile** (*Via Castello 27*) houses a little **Museo d'Arte Sacra** (🖾 *open Sun summer 4–7pm, winter 3–6pm*), where ecclesiastic vestments and objects and a late 14thC Sienese school triptych are displayed in one frescoed room. In the old Palazzo dei Priori is the **Museo Civico** (🖾 *open Tues–Sun 9am–noon, 2–5pm*), with pictures by R. Manetti, P. F. Fiorentino and others; under a loggietta are frescoes by S. Ferri of *David and Goliath* and *Judith and Holofernes*. Toward the bottom of Via Castello, no. 63 is the early 13thC **tower-house of Arnolfo di Cambio**.

R **La Cartiera**
Via Oberdan 1 🕿 *(0577) 921107* Ⅲⵖ 🖵 ⊒ 🍽 *Closed Mon, July.*
A popular restaurant in an old paper mill. ***Specialty:** Game.*

Collodi

*Map **15**D4. 63km (39 miles)* NW *of Florence, 17km (10 miles)* NE *of Lucca. 51014. Pistoia. Population: 2,233.*

Just to the w of *Pescia* is the picturesque village where Carlo Lorenzini, author of *Pinocchio*, spent his youth and gained his pen name, Carlo Collodi.

Sights and places of interest
Parco di Pinocchio
🖾 ⚘ *Open daily 8am to sunset.*
Games, statues and pavilions on the theme of Pinocchio and his creator.
Villa Garzoni Gardens ☆
🖾 *Open daily summer 8am–1pm, 2:30pm to sunset; winter 9am–noon.*
This sparkling beautiful and well-preserved garden, which flows downhill from the *castello*, was laid out in the mid-1600s by the Garzoni family. The villa assumed its present form in the late 18thC.

R **Gambero Rosso** (*Via S. Gennaro 2* 🕿 *(0572) 49364* Ⅲⵖ *to* Ⅲⵖ *closed Tues, Nov*), dull but convenient. See also *Pescia*.

Cortona ☆

*Map **13**G8. 102km (63 miles)* SE *of Florence, 32km (20 miles)* SE *of Arezzo. 52044. Arezzo. Population: 22,561* ℹ *Piazza Signorelli 10* 🕿 *(0575) 603056.*

The mythical founder of Cortona was Corythus, father of Dardanus, which suggests that Cortona was older than Troy; and certainly the town was already long established when it was occupied by the Etruscans in the 8th–7thC BC. The Romans took over in the 4thC BC; and in 217 BC the main Roman army was destroyed nearby at Lake Trasimeno by the Carthaginian general Hannibal. The commune which emerged from the Dark Ages in the 12thC was brutally sacked by Arezzo in 1258, recovered in the 14thC under the steadying rule of the Casali lords, and was eventually sold to Florence in 1411. The new association with Florence and the arrival of Fra Angelico, who spent some 10yr in the monastery then attached to San Domenico, freed the art of Cortona from the archaizing domination of Siena. In the second half of the 15thC Cortona produced its own great native painter, Luca Signorelli, whose work can be seen in the Diocesan Museum and the church of San Nicolò. The painters Pietro da Cortona and the Futurist Gino Severini were also natives of Cortona.

Modern Cortona, the principal town of the Valdichiana, is a serious place inhabited by farmers and bookish foreigners.

The brown sandstone buildings of the old town are scattered down the steep upper slope of Monte Sant'Egidio and wrapped in medieval walls which incorporate large sections built by the Etruscans. The main street, Via Nazionale, known locally as Ruga Piana because it is the only level street in the town, leads from Piazza Garibaldi to the medieval nucleus of Cortona, Piazza Repubblica – the first bar on the left of Via Nazionale as you leave Piazza Garibaldi serves fine ice cream.

Events: Market day is Sat. There is an annual antique fair from Aug 25 – Sept 25.

Sights and places of interest

Leave time to explore some of its atmospheric old streets: Vie Benedetti, Maffei, Guelfa, Roma, Dardano, and Berretini.

Museo dell'Accademia Etrusca ▥▥
Palazzo Pretorio, Piazza Signorelli ▨ *Open Tues – Sun 10am – 1pm, 4 – 7pm.*

The Palazzo Pretorio, which houses the Etruscan Academy, was built in the 13thC and was later the residence of the Casali rulers; it was extended in the 17thC. In the main hall is the centerpiece, the famous but repulsive **Etruscan Lamp ★** (5thC BC), the largest and most elaborate Etruscan object of its kind. Small Etruscan objects are displayed in the glass cases, and among the pictures are the entrancing Greco-Roman painting on slate of the *Muse Polyhymnia* and a very fine Pietro da Cortona *Madonna and Saints*. The following rooms are filled with an intriguing, badly-labeled miscellany of Egyptian objects, porcelains, a good coin collection and, at the end, a small room devoted to Gino Severini.

Museo Diocesano ▥▥
Piazza Trento Trieste ▨ *Open daily summer 9am – 1pm, 3 – 6:30pm, winter 9am – 1pm, 3 – 5pm.*

This important museum is opposite the Duomo in a former church which was modified and partly frescoed by Vasari. Its rather gloomy atmosphere is lit up with the glowing spirituality of Fra Angelico's *Annunciation ★* (1433); the predella is unusually fine, especially the episode of the *Meeting at the Golden Gate*. The other Angelico, a triptych of the *Madonna and Child with Saints*, also has a superb predella depicting *Scenes from the Life of St Dominic*. Most notable among a number of Signorellis are his *Deposition* and *Communion of the Apostles*. Other highlights are the Sassetta *Madonna and Saints*; P. Lorenzetti's *Crucifix* and *Madonna and Angels*; and the Roman **sarcophagus decorated with Amazons and Centaurs**, admired by Brunelleschi and Donatello.

At the far end of Via Dardano is the **Porta Colonia**, the best-preserved section of Etruscan wall, which commands a wonderful view.

Other sights

The most charming of the churches is **San Domenico**, and behind it are public gardens where one may walk and enjoy fine views of the plain below. The **Sanctuary of St Margaret**, farther along Via S. Margherita, is an ugly 19thC church which conserves the beautiful Gothic **tomb of St Margaret**, by Angelo and Francesco di Pietro. From there it is a short climb to the **Fortezza Medicea**, commanding another magnificent view.

Nearby sights

Madonna del Calcinaio ▥▥ ✝ ★
3km (2 miles) s, off Camucia road ▣ *For entry ask custodian, who lives in adjacent farmhouse.*

A masterpiece of church architecture, designed (1485 – 1513) by the military engineer Francesco di Giorgio, and notable for the springing energy of the interior space, organized so that the crossing is lighted at all times of day by the round windows above. Vasari's answer, the church of **Santa Maria Nuova** (1554), is above the town.

There are four **Etruscan tombs** in the vicinity. Those at Sodo, to the NW towards Arezzo, and at Camucia, to the s towards Lake Trasimeno, are

under huge mounds of earth known as *meloni*, and date from the
7th–6thC BC. The two near the Madonna del Calicinaio, the Grotta di
Tanella and the Tanella Angora, may date from the 4thC BC.

3.5km (2 miles) to the NE, in a lovely location, is the **Convent Le
Celle**, founded by St Francis between 1211–21; one may visit St Francis'
cell and the little 16thC church.

H **Gugliemesca** ✿
Villa Gugliemesca, 52044 Cortona ☎ *(0575) 603365* ▮☐ ☜ *26* ▭
26 ☛ ☎ ☶ AE ⑥ ⑩ VISA *Closed Nov–Mar.*
Location: 10km (6 miles) to N, on road for Città di Castello. This delightful,
unpretentious hotel is perched in a wood on Monte Sant'Egidio.
◠ ❧

H **L'Oasi**
Via Contesse 1, 52044 Cortona ☎ *(0575) 603188* ▮☐ ☜ *36* ▭ *36*
☛ ☎ ☶ *Closed Nov–Mar.*
Location: Just outside walls to the S. L'Oasi retains the hushed atmosphere
of the former convent in which it is housed. It is a clean, somber hotel.
◠ ☇ ❧ ♨

R **La Loggetta**
Piazza Pescheria ☎ *(0575) 603777* ▮▮☐ ☐ ☒ AE ⑩ *Closed Mon,
Jan.*
In the cool, intimate, brick-vaulted rooms local dishes are served.

R **Tonino**
Piazza Garibaldi 1 ☎ *(0575) 603787* ▮▮☐ ☐ *Closed Tues, Nov.*
A noisy restaurant annexed to the modern hotel **San Luca**.

Elba ★

*Map **10**/2–3. Province: Livorno. Getting there: By ferry, from
Piombino, 1hr by car ferry, 30min hovercraft – ferries run
frequently throughout the day, booking advisable in
July–Aug – from Livorno, daily boat takes 3hr direct to
Portoferraio or 5hr with stops at islands of Gorgona and
Capraia; by air, in summer, flights from Pisa. Getting around:
By bus, the service is run by ACIT; by car, main car rental
agencies are Avis, Arrighi (travel agents), Porto Azzurro
☎ (0565) 95000, Maggiore, Tessi (travel agents),
Portoferraio ☎ (0565) 92386. Population: 28,429 i Calata
Italia 26, Portoferraio ☎ (0565) 92671.*

Elba is the largest of the Tuscan islands, at 27km (17 miles) long
and 18km (11 miles) across at its widest, E end, with an
extremely irregular coastal perimeter measuring nearly 150km
(93 miles). The highest point is the summit of the granite Monte
Capanne (1,018m; 3,340ft.) which dominates the wild western
lobe of the island. Around the rest of the coast majestic cliffs
alternate with inviting sandy bays backed by evergreens.

The iron ore of Elba has been mined for at least 3,000yr. The
Greek name for the island was Aethalia (Soot Island) and the
Etruscans transported the iron ore in great quantities to the
mainland for smelting at *Piombino*; the main port was named
Portoferraio (Port Iron) in the 8thC.

The more recent history of Elba was affected by two of the
great modern imperialists: Duke Cosimo I of Florence and
Napoleon. In 1548 Cosimo built and fortified the city of
Portoferraio, and called it Cosmopolis. His ostensible purpose
was to police the pirate-infested Tyrrhenian Sea; his more
compelling motive was to gain a stronghold against the forces of
Spain and France. In the end he was obliged to share control of
the island with the Spanish, who built their own fortress at
Porto Azzurro.

In 1814 the Congress of Vienna ceded Elba to Napoleon as his dominion in exile. He spent nine restless months here, reforming the administration of the island, furnishing his two villas, and plotting his escape, which took place on Feb 26, 1815. The island then passed to Tuscany.

The island can offer vacationers facilities for sailing, waterskiing, spearfishing, tennis, golf and riding.

Hotels and restaurants on Elba

The standards of the 140 hotels on the island are extremely variable. Many hotels insist on half-board, which is a pity, because their kitchens can rarely cope with the fresh fish which is the great gastronomic treat of Elba.

Nearly every species of Mediterranean fish is caught in the clear waters around the island; which you order will determine the price of your meal. All the local wines are excellent, with a distinctive flavor from the minerals in the soil.

A–Z of towns

Capoliveri

Map 10I3. 5km (3¼ miles) sw of Porto Azzurro. Population: 2,397.

An isolated mining, fishing and wine-producing village on the SE lobe of the island below the iron mountain of Monte Calamita. Stunning views to the w.

Lacona

Map 10I3. 14km (9 miles) s of Portoferraio. Population: 200.

A quiet bathing resort on the S coast at the head of the long promontory which Napoleon made into his hunting estate.

H **Capo Sud**

Lacona, 57037 Portoferraio, Isola d'Elba ☎ *(0565) 964021* ▯ *to* ▯▯ 🕿 *34* 🛏 *34* 🍴 🏠 ⇌ *Closed Oct–Apr.*

A quiet and comfortable group of cottages.

▱ ▱ ▱ ⚓ ⚘ 🎣 ✎

Marciana

Map 10I2. 27km (17 miles) w of Portoferraio. Population: 2,272.

This wine-producing village on the slope of Monte Capanne is dominated by the ruined castle of the Appiano, the hereditary rulers of Elba in the Middle Ages. The **Antiquarium** (🕮 *open Thurs–Tues 10am–noon, 4–7:30pm, closed Wed; apply to custodian in Via della Fonte*) displays pre-historic, Etruscan and Roman material.

The **summit of Monte Capanne** ☆ is reached by funicular (🕮 ✳ *open daily 10am–noon, 2:30–6pm*) in 30 min or by mule in about 2¼ hr. A 40min drive to the NW is the sanctuary of the **Madonna del Monte**, where Napoleon stayed in 1814.

Marciana Marina

Map 10I2. 20km (12½ miles) w of Portoferraio. Population: 1,907.

A relatively unspoiled fishing village in a lovely open position.

H **Gabbiano Azzurro**

57033 Marciana Marina, Isola d'Elba ☎ *(0565) 99226* ▯ 🕿 *39* 🛏 *39* ▦ 🍴

Modern, straightforward, friendly. No dining-room.

R **Rendez-Vous da Marcello**
On the harbor ☎ *(0565) 99251* ⬛️□ *to* ⬛️□□ ▭ ◁€ *Closed Wed,
Jan–Feb.*
Popular fish restaurant on the harbor.

Marina di Campo
Map **10***/2. 17km (10½ miles) sw of Portoferraio. Population:
1,732.*

This fishing village and beach resort commands a wide arc of
sand on the Gulf of Campo on the s coast.

H **Lo Scirrocco**
Loc. Fetovaia Casa 19, 57034 Campo nell'Elba ☎ *(0565) 987060*
⬛️□ ⬟ 16 ⬛ 16 ⬛ ⬛ ⬛ AE ⓪ VISA *Closed Oct–Mar.*
Location: 9km (6 miles) w at Fetovaia. A handsomely decorated and
comfortable private hotel overlooking a pleasant, isolated sand beach.
⌂ ⧗ ⊡ ⚡ ⚓ ◁€ ⬟ ⬗

H An alternative is **Galli** (☎ *(0565) 987065* ⬛️□ *closed Oct–Apr*).

R **Bologna**
Via Firenze 27 ☎ *(0565) 97105* ⬛️□ □ ▭ AE ⓪ VISA *Closed Tues
except summer.*
A big, cheerful fish restaurant in an old boathouse.

R **Da Gianni**
2.5km (1½ miles) N at La Pila Airport ☎ *(0565) 976965* ⬛️□ *to* ⬛️□□
▭ ▦ *Closed Fri (except July–Aug) and Nov–Mar.*
A small, welcoming restaurant. *Specialty: Risotto di mare al forno.*

Porto Azzurro
Map **10***/3. 15km (9 miles) se of Portoferraio. Population:
2,960.*

The center of the Spanish protectorate in the 16th–17thC,
Porto Azzurro is still a charming sight from the Narengo side of
the Gulf of Mola, although the harborfront has been spoiled by
timid development. To the N is the massive Fortezza di
Portolongone, built by the Spanish in 1603; soon afterward they
built the nearby sanctuary of the **Madonna di Monserrato**,
which still stands 1.5km (1 mile) to the N of the town.

Portoferraio
Map **10***/3. Population: 11,135* *i* *Calata Italia 26*
☎ *(0565) 92671.*

The busy main town of Elba is magnificently situated on a
promontory which shelters its fine harbor. The old port is
guarded by two fortresses built by Cosimo I in 1548, the large
Forte del Falcone and the picturesque **Forte della Stella**.

Sights and places of interest
Palazzina Napoleonica dei Mulini ☆
▦ *Ticket also good for Villa Napoleonica. Open Tues–Sat
9am–1:30pm, Sun, hols 9am–12:30pm.*
Napoleon created his residence in exile from two old windmills above the
city near the Forte della Stella. The furnishings for this delightful little
palace were commandeered from his sister Elisa's house at Piombino; the
plate and library were brought from Fontainebleau.
Villa Napoleonica di San Martino ☆
6km (4 miles) to w, on Marciana road ▦ *ticket also good for
Palazzina Mulini. Open Tues–Sat 9am–1:30pm, Sun, hols 12:30pm.*
Even in exile, an emperor must have a country estate; Napoleon filled
this modest villa with personal symbols.
  The long Neoclassical **Pinacoteca Foresiana** (1851), nearby, houses a
large collection of 16th–19thC art.

141

🄷 **Hermitage**
La Biodola, 57037 Portoferraio ☎ *(0565) 969932* Ⓣ*500219
(summer) 211116 (winter)* ⅢⅢ ♎ *100* ▭ *100* ← ⚊ 🖻 🅰🅴 🆅🆂🅰
Closed Nov–Apr.
Location: 10km (6 miles) sw at La Biodola. Discreetly set into a hillside
overlooking a beautiful bay. **La Biodola** (☎ *(0565) 969966* ❙☐) is under
the same management.
🖾 🗠 🗻 🐙 ≈ 🗠 ✍ 🏌 ← 🏖

🄷 **Picchiae Residence**
57037 Portoferraio ☎ *(0565) 966072* ⅢⅢ ♎ *95* ▭ *95* ← 🏠 ⚊
Closed Oct–Apr.
Location: 8km (5 miles) s of Portoferraio, off Porto Azzurro road. A
modern, peaceful hotel offering marvelous views.
🖾 🗠 🗻 🗠 ≈ 🗠 🏌

🆁 A restaurant in the town with pleasant outdoor tables is: **La Ferrigna**
(*Piazza Repubblica* ☎ *(0565) 92129* ❙☐ *closed Tues, Jan–Feb*).

Procchio
*Map 10I2. 10km (6 miles) sw of Portoferraio. Population:
532.*
One of the chief sand-beach resorts on the N coast.

🄷 **Desirée**
Lido di Spartaia, 57030 Procchio ☎ *(0565) 907502/3* Ⓣ*590220* ⅢⅢ
to ⅢⅢ ♎ *69* ▭ *12* ← ⚊ 🖻 🅰🅴 Ⓟ 🆅🆂🅰 *Closed Nov–Apr.*
A modern and anonymous but efficiently managed hotel.
🗠 🗠 🗻 ≈ 🗠 🗠 ← 🏖

🄷 🆁 **Golfo**
57030 Procchio ☎ *(0565) 907445* Ⓣ*590690* ⅢⅢ *to* ⅢⅢ ♎ *75* ▭
75 ← ▦ ⚊ 🖻 🅰🅴 Ⓟ 🆅🆂🅰 *Closed Nov–Apr.*
A large, modern hotel in a pine forest with an especially attractive beach,
and an unusually good restaurant.
🗠 ≈ 🗠 🗠 ← 🍷

Rio Marina
*Map 10I3. 20km (12 miles) E of Portoferraio. Population:
2,420.*
This is the principal mining town of Elba, and on the third floor
of the Palazzo Comunale is an interesting little **mineral
museum** (🔲 *open Apr–Sept Mon–Sat 9am–noon, 3–6pm, Sun
9am–noon*). The **iron mines** may be visited on Sat in summer
by appointment (☎*(0565) 962001*).

Excursions
Island of Capraia
Boats depart from Portoferraio on Tues, Wed, Fri and Sat for a
day trip; the journey takes 2–3hr each way.

🄷 🆁 **Il Saracino** (☎ *(0565) 95018* ❙☐ *closed Oct–Mar*).

Island of Montecristo
Hotels and travel agents will arrange party bookings to visit the
deserted island now designated as a nature reserve.

Empoli
*Map 15E5. 33km (20 miles) w of Florence. 50053. Firenze.
Population: 45,802* **i** *Piazza Farinata degli Uberti*
☎ *(0571) 76115.*
The vast and unlovely sprawl around Empoli, an important
center of glass manufacture, disguises exceptional works of art.

The painters Pontormo and Jacopo Chimenti, called Empoli, were born here. The modern composer Ferrucio Busoni was also a native of the area. There is a festival of Busoni's works in the autumn.

Sights and places of interest
Collegiata ▥ †
At the historic center of Empoli is the church which marks the western limit of the influence of Florentine Romanesque; the lower section of the facade dates from 1093. The upper part is a post-World War II reconstruction of F. Ruggieri's late-18thC 'rationalization.'

Museo della Collegiata ☆
Piazzetta San Giovanni, to the right of the Collegiata ▧ *Open Tues–Sun 10am–noon.*

The museum incorporates the Baptistry of the Collegiata.

Ground Floor: A 15thC stone emblem shows the original appearance of the Collegiata facade; there is also a School-of-Donatello baptismal font, and a 16thC English brass lectern.

First floor: **Rm. 5** contains Bicci di Lorenzo's *St Nicholas of Tolentino defends Empoli from the Black Death* (1445), interesting for the view of early 15thC Empoli. In **Rm. 6**: Lorenzo Monaco's *Madonna Enthroned with Saints* (1404); Bicci di Lorenzo's *Madonna Enthroned with Saints* (1423); two works by Pontormo, *St John the Evangelist* and *St Michael Archangel*; and a tabernacle of *St Sebastian*, sculpted by A. Rossellino and painted by Francesco Botticini. In **Rm. 7** are two free-standing sculptures of the *Madonna Annunciate* and the *Angel Gabriel* (1447) by B. Rossellino; a *Madonna and Child*, usually attributed to the young Filippo Lippi; a tabernacle of the *Holy Sacrament* (1484) by Francesco and Raffaello Botticini. Two more images of the Madonna in this room are the relief sculptures by Tino da Camaiano (early 14thC) and by Mino da Fiesole (c.1465–70). **Rm. 8**: *Pietà* and other detached frescoes (c.1425) by Masolino, from the church of Santo Stefano; and frescoes of *St Andrew* and *John the Baptist*, rare works by Gherardo Starnina. **Rm. 9**: Terra-cottas from the Della Robbia workshop.

In the 14thC church of **Santo Stefano** in Via S. Stefano there is a *Madonna and Child* (1424) and other frescoes by Masolino.

Fiesole ☆
Map 12E6. 8km (5 miles) NE of Florence. 50014, Firenze. Population: 14,788. Getting there: No. 7 bus from Florence i Piazza Mino da Fiesole 45 ☎ (055) 598720.

When Florence was a mere cluster of buildings on the Arno, Fiesole, on its conical hill overlooking the valleys of the Arno and the Mugnone, was one of the chief cities of Etruria. Some scholars place the Etruscan settlement as early as the 8thC BC, although the town is not recorded until 225 BC. Faesulae was an important Roman military colony from 80 BC and later the capital city of Roman Etruria. In 1125 Florence sacked and superseded its mother city. *Pietra serena*, the cool gray stone employed so effectively by Florentine architects, comes from the nearby quarries of Monte Ceceri.

Fiesole is slightly cooler than Florence in summer, although the difference is often wishfully exaggerated.

Event: The *Estate Fiesolana*, a festival of concerts and films, takes place in the Roman Theater in July–Aug.

Sights and places of interest
The main square, on the site of the Roman forum, is the **Piazza Mino da Fiesole**.
Duomo †
The exterior of the Duomo (San Romolo), enlarged in the 13thC, was made dreary by a 19thC restoration. The **Cappella Salutati**, to the right of the choir, contains two fine works by Mino da Fiesole: the **tomb of Bishop Salutati**, and an altar front of the *Madonna and Saints*.

Museo Bandini

Via Dupré ☎ _(055) 59061_ 🔄 _Open Tues–Sun Mar–Apr, Oct 10am–12:30pm, 2:30–6pm; Nov–Feb 9:30am–12:30pm, 2–5pm; May–Sept 10am–noon, 3–7pm._

A miscellany of furniture, majolica, Renaissance pictures and Etruscan fragments.

San Francesco †

Above the public gardens is this 14thC church enlarged in the 15thC but now nearly ruined by ill-considered restoration in the early 20thC. The cloisters are charming, and there are magnificent views.

Below S. Francesco is the ancient basilica of **S. Alessandro**, on the site of the Roman temple of Bacchus. The wonderful marble columns dividing the interior space are Roman.

Teatro Romano 🏛 ☆

Via Marini ☎ _(055) 59477_ 🔄 _Hours as Museo Bandini._

Atmosphere and views as well as the Roman theater (c.80 BC), which has a capacity of 3,000; it was rediscovered in 1809 and excavated in 1873. To the right are the baths, discovered in 1891, and to the left the Roman-Etruscan temple, first fully revealed in 1918. Behind is a stretch of **Etruscan wall**.

Nearby sights

Badia Fiesolana 🏛 † ☆

Ask at porter's lodge for entry.

300m NW of San Domenico, this was the cathedral of Fiesole until the 11thC. Cosimo il Vecchio commissioned an unknown architect to rebuild this church in the mid-15thC. The unfinished facade (1464) incorporates the little green and white Romanesque facade of the earlier church. The superb cruciform **interior** is one of the glories of Renaissance architecture.

San Domenico 🏛 † ☆

In this hamlet, 1.5km (1 mile) SW of Fiesole, is the monastery of S. Domenico, built for Domenican monks in the early 15thC, now the seat of the European University. Fra Angelico took religious orders here and was prior from 1449–52. The church portico and campanile were added in the 17thC by Matteo Nigetti, and the **interior** remodeled in the late 15th–early 16thC, when the elegant stone arches to the nave chapels, some by Giuliano da Sangallo, were added. Over the first altar on the left is an **altarpiece** (c.1428), with its background repainted by Lorenzo di Credi (c.1501), and recently cleaned.

In the convent, to the right of the church portico (_ring for admission_), the Chapter House has a fresco of the _Crucifixion_ by Fra Angelico. His fresco of the _Madonna and Child_, now damaged, was in the church.

Villa Medici

Just to the W of the center of Fiesole. Not open to the public.

This was one of the first pleasure villas of the Renaissance, probably built for Cosimo il Vecchio by Michelozzo.

🏨 **Villa San Michele** 🏰

Via Doccia 4, 50014 Fiesole ☎ _(055) 59451_ 🏠 🔄 _32_ 🛏 _32_ 🍴
🗧 🚗 AE ⦶ ⦿ VISA _Closed Nov–Mar._

In a 14thC villa enlarged in the 15thC by Santi di Tito, the hotel is furnished like a private villa, with four-poster beds, old oak wardrobes and original fireplaces.
⬇

🏨 At San Domenico: **Bencistà** (☎ _(055) 59163_ 💶 _to_ 💶💶 _closed Nov–Mar_) is a comfortable old villa, as is **Villa San Girolamo** (☎ _(055) 59321_ 💶), run by Irish sisters.

🍴 Unpretentious favorites in the center are: **Mario** (☎ _(055) 59143, closed Tues_); **Pizzeria Etrusca** (☎ _(055) 5998838_ 💶), both in Piazza Mino da Fiesole; nearby, **La Romagnola** (_Via Gramsci 43_ ☎ _(055)59258_ 💶 _closed Mon_); at San Domenico, **Le Lance** (_Via Mantellini 2b_ ☎ _(055) 599090, closed Mon, Jan_) is a superior pizzeria with a terrace. At Pratolino, **Zocchi** (☎ _(055) 409202_ 💶 _closed Mon_) is a big, sunny restaurant offering a huge array of antipasti and meat from the charcoal grill. See also _Bivigliano, Settignano._

Forte dei Marmi

*Map **14**D2. 104km (65 miles) w of Florence, 34km (21 miles)
nw of Lucca. 55042. Lucca. Population: 10,193* **i** *Piazza
Marconi* ☎ *(0584) 80091.*

Forte dei Marmi is the quiet, discreet upper-class resort of the
Versilia laid out in neat, straight rows among the pine wood and
used mainly by Italians. The fort built in 1788 stands in the
central piazza.

Hotels

If you have not booked a hotel, you will find a good selection in
all categories in Viale Morin.

Augustus
Viale Morin 169, 55042 Forte dei Marmi, Lucca ☎ *(0584) 80202*
Ⓣ *590673* ▥ *to* ▥ ☞ *59* 🛏 *59* ▤ 🚗 🏠 ⇄ Ⓐ🄴 ⓥ ⓥⓘⓢⓐ *Closed
Oct to mid-May.*
A modern hotel near the beach.
🏠 ♨ ⑂ 🛄 🖼 🐾 🎿

Hermitage
Via Cesare Battisti ☎ *(0584) 80022* ▥ ☞ *40* 🛏 *40* ▤ 🚗 🏠 ⇄
Ⓐ🄴 ⓥ ⓥⓘⓢⓐ *Closed Oct–May.*
A luxury hotel noteworthy for its unusually good restaurant, **Il Pozzetto**.
🏠 🎿 ⑂ ≈ 🐾

Tirreno
Viale Morin 7, 55042 Forte dei Marmi, Lucca ☎ *(0584) 83333* ▥
☞ *59* 🛏 *59 Closed Nov–Mar.*
An attractive second-category hotel in an old villa.
🖼 🥀 ⑂ 🐾

Also: **Astoria Gardens** (*Via Leonardo da Vinci 10* ☎ *(0584) 80754* ▥
closed Nov–Mar); **Bell'Ombra** (*Viale Morin* ☎ *(0584)82225* ▯ *closed
Nov–Mar*), a decent, cheerful *pensione*; **Raffaelli Park** (*Via Mazzini 37*
☎ *(0584) 81494* ▥ *closed Nov–Apr*).

Ⓡ **La Barca**
Viale Italico 3 ☎ *(0584) 89323* ▥ ▱ 🚗 *Closed Mon eve, Tues,
Nov.*
Overlooking the beach, one of the most pleasant fish restaurants.

Ⓡ Also: **Bagno Bruno** (*Via Arenile 22* ☎ *(0584) 89972* ▥ *closed
Mon*); **Cervo Bianco** (*Via Risorgimento 9* ☎ *(0584) 89640* ▥ *closed
Wed, Nov*).

Gaiole in Chianti

*Map **12**F6. 69km (43 miles) se of Florence, 28km (17 miles)
ne of Siena. 53013. Siena. Population: 2,627.*

The medieval lord of this market town in the Chianti Classico
zone was one of the founders of the original Chianti league. The
Pieve di Spaltenna (1298), with an intact tower and pretty little
cloister, is just above to the w. On a hill to the e, which can be
climbed in 15min on foot, is the medieval village of **Barbischio**.
The fortified **Fattoria Meleto** stands in the midst of its
vineyards 2.5km (1½ miles) to the s.

Ⓡ **Badia a Coltibuono** ▥
Coltibuono, 5km (3 miles) to ne ☎ *(0577) 749424* ▥ ▱ 🍴 🚗
⬕ *Closed Mon, early Sept.*
The 11thC ex-monastery buildings and church are now part of an
active wine estate that includes a popular restaurant. Children
like the relaxed, chaotic atmosphere and the good fried potatoes.
Wine and oil are sold. ***Specialty: Spaghetti Genetto.***

Tuscany/*Galluzzo*

Galluzzo (Certosa del) 🏛 † ☆
Map 6E3. 6km (4 miles) s of Florence. Bus no. 36 or 37 from Florence 🖪 *but offering expected* 🖪 *Open daily summer 9am–noon, 4–7pm; winter 9am–noon, 2:30–5pm.*

The monastery which stands impressively above the Via Cassia was founded by the Florentine Niccolò Acciaiuoli in 1342. The **Pinacoteca** is housed in the Gothic Palazzo degli Studi; the dominating works are Pontormo's damaged **lunettes of the Passion cycle** (1522–25), detached from the *chiostro grande*. They were painted while he was living in the monastery during a plague in Florence and, although deeply influenced by Dürer, are striking examples of the Mannerist style Pontormo helped to invent. There are also paintings by Mariotto di Nardo, Dürer and Ridolfo del Ghirlandaio. The church of **S. Lorenzo**, in its large 16thC courtyard, has a high *pietra serena* facade (1556). The interior is divided into two sections: the Monks' Choir (with good 16thC stalls) and the Lay Brethren's Choir. A staircase leads to the subterranean chapels where members of the Acciaiuoli family are buried. The superb **tomb slab of Cardinal Agnolo II Acciaiuoli** was attributed to Donatello by Ruskin and others, but is now thought to be 16thC. Notice also especially the Gothic **monument to N. Acciaiuoli**.

The monastic complex includes the *parlatorio*, with 16thC stained glass; the *sala capitolo*, with a frescoed *Crucifixion* by Mariotti Albertinelli; the *chiostro grande*, embellished with 66 terra-cotta medallions of *Saints and Prophets* by Andrea and Giovanni della Robbia. Off the *chiostro grande* are the cells. The pharmacy sells liqueurs distilled in the monastery.

Gargonza
Map 12G7. 80km (50 miles) SE of Florence, 28km (17 miles) SW of Arezzo. 52048. Arezzo.

The 13thC houses in this tiny fortified village, where Dante took refuge after learning of his exile from Florence, can be rented by the week or, out of season, by the night. Gargonza is freely open to visitors, complete and unspoiled within its walls.

⊞ ℝ **Castello di Gargonza**
Info and bookings: Count Roberto Guicciardini, Castello di Gargonza, 52048 Monte San Savino, Arezzo 🕿 *(0575) 847021 or (055) 241586* 🌐*571466* 🖩 *to* 🖩🖩 🐕 *45 in 20 houses* 🖭 *in each house* 🍽 *outside walls only* 🍴 ⊟ *Closed Jan.*
The interiors have been attractively modernized, and the high position, surrounded by woodland, is open to cooling breezes and extensive views of the Valdichiana. The restaurant, **Il Castello** (🕿 *(0575) 847065* 🖩 *closed Mon*), just outside the walls, offers plain Tuscan cooking.
🞢 🖙 � 🞠 🗦 ⏷ ⏵

Giglio
Map 8K4. 14km (9 miles) SE of Monte Argentario. Getting there: By boat, 1hr from Porto Santo Stefano. 58013. Grosseto. Population: 1,706 **i** *Via Umberto 1, Giglio Porto* 🕿 *(0564) 809265.*

The second largest island in the Tuscan archipelago, Giglio is wilder, poorer and much smaller than *Elba*, being only 8.5km (5 miles) long and 5km (3 miles) across at its widest. The three centers – Giglio Porto, Giglio Castello, a hilltop town, whose maze of steep traffic-free streets is surrounded by anti-pirate walls, and Campese – are linked by a hair-raising bus service. Campese is the main sand-beach resort and there are other sand beaches at Cala dell'Arenella and Cala delle Cannelle.

H The **Arenella** (☎ *(0564) 809340* ◫ *to* ◫◫) is quiet and adequately comfortable; in Giglio Porto is the bright, clean and modest **Il Saraceno** (☎ *(0564) 809006* ◫ *to* ◫◫).

R In Giglio Porto: **Il Doria** (*Via Thaon de Revel* ☎ *(0564) 809000* ◫ *closed Oct to Easter*); **Da Ruggero** (*Via Umberto 1* ☎ *(0564) 809253* ◫ *closed Oct to Easter*); at Giglio Castello, open in the evenings only, is **La Galera** (*Via della Casa Matta* ☎ *(0564) 806106* ◫).

Greve

Map 12F6. 27km (17 miles) s of Florence, 40km (25 miles) n of Siena. 50022. Firenze. Population: 10,232.

The main market town of the Chianti is graced with a delightful asymmetrical central square, Piazza Matteotti, lined with porticoed 17thC buildings.

Events: Market day is Sat, and a wine fair is held in Sept.

H **Villa le Barone**
Via San Leoncino 13, 50020 Panzano in Chianti, Firenze
☎ *(055) 852215* ▥ ⌖ *17* ▭ *17* ⇒ ⇌ ▤ *Closed Nov–Mar.*
An exceptionally attractive country villa in an isolated location.
◰ ❦ ⇝

R The calm, pleasant **Giovanni da Verrazzano** (*Piazza Matteotti* ☎ *(055) 853189* ◫◫ *closed Mon*), has some rooms. Outside the town, **Trattoria Cappelli** (*s on the SS222* ☎ *(055) 852014* ◫◫ *closed Mon*) is part of the Montagliari wine estate, and serves good *chianina* beef.

R **Casprini** ❀
Passi dei Pecorai, 5km (3 miles) to n ☎ *(055) 85716* ◫ □ ▭ ⇐ ⊜
Closed Wed, Aug.
A classic family restaurant. **Specialty:** *Cannoli alla ricotta e verdura.*

Grosseto

Map 8I5. 141 km (87 miles) s of Florence, 73km (45 miles) s of Siena. 58100. Grosseto. Population: 69,301 i Viale Mongerosa 206 ☎ (0564) 22534.

Grosseto is the principal city of the Tuscan Maremma, the coastal plain where the natives regard themselves as a special and separate breed of Tuscans, toughened by centuries of hardship and proud of their land's recently restored fertility.

In the period of the great Etruscan cities which flourished here, the area to the NE of Grosseto was a navigable gulf. By the Middle Ages it was a freshwater lake, which eventually subsided into malaria-infested swampland.

The history of the Maremma after the fall of the Roman Empire was that of a battlefield contested by Florence, Siena, the Papal States and pirates from the Barbary Coast. When it became part of the Sienese territories in the late Middle Ages it was scantily populated; and in the mid-18thC, two centuries after the Florentine conquest of Siena, the area was nearly deserted. The first effective efforts to reclaim the land and rid the Maremma of malaria were initiated by the Lorraine grand duke Leopold II in 1828, but it was not until the early years of this century that significant progress was made. In 1943–44, Grosseto was the victim of severe bombing raids. The early 1950s saw a systematic program of agricultural incentives and repopulation, and since then the population of Grosseto has grown by more than five times.

It is against this violent background that Grosseto today must be seen. Its spirit is that of a modern city which has not quite discovered its own character.

Sights and places of interest

The main square is Piazza Rosselli, just to the N of Porta Nuova. What remains of the original urban nucleus is contained within an impressive hexagon of bastioned **brick walls** built by the 16thC Medici. Traffic is prohibited in the center.

Duomo †

Originally built in 1294–1302, but the imitation Romanesque facade dates from 1845; inside is a 15thC font and, in the left transept, an *Assumption* by Matteo di Giovanni.

Museo Archeologico e d'Arte della Maremma ☆

Piazza Baccarini 3 🕾 *(0564) 27290* 🖭 *Open Mon, Tues, Thurs–Sat 9:30–12:30pm, 4:30–7pm, Sun, hols 9:30–12:30pm. Closed Wed.*

The collection is displayed chronologically beginning with prehistory and ending with 13th–17thC paintings on the second floor.

The ground floor is largely devoted to material excavated from *Roselle*. On the first floor is a topographical explanation of the Etruscan Maremma and material from the sites. On the second floor are 13th–17thC Sienese pictures of which the most noteworthy are Sassetta's *Madonna of the Cherries* and Pietro di Domenico's *Pietà*.

San Francesco †

Piazza della Independenza.

Over the high altar of this 13thC Gothic church is a *Crucifixion*, an early work by Duccio.

🛈 Near the museum is the sensible, modest **La Maremma** (*Via Fulceri P. dei Calboli 5* 🕾 *(0564) 21177* ▮ *closed Tues*); near the station, **Enoteca Ombrone** ▬ (*Viale Matteotti 63–73* 🕾 *(0564) 22585* ▯▯▯ *closed Sun, early July, early Jan*) has a large wine cellar. Outside the town, **La Casareccia**, to the N on the road to *Roselle* at Poggione (*Via Senese 202* 🕾 *(0564) 414470* ▮ *to* ▮▮ *closed Wed, Aug*) is a friendly little restaurant with variable gastronomic standards.

Impruneta

Map **12**E6. *14km (9 miles) s of Florence. 50023. Firenze. Population: 14,884.*

This large agricultural village is located on a plateau overlooking the Greve and Ema valleys.

Event: The lively agricultural fair of St Luke in mid-Oct.

Sights and places of interest

Santa Maria dell'Impruneta ▥ †

The fine porticoed facade which overlooks the main square was added in 1634; the tall bell tower is 13thC. The design of the handsome **aedicules** (1456) flanking the entrance to the polygonal presbytery is attributed to Michelozzo, and they are embellished with terra-cotta decorations by Luca della Robbia. To the right of the church are two pretty cloisters.

🛈 **Bellavista**

Via della Croce 2 🕾 *(055) 2011083* ▮▮▯ ▭ ▬ *Closed Thurs, Nov.*

This unpretentious, cosy, small-town restaurant specializes in traditional Florentine cooking.

🛈 **I Tre Pini**, 6km (4 miles) N at Pozzolatico (🕾 *(055) 208065* ▮▮▯ *closed lunch, Tues, Nov–Dec*) is worth a visit.

Istia d'Ombrone

Map **11**I5. *140 km (87 miles) s of Florence, 7km (4⅔ miles) NE of Grosseto. 58040. Grosseto. Population: 1,405.*

A medieval village with one of the best restaurants of the Tuscan Maremma.

Nearby sights

13km (8 miles) to the SE, taking the road for Scansano, an unpaved road near Pancole leads to the **Castello Sergardi di Montepo**, a romantic fortified 16thC castle.

Ⓡ Terzo Cerchio ✿
Piazza del Castello 1 ☎ *(0564) 409235* ⑊⑊ ▬▬ ▙▜ ⚐ Ⓐ🄴 🆅🅸🆂🅰
Closed Mon, Nov.

It was in the third circle (*terzo cerchio*) of hell that Dante observed the fate
of gluttons, and if this outstanding restaurant has a fault it is the
temptation to commit gluttony. You choose from a succession of courses
brought to your table. The unlabeled Scansano wine is excellent.

La Verna

Map **13***E8. 75km (47 miles)* SE *of Florence, 58km (36 miles)* N
of Arezzo. 52010. Arezzo.

Monastery †
This monastery, reached by a beautiful twisting road of 26km (16 miles)
from *Bibbiena*, was founded in 1214 by St Francis, who received the
stigmata here on Sept 14, 1224. The chief artistic attractions are the
Andrea della Robbia terra-cottas in the churches, of which the loveliest
are the *Annunciation* and *Adoration of the Child* in the Chiesa Maggiore.
 Above the monastery is a magnificent **forest** of old beeches and firs.

Livorno

Map **10***F3. 116 km (72 miles)* W *of Florence, 19km (12 miles)*
S *of Pisa. 57100. Livorno. Population: 177,101*
i *Piazza Cavour* ☎ *(0586) 33111; at the port, Palazzo Dogana*
☎ *(0586) 25320.*

The major commercial port of Tuscany and still one of the
greatest in the Mediterranean, Livorno was the creation of the
Medici grand dukes – their most ambitious and successful
project. The transformation of the medieval fishing village into
a port which would more than compensate for the silted-up port
of Pisa was initiated by Cosimo I in 1571. Six years later, the
new 'ideal city' of Livorno designed by Buontalenti was
founded. In 1593 Ferdinand I declared Livorno an open city,
guaranteeing tax exemptions, free trade with all international
ports, and freedom of worship for all religions; and in 1621 that
remarkable Englishman, Robert Dudley, the marine engineer
in the service of the grand dukes, completed the extension of the
harbor with his great Medicean *mole* (harbor wall).
 By 1600 Livorno had a population of 5,000, enlivened, then
as now, by a substantial Jewish community. 18thC foreign
visitors found it a charming as well as prosperous city with
many fine contemporary palaces. These disappeared along with
the charm and the historic center during the bombardment of 1943.
 The old English name Leghorn, from the early Italian
Legorno, is rarely used today except, of course, to describe the
type of straw hat first made here in the 19thC.

Sights and places of interest

The old pentagonal center envisaged by Buontalenti is bisected
by its main street, Via Grande, which links the huge harbor
complex with the Piazza Repubblica. The city is guarded by
two fortresses: the Fortezza Nuova (1590) above Piazza
Repubblica, and the Fortezza Vecchia (1534), designed by
Antonio da Sangallo the Younger, in the harbor.
Monument to Ferdinand I (*'Quattro Mori' or 'Four Moors'*)
Piazza Micheli.
Facing the old harbor, this esthetically controversial monument
consists of a statue of *Ferdinand I* (1595) wearing the order of St Stephen
by G. Bandini and the **four bronze Moors** added by P. Tacca in 1626.
Some admire these straining Michelangeloesque figures; others would
say that they combine ineptitude with unfeeling virtuosity. The diarist
John Evelyn, who was of the first opinion, described the scene he

witnessed in this piazza in 1644 when Livorno was the chief slave port of the northern Mediterranean: "Here. . . . is such a concourse of slaves, Turcs, Moors and other nations, that the number and confusion is prodigious; some buying, others selling, others drinking, others playing, some working, others sleeping, fighting, singing, weeping, all nearly naked, and miserably chained."

The **English Cemetery** at Via Verdi 63 was the first Protestant cemetery in Italy. Tobias Smollett is buried here.

Museo Civico G. Fattori
Villa Fabbricotti ⬚ *Open Tues–Sat 10am–1pm, Thurs, Sat also 5–8pm in summer, 4–7pm in winter.*
A collection of paintings by the Macchiaioli, and several Modiglianis.

H The **Gran Duca** (*Piazza Micheli 16* ☎ *(0586) 32024* ▮▮) faces the harbor; the **Palazzo** (*Viale Italia 95* ☎ *(0586) 805371* ▮▮▮) is the grand hotel and faces the sea.

R La **Banditella da Cappa** (*Via Diego Angioletti 3* ☎ *(0586) 501246* ▮▮▮ *closed Sun, Aug*) and **Oscar** (*Via O. Franchini 78* ☎ *(0586) 501258* ▮▮ ⊡ ↽ *closed Mon, early Sept, late Dec.*), both at Ardenza, are the best fish restaurants.

R Also: **Antico Moro** (*Via di Franco 59* ☎ *(0586) 34659* ▮▯ *closed Wed, Aug*); **La Barcarola** (*Viale Carducci 63* ☎ *(0586) 402367* ▮▯ *to* ▮▮ *closed Mon, July*); **La Parmigiana** (*Piazza Luigi Orlando* ☎ *(0586) 807180* ▮▯ *closed Sun*), near the harbor.

Lucca ★
Map **14E3***. 74km (46 miles) w of Florence, 22km (14 miles) NE of Pisa.* 55100. *Lucca. Population: 91,814* **i** *Via Vittorio Veneto 40* ☎ *(0583) 46915.*

Alone of all the Tuscan city-states, Lucca resisted the thrust of Florentine imperialism and remained independent of united Tuscany until the 19thC. The town is still a separate and special place, its narrow medieval streets, red-brick palaces and tower houses and elaborate Romanesque churches encircled by the best-preserved 16th–17thC walls in Italy.

A Roman colony from 180 BC, capital city of Tuscany under the medieval Lombard and Frankish emperors, and a free commune from 1119, Lucca emerged in the early 14thC as the second richest city in Tuscany. Under the forceful leadership of the merchant-soldier Castruccio Castracani, Lucca became a serious threat to Florence; but Castracani's death in 1328 left the government divided and open for short periods to subjection by its enemies.

In 1369 Lucca was granted a charter of independence by the Emperor Charles IV. Representative governments alternated with periods of signorial rule until the mid-16thC when the oligarchy closed ranks against the populace. Thus protected from internal opposition the Republic fortified itself against the threat of Cosimo I's pan-Tuscan policies with its new ring of walls and retained its autonomy until 1799. Napoleon gave Lucca to his sister Elisa Baciocchi as a principate in 1805; in 1817 it passed as a duchy to Maria Louisa de Bourbon; and in 1847, Lucca was finally absorbed into the Tuscan grand duchy.

The Romanesque churches of the Tuscan silk town are in the Pisan style, richly embroidered with polychrome marble insets and relief carvings executed for the most part by visiting Lombard and Pisan sculptors. Another, later visitor, Jacopo della Quercia, carved a number of works for Lucca including his early masterpiece, the tomb of *Ilaria del Carretto* in the Duomo. The most talented local sculptor, hardly represented outside his native city, was Matteo Civitali, active in the 15thC.

In the 16th–18thC the Lucchese nobility built grand summer retreats in the cool hills to the NE. These villas (see *Excursions*) are among the most exhilarating examples of Mannerist and Baroque architecture in Tuscany. The Anglicized gardens of many of the villas testify to Lucca's long-standing special relationship with Britain.

Events: The birthplace of Luigi Boccherini and Giacomo Puccini is still musically active. In spring and early summer there is a festival of sacred music performed in the churches. Concerts of contemporary and classical music are held throughout the *Estate Musicale* from July to Sept, and in Aug a festival of music and theater takes place in the Villa at Marlia.

The feast of the Holy Cross is celebrated on the previous evening with a procession from S. Frediano to the Duomo.

An itinerant antique market comes to Piazza San Martino on the second Sun of each month.

Sights and places of interest

Piazza Napoleone is the main square. The Neoclassical monument to *Maria Louisa de Bourbon* in the center is by L. Bartolini. The Palazzo della Provincia (begun 1578) on the W side is based on designs by Ammannati; its early 19thC interior is by L. Nottolini.

A delightful walk can be taken along the tree-shaded path on the 4.2km (3 miles) ring of **ramparts**. Be sure also to see **Via Guinigi** and **Via Fillungo**, well-preserved medieval streets.

Duomo 🏛 † ★

Erected in the 11th–13thC, the cathedral's asymmetrical facade (1204) is largely the work of Guidetto da Como. Under the portico are fine relief carvings (begun 1233) by a Lombard master. The interior was Gothicized in the 14th–15thC. Four of Puccini's ancestors served here as organists and choir-masters.

In the left transept is Jacopo della Quercia's **tomb of Ilaria del Carretto** ★ (c.1406), his earliest surviving masterpiece and the first sculptural creation of the Renaissance to use Roman decorative motifs. The statue of *St John the Evangelist* nearby is also by Jacopo. In the adjoining chapel is an exceptionally fine panel of the *Madonna with Sts Stephen and John the Baptist* by Fra Bartolommeo. In the left nave is the **tempietto** (1484) by Matteo Civitali which houses the Volto Santo, the 11thC effigy of Christ carried through the city in procession on Holy Cross eve. Other works in the Duomo by Civitali include the pulpit (1498) in the right nave, and, in the right transept, two angels (1477) and the monumental S. Regalo altarpiece.

Museo Nazionale 🏛

Villa Guinigi 🎫 *Open Tues–Sat 9am–2pm, Sun, hols 9am–1pm.*

The Villa Guinigi was built in 1418 for Paolo Guinigi, political leader of Lucca from 1400–30.

Ground floor: Etruscan and Roman pieces excavated locally; works by Lucchese sculptors of the 8th–15thC, including M. Civitali.

First floor: 13th–19thC paintings, intarsia work, furniture and textiles. One of the painted crosses in Rm. XI is signed by Berlinghieri. In Rm. XIV are two altarpieces by Fra Bartolommeo.

Pinacoteca Nationale 🏛

Palazzo Mani, Via Galli Tassi 43 🎫 *Open Tues–Sat 9am–2pm, Sun, hols 9am–1pm.*

This collection of Renaissance to 19thC pictures from the Medici collection was given to Lucca by Leopold II. The 17thC palace retains much of its elaborate furniture.

San Frediano 🏛 † ★

Erected from 1112–47 on the site of a 6thC basilica. The mosaic of the *Ascension* on the facade, possibly by Berlinghieri, was heavily restored in the 19thC. Inside, the 12thC font at the top of the right nave is decorated with relief carvings of the story of *Moses*, the *Good Shepherd* and the *Apostles*. In the Trenta Chapel at the bottom of the left aisle are reliefs by

Jacopo della Quercia and assistants, notably a Gothic polyptych **altarpiece** (1422) with a superb predella.

Across the Via Fillungo the oval outline of the Roman amphitheater is traced by medieval houses forming the intensely picturesque **Piazza Anfiteatro** ☆ Via Cesare Battisti, which twists s towards S. Michele in Foro, is flanked by 17th–18thC palaces.

San Michele in Foro Ⅲ † ☆

A few steps to the N of Piazza Napoleone, Piazza San Michele occupies the site of the Roman forum. On the corner of Via Vittorio Veneto is the Renaissance **Palazzo Pretorio**, designed by M. Civitali, altered in the 16thC.

Begun in 1143, the church of S. Michele is a typical example of Pisan-Lucchese architecture. The high white marble facade belongs to the 13thC and the Lucchese tradition of rich decoration; the apse is in the Pisan style, possibly by Diotisalvi. Inside is a *Madonna and Child* by Andrea della Robbia and, in the left transept, a panel painting of *Four Saints* by Filippo Lippi.

Among other notable churches in Lucca are S. Giovanni, S. Maria Forisportam, S. Giulia and S. Alessandro.

Ⓗ **Napoleon**

Viale Europa 1 ☎ *(0583) 53141* ⅢⅢ ⬛ *63* ▭ *63* ▦ ▢ ▱ ⇥
Location: Outside the walls to the sw. Thoughtfully modernized behind the earlier villa facade.
‡ ▢ ▱ ⎌

Ⓡ **Buca di San Antonio**

Via della Cervia 3 ☎ *(0583) 55881* ⅢⅠ ▭ ⬛ ⬛ ▦ ⬛ AE CB ⓦ
Ⓒ Ⓥ️ⓈⒶ *Closed Sun eve, Mon, late July.*
An agreeably intimate restaurant. Regional specialties.

Ⓡ **Solferino**

San Macario in Piano ☎ *(0583) 59118* Ⅰ▢ *to* ⅢⅠ ▭ ⬛ ▭ ⬛ AE
CB ⓦ *Closed Tues eve, Wed. Aug.*
The ambitious cuisine includes local and international dishes.
Specialties: *Spaghetti alla beppe, pappardelle in salsa di melograno, filetto di bue in crosta.*

See also *Excursions* below.

Shopping

Many gourmets consider the olive oil of Lucca to be the best produced in Italy – be careful that you are buying real Lucca oil.
Ice cream parlor
Gelateria Veneta di Arnoldo (*Via Vittorio Veneto 74*
☎ *(0583) 47037*) serves the best ice cream in town.

Excursions

1. Villas outside Lucca ★
Head N from Lucca on the *Abetone* road, along the E bank of the River Serchio. After 16km (10 miles) is the 11th–12thC Pieve di Brancoli.

Then make for Marlia, near Fraga.
Villa Imperiale Ⅲ

Marlia ▰ ▮▮ *Open July–Oct Tues, Thurs, Sun 9am–noon, 3–6pm; Nov–June Tues–Sat 9am–noon, 3–6pm.*
The most famous and imposing of the villas near Lucca, adapted and redecorated in First Empire style when it was the summer residence of Elisa Baciocchi. Magnificent 17thC park.

Take the road for Segromigno Monte.
Villa Mansi Ⅲ

3km (1¾ miles) E of Marlia ▰ ▮ *Open daily 10am–12:30pm, 3–6pm.*
A late-16thC villa transformed in the early 18thC with a charming facade and good Baroque furnishings and pictures on the first floor. A tavern attached to the villa serves produce from the estate.

Take the road for Camigliano.

Villa Torrigiani 🏛
1.5km (1 mile) s of Segromigno 🔲 *Open daily Easter to Nov 9am–1pm, 2–6pm; park always open in daylight.*
Built in the 16thC, with a spectacular Mannerist facade. The 17thC park was Anglicized in the 19thC except for the sunken garden and the ingenious surprise fountains.

🍴 **La Mora**
Sesto Moriano ☎ *(0583) 57109* 🔲 to 🔲 🔲 🍽 🚗 🚐 *Closed Thurs, Oct.*
Near Ponte a Moriano, 9km (6 miles) from Lucca. The shop sells wines and olive oil. *Specialties: Garfagnana soups.*

---

2. Santa Maria del Giudice 8km (5 miles) sw of Lucca
Two Romanesque churches in the Pisan-Lucchese style: **San Giovanni Battista**, and **Santa Maria Assunta**.

🍴 **Da Peppino** is large, modern, popular (☎ *(0583) 379482* 🔲 to 🔲 *closed Mon, Aug*).

Massa
Map **14**D2. *115km (71 miles) NW of Florence, 45km (28 miles) NW of Pisa. 54100. Massa–Carrara. Population: 65,814.*
A booming, untidy frontier town at the mouth of the Frigido valley below the foothills of the Apuan Alps, Massa did not become part of Tuscany until 1859, and it is still the least 'Tuscan' of Tuscan provincial capitals.

Piazza Aranci, the old center, is dominated by the startling 17thC Palazzo Cybo Malaspina, which encloses an attractive loggiaed courtyard (1665) by G.F. Bergamini. The Duomo has a modern facade and a Baroque interior.

Above the town is the medieval **Rocca** (🔲 *open Tues–Sat 9am–noon, 4–7pm*) and a Renaissance palace which was the residence of the 16thC Malaspina dukes.

Massa Marittima
Map **10**H4. *132km (79 miles) SW of Florence, 64km (40 miles) SW of Siena. 58024. Grosseto. Population: 10,297* **i** *(summer only) Palazzo Comunale* ☎ *(0566) 902296.*
The mineral-rich territory of Massa Marittima was mined by the Etruscans and Romans; the copper and silver mines were the economic base of the independent republic which was constitutionally established in 1225 and flourished proudly until it was conquered by Siena in 1335. The Duomo, one of the most beautiful and richly decorated churches in Tuscany, was erected during the period of communal independence; and the first miners' code in Europe was drawn up in the city in 1310.

Event: The *Balestra del Girofalco*, a crossbow competition with a mechanical falcon as target, takes place in medieval costume on May 20 and second Sun in Aug.

Sights and places of interest
The town is in two distinct parts: the Romanesque lower town or Città Vecchia is linked by Via Moncini to the Gothic upper town or Città Nuova, built after the Sienese conquest.

The center of the old town is Piazza Garibaldi.
Duomo 🏛 † ★
This lovely cathedral in the Pisan Romanesque-Gothic style was completed between 1287–1304. The **relief carvings** over the portal

depict five episodes in the life of San Cerbone, patron saint of the
cathedral, with the beguiling beasts that helped him. The campanile
rising from the arcaded left flank was largely reconstructed in the 1920s.

At the top of the right aisle is the font, where St Bernardino was
baptized in 1380, with relief carvings (1267) by Giraldo da Como and a
15thC tabernacle rising from its center. In the chapel to the left of the
high altar is a panel painting of the *Madonna della Grazie* (c.1316),
closely influenced by Duccio's *Maestà* in *Siena*.

Ask the sacristan to unlock the access door to the subterranean
chapels. In the polygonal undercroft is the exquisite **Arca di San
Cerbone** (1324), San Cerbone's tomb, by the Sienese sculptor Coro da
Gregorio in a painterly style influenced by illuminated manuscripts.

Opposite the Duomo is the **Palazzo Comunale**, the town hall created
from a complex of 14th–15thC tower houses.

Museo/Palazzo del Podestà IIII
☒ *Open summer Tues–Sun 10:30am–12:30pm, 4–7pm.*
The magistrate's palace, built in c.1230, now houses a small
archeological collection and Sienese pictures; outstanding is A.
Lorenzetti's *Maestà*.

Upper town (*Città Nuova*)
The upper town is guarded by the huge **Fortezza dei Senesi**, built by the
Sienese after their conquest of Massa Marittima in 1334. Its center is
Piazza Matteotti, from where the Corso Diaz leads to the Gothic church
of S. Agostino (1299–1313), which possesses interesting 16th–17thC
pictures by Empoli, Pacchiarotti, Lorenzo Lippi and others.

Nearby sights
Museum of Mining (Museo della Miniera) in Viale Martiri di Niccioleta
(☒ *hours as museum in Palazzo del Podestà*).

Ⓡ **Roma** (*Via Norma Parenti 17–19* ☎ *(0566) 902644* ⅢⓁ *closed Fri*).

Montalcino

*Map **8**H6. 109km (67 miles) s of Florence, 41km (25 miles) s
of Siena. 53024. Siena. Population: 5,702 i Via Mazzini 41
☎ (0577) 848242.*

Montalcino stands on an olive-clad hill above the Ombrone and
Asso valleys. The site was inhabited by the Etruscans and
Romans, and in the early Middle Ages belonged to the
Benedictine abbey of **Sant'Antimo** (see opposite). A period of
communal independence came to an end in 1260 when the town
was subjected to Sienese rule after the battle of Montaperti.
Montalcino provided sanctuary for Sienese aristocratic
Republicans who fled their besieged city in 1555. Sienese
gratitude is still expressed twice a year when the standard
bearers representing Montalcino occupy the place of honor in
the procession which preceeds the Palio.

Brunello di Montalcino is one of the great Italian wines.

Sights and places of interest
Piazza del Popolo is the main square; the **Palazzo Comunale**
with its high tower dates from the 13th–14thC; the imposing
loggia was added in the 14th–15thC. Above, in Piazza
Garibaldi, is the church of **Sant'Egidio** built by the Sienese in
1325. Over the first altar on the left notice the wooden
Crucifixion (15thC) framed by 16thC inlaid wooden doors.

The **Rocca** which dominates the town was built by the
Sienese in 1361 and was one of the most crucial defense posts of
the Republic. Inside is an *enoteca* of local wines.

Museo Civico e Diocesano
Via di Ricasoli 29 ☒ *Open daily summer 10am–noon, 4–6pm;
winter 10am–noon, 3–5pm.*
Below the Rocca, this museum houses 14th–15thC Sienese pictures;
ecclesiastic objects including a 12thC illuminated bible; 15thC

polychrome wooden statues; and a separate archeological collection.

In Piazza Cavour is the former pharmacy of the Hospital of Santa Maria, frescoed by V. Tamagni.

Nearby sights
Sant'Antimo Ⅲ † ★
Near Castelnuovo Abate, 8km (5 miles) to s. Apply for entry to custodian at Via del Centro 12, Castelnuovo Abate.

This radiantly lovely Romanesque church, set in a gentle golden valley, is built of travertine with architectonic decorations in alabaster and translucent onyx quarried locally. It dates mostly from the early 12thC. The monastery was founded, according to tradition, by Charlemagne early in the 9thC. The doorway on the left flank, adorned with geometric carvings in the Lombard style, and the crypt survive from the earlier building. The beautiful **interior** is embellished with fine capitals. There are frescoed apartments off the clerestory.

R The best of the restaurants in the center of the town is **Il Giglio** (*Via S. Salone 49* ☎ *(0577) 848167* **◫** *closed Mon*).

R **Taverna dei Barbi**
2km (1¼ miles) s of Montalcino, off the Sant'Antimo road
☎ *(0577) 848277* ▭ ➤ ◉ *Closed Wed, two weeks in June.*
Superb Brunello wines with a limited selection of plain Tuscan food.

Monte Amiata
Map **8***H6.*

The isolated conical peak of this extinct volcano 1,738m (5,702ft.) high is visible from Siena and in much of its art.

"Surely here, if anywhere in the world," wrote the Sienese Pope Pius II in his *Commentaries*, "sweet shade and silvery springs and green grass and smiling meadows allure poets." The upper slopes are equipped for skiing and climbing.

The summit is most easily reached from *Abbadia San Salvatore*, the most populous center. Other, more picturesque villages, are Arcidosso, Bagnone, Castel del Piano, Piancastagnaio and Santa Fiora.

Montecatini Terme
Map **15***D4. 49km (30 miles)* NW *of Florence, 49km (30 miles)* NE *of Pisa. 51016. Pistoia. Population: 21,764* **i** *Viale Verdi 66* ☎ *(0572) 70109. The season is Apr–Oct.*

One of the most famous and fashionable spas in Europe, Montecatini Terme was laid out in the early 20thC around a stately park. The warm saline waters are recommended for liver ailments and skin problems. The café of the **Stabilimento Tettuccio** is the main meeting place.

From Viale A. Diaz, a funicular railway ascends to the beautifully situated old town, Montecatini Alto. To the N there is lovely walking country in the Valdinievole.

Nearby sight
8km (5 miles) s at Ponte Buggianese is the church frescoed by the modern painter Pietro Annigoni.

H Montecatini has some 500 hotels, mainly clustered around the **Parco delle Terme**; most open only during the season. The best-known luxury hotel is the **Grand Hotel e la Pace** (*Via della Torretta 1* ☎ *(0572) 75801* **▥** *closed Nov–Mar*); and equally central is the first-class **Manzoni** (*Viale Manzoni 28* ☎ *(0572) 70175* **◫** *to* **▥** *closed Nov–Mar*).

Reliable hotels in the less expensive range include: **Rigoletto** (*Via Baragiola 5* ☎ *(0572) 70063* **◫**); and **Torretta** (*Viale Bustichini 27* ☎ *(0572) 70305* **◫** *closed Nov–Mar*).

Montefollonico

Map 12H7. 112km (70 miles) SE of Florence, 60km (37 miles) SE of Siena. 53040. Siena. Population: 820.

A walled hill village overlooking the valleys of the Orcia and Chiana. There is also an unpaved road from *Montepulciano* which can be walked in 45min.

Ⓡ **La Chiusa**

☎ *(0577) 65484* ⅢⅢ ⌷ 🚗 🚙 ◁€ *Closed Tues, Nov–Mar.*

The young owners of this outstanding country restaurant combine deep interest in the culinary traditions of the area with an irrepressible inventiveness. Do not refuse the array of delicate antipasti, the soups (even better than the pasta) or the *gelato 'Dania,'* a soft caramel ice cream.

Monte Oliveto Maggiore

Map 8J6. 104km (65 miles) SE of Florence, 36km (22 miles) SE of Siena. 53020. Siena.

The abbey †

⌷ 🚗 *Open daily 9am–12:45pm, 3–7pm.*

Magnificently situated above the barren clay hills near *Siena*, the red-brick buildings of this abbey date from the 14th–18thC; their institutional appearance is the result of a 19thC restoration.

The **chiostro grande** is decorated with important but heavily restored and overpainted frescoes of *Scenes from the Life of St Benedict*. Nine are by Signorelli (1497–98), the rest by Sodoma (from 1505). In the church the intarsiaed **choir stalls** (1503–05) by Giovanni da Verona are exceptionally sophisticated exercises in perspective.

Ⓡ **La Torre** (☎ *(0577) 707022, closed Tues* ⅢⅢ).

Montepulciano ☆

Map 12H7. 119km (74 miles) SE of Florence, 65km (40 miles) SE of Siena. 53045. Siena. Population: 14,297 i Via Cavour 15 ☎ *(0578) 77049.*

Like *Pienza*, 14 km (9 miles) to the w, Montepulciano is neither town nor village, but a miniature Renaissance city. See these two little hill cities one after another and you will have captured the essence of the 15thC urban ideal as realized by some of the most distinguished Italian architects of the period. From the 12thC, Montepulciano modeled itself on Florence and Siena, its political masters. Its fortifications were rebuilt when Montepulciano fell to the Sienese in 1495–1511.

Agnolo Ambrogini, the leading humanist poet and scholar of the 15thC and tutor to Lorenzo de' Medici's children, was born in Montepulciano and called himself Poliziano after the medieval Latin name of his birthplace, Mons Politianus. The Jesuit Cardinal Robert Bellarmine was largely responsible for the flourish of Baroque architecture which followed.

Vino Nobile di Montepulciano is a redoubtable Tuscan wine.

Event: An annual music festival, the *Cantiere Internazionale d'Arte*, takes place here in early Aug. Founded in 1975 and run by a distinguished international committee, it emphasises community involvement in performances of 20thC music.

Sights and places of interest

Follow the Corso from Porta al Prato to the far end of the town and loop back along its western edge.

The Corso

Via Gracciano nel Corso: The Corso is lined with good Renaissance palaces. No. 99, Palazzo Avignonesi, is attributed to Vignola; no. 72, the

Cocconi, is attributed to Antonio da Sangallo the Elder. The lower story of no. 81, the Palazzo Bucelli, is faced with a mosaic of Etruscan and Roman tombs and cinerary urns. On the right is Michelozzo's delightful, Gothic-Renaissance church of **Sant'Agostino**; the lovely terra-cotta relief over the portal of the *Madonna and Child with Sts John the Baptist and Augustine* is also by Michelozzo.

Via di Voltaia nel Corso: The palace on the left, the Cervini, no. 21, with graduated rustication and a breaking-wave frieze, was designed by Antonio da Sangallo the Elder but not completed. Farther along on the left is the church of Gesù, which has a charming curved Baroque interior.

The last stretch of the Corso, **Via dell'Opio**, leads to the Via del Poliziano past no. 5, the house where Poliziano was born in 1454, to the Gothic church of S. Maria dei Servi, which has a Baroque interior.

The highest point of Montepulciano is its center, the wide and splendidly various **Piazza Grande**.

Duomo †

Designed by Ippolito Scalza and built on the site of the earlier parish church from 1592–1630, the Duomo contains a superb altarpiece of the *Assumption* (1401), possibly Taddeo di Bartolo's best work. Michelozzo's **Tomb of Bartolomeo Aragazzi**, dismantled in the 17thC, is now displayed in fragments placed to the left of the entrance, on the first two pillars of the nave, on either side of the altar and elsewhere. Notice also, in the right nave, the 15thC Sienese school polychrome *Annunciation*.

The **Palazzo Comunale**, next to the Duomo, was begun in the late 14thC, but its facade is later, possibly designed by Michelozzo. Opposite are the Tarugi (no. 3) and Contucci (no. 6) palaces by Antonio da Sangallo the Elder.

Museo Civico Ⅲ

Via Ricci 11 🔄 *Open Tues–Sun*

The Gothic Neri-Orselli Palace houses 13thC–17thC paintings, terracottas and 15thC illuminated choir books.

Nearby sight

San Biagio Ⅲ † ★

Situated just outside the town to the sw, this church (1518–45) is the masterpiece of Antonio da Sangallo the Elder. The densely classicizing interior, all in the same pale-honey travertine, is weighted with loyalty to the architectural principles of Bramante. The **Canon's House** and **well-head** were also designed by Sangallo but completed posthumously.

Ⓗ Ⓡ **Il Marzocco**

Piazza Savonarola 🕿 *(0578) 77262* ⅢⅢ 🔄 *17* 🔄 *7* 🔄 🔄 *VISA*
Conveniently located inside the walls, this small hotel-restaurant offers clean, cosy rooms and good, simply prepared food.
🔽

Ⓡ **Porta di Bacco**

Porta di Bacco 2 🕿 *(0578) 77907* ☐ *AE*
Light, wholesome snacks and local wines, oil and cheese on sale.

Ⓡ **Pulcino**

Pulcino, 2.5km (1½ miles) to se 🕿 *(0578) 77905* ⅢⅢ 🔄 🔄 🔄 🔄
Closed Mon.
A big, heartily informal country restaurant with long, shared tables and ravishing views. See also *Montefollonico*.

Monteriggione

*Map **11**F5. 55km (34 miles) s of Florence, 15km (9 miles) NW of Siena. 53035. Siena. Population: 6,573.*

A complete medieval village encircled by 13thC walls built by the Sienese against the Florentines: Dante compared the 14 towers to giants (*Inferno, XXXI*).

Nearby sight

Abbadia Isola †

Less than 3km (1¾ miles) sw, this tiny village conserves a Romanesque church in the Lombard style from the 11thC Cistercian abbey of

S. Salvatore. The church possesses an altarpiece (1471) by Sano di Pietro; a fresco of the *Madonna and Child with Saints* by Taddeo di Bartolo; an early 15thC font; and an Etruscan-Roman cinerary urn. In the priest's house is a *Madonna and Child*, possibly by Duccio.

H R **Casalta**
Strove, 53035 Monteriggioni, Siena ☎ *(0577) 301002* ▮▯ ⬥ 10
🛏 10 ⬥ ⬛ ⬛ ≡ ▣ *Closed Nov–Feb. Restaurant closed Wed.*
A well-managed hotel and restaurant serving above-average Tuscan food, 6km (4 miles) sw past Abbadia Isola.

R **Il Pozzo**
Piazza Roma 2 ☎ *(0577) 304127* ▮▯ ⌑ *Closed Sun eve, Mon, Aug.*
An elegant and efficient country restaurant.

Monte San Savino

Map **12***G7. 86km (53 miles) SE of Florence, 22km (14 miles) sw of Arezzo. 52048. Arezzo. Population: 7,565.*
An agricultural hill village, the birthplace of the sculptor Andrea Sansovino. The main street is the Corso Sangallo, which is lined with fine palaces and churches. The little church of Santa Chiara in Piazza Gamurrini contains terra-cottas by Sansovino and other sculptors. Sansovino is thought to have designed the handsome **Loggia dei Mercanti** farther along the Corso. The **Palazzo Comunale** opposite is by Antonio da Sangallo the Elder.

H **Sangallo** (*Piazza Vittorio Veneto* ☎ *(0575) 843010* ▮▯), a modern, quiet hotel.

H R See also *Gargonza*.

Monti dell'Uccellina, Parco Naturale della Maremma ☆

Map **11***I–J5. 157km (98 miles) s of Florence, 17km (10 miles) s of Grosseto. Entrance at Alberese* ☎ *(0564) 407098* ▨ ▮
on foot ✿ *Open Wed, Sat, Sun, hols.*
The extremely varied ecological balance of the coastal terrain is protected in the Maremma Nature Reserve. Demonstrations of cattle roping are sometimes given by the local *butteri* (cowboys).

R **Tonale**, an isolated farmhouse at Podere Tonale near Alberese (☎ *(0564) 407027* ▮▯ *closed Thurs*). See also *Talamone*.

Orbetello

Map **8***J5. 183km (113 miles) s of Florence, 43km (27 miles) s of Grosseto. 58015. Grosseto. Population: 14,749* **i** *Corso Italia 121* ☎ *(0564) 867389.*
The capital of the Spanish Garrison States, the *Presidii*, from 1557 retains something of the atmosphere (and the faces) of a Spanish colonial town. The fortifications on the mainland side were initiated by the Sienese and extended by the Spanish.

The **Duomo** (1376) has a pretty Gothic facade decorated in the Sienese style. In the first chapel on the right is a rare pre-Romanesque marble **altar front**.

The **Orbetello Oasis**, a sanctuary for migrating birds, is nearby. For information ☎ (0564) 860239.

H **Nazionale** (*Corso Italia 48* ☎ *(0564) 867062* ▮▯) is old-fashioned and basic; **Presidi** (*Via Mura di Levante* ☎ *(0564) 867601* ▮▯ *to* ▮▯) is a sensible, friendly hotel on the lagoon.

Ⓡ **Da Egisto** (*Corso Italia 186* ☎ *(0564) 867469* Ⅲ□ *closed Mon, Nov*) is at one end of the Corso; **La Pergola** (*Via Roma 14* ☎ *(0564) 867585* Ⅲ□ *closed Thurs, Oct*) is at the other; **Il Cantuccio** (*Via Mentana 7* ☎ *(0564) 867587* Ⅲ□ *closed Mon*) specializes in imaginative antipasti.

Two restaurants 7km (4¾ miles) NE on the Via Aurelia near Orbetello Scalo, both with rooms, are: **Il Cacciatore** (☎ *(0564) 862020* □ *closed Wed*); and **La Ruota** (☎ *(0564) 862137* Ⅲ□ *closed Wed*). See also *Port'Ercole, Porto Santo Stefano.*

Pescia
Map 15D4. 61km (38 miles) NW of Florence, 19km (12 miles) NE of Lucca. 51017. Pistoia. Population: 18,979.

This horticultural and papermaking center in the Valdinievole is renowned for its carnations and asparagus. The town has been divided into five districts or *quinti* since the 13thC. The civic center, Piazza Mazzini, is on the right bank of the River Pescia; the religious center, Piazza del Duomo, is on the left bank.

Sights and places of interest
Piazza Mazzini
The long, narrow square is a lively architectural farrago of 14th–19thC houses, closed at the S end by the 15thC **Oratory of the Madonna di Piè di Piazza**, possibly designed by Brunelleschi's adopted son Buggiano, and at the N end by the 13th–14thC Palazzo dei Viacri.

In the nearby Piazza S. Stefano is the **Museo Civico** (🔲 *open Mon, Wed, Fri 4–7pm*) with Tuscan paintings of the 14th–16thC.
Duomo †
The Baroque Duomo (1693) has a late 19thC facade and a sturdy Romanesque-Gothic campanile. Inside is the Renaissance **Turini Chapel** by Giuliano di Baccio d'Agnolo, and the remains of a 13thC ambo.
San Francesco †
Via Battisti.
The restored interior of this Gothic church contains a rare Romanesque painting by Bonaventura Berlinghieri of *St Francis* (1235), executed only 9yr after the death of the saint. The Brunelleschian **Orlandi-Cardini Chapel** (1451) may have been designed by Buggiano.

Also in Via Battisti is the 11th–14thC Oratory of Sant' Antonio containing a moving wooden group of the *Deposition.*

The huge steel and glass flower market, the **Nuovo Mercato dei Fiori**, occupies a site of 48,000sq.yd. on the road to Chiesina Uzzanese.

Nearby sights
3km (1¾ miles) to the E of Pescia is the beautifully located village of Uzzano, and 12km (7 miles) to the N is the isolated **Pieve di Castelvecchio** (11th–12thC), the area's best Romanesque church.
See also *Collodi.*

Ⓡ **Cecco** ✿
Viale Forti 84 ☎ *(0572) 477955* Ⅲ□ 🔲 ≧ 🛋 🚗 *Closed Mon, early July, Nov.*
Pleasant service and exceptional food. In Apr and May try the local *asparagi giganti.* **Specialties**: *Pastas, pollastrino al mattone.*

Pienza ★
Map 9H7. 120km (75 miles) S of Florence, 52km (33 miles) of Siena. 53026. Siena. Population: 2,622 i Vicolo della Canonica 1 ☎ *(0578) 74558.*
Few men have left such a vivid and complete picture of their period as did Enea Silvio Piccolomini, born in 1405 of an impoverished branch of a noble Sienese family, Pope as Pius II from 1458–64, in his remarkably candid autobiography, the *Commentaries.*

Pienza, the Utopian city with which he glorified his humble birthplace, Corsignano, is the first modern example of considered town planning. This joyous little Renaissance new town is a celebration of the bracing winds of change that blew from every direction through the culture of 15thC Italy. It is a meeting ground of the Gothic and Renaissance styles, of the German church architecture Pius had seen on his travels and the strict Classical principles laid down by Alberti, of Florentine and Sienese art, of the Tuscan countryside and the sophisticated urbanity of the Tuscan quattrocento spirit.

As soon as Pius was elected Pope he commissioned Bernardo Rossellino to rebuild Corsignano. Work began in 1459. Three years later the piazza and street grid were complete and the new city was renamed Pienza by Papal bull. Pius left instructions that his cathedral, "the finest in all Italy," should never be altered in the smallest detail. The remote location of Pienza has ensured that his order has been carried out.

Sights and places of interest

The central **Piazza Pio II** is like an open-air room looking S through the two window spaces on either side of the cathedral, which is flanked by the Palazzo Piccolomini on the right and the Palazzo Vescovile (Bishop's Palace) on the left. The N side is closed by the Palazzo Comunale and a wing of the Ammannati Palace, built by one of Pius' cardinals. The beautifully carved wellhead (1462) was designed by Rossellino.

Cattedrale ⅢⅢ †
The travertine facade follows Alberti's Classical principles of organization. On the pediment is the papal coat of arms. The interior was inspired by the German *Hallenkirchen* Pius admired.

He specially commissioned the **paintings** by illustrious Sienese artists: Giovanni di Paolo, Matteo di Giovanni, Vecchietta and Sano di Pietro. The Classical frames and the decorative carvings elsewhere in the church were executed by Sienese craftsmen. The Gothic **canons' stalls** (1462) in the central chapel are magnificent. In the crypt, below the apse, is a **baptismal font** by Rossellino.

Museo della Cattedrale
Open daily Nov–Feb 10am–1pm, 2–4pm; Mar–Oct 10am–1pm, 3–6pm.

In the Canon's House. Sienese paintings, Flemish tapestries, illuminated choir-books and ecclesiastic vestments including, most notably, the **cope** embroidered for Pius II in England.

Palazzo Piccolomini ⅢⅢ
Piazza Pio II. First floor open daily 10am–12:30pm, 3–6pm; ring bell for admission.

The papal residence is a rougher version of Alberti's and Rossellino's *Rucellai Palace, Florence*, with one important addition, the three-tiered loggia on the S side. The elegant courtyard gives access to the hanging gardens below the palace.

Palazzo Vescovile
Pius acquired for Rodrigo Borgia, the future Pope Alexander VI, the old Gothic Palazzo Pretorio, which Borgia adapted and later gave to the city as the Bishop's Palace. †

Pieve di Corsignano †
Below the town, 1km (⅝ mile) from the Porta al Ciglio. Pius II was baptized in the rough stone font which remains in this endearing little Romanesque church which now stands alone in a sloping olive grove.

Il Prato (*Piazza Dante 25* ☎ *(0578) 74601* ▯ *closed Wed, July*). See also *Montalcino*, *Montefollonico* and *Montepulciano*.

Shopping
The **Bottega Verde** (*Corso Rossellino 38*) sells wine and herbs.

Pietrasanta

*Map **14**D3. 104km (64 miles) NW of Florence, 35km (22 miles) N of Pisa. 55045. Lucca. Population: 25,722 **i** Via Donizetti 14, Tonfano ☎ (0584) 20332.*

The main town of the Versilia and center of marble working is 3.5km (2 miles) inland from its coastal resort Marina di Pietrasanta. The imposing 13th–14thC Duomo is much restored.

Event: An exhibition of marble work by local artisans is held July–Sept in the Consorzio Artigiani.

R **Baffardello**, 2.5km (1½ miles) S at Tonfano (☎ (0584) 21788 ▯ *closed Mon, Aug*); **Wagener**, 3.5km (2 miles) E at Valdicastello Carducci (☎ (0584) 772018 ▯ *closed Thurs*) offers homey food in an old marble workshop. See also *Forte dei Marmi*.

Pisa ★

*Map **14**E3. 91km (56 miles) W of Florence, 3km (2 miles) N of Galileo Galilei international airport at S. Giusto. 56100. Pisa. Population: 103,849 **i** Piazza del Duomo ☎ (050) 23535.*

The golden age of Pisa was the 12thC, when the Duomo was completed and the Baptistry and Campanile were begun. Pisa had enjoyed a modest maritime economy even during the Dark Ages, thanks to its natural harbor at the mouth of the Arno, and was favored by successive emperors who needed the support of its strong navy. In 1162 Emperor Federico Barbarossa granted the commune control of a large coastal territory stretching to the N and S beyond the modern Tuscan borders.

The Duomo, a mix of the Italian and Oriental styles familiar to Pisan sailor merchants, was widely copied and infused

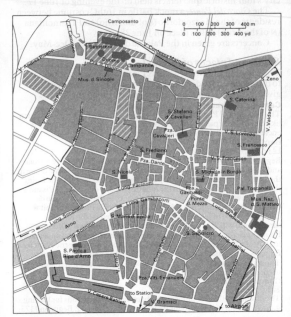

Tuscan Romanesque architecture with new vigor. In sculpture, too, Pisa led the way, producing in Nicola and Giovanni Pisano the first great modern figure sculptors.

After the destruction of its fleet by the Genoese at the battle of Meloria in 1284, the communal government, distracted by internal conflict, neglected the shallow harbor, which began gradually to silt up. The city fell to Florence in 1406, the port in 1421. There was one final bid for independence in 1495 when Pisa, under the protection of Charles VIII, revolted, not to be retaken until 1509.

The Florentines paid special attention to the welfare of their prize conquest, which remained commercially active even after the harbor had finally silted up in the 16thC. The University, which is today one of the most respected in Italy, was revived in 1472 by Lorenzo de' Medici, who temporarily forbade Florentines to study elsewhere, and in 1561 Cosimo I made Pisa headquarters of his new Crusading Order of St Stephen.

Pisa's most illustrious son was Galileo, who taught at the University (which has had a strong science faculty ever since). In the 19thC when Walter Savage Landor, Shelley, Byron and later the Brownings all made their homes in Pisa for short periods, the city was a brooding backwater shrouded in the mists of its Maremma where the rich grazing lands had once been a source of its republican prosperity. Elizabeth Barrett Browning found it "very beautiful and full of repose"; but to Shelley's more feverish imagination Pisa sometimes seemed "a desolation of a city, which was the cradle, and is now the grave of an extinguished people." In the last years of World War II some of Pisa's greatest monuments were severely damaged.

Events: The annual *Regatta di San Ranieri*, a race among the city's four historic quarters, is held on the evening of June 17.

The *Gioco del Ponte*, a mock battle in 16thC costume between residents of the Mezzogiorno (s of the Arno) and Tramontana (N of the Arno), takes place on June 28.

Concerts are given in the Palazzo dei Cavalieri, Dec-May.

Sights and places of interest

The center of the modern city is Piazza Garibaldi. Immediately to its s is the **Ponte di Mezzo**, the city's oldest bridge, which gives the best view of the elegant palaces lining the Arno.

Campo dei Miracoli *(Piazza del Duomo)* ★

The buildings of Pisa's religious center are placed on their emerald lawn like carved ivory pieces in a great ecclesiastical game. The complex is enclosed on the w and N sides by sections of the 13thC city walls.

Baptistry ⅢⅢ † ★

○ Open daily 9am–1pm, 3pm to sunset.

Begun in 1152 by Diotisalvi, carried forward from 1260–84 by Nicola and Giovanni Pisano, the Baptistry was completed by its Gothic dome in the 14thC. Of the four beautiful portals notice especially the one facing the Duomo. The *Madonna* in the lunette is a copy of Giovanni Pisano's original now in the Museo Nazionale. Inside, to the left of Guido da Como's octagonal **baptismal font** (1246), is Nicola Pisano's **pulpit** ★ (1260); the style of his relief carvings was affected by the Roman sarcophaghi which in the 13thC were used as the tombs of Christian Pisans buried around the Duomo; this pulpit marks the first appearance in Italy of Classical Gothic sculpture. The panels illustrate the *Nativity*, *Epiphany*, *Presentation at the Temple*, *Crucifixion* and *Last Judgement*. The statues around the walls, by Nicola and Giovanni Pisano, were originally on the exterior of the Baptistry.

Campanile ⅢⅢ † ★

○ ✳ Open daily 9am to sunset.

The circular bell tower of Pisa is perhaps even more famous for leaning 4.5m (15ft) out of line than for its architectural elegance. Begun in 1173, its foundations were tilted by a settling of the soil when the third story was half built. After a pause of 100yr the tower was completed in the mid-14thC. It is, of course, from this tower that Galileo is supposed to have dropped the three metal balls of different masses which disproved Aristotle's theories about the acceleration of falling bodies. A spiral staircase of 294 steps leads to the top.

Camposanto *(Cemetery)* ☆
🚇 *Open daily 9am to sunset.*

Legend has it that earth for the cemetery of Pisa was brought in shiploads from the Holy Land early in the 13thC. This sacred ground was enclosed by a rectangular building begun in 1277 and completed in the 15thC. The walls of the interior portico were frescoed by leading Italian artists including Taddeo Gaddi, Spinello Aretino and Benozzo Gozzoli. Over the centuries, a precious collection of antique sarcophaghi was assembled here. What could be salvaged from wartime damage has been painstakingly pieced together; but the ghostly frescoes speak more eloquently through their sinopias, now in the **Museo delle Sinopie**.

The most interesting works are in the N section. In the N portico are the remains of Gozzoli's popular *Grape Harvest* and *Drunkenness of Noah*; and, among other fine sarcophaghi, the 2ndC AD sarcophagus depicting *Phaedra and Hyppolitus* which affected the style of Nicola Pisano's Baptistry pulpit. Off the portico, to the left of the Cappella Ammannati, is the **Salone degli Affreschi**, where the greatest of the Camposanto frescoes, detached and restored, are hung. The most famous is the *Triumph of Death* (*Trionfo della Morte*) by an unknown late-14thC master, which inspired Liszt's *Totentanz*, hence the bust of the composer near the entrance. Among the sculptures are Giovanni Pisano's *Madonna and Child*, and five statues from Tino da Camaiano's *Tomb of the Emperor Henry VII* in the Duomo.

Duomo 🏛 † ☆
Open daily 7:45am–1pm, 3pm to sunset.

The most influential Romanesque building in Tuscany and the first to be dressed in black and white horizontal stripes, the Duomo was begun in 1064 by Buscheto; its tiered facade was added in the 12thC by Rainaldo. Entrance is normally by the Porta di San Ranieri on the S transept; the crudely energetic and touching bronze doors (1180) by Bonanno represent *Scenes from the Life of Christ*.

The grandly proportioned interior consists of a nave with double aisles crossed by unusually deep transepts. The interior was heavily restored in the early 16thC after a devastating fire. At the bottom of the left side of the nave is Giovanni Pisano's **pulpit** ★ (1302–10). It bears an inscription suggesting that this extremely complex work caused the artist considerable worry. The result was one of the most personal and dramatic sculptural masterpieces of its own or indeed any time. The relief panels divided by figures of prophets and saints, depict scenes from the New Testament beginning with the *Birth of the Baptist*, facing the column. The sequence continues with the *Annunciation, Visitation, Nativity, Adoration of the Magi, Presentation at the Temple, Flight into Egypt, Slaughter of the Innocents, Kiss of Judas* and *Passion, Crucifixion, The Elect*, and *The Damned*.

In the E corner of the right transept is a reconstruction of Tino da Camaiano's **tomb of Emperor Henry VII**, commissioned when the sculptor was made Head of Works of the Cathedral in 1315. On the balustrade flanking the entrance to the presbytery are two **bronze angels** by Giambologna, who also made the *Crucifix* over the high altar. On the right as one enters the presbytery is Andrea del Sarto's charming *St Agnes*. More paintings by Andrea hang below the choral galleries. The 13thC mosaics of the *Redeemer in Glory* in the vault of the apse were completed with the head of *St John the Evangelist* by Cimabue in 1302. Below hang good canvases by Beccafumi.

Museo delle Sinopie ☆
🕿 *(050) 22531* 🚇 *Open 10am–1pm, 3–5pm.*

Opposite the S side of the piazza, in the Ospedale Nuovo della Misericordia, this fascinating display of preparatory drawings, revealed by the detachment of the Camposanto frescoes, is a unique opportunity to study the technique of some of the leading artists of the 13th–15thC. They include the *Triumph of Death* and Gozzoli's *Scenes from the Old Testament* and *Annunciation*.

Museo Nazionale di San Matteo ★
Lungarno Medfceo ☎ *(050) 23750* 📷 *Open Mon–Sat 9am–2pm,
Sun, hols 9am–1pm.*

Behind the church of San Matteo on the Lungarno Medfceo, a former
convent, once used as a prison, now houses a superb collection of Pisan
sculpture and 12th–15thC Tuscan pictures. Among the many
outstanding pieces, notice especially: **figures from the exteriors of the
Duomo and Baptistry** by Giovanni Pisano; the *Madonna of the Milk* by
Andrea Pisano, formerly in Santa Maria della Spina; two *Crucifixes* by
Giunta Pisano; the *Madonna and Child* and *Scenes from the Childhood of
Christ* by the Master of San Martino; Simone Martini's polyptych of the
Madonna and Child with Saints; Masaccio's *San Paolo*, part of a
polyptych (of which the other sections are now scattered or lost) that was
the master's first major work.

Nearby on the Lungarno Medfceo is the Toscanelli palace where
Byron lived in 1821–22.

Piazza dei Cavalieri ☆

Five minutes' walk from the Duomo is the central square of medieval
Pisa, rebuilt in the 16thC by Vasari as headquarters of the Knights of the
Order of St Stephen. The **Palazzo dei Cavalieri** (1562) is decorated with
splendid and fantastic *sgraffiti* incorporating the busts of six Medici
grand dukes. To its right is the church of **S. Stefano dei Cavalieri**
(1569), also designed by Vasari but with a later facade. The **Palazzo
dell'Orologio**, on the N of the square, was adapted in 1607; it stands on
the site of the tower where Count Ugolino della Gherardesca and his male
heirs were starved to death by their political rivals in 1288; this episode,
grimly described by Dante in *Inferno, XXXIII*, inspired Shelley's poem
The Tower of Famine.

Santa Maria della Spina 🏛 † ★
Lungarno Gambacorti. Open daily 8am–noon.

Named after a thorn from Christ's crown brought from the Holy Land by
a Pisan merchant, this beautiful church was the swan song of the Pisan
Gothic style. The last of the great Pisan churches and perhaps the
loveliest, it assumed its present size in the 1320s. The building originally
stood closer to the Arno; in 1871 it was moved, stone by stone, to its
present drier site.

Other sights

Other Pisan churches well worth visiting are S. Caterina, S. Francesco,
S. Michele in Borgo, S. Paolo a Ripa d'Arno, S. Nicola, S. Sepocro, S.
Zeno, S. Frediano.

🅷 **Dei Cavalieri**
Piazza della Stazione 2 ☎ *(050) 43290* ☎ *590663* 𝄞 🛏 *102*
🛏 *102* ▦ 🚗 🎱 ⚌ 𝔸𝔼 ⓘ 🅲🅳 𝒱𝐼𝒮𝐴

Conveniently located near the station and air terminal, this modern hotel
is now part of the Ciga chain.
🍴 📠 ⛷

🅷 **La Pace**
Viale Gramsci 14 ☎ *(050) 502266* 𝄞 *to* 𝄞𝄞 🛏 *67* 🛏 *67* ▦ 🚗
𝔸𝔼 🅲🅱 🅲🅳 ⓘ 𝒱𝐼𝒮𝐴

Another modern, quiet hotel near the station.
🍽 🍴 📠 ⛷

🆁 **Buzzino**
Via Carlo Cammeo 44 ☎ *(050) 27013* 𝄞𝄞 ⚏ ⚌ 🚗 𝔸𝔼 ⓘ 🅲🅳 𝒱𝐼𝒮𝐴
Closed Tues, two weeks in Nov.

Imaginative variations on regional cuisine, but regular clients get the best
advice and fastest service.

🆁 **Sergio**
Lungarno Pacinotti 1 ☎ *(050) 48245* 𝄞𝄞 *to* 𝄞𝄞𝄞 ⚏ ⚌ 𝔸𝔼 ⓘ 𝒱𝐼𝒮𝐴
Closed Sun, Mon lunch, mid-July to mid-Aug.

The fashionable restaurant of Pisa and the most reliable cuisine. Service
is attentive and practiced. *Specialties*: *Penne alla zingara*, *portafoglio
alla Sergio*.

🆁 See also *Excursions* opposite.

Excursions

1. S. Piero a Grado †
6km (4 miles) sw of Pisa is a Romanesque basilica (*open daily
9am–6pm*) of the mid-11thC built on the site where St Peter is
thought to have landed on his way from Antioch to Rome.

> ℝ There is a good choice of fish restaurants on the coast near S. Piero.
> At Marina di Pisa, try **Janett** (*Via Maiorca 34* ☎ *(050) 36521* ▮▮▯ *closed
> Mon*); or **Toto** (*Via Montefeltro 32* ☎ *(050) 36605* ▮▯ *to* ▮▮▯ *closed Mon
> eve, Tues, Nov*). At Tirrenia, **Belvedere** (*Largo Belvedere*
> ☎ *(050) 37673* ▮▯ *to* ▮▮▮▮).

2. Tenuta di San Rossore
6km (4 miles) w of Pisa is a protected littoral wood of oaks and
pines (*open Sun, hols 9am–sunset*), formerly a royal estate,
between the mouths of the Arno and the Serchio.

> ℝ North of the Serchio, at Migliarino, is the excellent family restaurant
> **Ugo** (*Via Aurelia 342* ☎ *(050) 811055* ▮▮▯ *closed Mon, Tues eve, late
> July*).

Pistoia★
*Map **15**D5. 37km (23 miles) nw of Florence. 51100. Pistoia.
Population: 94,637 i Via XXVII Aprile 13* ☎ *(0573) 21622.*

In 62 BC the Roman revolutionary Catiline was cornered by
Roman legions near Pistoia; facing defeat he plunged through
the enemy ranks to his death. Dante considered the Pistoiesi to
be even more dangerous than Catiline; and certainly their past is
deeply scarred by factional conspiracy and violence. It was in
Pistoia, as Dante recounts in the *Inferno, XXIV*, that the fierce
political contest between Blacks and Whites originated.

For at least 200yr after the commune had surrendered to
Florence in 1329 its citizens retained their reputation for rude
manners and rough justice. Machiavelli described them as
"brought up to slaughter and war"; and when the first pistols
were made in Germany in the 16thC, they were named after the
vicious little daggers worn by Pistoiesi and known as *pistolese*.
Today Pistoia is a peaceful provincial capital surrounded by the
orchards and nursery gardens which are the basis of its
economy. Its main attraction for tourists is the wealth of
Romanesque sculpture, especially the three pulpits in S.
Bartolommeo, S. Giovanni Fuorcivitas, and S. Andrea, which,
if seen in that order, will enable one to follow the first
'renaissance' of Tuscan sculpture as it evolved from
1250–1300.

Sights and places of interest
The early 14thC walls, still partly intact, were later
strengthened with bastions by the Medici. But the main historic
monuments of the town lie within the earlier walls, the outline
of which is traced in part by Corso Gramsci.

Duomo ▥ †
The marble porch, which gives the cathedral the appearance of
crouching ready to pounce, was added in the mid-14thC to the
12th–13thC Pisan-style facade. The terra-cottas (1505) over the central
portal and in the vault above are by Andrea della Robbia. The interior
walls are decorated with fragments of 13th–14thC frescoes uncovered
during a recent restoration. At the top of the right aisle is the 14thC **tomb
of Cino da Pistoia**, who was Dante's friend. In the Cappella di San
Jacopo, off the right aisle, is the extraordinary silver **St James Altar**, one
of the supreme examples of the Italian goldsmiths' art and crowded with
many endearing details. It was created from 1287–1456 by a succession
of Tuscan sculptors including Brunelleschi, who made the two **figures**

on the left side. In the chapel to the left of the high altar is a *Madonna and Saints* (1485) by Lorenzo di Credi, possibly begun by Verrocchio; also the bust of *Archbishop Donato de' Medici* by A. Rossellino or Verrocchio.

Baptistry †

Opposite the cathedral is the tall, hexagonal Gothic Baptistry (1338–1359), by Cellino de Nese to a design by Andrea Pisano. The interior is bare except for the original font, rediscovered during a recent restoration, and the shameful commercial art exhibitions which are, incredibly, permitted to take place here from time to time.

Palazzo del Comune ▥

Open Tues–Sat 9:30am–12:30pm, Sun, hols, 10am–1pm.

The town hall, a very fine example of Gothic civic architecture, was founded in 1294 by the enlightened Florentine governor Giano della Bella but building was delayed by political upheavals and not completed until 1355. Over the central door and on the corners are the crests of Medici Popes. The aerial corridor from the Sala Maggiore to the Duomo was added in 1637. The **Marino Marini Center** (the sculptor was born in Pistoia in 1901) is off the courtyard; among the works on display are portraits of *Thomas Mann*, *Henry Miller* and *Chagall*. The **Museo Civico**, opened in 1981, occupies rooms on the first and second floors.

Palazzo del Podestà

This 14thC building is still the city's tribunal. To the left of the entrance is the old court, complete with judge's seat, table of justice and bench of the accused.

Ospedale del Ceppo ▥

Piazza Giovanni XII. Not open to the public.

The startling frieze over the porch of the hospital looks at first glance like the work of a Russian social realist. It was executed in the early 16thC by members of Andrea della Robbia's workshop and illustrates the *Seven Works of Mercy*, a fascinating picture of poverty and illness in the 16thC. The lovely Verrocchiesque tondi over the columns are probably by Andrea himself. The hospital is still in use.

Sant'Andrea ▥ †

The 12thC church has an enchanting but unfinished facade. The reliefs (1166) of the *Journey and Adoration of the Magi* over the central portal are by the brothers Gruamonte and Adeodato. The blonde, barnlike interior is dominated by the city's outstanding work of art, the **pulpit ★** (1298–1301) by Giovanni Pisano. This pulpit was finished a year before Giovanni started work on the pulpit of the **Duomo** in *Pisa*. These carvings are so intensely dynamic that one can scarcely believe they were created two centuries before the age of Michelangelo. Their subject is the *Life of Christ* and the *Last Judgment*. Opposite the pulpit is a wooden *Crucifix* also by Giovanni, in a fine 15thC tabernacle frame.

San Bartolomeo in Pantano †

Piazza S. Bartolomeo. Hours very irregular.

This 12thC church contains a reconstructed **pulpit** (1250) by Guido da Como.

San Giovanni Fuorcivitas †

Via Francesco Crispi.

The name refers to the original 8thC church which stood outside the city walls. The building was erected from the mid-12th to 14thC and restored after damage during World War II. The entrance is by the decoratively vivid but scarred N flank. Inside, the **holy water stoup** in the center is notable for the four busts of cardinals by the young Giovanni Pisano. On the right wall is the **pulpit** (1270) by Gugliemo da Pisa, a follower of Nicola Pisano; the reliefs illustrate *Scenes from the New Testament*. On the left wall are the glazed terra-cotta figures of the *Visitation*, a moving work attributed to Luca or Andrea della Robbia. To the left of the altar is a large polyptych (1353–55) by Taddeo Gaddi.

Zoo *(Giardino Zoologico)*

Via Pieve a Celle 160 ☎ (0573) 571280 ▥ ▣ ⚹ Open daily 9am to sunset.

The new and attractively planned zoo is 4km (2½ miles) sw of Pistoia.

Other sights

Visitors with leisure should also look at the churches of S. Francesco; S. Domenico; S. Paolo; S. Maria delle Grazie, designed by Michelozzo; and the Cappella Tau, decorated with 14th–15thC frescoes.

H **Arcobaleno**
Via Valdi e Collina 37, Sanmommè, 51020 Pistoia
☎ *(0573) 470030* ❙❙ 🗖 *28* 🗖 *24* 🍴 ☰🗢🗖 *summer* 🄲🄳 *Closed
Jan – Feb.*
Location: 15km (9 miles) to N at Sanmommè. A holiday hotel in the
mountains popular with children for the sports facilities and disco.
🏠 ⚓ ⫷ ⇌ 𝄢 ⚓ ●

H **Residence il Convento**
Via S. Quirico 33, 51100 Pistoia ☎ *(0573) 452651* ❙❙❙ 🗖 *24* 🗖 *24*
🍴 🏠 ☰ AE VISA
Location: 5km to NE near Ponte Nuovo. A peaceful retreat in an 18thC
ex-convent overlooking Pistoia.
🏠 🖼 🎣 ⚓ ⫷

R In the center is the unfussy and comfortable **Chiavi d'Oro** (*Via Pacini
19* ☎ *(0573) 24301* ❙❙ *closed Mon, early June*). Just outside are: **Checco**
(*Via Dalmazio 454* ☎ *(0573) 22135* ❙❙❙ *closed Wed, Aug*); and **Rafanelli**
(*Via S. Agostino 47* ☎ *(0573) 23046* ❙❙❙ *closed Mon, early Aug*).

R **Osteria del Contadino**
Via Provinciale Pratese 58, Agliana ☎ *(0574) 71450* ❙❙❙ 💬 🍴 🍴
Closed Mon, Aug.
This rustic, friendly country place, halfway between Pistoia and Prato,
prepares Tuscan home cooking with a daily set menu which includes
various Chianti wines. *Specialties: Soups, grilled meats, game birds,
beans, polenta.*

R **Signorino**
Via Bolognese 207 ☎ *(0573) 475028* ❙❙❙ 💬 🍴
A cheerful and popular country restaurant 10km (6 miles) N of Pistoia
with a good cold table as well as hearty regional specialties.

Pitigliano
*Map **9***J7. 218km (134 miles) s of Florence, 74km (46 miles)
SE of Grosseto. 58017. Grosseto. Population: 4,443.*
Pitigliano from a distance is one of the most amazing sights in
Tuscany. Carved out of a rock escarpment above a natural moat
formed by three deep ravines, this was the seat of the Roman
Orsini barons when they took control of the area in 1293. It
retains the dour, impressive stamp of a warlord's headquarters,
remarkably intact, charmless but fascinating.
   The main square, Piazza della Repubblica, is dominated by
the 14th–15thC **Palazzo Orsini**, modified in the 16thC by
Guiliano da Sangallo. The strongly atmospheric medieval *borgo*
straddles the escarpment beyond the Duomo.

Poggibonsi
*Map **11**F5. 41km (25 miles) s of Florence, 33km (20 miles) NW
of Siena. 53036. Siena. Population: 25,784.*
A commercial and industrial center (wine and furniture).

Nearby sights
2km (1¼ miles) s is the 13thC Gothic church of San Lucchese,
reconstructed after World War II, containing frescoes by Bartolo di
Fredi.
   8km (5 miles) SE on the Siena road is the fortified medieval hamlet of
Staggia, where the museum (🖾 *apply at sacristan's house*) attached to the
parish church possesses a panel of the *Communion of the Magdalen* by A.
del Pollaiuolo.

H R **Alcide** (*Viale Marconi 67a* ☎ *(0577) 937501* ❙❙ *to* ❙❙❙ *closed
Wed, July*). See also *Sovana*.

Poggio a Caiano

Map **15***E5. 17km (10 miles)* w *of Florence. 50046. Firenze.
Population: 5,892.*

Villa Medicea di Poggio a Caiano 𝕀𝕀𝕀 ★
▨ *Gardens only open 8:30am to sunset.*
The most innovative and influential of all Medici country houses, built
for Lorenzo de' Medici from 1480–85, and the only important surviving
building for which he was personally responsible. The architect was
Giuliano da Sangallo, who adapted the antique Roman villa type to the
requirements of Renaissance country life.

The arcaded ground floor provides a balcony for the *piano nobile*. The
central loggia with its Robbianesque terra-cotta frieze was probably
added in the 16thC. The curved staircases were added in the 17thC.

The traditional central courtyard is replaced by a two-story high
salone frescoed by Andrea del Sarto (until 1512), Franciabigio (until
1520), Pontormo (until 1532) and completed by A. Allori (1582). The
Classical subjects refer to events in Medici history. The high point is
Pontormo's fresco in the lunette of the right wall of *Vertumnus and
Pomona* (1521), an idyllic and graceful picture of a Tuscan summer's day
and a masterpiece of design.

ℝ See *Carmignano, Artimino*.

Pontassieve

Map **16***E6. 18km (11 miles)* e *of Florence. 50065. Firenze.
Population: 19,752.*
A commercial wine town. The Wed market is good for shoes.

ℍ **Castello di Sanmezzano**
Leccio, 50066 Reggello, Firenze. ☎ *(055) 867911* ▥ ☙ *14* ▭ *14*
▱▭◻
Location: Near the Incisa autostrada exit from Florence. A 17thC castle
eccentrically decorated in 19thC Moorish style.
▱◻◻◪✿⚲☇⛄✦◁

ℝ **Il Girarrosto ❖** (*Via Garibaldi 23–35* ☎ *(055) 8302048* ▮▢ *to* ▮▮▢
▭ ◉ *closed Mon, July.*) **Specialty**: *Game.*

Pontremoli

Map **14***B2. 164km (102 miles)* nw *of Florence, 53km (33
miles)* nw *of Massa. 54027. Massa-Carrara. Population:
10,335 i in the Municipio* ☎ *(0187) 831180.*
The principal town of the Lunigiana, named after the Etruscan
city of Luni (which is now in Liguria).

A 19thC Neoclassical facade has been added to the Baroque
cathedral. The town boasts a pretty oval Rococo church, the
Madonna del Ponte (1738).

Other sights
In the **Castello** on the hill of Piagnaro is a museum (▨ *open Tues–Sun
9am–noon, 2–5pm summer, 4–7pm winter*) exhibiting the strange,
totemic *stela* statues and other pre-Etruscan material discovered in the
area.

1.5km (1 mile) to the se of the center, the church of SS Annunziata has
a fine 16thC interior with a marble *tempietto* (1527) attributed to Jacopo
Sansovino.

ℍ **Golf** (*Via Pineta* ☎ *(0187) 831573* ▥).

ℝ **Da Bussè** (*Piazza Duomo 9* ▮▢ *closed Fri, late July*), an old-
fashioned rustic trattoria. 15km (9 miles) se at Bagnone is **I Fondi** (*Via
della Repubblica 22* ☎ *(0187) 496086* ▮▢ *closed Wed, two weeks in
Sept–Oct*).

Poppi
Map 12E7. 53km (33 miles) SE of Florence, 38km (24 miles) N of Arezzo. 52014. Arezzo. Population: 5,790.
Poppi is the starting point for the beautiful drive to *Camaldoli*. It is worth pausing here to admire the arcaded old streets.

Sights and places of interest
Palazzo Pretorio 🏛
Piazza Grande ⌖ Open Mon–Sat 9am–2pm.
Originally the castle of the Guidi lords, the palace was rebuilt in 1274 and extended in 1291. Its resemblance to the *Palazzo Signoria, Florence* suggests that Arnolfo di Cambio may have had a hand in the design.
Primo Parco Zoo
☎ *(0575) 58602* ▨ ▯ ☗ *Open daily 8am to sunset.*
Just outside the town, in a ravishing setting, this is the first zoo in Europe to be devoted exclusively to European animals.

Populonia
Map 10H3. 149km (93 miles) SW of Florence, 89km (55 miles) NW of Grosseto. 57020. Livorno. Population: 122.
The only Etruscan town built on a coastal site, Populonia was inhabited from the 9thC BC and in the 7thC BC became a rich industrial city – the blast furnace of the ancient world. Iron ore imported from *Elba* was smelted here in such quantities that the necropolis was buried in slag and the beaches are still streaked with black. The inhabitants may have been the first Etruscans to mint coins, in the 5thC BC. Populonia fell under the influence of Rome in the 3rdC BC, and by the 4thC AD was nearly empty.

The village is dominated by its restored medieval **rocca**. A privately owned **Etruscan museum** on the main street (*apply to custodian at no. 11*) houses an interesting collection of small, sacred and domestic objects from the necropolis.

Necropolis ☆
3km (2 miles) E of village ⌖ 🚏 tours roughly on the hour. Open daily 9am–noon, 4–8pm summer, 9am–noon, 2–6pm winter.
This complex comprises tombs of the 9th–3rdC BC.

Port'Ercole
Map 8J5. 190km (118 miles) S of Florence, 50km (31 miles) S of Grosseto. 58018. Grosseto. Population: 3,400.
A fashionable sailing resort on the E coast of Monte Argentario which has attracted a faithful English summer colony. The Etruscans gave it the name of Port of Hercules. The three fortresses which guard it testify to its strategic importance; there is nowhere else except Malta where one can see Renaissance principles of fortification so well defined.

Sights and places of interest
Forte Filippo 🏛
▨ 🚏 *Tours on Wed.*
The best demonstration of late-Renaissance fortification in the Mediterranean. Mathematically and technically flawless, it is in an excellent state of preservation. Now converted into private apartments.
Forte Stella 🏛
South of the harbour, this now abandoned hexagonal fort on a four-sided bastion base was built by the Spanish in the 17thC.
Rocca Spagnola 🏛
⌖ *Open Apr–Dec 20 10am–1pm, 4pm to sunset; Dec 21–Mar 10am–1:30pm, 3:30pm to sunset. Permission necessary from mayor's office (easily obtained).*
The Rocca Spagnola is the original nucleus of the medieval fortress, refined and extended in the 15th–16thC, which dominates the historic

center of the town, Piazza Santa Barbara. It forms a complete village.

On the Tombolo di Feniglia is a protected pine forest and a sandy beach where Caravaggio died in 1610.

H **Don Pedro**
Via Panoramica 23, 58018 Port'Ercole, Grosseto ☎ *(0564) 833914*
▥▥ ⬮ 44 ▭ 44 ▦ ▣ ▣ ≈ *Closed Dec–Mar.*
The most attractive and best managed medium-price hotel in the area.
✲ ▨ ✇ ◁⟨

H **Il Pellicano**
Via Panoramica, 58018 Port'Ercole, Grosseto ☎ *(0564) 833801*
☏ *500131* ▥▥ ⬮ 27 ▭ 27 ▦ ⇌ ⇌ ⊜ AE ⊕ VISA *Closed Nov to mid-Apr.*
Location: 3km (2 miles) N towards Porto Santo Stefano. Luxurious American country house decor and isolated location.
⌂ ▨ ✇ ⚓ ◁⟨ ⇌ ⇗ ⟓

H **Stella Marina** (*Lungomare A. Doria* ☎ *(0564) 833055* ▮▯).

R **Il Gambero Rosso** (*Lungomare A. Doria 60* ☎ *(0564) 833907* ▥▥ *closed Thurs, Nov, Jan*) is a good fish restaurant, as is the nearby **Grotto dei Pescatore** (☎ *(0564) 833099* ▮▯ *closed Tues*).

Excursion
The island of Giannutri

23km (14 miles) to the S, the island is reached from Port'Ercole. Near Cala Maestra is a 1stC AD Roman villa. Good spear-fishing in the clear waters of the Cala dei Grottoni.

Porto Santo Stefano

*Map **8**J5. 193km (121 miles) s of Florence, 53km (33 miles) s of Siena. 58019. Grosseto. Population: 10,100 **i** Corso Umberto 55a* ☎ *(0564) 814208.*
This active fishing port on the N coast of Monte Argentario retains some of its charm. Boats depart frequently for *Giglio*.

H **Torre di Cala Piccola** ▦
58019 Porto Santo Stefano, Grosseto ☎ *(0564) 825133* ▥▥ ⬮ 56
▭ 56 ⇌ ≈ ▣ *summer* VISA *Closed Nov–Feb.*
Location: 8km (5 miles) W. The main luxury hotel on the Argentario coast.
✲ ☐ ▨ ✇ ⚓ ⇌ ⇗ ➤

R **Il Moresco da Valli** (*Via Panoramica 156* ☎ *(0564) 824158* ▮▯ *closed Tues, Nov–Mar*). Fish restaurants include: **Armando** (*Via Marconi 1/3* ☎ *(0564) 812568* ▥▥ *closed Wed and Nov*); the simpler but equally attractive **La Fontanina di San Pietro** (☎ *(0564) 812029* ▮▯ *to* ▥▥ *closed Tues*); and **Il Palombaro** (*Lungomare dei Navigatore* ☎ *(0564) 814646* ▥▥ *closed Mon*).

Nightlife
La Strega del Mare at Calagrande (☎ *(0564) 812791* ▥▥) is a popular nightclub serving good food.

Prato ★
*Map **15**D5. 19km (11 miles) NW of Florence. 50047. Firenze. Population: 156,955 **i** Via L. Muzzi 51* ☎ *(0574) 35141.*
Florentines say that if you listen closely in Prato late at night when the textile factories are closed you will hear a whirring: it is the sound of the inhabitants spinning in their back parlors. 75% of the manufactured wool exported from Italy comes from Prato, and most of it is produced by small, privately owned

firms. Its population has doubled in 30yr and is now the fourth largest and possibly the most affluent in Central Italy. Florentines also call Prato the tail that tries to wag the dog.

The first cloth mills on the banks of the Bisenzio were in operation in 1108, half a century earlier than the first in Florence. But the prosperous city which grew up around a meadow (*prato*) was no more successful than most Tuscan communes at self-government. Unable to control its political factions, Prato placed itself under the protection of the Anjou rulers of Naples in 1313. In 1351, the Queen of Naples sold her rights to the city to Florence for 17,500 florins. The commercial fortunes of Prato were given an enormous boost later in the 14thC by the business operations of Francesco di Marco Datini, subject of Iris Origo's admirable biography, *The Merchant of Prato*. But although Prato enjoyed a greater economic and political autonomy than many Florentine-dominated cities, it rebelled on several occasions; and in the 16thC Florence punished it by rationing its permitted production of wool.

Apart from its distinctive green-and-white striped churches, there are two artistic masterpieces, both by Florentines, which compel a visit to Prato: Filippo Lippi's frescoes in the Duomo and Giuliano da Sangallo's church Santa Maria delle Carceri.

Events: The Metastasio Theater in Via Benedetto Cairoli is the home of an enterprising experimental company which plays from Oct–Apr. In spring and summer, concerts are given in the Metastasio and in the Castello.

The *Ostensione del Sacro Cingolo*, which is the ceremonial display of the Virgin's Holy Girdle from the external pulpit of the Duomo, takes place on May 1, Easter Day, Aug 15, Sept 8, and Dec 25.

Sights and places of interest

The old town sits within a partly intact hexagon of 13thC walls on the sw bank of the River Bisenzio.

Castello dell'Imperatore
⊡ *Open Mon, Tues, Thurs–Sat 9am–noon, 4–7pm.*
For a good orienting view walk around the battlements of this castle, built in the 13thC for the Emperor Frederick II.

Opposite the Castello is **Santa Maria delle Carceri** (see over).

Duomo Ⅲ † ★
The striped facade was applied to the Romanesque building in 1384–1457. The glazed terra-cotta lunette of the *Madonna with Sts Stephen and Lawrence* (1489) over the portal is by Andrea della Robbia. Projecting from the right corner is the covered **pulpit of the Holy Girdle** (1428–38) by Donatello and Michelozzo. The originals of Donatello's carvings of *Dancing Putti* have been removed to the Cathedral Museum.

The sturdy green and blonde interior conserves remarkable works of art, but the nave is bare except for the pulpit (1473) by Mino da Fiesole and A. Rossellino. Left of the entrance is the **chapel of the Holy Girdle** (1385–95); the legend of the Holy Girdle is illustrated by Agnolo Gaddi's frescoes (1392–95). The Holy Girdle was brought from the Holy Land to Prato in the 12thC, and its story is still popular in Tuscany. Over the altar is a *Madonna and Child* (c.1317) by Giovanni Pisano. Behind the high altar of the cathedral, in the choir, are Filippo Lippi's frescoes ★ (1452–66) of the martyrdom of *St John the Baptist*, on the right wall, and of *St Stephen*, on the left (a coin-operated light switch is on the left of the last chapel in the left transept). Filippo labored over these frescoes for 14yr during which he was tried for fraud and fathered a child by the nun Lucrezia (who may be the model for the dancing Salome). They are the considered masterpieces of his troubled maturity, and yet they glow with a clear-eyed vivacity and apparently spontaneous grace which make them among the most immediately pleasing of Renaissance paintings.

The chapel to the right of the altar is frescoed with scenes from the *Lives of the Virgin and of St Stephen*, begun by Paolo Uccello or a disciple and completed, still in the early 15thC, in a strange quasi-Mannerist style by Andrea di Giusto. In the right transept is a tabernacle of the *Madonna of the Olive* (1480) by all three Maiano brothers; also a panel painting of the *Death of St Jerome* by Filippo Lippi.

Museo dell'Opera del Duomo (*Cathedral Museum*)
🚋 *Open Mon, Wed–Sat 9am–12:30pm, 3–6:30pm, Sun, hols 9:30am–12.30pm. Closed Tues.*

In the Bishop's Palace to the left of the Duomo. The main attractions are Donatello's reliefs of *Dancing Putti* from the exterior pulpit, but they are less good than the miniature frieze of dancing putti on the exquisite **reliquary of the Holy Girdle** (1446) by Maso di Bartolomeo.

Galleria Comunale
Piazza Comune 🚋 *Open Tues–Sat 9am–7pm, Sun, hols 9am–noon.*

The gallery occupies three floors of the 13th–14thC Palazzo Pretorio. The large collection includes minor 14th–15thC altarpieces in good condition, two panels by Filippo Lippi, Neapolitan fruit paintings, and plaster models by L. Bartolini.

Santa Maria delle Carceri ⌂ † ★
The interior, begun in 1485, is one of Giuliano da Sangallo's most important works, a perfect restatement of Brunelleschian principles.

Other sights

Palazzo Datini in Via Rinaldesca, which Francesco di Marco Datini had built for himself in the late 14th–early 15thC; Datini's tomb is in the nearby church of **San Francesco**; the late 14thC frescoes in the chapter room off the cloister include a picture of *St Matthew as a Money Changer*, a rare, but in Prato appropriate, genre subject.

Ⓡ **Il Piraña**
Via Valentini 110 ☎ *(0574) 25746* ▥ ☐ ⊞ AE ⬤ *Closed Sat, Aug, late Dec to early Jan.*

Do not be deterred by the location of this restaurant, which is 10mins' drive from the center opposite a string of factories. Even the Florentines will tell you that this is now one of the best fish restaurants in Italy, although the decor is an excessively fussy attempt to be ultramodern.

Ⓡ Restaurants in the center include **Baghino** (*Via dell'Accademia 9* ☎ *(0574) 27920* ▥ *closed Sun, Mon, lunch during Aug*); **Livio** (*Via G. Guasti 62–66* ☎ *(0574) 23709* ▥ *closed Sat, Aug*), simple and inexpensive; and **Stella d'Italia** (*Piazza del Duomo 8* ☎ *(0574) 27910* ▥ *closed Mon eve, Sat, Aug*), with tables on the piazza.

Punta Ala

Map 10I5. 150km (93 miles) sw of Florence, 40km (25 miles) w of Grosseto. 58040. Grosseto. Population: 190.
This luxurious resort on a headland overlooking the island of *Elba* was founded in 1960. It offers golf, sailing, riding, polo, tennis, sand beaches and is near the Etruscan sites.

Hotels

Alleluja
58040 Punta Ala, Grosseto ☎ *(0564) 922050* 📺 *500449* ▥ ⚘ 42 ☐ 42 ⊞ ◚ ☎ ▦ AE
The most attractive of the hotels, which preserves something of the mood of the old Tuscan farmhouse, the nucleus of the original estate.
⌂ ☐ ▱ ⩘ ⤳ ⁌ ᔆ ✔ ⭢ ⬤

Gallia Palace Hotel
Via delle Sughere, 58040 Punta Ala, Grosseto
☎ *(0564) 922022/3/4/5* 📺 *590454* ▥ ⚘ 98 ☐ 98 ⊞ ◚ ☎
AE *Closed Oct–Apr.*
The modern luxury hotel of Punta Ala is an architecturally impersonal building set in a splendid garden. Good service.
⌂ ‡ ⛄ ▱ ◔ ⩘ ⤳ ⁌ ᔆ ✔ ⭢ ⬤ ᨊ

Golf
58040 Punta Ala, Grosseto ☎ *(0564) 922026* ⬛⬛ ⬢ *180* 🛏 *180*
⬛⬛ ⬟ ⬛ ⮕ AE ⓞ *Closed Oct–Apr.*
The only moderately priced hotel in the resort.
🏠 ⁑ 🗖 🗗 🚿 🛲 🍴 🕭 ⚓ ✦ 🍶 ➡

R̄ The restaurants on the port are unnecessarily expensive. Instead, try those at *Castiglione della Pescaia* and *Tirli*.

Radda in Chianti
Map **12***F6. 58km (36 miles)* s *of Florence, 34km (21 miles)* n *of Siena. 53017. Siena. Population: 1,588.*
A little hill village which became headquarters of the Chianti League in 1415. The medieval street plan and sections of the fortifications survive.

3km (1¾ miles) N is **Volpaia**, the prettiest of the small medieval Chianti villages.

Ⓗ R̄ **La Villa** (☎ *(0577) 738021* ⬜) 3.5km (2 miles) E at La Villa, a modest but eccentric country inn.

Roselle
Map **11***I5. 131km (81 miles)* s *of Florence, 10km (6 miles)* NE *of Grosseto. Grosseto.*
Etruscan Roselle, like *Vetulonia*, was an island dominating the waters of the gulf which then filled part of the Grosseto Maremma. Excavations have revealed layers of civilization stretching back to the Neolithic age. The Etruscan city, one of the federation of 12, was taken over by Rome early in the 3rdC BC. Portable material uncovered is now in *Grosseto*.

The **ruins** ✪ (⬛ *hours unrestricted*) are in a remarkably complete state of conservation, surrounded by a nearly intact ring of Etruscan- and Roman-built walls. Remains of the Roman city include the forum, a stretch of paved street, basilicas, villas, amphitheater and baths. Etruscan remains include rare artisans' cottages of the 7th–6thC BC.

R̄ See *Istia d'Ombrone* and *Grosseto*.

San Casciano in Val di Pesa
Map **15***E5. 17km (10½ miles)* s *of Florence. 50026. Firenze. Population: 14,522.*
A busy agricultural-industrial town graced by the church of the **Misericordia** which possesses several fine Sienese paintings, including a *Crucifixion* on panel by Simone Martini.

Nearby sights
3km (1¾ miles) to the N is the one-street hamlet of **Sant'Andrea in Percussina**, where Machiavelli spent 15yr in exile from Florence during which he wrote his six great works, including *The Prince*. His house is privately owned but sometimes open to the public.

R̄ **Albergaccio Taverna Machiavelli**
Via degli Scopeti 64 ☎ *(055) 828471* ⬛⬜ to ⬛⬛ ⬜ ⬟ *Last orders at 8pm.*
The tavern opposite Machiavelli's house serves and sells wines from the Serristori vineyards.

R̄ **La Tenda Rossa**.
Piazza Monumento 9/14, Cerbaia Val di Pesa ☎ *(055) 826132* ⬛⬛⬛⬛
⬜ ⬟ AE *Closed Wed, Thurs lunch, three weeks from Aug–Sept.*
This outstanding trattoria, 6km (4 miles) to the N, excels in pastas.

San Galgano 🏛 † ★
Map 11G5. 101km (63 miles) sw of Florence, 33km (20 miles) sw of Siena.

The ruined church of San Galgano is one of the most moving sights in Tuscany. Although meadow grass now grows in the roofless nave, the magnificence of the once-powerful Cistercian foundation is still apparent. Built between 1218–80, the church introduced French Gothic architecture to Tuscany.

On a hill above is the little Romanesque church of **San Galgano**, with the 14thC chapel frescoed by A. Lorenzetti.

San Gimignano ★
Map 11F5. 55km (34 miles) sw of Florence, 38km (24 miles) nw of Siena. 53037. Siena. Population: 7,501 i Piazza del Duomo ☎ (0577) 94008.

San Gimignano '*delle belle torri*' (of the beautiful towers) is the best-preserved medieval town in Tuscany. Its defense system once involved more than 70 towers, of which 13 survive. Warring factions dropped rocks and burning tar on their enemies from these towers, which were also important status symbols. Height meant prestige for medieval Tuscan noblemen, as for 20thC American tycoons; and from a distance San Gimignano bears an eerie resemblance to a tipsy, miniature New York.

Most Italian cities looked very like San Gimignano in the 12th–13thC. The skyline of medieval Siena bristled with over 50 such towers, and that of Florence with over 100. E.M. Forster's early novel, *Where Angels Fear to Tread*, is set in San Gimignano, which he calls "Monteriano".

The narrative painter Benozzo Gozzoli was born here. His charming frescoes in the Collegiata and the church of San Agostino are not great art, but are easy to enjoy.

Events: Colorful masked processions take place on the first and last Sun of the carnival period before Lent.

There is an opera season in Aug in Piazza del Duomo.

Sights and places of interest
Porta San Giovanni (1262), the finest of the town gates, is the main entrance; there is a car park nearby. The town is in any case best toured on foot.

There are marvelous views from the 13thC town **walls** and from the **Rocca**, built by the Florentines in 1353.

Piazza della Cisterna
The main square is actually triangular, and retains at its center the original 13thC cistern. The buildings are 13th–14thC, of which the finest is the 14thC Palazzo Tortoli (no. 7), in the Sienese style.

Piazza del Duomo
The monumental buildings and seven towers of the Piazza del Duomo are all pre-1400. On the w of the square is the Collegiata. The Palazzo del Popolo is on the s side and the Palazzo del Podestà on the E.

Collegiata †
The Romanesque facade of the Collegiata was enlarged by Giuliano da Maiano in the 15thC, but has been often restored since. The interior is notable for its 14th–15thC frescoes. On the interior facade the frescoes include the *Martyrdom of St Sebastian* (1465) by Gozzoli; polychrome statues of the *Annunciation* (1421) by Jacopo della Quercia. On the right wall are *New Testament Scenes* (c.mid-14thC) by Barna da Siena, completed by Giovanni d'Asciano.

Off the right nave is the **Cappella di Santa Fina** ★ – 1468 (🎫 *ticket also good for Pal. del Popolo, hours as Pal. del Podestà*), one of the high points of Renaissance architecture, built by Giuliano da Maiano with an **altar** by Benedetto da Maiano. The beautiful frescoes (1475) by

Domenico Ghirlandaio and assistants depict two *Scenes from the Life of Santa Fina*; according to the legend, wallflowers sprang from the towers on the day she died.

In the presbytery, the ciborium over the high altar is by B. da Maiano. The choir stalls in the apse are by Antonio da Colle. On the left nave wall are frescoes of the *Old Testament* (c.1367) by Bartolo di Fredi, and in the 14thC Baptistry loggia, off the left nave, is a fresco of the *Annunciation* by Domenico Ghirlandaio.

Palazzo del Podestà ▥

🖼 *Open Apr–Oct Tues–Sun 9:30am–12:30pm, 3:30–6:30pm; Nov–Mar Tues–Sun 10am–1pm, 2:30–5:30pm. Closed Mon.*

On the E side of the square, this 13thC building was enlarged in the 14thC. Its imposing Torre dell Ragnosa at 51m (167ft) was meant to set the maximum legal height for towers, but tower-building rivalry continued.

Palazzo del Popolo

Piazza del Duomo 🖼 *ticket also good for Cappella di Santa Fina in Collegiata. Hours as Pal. del Podestà.*

On the S side of the square, this building houses the Pinacoteca Civica, and offers a spectacular view from the top of its tower, the **Torre Grossa**. Inside, on the first floor, the Sala di Dante, so called because the poet spoke here in 1300 in favor of an alliance with Florence, contains an important *Maestà* (1317) by Lippo Memmo. The **Pinacoteca**, on the next floor, houses a beguiling collection of 13th–15thC Sienese and Florentine paintings.

Sant' Agostino †

A Romanesque-Gothic church (1290–98) of impressive simplicity. In the Cappella di S. Bartolo, right of the main entrance, is a marble altar (1494) by B. da Maiano. Over the high altar, the *Coronation of the Virgin* (1483) is a major work by Piero del Pollaiuolo. In the choir Gozzoli's *Life Story of St Augustine* has 17 frescoed scenes (1464). In the left nave is Gozzoli's *St Sebastian* (1464).

Via San Matteo

The main street has travertine paving and medieval buildings, especially the Romanesque church of San Bartolo and the *casa-torre* Pesciolini at no. 32.

Other sights

Of the many more Romanesque churches within the walls, the most interesting is San Jacopo, at the NE corner.

Outside the walls, 4.5km (3 miles) from Porta San Matteo, is the Romanesque **Pieve di Cellole** (1237).

Ⓗ Ⓡ **Bel Soggiorno**
Via San Giovanni 91, 53037 San Gimignano, Siena
☎ *(0577) 940375* ☎ *573347* ▥ 🛏 *27* 🛏 *27* 🖼 ⇌ 🏠
Restaurant closed Mon.
Wonderful views of the town from this 13thC house.
✛ 🦻 ◁€

Ⓗ Ⓡ **La Cisterna**
Piazza della Cisterna 23, 53037 San Gimignano, Siena
☎ *(0577) 940328* ▥ 🛏 *48* 🛏 *48* 🚗 ⇌ 🏠 🅰🅴 ⓒⓞ
Huge rooms in a 13thC palace with an Edwardian atmosphere. The restaurant, **Le Terrazze**, offers splendid views from spacious rooms with low ceilings with exposed beams.
✛ 🖼

Ⓗ Ⓡ 5km (3 miles) N at Pancole is the country inn **Leonetto**
(☎ *(0577) 955044, restaurant closed Tues*) with quiet rooms.

Ⓡ **Ponte a Rondolino**
Via Sevestro 32 ☎ *(0577) 941029* ▥ 🗋 🍴 ⇌ 🏠 🚗 🅰🅴 *Closed Mon eve, Tues, Jan–Mar.*
In this rustic trattoria imaginative versions of French and Tuscan dishes are served, with wines made on the estate. Guests can spend the night in simple rooms in the attached *foresteria*. **Specialties: Risotto with Vernaccia, veal fillet Louis XV.**

San Giovanni Valdarno
Map 11F6. 45km (28 miles) SE of Florence, 37km (23 miles) W of Arezzo. 52027. Arezzo. Population: 19,908.

The birthplace of the painters Masaccio and Giovanni da San Giovanni is now the chief industrial town of the Valdarno.

See also *Pontassieve*.

2km (1¼ miles) to the S, in the church of the convent of Montecarlo, is one of Fra Angelico's masterpieces, an *Annunciation* (c.1440), with a fine predella. 13km (8 miles) to the NE, near Loro Ciuffena, is the tiny farming hamlet of Gropina. Its Romanesque church, **S. Pietro**, has unusual capitals and primitive carvings on its pulpit.

5km (3 miles) SE is Montevarchi where a market is held on Thurs.

San Miniato
Map 15E4. 44km (27 miles) W of Florence, 39km (24 miles) E of Pisa. 56027. Pisa. Population: 24,701.

Medieval San Miniato was the seat of the Lombard Imperial Vicariate in Tuscany and therefore known as S. Miniato al Tedesco ('of the German'). The fortifications, of which only two towers remain, were rebuilt in 1240 by Frederick II.

Sights and places of interest
The 13thC **Duomo** has been rebuilt and restored many times and its pompous interior decorations are 18th–19thC. Its bell-tower, the **Torre di Matilde**, predates the Duomo and was built as a defense tower.

The **Museo Diocesano** (🖾 *open Tues–Sun summer 9am–noon, 4–7pm; winter 9am–noon, 2:30–5pm*), to the left of the Duomo, retains sacred art from the region including works by Filippo Lippi, Neri di Bicci, Fra Bartolommeo, Empoli and Verrocchio.

A short, stiff climb from the Prato del Duomo brings one to the tower which is the last surviving reminder of Frederick II's **Rocca**, a reconstruction of the original which was destroyed during World War II. On a clear day the view embraces the whole of the Arno plain. Below the Prato del Duomo is **Piazza della Repubblica**, the most picturesque in the town. The Seminario retains 14thC storefronts and 17thC *sgraffiti*.

Ⓗ Ⓡ **Miravalle** (*Piazza Castello 3* ☎ *(0571) 43007* 🔲).

San Quirico d'Orcia
Map 8H6. 111km (64 miles) SE of Florence, 43km (29 miles) SE of Siena. 53027. Siena. Population: 2,231 **i** *Piazza Liberta 2* ☎ *(0577) 43252.*

A village overlooking the Orcia and Asso valleys.

Collegiata †
The Romanesque-Gothic Collegiata has three magnificent **portals**: on the facade (1080); on the right flank (late 13thC), adorned with lions and caryatids by a follower of Giovanni Pisano; and at the head of the right transept (1298). Inside is an unusually fine triptych by Sano di Pietro and good choir stalls (1502) by Antonio Barili.

Nearby sights
San Giovanni d'Asso, 15km (9 miles) N, dominated by its 12thC Castello; and **Castiglione d'Orcia**, 5km (3 miles) S, hometown of the artist Vecchietta, which is near the atmospheric medieval village of **Rocca d'Orcia**. 6km (4 miles) SE is the little spa town of **Bagno Vignoni**, now rather run down.

Ⓗ Ⓡ **Posta-Marcucci** ✿
53027 Bagno Vignoni, Siena ☎ *(0577) 887112* 🔳 🛏 *48* 🛌 *43* 🆅🆂🅰

Location: 6km (4 miles) S, off the Via Cassia. Its thermal baths, used by St Catherine of Siena and Lorenzo the Magnificent, make this simple but comfortable hotel a restful place to take the waters.

🏠 ♿ ⚓ ♨ ⚲

Sansepolcro

*Map 13F8. 114km (71 miles) SE of Florence, 39km (24 miles)
NE of Arezzo. 52037. Arezzo. Population: 15,695.*

In this somewhat mournful town close to the Umbrian border
Piero della Francesca was born after 1420 and spent the last
14yr of his life writing his treatises on *Perspective* and the *Five
Regular Bodies*. It was probably in the early 1460s that he
executed his masterpiece, the *Resurrection*, in his native town.

Museo Civico

Via Aggiunti 65 ▄▄ *Open daily 9:30am–1pm, 2:30–6pm.*

Piero's hypnotic *Resurrection* ★ has been called the greatest picture in
the world. Sir Kenneth Clark describes the spell it casts.

"Before Piero's Risen Christ we are suddenly conscious of values for
which no rational statement is adequate; we are struck with a feeling of
awe, older and less reasonable than that inspired by the Blessed
Angelico. This country god, who rises in the gray light while humanity is
asleep, has been worshipped ever since man first knew that the seed is not
dead in the winter earth, but will force its way upward through an iron
crust. Later He will become a god of rejoicing, but His first emergence is
painful and involuntary. He seems to be part of the dream which lies so
heavily on the sleeping soldiers . . . ."

Opposite is Piero's early polyptych, the *Madonna della Misericordia* ★
(1446–c.1458). Like the *Madonna del Parto* at **Monterchi** (see below),
this Madonna of Mercy is both a pretty, young peasant girl and icy
goddess, whose state of spiritual detachment has been likened to that
evoked by Buddhist and African sculpture. The whole polyptych is in
uneven condition and other sections were painted by assistants. Also by
Piero are the frescoes of *St Julian* and *St Louis of Toulouse*.

Notable among the other works in the museum are a processional flag
representing the *Crucifixion* by Signorelli; Pontormo's *St Quentin*; and
battered but fine 15thC choir stalls which demonstrate the influence of
Piero on perspective intarsia work.

Other sights

In the Romanesque-Gothic **Duomo**, paintings include two panels by
Matteo di Giovanni, part of a polyptych of which the central panel, the
Baptism of Christ by Piero, was purchased for the London National
Gallery in 1861 – for £241 (about $1200).

The church of **San Francesco** retains it Gothic high altar (1304) for
which Sassetta painted his *St Francis* altarpiece, an early influence on
Piero, now scattered, parts being in London and Paris.

In the 16thC church of **San Lorenzo** is a dramatic *Deposition*
(c.1528–30) by Rosso Fiorentino.

H R **La Balestra** (*Via dei Montefeltro 29* ☎ *(0575) 76217/76345* ▮▯
restaurant closed Tues). See also **Anghiari**.

Excursion

17km (11 miles) S of Sansepolcro, in the tiny cemetery chapel on
the edge of the village of **Monterchi**, is another masterpiece by
Piero, the *Madonna del Parto* ★ (▄▄ *custodian always on duty*).
Pointing proudly to her pregnant womb, she is revealed to us by
two triumphant angels, reverse images of the same cartoon.

Saturnia

*Map 9K7. 215km (134 miles) S of Florence, 57km (35 miles)
SE of Grosseto. 58050. Grosseto. Population: 631.*

The Etruscan town on this site was called Aurinia. The Romans
named it Saturnia because they believed it had been founded by
Jupiter's father. The walls built by the Sienese in the 15thC
incorporate Etruscan and Roman sections.

The Etruscan necropolis lies to the N of the walls, the most
interesting tombs being in the Puntone area.

The spa of **Terme di Saturnia**, where sulfurous water springs at a
constant temperature of 106°F (37°C), is 3km (2 miles) to the s.

The road N to *Monte Amiata* passes through a beautiful, sparsely
populated landscape dotted with medieval castles and villages.

Ⓗ **Terme di Saturnia**
Strada della Follonata, 58050 Saturnia, Grosseto
☎ *(0564) 601061* ✆ *500172* ▥▥▥ ☎ 104 ▭ 104 ━ ▥ ⇌ AE ⊙
A serious first-class spa hotel offering a wide range of treatments.
▱ ♨ ⎘ ⚘ ≈ ⁓ ♣ ♨

Ⓡ **I Due Cippi-da Michele** (☎ *(0564) 601474* ▮▯ *closed Tues except
summer*) is in the main square of Saturnia; also **La Volpe** (*Le Croste*
☎ *(0564) 601474, closed Mon*), 6km (4 miles) s of Montemerano.

Ⓡ **Laudomia**
9km (6 miles) s at Poderi di Montemerano ☎ *(0564) 629224* ▭
▱ ⎘ *Closed Wed, June.*
A welcoming traditional rustic restaurant with rooms.

Scarperia

*Map **16**D6. 30km (19 miles) N of Florence. 50038. Firenze.
Population: 5,190.*
An industrial and crafts center (furniture, wrought iron,
knives, copper) in the Mugello with a fine Palazzo Pretorio of
1306 and, in the church opposite, a tondo of the *Madonna and
Child* by B. da Maiano.

Event: International motorcycle rallies take place at the
autodrome on Sun.

Nearby sights

The road to the N climbs through the mountain **pass of Scarperia** at
882m (2,920ft), the 'little Switzerland' of the Mugello, known as '*il
Giogo*,' which links the Mugello to the Santerno Valley.

3.5km (2 miles) NE of Scarperia is the village of **Sant' Agata**, with a
strikingly unusual Romanesque **pieve**.

Ⓡ The homey, delightful **Molinuccio** (☎ *(055) 8406952* ▮▯ *closed
Mon*), 2km (1½ miles) beyond Sant'Agata at Molinuccio, has a trout pond.

Shopping

Coltelleria Artigiana Giglio (*Via dell'Oche 48* ☎ *(055) 846148*
▮▯); knives of all kinds at low prices.

Sesto Fiorentino

*Map **6**B2–3. 9km (6 miles) NW of Florence. 50019. Firenze.
Bus 28 from Florence station. Population: 44,458.*
An important center of the porcelain and ceramics industry. In
the central square, Piazza Ginori, is the 15thC Palazzo Pretorio.
Museo delle Porcellane di Doccia
Via Pratese ▨ *Open Tues–Sat 9:30am–1pm, 3:30–6pm.*
In a park along the Via Pratese, this modern museum (1965) exhibits a
superb collection of 18th–20thC porcelains from the Doccia factory
founded in 1737 by Carlo Ginori.

Nearby sight

To the E of Sesto is **Quinto**, where the imposing 7thC BC Etruscan **tomba
della Montagnola** is in the Via Fratelli Rosselli (custodian at no. 95).

Ⓗ **Villa Villoresi**
Via delle Torri 63, 50019 Sesto Fiorentino, Firenze
☎ *(055) 4489032* ▥▮ ☎ 27 ▭ 27 ━ ▥ ⇌
A beautifully maintained 14thC villa.
▱ ⎘ ⚘ ◁≈ ≈

H R **Motelagip** (*Campo Bisenzio* ☎ (055) 440081 ▥▯ to ▥▥▥).

R **Giuseppe Alessi**
Via Bolognese 11, Montorsoli ☎ (055) 401059 ▥▥▥ ▭ ▤ *Closed
Sun, Wed lunch, Thurs lunch, Aug.*
This is a restaurant for serious eaters only. You must book a table 3–4
months in advance. The proprietor is a scholar of Renaissance cooking,
and his great dishes are carefully researched historic re-creations that
are prepared with the best ingredients still to be found in the Tuscan
countryside.

R **La Terrazza** (☎ (055) 8879078 ▥▯ to ▥▥▥ *closed Sun, Mon, Aug*) is
in the Castello of Calenzano; **Vecciolino** (*Via Colli Alti* ☎ (055) 448194
▥▯ *closed Tues*).

Settignano
Map **7***D5. 8km (5 miles)* E *of Florence. Bus 10 from Piazza
San Marco, Florence. 50135. Firenze. Population: 1,563.*
A Florentine suburb in the Fiesolan Hills graced by cypresses,
olive groves and fine old villas. Renaissance sculptors who were
born or made their home for a time in the area near the *pietra
serena* quarries of Monte Ceceri include Desiderio, the
Rossellino brothers, the Maiano brothers, Benedetto da
Rovezzano, and Michelangelo. Boccaccio set the *Decameron* in
these hills, and D'Annunzio lived here during his love affair
with Eleanora Duse in the Villa Capponcina.
   One of the many foreign literary residents was Walter Savage
Landor, author of *Imaginary Conversations*, who lived in the
15thC Villa Gherardesca in the 1820s; another was the art
historian Bernard Berenson, whose Villa I Tatti is now run by
Harvard University as a center for Renaissance studies. The
English attachment to this countryside reached a peak late in
the 19thC when Queen Victoria visited the Castle of **Vincigliata**
(see below). The gushing sensibilities of English esthetes were
satirized by Anatole France in his novel *Le Lys Rouge*.
   See also *Fiesole*.

Sights and places of interest
Approaching from central Florence, the Via G. D'Annunzio leads past
Nervi's concrete **Stadium** in the Campo dei Marti to Ponte a Mensola
where the church of **S. Martino a Mensola** (*ring for entrance*) has an
elegant *quattrocento* interior with a triptych by Taddeo Gaddi. The Via
d'Annunzio then climbs to the village of Settignano. There is a good view
of Florence from Piazza Desiderio and, in the 16thC church of the
Assunta, a pulpit designed by Buontalenti, and a Della Robbia *Madonna*.
   1km (⅔ mile) SE is the **Villa Gamberaia** which has one of the great
Italian gardens (*rarely open to the public*).
   To the NE is Montebeni, Berenson's favorite walking country and still
unexpectedly rural. A left turn off the Montebeni road leads to the Castle
of **Vincigliata**, Victorianized in 1855 by John Temple Leader.

H **The Villa Linda**, on the Maiano road (☎ (055) 603913 ▭) is a
simple *pensione*.

R **Le Cave**
Via delle Cave 16, Maiano ☎ (055) 59133 ▥▯ ▭ ⌂ ▬ *Closed
Thurs, Sun eve, Aug.*
An old *bottega* which once served the quarry workers. The food is not
above ordinary and the interior is noisy; but the location is magical.

R **Osvaldo**
Via G. d'Annunzio 51 ☎ (055) 602168 ▥▯ to ▥▥ ▭ ▬ *Closed
Tues eve, Wed.*
A favorite with fellows of **I Tatti**.

Siena ★
Map 11G6. 68km (42 miles) s of Florence. 53100. Siena.
Population: 64,251 **i** *Piazza del Campo 55*
☎ *(0577) 280551; Via di Città 5* ☎ *(0577) 47051.*

Soft Siena, City of the Virgin, stands on her pedestal of three
hills, vain of her beauty, absorbed in her past. She is the other
half of Tuscany, feminine counterpart to the hardheaded
masculinity of Florence. According to a persistent legend,
Siena was founded by Senius, son of Remus; hence the wolf,
one of the city's most prominent emblems. But the earliest
certain knowledge we have of Siena, apart from evidence of an
Etruscan settlement, is of the Roman colony Saena Julia.

During the early Middle Ages Siena enjoyed a privileged
relationship with the Hohenstaufen emperors; and as a free
republic from the early 12thC she attained a precocious pre-
eminence in banking and trade, and became the leading
Ghibelline center in Tuscany and the natural rival of Guelf
Florence. Although the defeat of Florence at the Battle of
Montaperti in 1260 is still celebrated in Siena as a glorious
event, it was less significant than the Florentine victory 9yr later
at Colle di Val d'Elsa. Then Siena joined the Guelf alliance and
from 1287 was governed as an oligarchy by a Council of Nine
'Good Men' chosen from the middle classes. The Republic
flourished under the balanced, methodical rule of the Nine; the
late 13th to early 14thC was an age of stability, prosperity and
artistic achievement. But the turmoil and discontent following
famines and the Black Death of 1348 led to the overthrow in
1355 of the Nine by the nobles assisted by the working class.

There is nothing in the world quite like Siena; it is a medieval
city that might be likened to a rare beast, with heart, arteries,
tail, paws and teeth. Only the skeleton is left, intact, and it is
enough to astound us.

Bernard Berenson

Spiritually Siena was guided through the turbulent post-
plague years by two remarkable religious reformers, later
canonized as St Catherine of Siena (1347–80) and St
Bernardino of Siena (1380–1444). Politically, the next two
centuries were marked by fruitless wars, voluntary submission
to foreign control – Charles IV from 1355, Gian Galeazzo
Visconti from 1399, Charles V in 1530 – and periods of unstable
independence when the power of nobility became increasingly
stronger.

In 1552 the city rebelled against the Spanish occupation, and
2yr later the combined forces of Charles V and Duke Cosimo I
of Florence advanced on Siena and laid siege for 18 months
during which the population was halved and the countryside
devastated. In 1557 Charles sold the city outright to Cosimo,
and in 1559 Siena and her territories were officially annexed to
the Tuscan grand duchy by the Peace of Cateau-Cambrésis.

As the unwilling bride of Florence, Siena was treated as a
second-class member of the Tuscan empire. No public banks
were permitted to operate until 1622; the wool industry
collapsed in the mid-17thC and by the mid-18thC most Sienese
noble families were deeply in debt. "Cracking, peeling, fading,
crumbling, rotting," Henry James wrote of the city in 1909.

And yet, visitors to Siena in the late 20thC will find more here
than art to admire and even envy. It seems that the ideal of the
Common Good, practised by the Nine and revealed to posterity

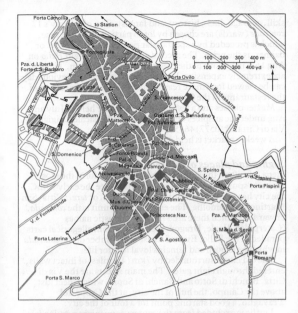

in Ambrogio Lorenzetti's famous frescoes in the Palazzo
Pubblico, may not have been forgotten.

Sienese art

Siena is a Gothic city. Its greatest buildings – the Duomo and
Palazzo Pubblico – and best known pictures – Duccio's *Maestà*,
Simone Martini's *Maestà* and *Guido Ricci da Fogliano*,
Ambrogio Lorenzetti's *Good and Bad Government* – were
created in the late 13th–14thC. In the 15thC the Sienese by and
large ignored the Florentine Renaissance. They continued to
build ogival palaces and even their major painters, Giovanni di
Paolo and Sassetta, made decorative, two-dimensional pictures
on gold backgrounds. It was not until the 16thC that
Renaissance painting arrived with Sodoma and Domenico
Beccafumi, the greatest Sienese Mannerist.

Most important works of art were commissioned by the
government or religious bodies, powerful, conservative groups
who knew exactly what they wanted as to style and subject
matter. Over half the pictures commissioned between
1350–1550 were of the Virgin, Queen of Siena; and
collaborative projects were more common than in Florence.

Sienese sculpture advanced earlier and further than its sister
arts, thanks partly to the influence of Giovanni Pisano, whose
figures for the facade of the Duomo are among the most
important examples of Gothic sculpture in Italy. The greatest
native Sienese sculptor, Jacopo della Quercia, effected the
transition to the Renaissance; his principal works in the city are
the Fonte Gaia and the Baptistry font.

Events: The *Palio*, the barebacked horse race around the
Campo on Aug 2 and 16, is the central event of the Sienese
calendar and the focal point of every Sienese citizen's life. It is
one of the strangest and most magnificent public spectacles
there are: a mixture of pomp, licensed violence and corruption,

skill, courage, luck, history, and fantasy. Ten of the city's 17 *contrade* (wards) are chosen by lot to participate in the race, which is preceded by a spectacular procession. The *palio*, or banner, is the prize. The second and more important *Palio* on Aug 16 is in honour of the Assumption of the Virgin. Tickets are extremely expensive, but the rehearsals on the previous days can be viewed for a more reasonable price from a seat at one of the restaurants in the Campo.

Master classes and a festival of concerts are held in July and Aug under the auspices of the Accademia Musicale Chigiana, 82 Via di Città ☎ (0577) 46152.

A weekly market is held on Sat morning.

Sights and places of interest

Siena is built on three landlocked hills which form the most westerly spur of the Chiana mountains. Since the early 13thC the city has been divided into three districts, or *terzi*: Città, San Martino and Camollia. The essential civic unit is the *contrada*, or ward, of which there are 17. Their fantastic names (Caterpillar, Eagle, Dragon, etc.) derive from allegorical carts paraded at the Palio. Every Sienese is a member of the *contrada* in which he is born and remains loyal to it for life.

The old city is surrounded by 7km (4⅓ miles) of intact walls, entered through eight gates. The main streets are the Via di Città, Banchi di Sotto and Banchi di Sopra, which meet just above the Campo, the hub of the city, at the **Croce del Travaglio**, a good starting point for a tour of the city.

Traffic is excluded from the center; convenient parking lots are near S. Domenico, the Stadium and the Lizza.

Campo ★

The central square of Siena, one of the most magical public spaces in Europe, lies at the confluence of the three hills on which the city is built. Its sloping, semicircular shape often elicits comparisons: to a fan, or shell, or amphitheater. For the Sienese it is a cloak – the cloak of the Madonna spread out to protect her favored city. The perimeter of the cloak is trimmed with lacy palaces of which the most striking is the curved **Sansedoni**, originally a group of 13 palaces extended in the 14thC and restructured in the early 18thC.

The brick paving is divided into nine sections symbolizing the government of the Nine Good Men, who were responsible for the systematic development of the Campo from the late 13thC. At the center of the curve is a reproduction of Jacopo della Quercia's Fonte Gaia, the original of which is now in the **Palazzo Pubblico**.

Palazzo Pubblico 🏛 ★

The structure of the most graceful Gothic civic building in Tuscany reflects that of the communal government for which it was erected from 1297–1342. The wings (raised by one story in 1681) were occupied respectively by the Podestà, responsible for justice, and the Nine, responsible for administration, and separated by the central body housing the Biccherna, or treasury, and the General Council. The black and white communal shield, the *balzana*, decorates all the openings of the facade. From the left corner, the bell tower (1325–48), known as the **Mangia** after the nickname ('wastrel') of its first bell-ringer, leaps – in William Dean Howell's vivid words – "like a rocket into the starlit air." The **Cappella di Piazza** at the base of the Mangia was built from 1352–76 and modified in 1468. To its right is the entrance to the Cortile del Podestà, which gives access to the sections of the palace open to the public. For a stunning view climb the 503 steps to the top of the Mangia.

Museo Civico ★

First floor 📷 *Open Apr–Sept Mon–Sat 8:30am–7:30pm; Oct–Mar 8:30am–7pm, Sun, hols 8:30am–1pm.*

Sala del Risorgimento: The six frescoes, by the best late 19thC-Sienese artists, relate episodes from the life of Victor Emmanuel II. **Sala di Balìa:** The only room in the palace decorated by non-Sienese artists. The frescoes (1407) by Spinello Aretino and Pari di Spinello depict the life of the Sienese Pope Alexander III. **Sala dei Cardinali:** Sculptures by followers of Jacopo della Quercia. **Sala del Concistro:** Portal by B. Rossellino, frescoes by Beccafumi of the *Political Virtues* (1529–36).

Antechapel: Frescoes (1414) by Taddeo di Bartolo. The huge *St Christopher* symbolizes the duty of the commune to care for the weak. **Chapel:** The elegant iron gate (1437) may have been designed by Jacopo della Quercia. The Gothic **choir stalls** (1428) illustrate the Nicene Creed. Frescoes of *Scenes from the Life of the Virgin* (1407) by Taddeo di Bartolo. Over the altar, the *Sacred Family with St Leonard* by Sodoma.

Sala del Mappamondo: The room where the city council met. The painted map after which the room was named no longer exists, but a recent restoration has revealed the existence of yet another 14thC fresco beneath the equestrian portrait of *Guido Riccio da Fogliano* ★ (1328), traditionally assumed to be by Simone Martini. Originally part of a cycle running around three walls of the room and illustrating the castles conquered by Siena after 1314, this fresco records the victory over the nobles of Montemassi and Sassoferrato. On the opposite wall is the *Maestà* ★ (1315) signed "Siena had me painted by the hand of Simone [Martini]." The Virgin is represented as the Queen of Heaven and Siena.

Sala della Pace: Sienese dedication to law and order received its most complete and vivid pictorial expression with Ambrogio Lorenzetti's *Allegory of Good and Bad Government* ★ (1338–40), painted for the council chamber as a reminder of the Augustinian and Thomist teachings that justice and common good are the first aims of good government. On the wall opposite the windows, *Good Government* is represented by a king wearing the colors of the *balzana* and surrounded by symbolic virtues and attributes. On the right wall, we see the *Effects of Good Government in the City and Country*. For all its didactic intricacy, this picture may still be enjoyed in the spirit as St Bernardino described it in the 15thC: "I see merchants buying and selling, I see dancing, the houses being repaired, the workers busy in the vineyards or sowing the fields. . . ." On the left wall is the ruined fresco of *Bad Government and its Effects*.

Sala dei Pilastri: Sienese pictures of the 14th–15thC, including Neroccio di Bartolommeo's diptych of *St Bernardino*. **Loggia:** The remains of Jacopo della Quercia's carvings for the **Fonte Gaia** ★ (1409–19). The fountain commemorated the appearance of water in the Campo.

Chigi-Saracini Palace ▥
Via di Città 89 🔲 🗺️ *Visits on request* ☎ *(0577) 46152.*
Built in the 14thC for one of the great Sienese banking families, this lovely stone and brick palace now houses the distinguished Accademia Musicale Chigiana, who hold some of their summer concerts here (see events opposite) and a collection of 14th–17thC Tuscan paintings.

Across the Via di Città, at no. 126, is the **Palazzo Piccolomini delle Papese** (1460–95), built for Pius II's sister, probably by B. Rossellino, in the Florentine Renaissance style.

Duomo ▥ † ★
The cathedral of Santa Maria dell'Assunta was the most expensive and carefully considered building project of Siena's golden age. Its construction, which occupied nearly two centuries, was in the beginning supervised by committees of Sienese citizens, and there was no Sienese artist or craftsman of any distinction who did not work at some time on the cathedral. Long after the structure was completed in the late 14thC, they continued to embellish the interior. The result is perhaps less satisfying as a work of architecture than for its individual components.

The site chosen for the building, which began in the late 12thC, was the Castelvecchio, the earliest inhabited part of the city. The basic structure was complete in 1215, the hexagonal cupola in 1264, and the facade was begun in 1284. In 1339 an extraordinary and hopelessly ambitious decision was made: Siena would build a new and greater cathedral, rivaling those of Florence and Orvieto, for which the old cathedral would serve as transept. This unwieldy and, as it turned out, prohibitively expensive scheme was abandoned after the 1348 plague, and the old cathedral was finally completed in 1382.

The skeletal remains of the new cathedral (**Duomo Nuovo**), now housing the Cathedral Museum (**see over**), stand to the right of the Duomo, behind Buontalenti's Palazzo della Prefettura. Opposite the

Duomo is the **Hospital of Santa Maria della Scala ▥** (▣ *open daily 9am–noon*), the most important institution in medieval and Renaissance Siena after the Duomo and Palazzo Pubblico. The building, which dates from late 13th to 14thC, is still in use as a hospital; in the Sala d'Infermeria modern patients are surrounded by frescoes illustrating the care of the sick in the Renaissance. Over the high altar of the adjoining church of **Santa Maria della Scala**, rebuilt in 1466, is Vecchietta's superb bronze *Risen Christ* (1476). To the left of the Duomo is the early 18thC imitation-Gothic Palazzo Arcivescovile (Archbishop's Palace), with Ambrogio Lorenzetti's enchanting, naturalistic *Madonna Lactans*.

The polychrome marble **facade of the Duomo** is best studied from the far right corner of the square. The lower section (1284–96), the first building project in Tuscany to reflect the Gothic influence of *San Galgano*, was designed by Giovanni Pisano. The statues are copies of the originals, by Giovanni or assistants, now in the Cathedral Museum (see opposite). The central bronze door dates from 1958, and the gabled upper section in the high Gothic style was begun in 1376; the mosaics are 19thC. From the right transept rises the Romanesque **campanile** (1313).

The **interior** is most immediately striking for the giddy optical effect of the black and white stripes. The **floor ★** is paved in marble with 56 designs produced by over 40 leading Sienese artists, executed by craftsmen in *sgraffiti* or intarsia, a remarkable collaborative work carried out between 1369–1547. Notice especially Beccafumi's *Old Testament Scenes* between the cupola and high altar.

Libreria Piccolomini ★
Off the left nave ▥ *Open daily 9am–7pm.*
The most brilliantly decorative room in Tuscany, this was built in the 1490s by Francesco Todeschini Piccolomini (Pope Pius III). The vividly charming frescoes (1502–05) by Pinturicchio depict ten *Scenes from the Life of Pius II*. In the center of the room is the beautiful and influential *Three Graces*, a 3rdC Roman copy of a Hellenistic statue. Fine illuminated choir books are displayed on late 15thC benches.

To the w of the library is the great **Piccolomini Altar** (1503), designed by Andrea Bregno. The statues of *Sts Peter and Pius* and *Sts Gregory and Paul* are by the young Michelangelo.

Left transept: The **chapel of St John the Baptist** (1481–98) is entered through an elegant marble portal. Frescoes include Pinturicchio's two portraits of *Alberto Arighieri*, in youth and old age. The vigorous bronze statue of the *Baptist* (1457) is by Donatello; that of *St Catherine of Alexandria* (1487) is by Neroccio. The **pulpit ★** (1266–68) is by Nicola Pisano, assisted by his son Giovanni and pupils including Arnolfo di Cambio; 6yr later than the great **Baptistry** pulpit at *Pisa*, this work is freer and more innovatory. The seven panels, separated by figures of prophets and angels, depict *Scenes from the Life of Christ*. The staircase was added by Riccio in 1570.

The **chapel of St Ansano** contains a **monument to Cardinal Petroni** (1317–18) by Tino di Camaiano and, in the pavement, the slab **tomb of Bishop Giovanni Pecci** by Donatello.

Presbytery: The **high altar** (1532) by Peruzzi bears a huge **ciborium** (1462–72) by Vecchietta. The two higher flanking *Angels* (1489) are by Giovanni di Stefano, those placed lower down (1499) by Francesco di Giorgio Martini. Eight serenely beautiful **candelabra-angels** (1548–50) on the nave pilasters are by Beccafumi, perhaps his masterpieces as a sculptor. In the apse are 51 finely carved **choir stalls** (14th–16thC). The **window** above (1288) is one of the earliest examples of Italian stained glass, made from cartoons by Duccio.

Right transept: The **Chigi chapel** (1661) was built for the morbidly pious Fabio Chigi, Pope as Alexander VII, to designs by Bernini. *St Jerome* and the *Magdalen* in niches on the entrance wall are by Bernini. The *Madonna del Voto* over the altar is by Guido da Siena or a follower.

Baptistry ★
Reached by a steep flight of steps to the right of the Duomo. Facing its own Piazza San Giovanni, the Baptistry is situated beneath the apse of the cathedral. The impressive Gothic **facade** (1317–82) is incomplete in the upper section. The **interior** was designed by Camaino and Tino di Camaino and frescoed by, among others, Vecchietta. At its center is Jacopo della Quercia's hexagonal marble **font ★** (1411–30), a masterpiece of artistic collaboration in the Gothic-Renaissance style. Two of the statues around the basin, *Faith* and *Hope*, are by Donatello.

The six gilded bronze relief panels include Jacopo della Quercia's powerful *Zacharias expelled from the Temple*, Ghiberti's *Baptism of Christ* and Donatello's *Herod's Feast*.

To the E of the Baptistry is the **Palazzo del Magnifico** (1504–08), designed by G. Cozzarelli for Pandolfo Petrucci, autocratic political leader of Siena from 1487–1524. The beautifully wrought bronzes on the handsome facade have been replaced by copies.

Museo dell'Opera del Duomo (*Cathedral Museum*) ★
In right aisle of the Duomo Nuovo 🔁 *Open daily 9am–7pm.*

Ground floor: Among the carvings from the cathedral facade, the **ten figures** ★ (1284–96) by Giovanni Pisano are among the most important Gothic sculptures in Italy. In the center is a bas-relief of the *Madonna and Child with St Anthony Abbot and Cardinal Antonio Casini*, a late work by Jacopo della Quercia.

First floor: Sala di Duccio. Duccio's *Maestà* ★ (1308–11), the inaugural work of the great period of Sienese painting, was carried to the Duomo when complete in a magnificent candlelit procession while the bells of Siena pealed the Gloria and the citizens offered prayers and alms to the poor. It stood over the high altar of the cathedral until removed to a side chapel in 1505. Originally painted on both sides, the panel was split and dismantled in the 18thC. The *Madonna Enthroned* now faces the 26 *Scenes from the Passion*. On the left wall are 19 **panels from the predella and upper section** (others are in London, Washington and New York).

On the right wall are P. Lorenzetti's triptych of the *Nativity of the Virgin* (1342) and a *Madonna and Child* (1283) by the young Duccio.

Sala del Tesoro: The finest treasures are Giovanni Pisano's tiny wooden *Crucifix* and F. da Valdambrino's busts of saints.

Second floor: Sala della Madonna degli Occhi Grossi. The room is named after the 13thC panel of a large-eyed *Madonna* in the center. The outstanding picture is Simone Martini's *Blessed Agostino Novello with Four of his Miracles* ★ (c.1330), formerly in Sant'Agostino. **Sala dei Conversari:** Works by Matteo di Giovanni, Beccafumi, Pomarancio and Luca Giordano. From the next room one may climb to the rim of the Duomo Nuovo for spectacular views.

The **Cripta delle Statue** (*hours as museum*) is entered from the steps leading to the Baptistry. It contains statues from the Duomo and fresco fragments (1270–80), the earliest known Sienese wall paintings.

Fonte Branda
The most famous and one of the oldest of the many Sienese wells.

Fontegiusta †
Via Fontegiusta, off Via Camollia.

The church of the Madonna di Fontegiusta was built in 1482–84 in gratitude for a Sienese victory over the Florentines. The elegant portico was added in 1489. The unusual square interior contains 16thC Sienese paintings and a large tabernacle by Marrina.

Via Camollia ends at the **Porta Camollia** (1604), the most northerly of the Sienese gates opening onto the Florence road. The famous Sienese welcome *Cor magis tibi Sena pandit* (Siena opens wide its heart to you) was inscribed when the gate was rebuilt in honor of a visit by Ferdinand I.

Forte di Santa Barbara
Built in 1560 by Duke Cosimo I, this fort now houses the Enoteca Italica Permanente (see *Tuscan wines*). The views from the ramparts are best at sunset. To the NE is the **Lizza**, the triangular public park of Siena.

Loggia della Mercanzia
Erected in 1428–44 where the three principal streets of Siena meet above the Campo, and now housing the Provincial Tourist Board. The statues of saints are by Vecchietta and A. Federighi. The upper story is 17thC.

Piccolomini Palace 🏛 ☆
Via Banchi di Sotto 👁 *Open Mon–Fri 9:30am–1pm,
Sat 9am–12:30pm.*

The palace, begun in 1469, was very likely designed by B. Rossellino. It resembles his *Rucellai Palace, Florence* and **Piccolimini Palace** at *Pienza*. With the nearby **Logge del Papa** (1462), designed by A. Federighi, this constitutes the most important Renaissance building complex in Siena. The palace houses the State Archives; among the documents on view are the **covers of the registers of Biccherna**, the treasury, illuminated by leading Sienese artists from 1258–1659.

The 16thC ex-monastery opposite the palace is the seat of the University of Siena. Via San Vigilio leads to the picturesque medieval buildings of the **Corte del Castellare degli Ugurgieri**.

Pinacoteca Nazionale ▥ ★
Via San Pietro 29 🚻 *Open Tues – Sun 8:45am – 1:45pm.*

The outstanding collection of 12th–early 17thC Sienese pictures is housed in the graceful early 15thC Gothic **Palazzo Buonsignori**. The display is arranged chronologically beginning on the second floor. The following is an introductory tour of some of the major works.

Rm. I: Altar frontal of *The Redeemer* with symbols of the Evangelists and scenes from the Passion (1215), the earliest dated Sienese painting. Rm. II: Works by Guido da Siena (13thC) the first of the great Sienese masters. Rms. III–IV: Duccio, especially the finely executed but damaged *Madonna dei Francescani*. Rm. VI: Simone Martini's *Madonna and Child*. Rms. VII–VIII: The *Two Views*, attributed to A. Lorenzetti, are the earliest known examples of pure landscape painting in pre-Renaissance European art. Also by A. Lorenzetti: *Madonna with Saints and Angels* and *Annunciation* (1344). P. Lorenzetti: *Madonna and Child* (1328–29), originally in the center of an altarpiece of which the superb *Stories of the Carmelite Order* formed the predella. *Birth of the Virgin* (c.1380–90) by Paolo di Giovanni Fei.

Rm. XIII: Giovanni di Paolo's *Last Judgment* and *Madonna of Humility*; Sassetta's *Last Supper* and *St Anthony Abbot*. Rm. XIV: Neroccio's *Madonna and Saints* (c.1475); Francesco di Giorgio's *Annunciation* and *Nativity*. Rm. XVIII: Sano di Pietro's *The Virgin Commending the City of Siena to Pope Calixtus II* (1456); Francesco di Giorgio's *Coronation of the Virgin*.

First floor. Rm. XXIII: Pinturicchio's *Holy Family with the Young St John*. Rms. XXX–XXXII: Sodoma's *Nativity, Scourging of Christ* (c.1511–14), *Deposition*. Rm. XXXIII: Beccafumi's *St Catherine Receiving the Stigmata* (c.1515) and *Birth of the Virgin* (1543). Rm. XXXVII: Beccafumi's *Descent into Hell* (c.1530–35). Sodoma's *Descent into Hell* and *Gethsemene* (c.1525).

Salimbeni Palace ▥
This beautiful 14thC palace is the headquarters of the Sienese-owned Monte dei Paschi bank. On the right side of Piazza Salimbeni is the Renaissance **Spanocchi Palace** (1470) by G. da Maiano, and on the left the 16thC Tantucci Palace.

Sant'Agostino †
The 13thC building, remade in the 18thC, retains important paintings, notably Perugino's *Crucifixion* (1506), A. Lorenzetti's *Madonna and Saints*, Matteo di Giovanni's *Slaughter of the Innocents* (1482) and, over the high altar, Sodoma's *Epiphany*.

Santa Caterina (*Santuario Cateriniano*) †
A complex of chapels created in and around the house of Catherine Benincasa, the eloquent mystic who was canonized in 1461. **The Oratory of St Catherine** (1465–74), facing Via S. Caterina, was built by the *contrada* of Fontebranda, whose symbol, the goose, adorns the facade. Inside is a wooden statue of *St Catherine* (1474) by Neroccio and five frescoed *Angels* by Sodoma. The Oratorio della Camera is built over St Catherine's cell. The Baroque Oratorio del Crocifisso contains the 13thC *Crucifix* before which the saint received the stigmata at Pisa in 1375. The Oratorio Superiore has a ceiling by Riccio, and a 17thC tiled floor.

San Domenico †
The stark red-brick Dominican preaching church crowns the hill above **Fontebranda**. The present building, incorporating the original early-13thC church, dates from the 14th–15thC. The campanile was completed in 1340. The only authentic portrait of *St Catherine*, who assumed the Dominican habit in this church, is that by her friend Andrea Vanni, in a chapel at the w end. In the Chapel of St Catherine, off the right side, are Sodoma's frescoes of *Episodes from the Life of St Catherine* (1526). The *Ciborium* and two *Angels* (1475) are by B. da Maiano.

San Francesco †
As in Florence, the Franciscan preaching church stands across the city from that built by the Dominicans. An earlier church on this site was begun immediately after the death of St Francis. The present building (1326–1475) was altered after a fire in the 17thC and again in the late 19thC. The Neo-Gothic facade was applied in 1913. In the N transept are detached frescoes (1331) by P. Lorenzetti of the *Crucifixion* and by A. Lorenzetti of *St Louis of Anjou before Pope Boniface VII* and the *Martyrdom of the Franciscans*.

On the s side of the piazza is the **Oratorio di San Bernardino** (*custodian at no. 19*). This oratory was built in the 15thC on the site where the Franciscan St Bernardino had preached. The upper chapel is elegantly decorated with 15thC stuccowork, carvings and frescoes by Sodoma, G. del Pacchia and Beccafumi. The Via del Comune descends to the 14thC **Porta Ovile**.

Santa Maria dei Servi †
Piazza Alessandro Manzoni
The building dates from the 13th–15thC; the interior naves and aisles were reworked in 1471–1528. Most important of the Sienese school pictures are: right aisle, Coppo di Marcovaldo's *Madonna* (1261); right transept, P. Lorenzetti's fresco of *The Slaughter of the Innocents*; left transept, Lippo Memmi's *Madonna*.

Nearby is the imposing **Porta Romana** (1327), from which the Via Cassia leads to Rome.

Santo Spirito †
Via dei Pispini
The brick Church of the Holy Spirit dates from 1498. The portal is attributed to Peruzzi and the cupola (1508) to Cozzarelli. Inside are works by Sodoma, Cozzarelli and Beccafumi. At the end of Via dei Pispini is the 14thC **Porta Pispini**, with the remains of a fresco of the *Nativity* (1531) by Sodoma.

Tolomei Palace ▥
11 Via Banchi di Sopra
The oldest private palace in Siena, now occupied by the Florentine Savings Bank, was built in 1208, and altered in c.1267.

Other sights outside the city walls

Diavoli Palace ▥
Just beyond Porta Camollia in Via Fiorentina is a medieval building, rebuilt in 1460 by A. Federighi. This palace is one of the first and most original pieces of Sienese Renaissance architecture.

Osservanza ▥ †
2.5km (1½ miles) from Porta Ovile, beyond the railway crossing, is the most interesting church in the environs of Siena, founded by St Bernardino in 1423 and rebuilt after damage in World War II to the original designs (1474–90) of Giacomo Cozzarelli. It contains a terracotta group of the *Annunciation* by Andrea della Robbia and, in the sacristy, a large *Pietà* by Cozzarelli.

Hotels

Certosa di Maggiano
Strada di Certosa 2, 53100 Siena ☎ *(0577) 288180*
Ⓣ*574221* ▥ ☎ *14 including 9 suites* ▭ *14* ⬛ ⬛ ⬛ AE Ⓟ VISA *Closed Nov–Feb.*
Location: *E of Porta Romana off the Arezzo/Rome road.* An exceptionally well-furnished, comfortably civilized and peaceful hotel around the cloister and church of a 14thC monastery.
▱ ☐ 🖻 ⚑ ⚓

Palazzo Ravizza
Pian dei Mantellini 34, 53100 Siena ☎ *(0577) 280462* ▯ *to* ▥ ☎ *13* ▭ ⬛ ⬛
Location: *5min walk from the Duomo and Campo.* This attractive first-class *pensione*, run by the same family for nearly 200yr in a 17thC villa, has maintained its old-fashioned character better than most.
‡ 🖻 ⚑ 《

Park Hotel
Via Marciano 16, 53100 Siena ☎ *(0577) 44803* Ⓣ*571005* ▥ ☎ *69* ▭ *69* ⬛ ⬛ ⬛ ⬛ AE CB ☎ VISA
Location: *2km (1½ miles) to NW.* A slick, modernized 15thC suburban villa. Standards have improved since it was taken over by the Ciga chain, but the service still doesn't live up to the luxurious accommodation. Good restaurant.
▱ ‡ ☐ 🖻 ⚑ ⚑ ⚓ ⚓ ⚒

Villa Scacciapensieri
Via di Scacciapensieri, 53100 Siena ☎ *(0577) 41411/41442* ▥ *to* ▥ ☎ *29* ▭ *29* ⬛ ⬛ ⬛ AE Ⓟ Ⓠ VISA *Closed Nov–Feb.*
Location: *3km (2 miles) to N.* A big, comfortable country villa set in a large garden with wonderful views of Siena. The generous breakfasts are a rare treat in Tuscany.
▱ ☐ 🖻 ⚑ 《 ⚓ ⚒

Restaurants

To dine in the Campo on a starlit evening is one of life's most magical experiences, but there isn't much to choose between the two restaurants: **Il Campo** (☎ *(0577) 280725, closed Tues*) and **Mangia** (☎ *(0577) 281121, closed Mon*).

Away from the Campo – and the tourists – the culinary standards are somewhat higher: **Guido** (*Vicolo Pettinaio 7* ☎ *(0577) 280042* ▮▯ to ▮▮▯ *closed Mon, two weeks in July*); **Mariotti da Mugolone** (*Via dei Pelligrini 8* ☎ *(0577) 283235* ▮▮▯ *closed Thurs*); **Tullio ai Tre Cristi** (*Vicolo Provenzano 1* ☎ *(0577) 280608* ▮▮▯ *closed Mon, Nov – Mar*).

La Taverna ✿
Via del Serpente 5, Vagliagli ☎ *(0577) 322532* ▯ ▭ ▬ ▭ *Closed Mon.*
This is a warm, cheerful tavern in a small hill town N of Siena.
Specialties: Homemade pastas.

Taverna Il Colombaio
SS 222, Querciagrossa, 2km N of Siena ☎ *(0577) 51144* ▮▮▯ ▯ ▭ ▬ ▭ ▭ [VISA] *Closed Sun eve, Mon.*
This charming old inn has comfortable rooms, and the restaurant serves its own versions of Sienese dishes. Chianti Classico is matched by wines from the Villa Colombaio estate of the Ugurgieri family. *Specialties: Cacciucco di pollo, sformati of vegetables.*

Vecchio Maniero
Via Stretta 5, Sovicille ☎ *(0577) 314340* ▮▮▯ ▯ ▭ ▬ ▭ [AE] [CB] [◉] [◉] [VISA] *Closed Mon, two weeks in July, two weeks in Jan.*
In an ancient manor house in the medieval village of Sovicille, 7km (4 miles) W of Siena. *Specialties: Pastas, filetto alla Vecchio Maniero.*

Sinalunga

*Map **12**G7. 103km (64 miles) SE of Florence, 45km (28 miles) SE of Siena. 53048.*
Hill town in the heart of the Valdichiana with good restaurants conveniently near the entrance to the autostrada A1.

Ⓡ Delle Grotte ✿
Viale Matteotti 35 ☎ *(0577) 60269* ▯ ▬ ▭ ▭ [VISA] *Closed Wed.*

Ⓡ Locanda dell'Amorosa
2km (1¼ miles) s ☎ *(0577) 69497* ▮▮▯ ▯ ▬ ▭ ▭ [AE] [◉] [VISA] *Closed Mon eve, Tues, Jan – Feb.*
An unusually elegant restaurant, with comfortable rooms, in the converted brick stables of a winegrowing estate.
Specialties: Pâté rustico, ravioli di ricotta, carpaccio, bistecca alla Fiorentina.

Sovana

*Map **8**I6. 226km (141 miles) S of Florence, 82km (51 miles) SE of Grosseto. 58010. Grosseto.*
A solitary, semi-abandoned village with Etruscan-Roman foundations on a plateau 8km (5 miles) NW of *Pitigliano*. The **Rocca** was built by the Aldobrandeschi lords in the 13thC. The main street is flanked by medieval houses. At one end is the 13thC **Palazzo Pretorio**, modified in the 15thC, and the Romanesque church of **Santa Maria** which contains a c.8th–9thC ciborium, a rare example of pre-Romanesque sculpture. At the far end is the splendid and dramatically situated Romanesque **Duomo**.

The **Etruscan necropolis** ☆ is in cool birch woods 1.5km (1 mile) below the town. (*A guide can be found at the Taverna Etrusca. Allow a minimum of 1hr.*) The architectonic tomb fronts are carved from the rock face of the gorge with burial grottoes beneath. The most sophisticated is the 2ndC BC Tomba Ildebranda in the form of a temple facade.

☐R☐ **Taverna Etrusca** ❦ (*Piazza Pretorio* ☎ *(0564) 616183, closed Mon, two to three weeks in June–July*).

Stia
Map **12***E7. 49km (30 miles) E of Florence. 52017. Arezzo. Population: 3,023.*
At the head of the Casentino just below **Monte Falterona**, where the Arno has its source. Its central Piazza Tanucci is a piece of first-class town planning, and the Romanesque church preserves a *Madonna and Child* (1437) by A. della Robbia and an *Annunciation* (1414) by Bicci di Lorenzo.

Nearby sights
In the late Middle Ages Stia was closely surrounded by the castles of the Guidi lords who ruled the upper Casentino and with whom the exiled Dante took refuge. The noblest of the ruined castles is the **Castello di Romena** (☒☒ ☒☒ *open daily 9am–noon, 3–7pm*), 3km (2 miles) S. Nearby, on a parallel road, is the 10th–12thC **Pieve di Romena** (*custodian in house next door*), the finest Romanesque church in the Casentino but over-restored.
 A magnificent 4hr walk N from Stia will take one to the summit of Monte Falterone via the source of the Arno on its S flank.

☐R☐ The proprietor of **Falterone** (*Piazza Tanucci 2* ☎ *(0575) 58631* **II**☐ *closed Sat*) is proud of his prizewinning *zuppa ripiena*.

Talamone
Map **8***J5. 164km (102 miles) S of Florence, 24km (15 miles) S of Grosseto. 58010. Grosseto. Population: 485 i See Porto Santo Stefano.*
A picturesque fishing village and tourist harbor on a headland S of *Monti dell'Uccellina* and overlooking Monte Argentario. The Sienese purchased Talamone from the Abbey of San Salvatore in 1303; their intention to make it into a port rivaling Pisa and Genoa was derided by Dante (*Purgatorio, XIII*). It became part of the Spanish Garrison States in 1556.

☐H☐ **Corte dei Butteri** ☒☒
58010 Fonte Blanda, Grosseto ☎ *(0564) 885547* **IIII** ☒ 87 ☒ 87
☒☒ ☒ ☒ ☒ *Closed Oct–Apr.*
Location: Fonte Blanda, 4km (2½ miles) NE. A modern luxury hotel.
☒☒☒☒☒☒☒☒

☐H☐ On the promontory is the **Capo d'Uomo** (☎ *(0564) 887077* **II**☐ *closed Oct–Mar*).

☐R☐ Restaurants in the center are more reasonably priced than those on the Argentario but are rather self-consciously geared to tourists. The two favorites are: **La Buca** (☎ *(0564) 887067* **II**☐ *closed Mon, Nov–Dec*); and **Da Flavia** (☎ *(0564) 887091* **II**☐ *closed Tues except summer, Dec–Mar*). For more genuine food of the region try **Da Dono**, 3km (2 miles) NE (☎ *(0564) 885523* **II**☐ *closed Mon*).

Tirli
Map **11***I5. 26km (16 miles) NE of Grosseto. 58040. Grosseto. Population: 597.*

☐R☐ **Tana del Cinghiale** (☎ *(0564) 945810* **II**☐ *to* **III**☐ *closed Wed, Oct*), a remote restaurant and hunting lodge (with rooms) in the hills specializing in wild boar.

Torre del Lago Puccini

Map 14E3. 95km (59 miles) w of Florence, 16km (10 miles) N of Pisa. 55048. Lucca. Population: 5,450.

Just to the E of the dull little village of Torre del Lago Puccini is **Lake Massaciuccoli**, the largest of the few lakes in Tuscany. The opera composer Giacomo Puccini, who settled here in 1891, once described this place as his "supreme joy, paradise, Eden, the Empyrean, turris eburnea, vas spiritualis, kingdom." He built himself a house on the shore of the lake, where he lived until shortly before his death in 1924.

Event: A festival of Puccini operas is held in early Aug. News and reservations: Segreteria del Festival Pucciniano, Piazza Puccini, 55048 Torre del Lago, Lucca ☎(0584) 342006.

Villa Puccini ☆

■■ 🖬 *Open daily summer 9am – noon, 3 – 7pm; winter 9am – noon, 2 – 5pm.*

The villa is preserved as it was in Puccini's lifetime, and he is buried here in a mausoleum built, appropriately, between his piano and his gun room. The house is thus a shrine as well as a vivid testimony to this lovable genius.

Ⓡ Next to the villa are **Butterfly-da Mario** (☎ *(0584) 341024* ◫ *closed Thurs, Nov*) with rooms; **Da Cecco** (☎ *(0584) 341002* ◫ *closed Mon, early July, two weeks in Nov – Dec*).

Across the lake, near Quiesa, 11km (7 miles) by road, are: **Colle Paradiso** (☎ *(0584) 93140* ◫ *to* ◫ *closed Tues, Jan*) with rooms; and the humbler **Oliva** (☎ *(0584) 93300* ◫ ❤ ◁ *closed Tues*).

Vallombrosa

Map 12E6. 33km (20 miles) SE of Florence. 50060. Firenze.

In the NE Pratomagno Hills, reached by beautiful twisting roads, is the monastery of Vallombrosa, the mother house of the order founded in the early 11thC by the Florentine religious reformer San Giovanni Gualberto.

Monastery Ⅲ †

🖾 *Open daily 9am – noon, 3 – 7pm.*

The imposing monastery, like a finely designed symmetrical castle, has a facade (1635 – 40) by G. Silvani. The campanile is 13thC, and the tower 15thC; the church itself is mainly 17thC. A plaque records that Milton stayed here in 1638. All around is a magnificent **forest**.

Nearby sights

9km (6 miles) above, near the summit of **Monte Secchietta** at 1,449m (4,216ft), is fine walking country, also equipped for skiing. **Saltino**, a modern summer and winter sports resort, is 2km (1½ miles) W, and **Consuma**, another holiday resort, is 10km (6 miles) NE.

Ⓗ **Vallombrosa**
50060 Vallombrosa, Firenze ☎ *(055) 862012* ◫ ❧ *76* ▭ *66* ▭
▱ 🖃 *Closed Sept – May.*
Location: At Saltino, 1km to W. A comfortable wooded summer retreat.
🏠 ‡ 🖾 ❤ ◁

Ⓡ **Sbaragli**, at Consuma (☎ *(055) 8306500, closed Tues*) with rooms.

Vetulonia

Map 11I5. 141km (87 miles) SW of Florence, 29km (18 miles) NW of Grosseto. 58040. Grosseto. Population: 615.

Vetulonia is the most enigmatic of the great Etruscan city-states. Like *Roselle*, Etruscan Vetulonia was a maritime city situated on an island rising from the navigable waters of the gulf which then filled part of the Grosseto plain. Its culture flourished from the 8th–6thC BC and then seems to have died out with mysterious suddenness. The Roman symbol of power, the fasces, was borrowed from archaic Vetulonia.

Sights and places of interest
Museo Archeologico
🔲 *Open Tues–Sun summer 9am–noon, 4–7pm; winter 9am–noon, 3–6pm.*

This small, interesting museum occupies the site of the acropolis at the entrance to the village. Above are remains of the **walls** (6thC BC) built of huge polygonal blocks of stone and commanding a magnificent view.
Necropolis ☆
3km (1¾ miles) to NE 🔲 🔳 🕇 *inquire about tours at museum.*

The most important tombs are the **tumulo della Pietrera**, domed in the manner of Mycenaean tombs, and, 400m (¼ mile) below, the **tumulo del Diavolino**; both probably late 7thC BC.

Ⓡ See *Tirli*.

Viareggio
*Map **14**D3. 97km (60 miles) w of Florence, 27km (17 miles) w of Lucca. 55049. Lucca. Population: 59,460 i Viale Carducci 10* ☎ *(0584) 42233; summer only, RR station, Piazza Dante* ☎ *(0584) 46382.*

The capital of the Versilia Riviera is one of the oldest seaside resorts in Italy. The climate is healthy and mild in winter, but the atmosphere today is that of a tough, citified seaside strip masking a sleazy but more congenial port area. Stately Liberty buildings and palm-fringed avenues were laid out at the turn of the century in strict parallel roads where the medieval King's Highway (Via Regia) once ran through the pine woods. The fine-sand beach is over 100m (325ft) wide and divided into well-equipped and expensive bathing establishments. The harbor is lively with fishing and tourist boats.

To the N, Viareggio merges with the modern and less expensive Lido di Camaiore. To the S, a protected pine forest stretches as far as *Torre del Lago* and there are free beaches.

The monument to Shelley in Piazza Shelley records that the poet's body was washed up on the beach in 1822.

Event: Viareggio Carnival, the most elaborate in Tuscany, takes place throughout the month before Lent. Festivities include processions of allegorical floats, masked balls, fireworks, and a soccer tournament.

Ⓗ **Astor**
*Viale Carducci 54, 55049
Viareggio, Lucca*
☎ *(0584) 50301* 📞 *573692* ▥
🛏 *71* 🔲 *71* ▦ 🔲 🔳 ⇌ 🅰🅴
💷 🔲
This ultramodern luxury hotel is part of the SINA chain. Service apartments available.
‡ 🔲 🗂 ≈ 🐇 ℅ 🛶 🛎

Ⓗ **Palace**
*Via Flavio Gioia 2, 55049
Viareggio, Lucca*
☎ *(0584) 46134* ▥ 🛏 *78* 🔲
78 🛶 🔳 ⇌ 🅰🅴 💷 🔲 💷 🆅🅸🆂🅰
An attractive first-class hotel decorated in red, white and gold Second Empire style.
🗂 🐇 🛎

Ⓗ **Principe di Piemonte**
*Piazza Puccini 1, 55049
Viareggio, Lucca*
☎ *(0584) 50122* ▥ 🛏 *123*
🛏 *103* ▦ *partial* 🔲 🔳 ⇌ 🅰🅴
💷 *Closed Oct–Apr.*
A spacious turn-of-the-century grand hotel decorated in sugared-almond colors with polished mahogany and fresh flowers.
🗂 🥂 ⟨⟨ ≈ 🐇 🛎

Ⓡ **Buonamico**
Via Sant'Andrea 27
☎ *(0584) 43038* ▥ 🔲 🛶
Closed Tues, Oct.
A small, dark restaurant on a side street near the fishing port. Next door is a tiny fish shop where you may choose your meal. Reserve.

R **Il Patriarca**
Viale Carducci 79
☎ (0584) 53126 |||| ⌷ ⬛ ⌷
⌷ AE CB ⊙ ⊙ VISA *Closed
Wed, four weeks in Oct–Nov.*
One of the super-smart restaurants
of the Versilia. Good soups,
risottos, *baccalà*.

R **Romano**
Via Mazzini 122 |||| ⌷ ⬛ ⌷
☎ (0584) 31382
Closed Wed, Nov–Dec.

Skillfully inventive variations on
the fresh fish motif. Ask advice.

R Also recommended among
Viareggio's excellent restaurants:
Il Cancello (*Viale Carducci 27a*
☎ (0584) 31320 |||| *closed Mon*);
Fedi da Gianfranco (*Via Verdi 111*
☎ (0584) 48519 |||| *closed Tues,
four weeks in Sept–Oct*); **Tito del
Molo** (*Lungomolo Corredo del Greco
3* ☎ (0584) 42016 |⌷ *to* |||
closed Wed, Jan).

Vinci

*Map 15E5. 43km (27 miles) w of Florence. 55009. Firenze.
Population: 13,577.*
Leonardo's birthplace is on Monte Albano, N of *Empoli*.

Museo Vinciano
🕭 *Open Mon–Sat 9:30am–noon, 3–6pm, Sun, hols, 10am–noon,
3–6:30pm.*
The town has dedicated rooms in its restored 13thC *castello* to a small
museum about its famous son, displaying models made from his designs.

Nearby sights
3km (2 miles) N at **Anchiano** is the farmhouse where Leonardo may
have spent his childhood, in a ravishing setting amidst olive groves.
   The drive N over Monte Albano to *Pistoia* is spectacularly beautiful.

Volterra ★

*Map 10F4. 81km (50 miles) sw of Florence, 57km (35 miles)
w of Siena. 56048. Pisa. Population: 14,911 i Via G. Turazza
2 ☎ (0588) 86150.*
Volterra was the northernmost and one of the most powerful of
the federated Etruscan city-states. Its name was Velathri, it was
three times the size of the present town, and it controlled a
territory stretching from Pisa to Populonia and from the sea
inland as far as the Pesa valley. 522m (1,712ft) above sea-level
and protected by 7km (4⅜ miles) of walls which were in places
12m (39ft) high, it became a prosperous Roman municipality in
the 4thC BC, but supported Marius against Sulla in the civil war
and was conquered by the latter in 82–80 BC.
   During the Middle Ages, Volterra's struggle against the
ecclesiastic lords for communal independence was bitter and
protracted but, in the 13thC, successful. Although taken under
the 'protection' of Florence from the mid-14thC the Republic of
Volterra remained technically independent until 1470. This
was the year when Lorenzo de' Medici, desperate to safeguard
the crucial Florentine rights to alum mining in Volterra's
territory, hired the Duke of Urbino to invade the city. The
brutality of the siege remained one of the few blots on Lorenzo's
diplomatic career; one of his would-be assassins in the Pazzi
Conspiracy 8yr later was a Volterran.
   Lorenzo built a new fortress, known as the Fortezza Nuova
or *'Il Maschio'* (now a prison) and fortified the old 14thC tower,
the Fortezza Vecchia or *'La Femmina.'* The city waited in the
shadow of these loathed symbols of foreign domination until the
final and futile rebellion of 1530, which was quickly subdued by
the Florentine general Federigo Ferrucci.
   Many travelers have remarked on the uncanny atmosphere of
Volterra, where a chill wind can spring up from nowhere on the

the balmiest summer day, and where the hill on which the town
stands has sheered off, forming the cliffs, the *Balze*, to the NE,
and carrying parts of the Etruscan city with them. D. H.
Lawrence saw the city "that gets all the wind and sees all the
world" as "a sort of inland island. still curiously isolated, and
grim." It is certainly very much its own place. Unlike its
neighbor and traditional enemy *San Gimignano*, Volterra does
not primp for tourists. The inhabitants are courteous, but there
is about them an air of brooding energy which can prompt the
fancy, especially when the wind is high, that Volterra is still
waiting, and for something more important than tourists.
Meanwhile, the town is economically if not politically
independent. The quarrying and carving of alabaster are
the chief occupations.

Sights and places of interest

The medieval city is contained within 13thC walls. The views,
on a clear day, extend to the mountains below *Carrara*, to
Corsica and inland to *Monte Amiata* and the Casentino.
    The parking lot nearest the Piazza dei Priori, the main
square, is in Piazza Martiri della Libertà, the s entrance to the
town. The following itineraries assume a day's visit, half
devoted to the medieval town and half to the remains of the
Etruscan city and to visiting the *Balze*.

Duomo Ⅲ †
The simple facade is 12thC, adapted to the Pisan style in the 13thC. The
interior, altered in the 16thC, has an attractive painted wooden ceiling.
In the right transept is a polychrome wooden *Deposition* (1228), an
unusual larger-than-life-size folk-Romanesque scene made by Pisan
sculptors, more religious theater than art. Over the high altar is Mino da
Fiesole's exquisite **ciborium** (1471) flanked by his two charming *Angels*
resting on 12thC twisted columns. In the left aisle is the **pulpit**, remade
from 12thC carvings, and an *Annunciation* (1497) by Albertinelli.
    In the chapel off the entrance to the nave are two niches containing
15thC polychrome terra-cotta groups by Zacchi Zaccaria of the *Epiphany*
(right) and *Nativity* (left). The background to the *Nativity*, a delightful
panoramic fresco of the *Magi*, is by Gozzoli.
    Inside the 13thC **Baptistry** is a **baptismal font** (1502) by A. Sansovino.

Museo di Arte Sacra
Via Roma ☎ *(0588) 86192* 🔁 *Open Mon–Wed, Fri–Sun*
10am–1pm, 3–6pm. Closed Thurs.
A display of architectural fragments, sculptures, reliquaries and
paintings, next to the Duomo. Notice particularly Andrea della Robbia's
bust of *St Linus*, the silver bust of *St Octavian* by A. Pollaiuolo, and a
gilded bronze *Crucifix* by Giambologna.

Museo Etrusco Guarnacci ★
Via Don Minzoni 15 ☎ *(0588) 86347* 🔁 *Open daily 9am–1pm,*
2:30–5:30pm.
This is one of the largest and most important Etruscan collections outside
Florence and Rome. There are some 600 cinerary urns in tufa, alabaster
or terra-cotta, dating from the 6th–1stC BC. For D. H. Lawrence these
urns were like "an open book of life"; for scholars they are like a book
about Etruscan beliefs about the afterlife. They are arranged according
to subject matter of the carvings. In Rm. 24 on the first floor is the tiny
Giacometti-like *Ombra della Sera* and other Etruscan bronze votives.

Piazza dei Priori
The central square retains its character thanks partly to some modern
imitations of the medieval architecture. The **Palazzo Pretorio**, on the NE
side, is a 13thC complex but much restored; its crenellated tower,
adapted in the early 16thC, is known as the *'porcellino'* (piglet).

Palazzo dei Priori/Galleria Pittorica Ⅲ
Piazza dei Priori ☎ *(0588) 86025* 🔁 *Open Mon, Wed–Sat*
10am–1pm, Sun, hols 10am–1pm, 3–6pm.
The town hall (1208–54) is the oldest civic building in Tuscany; on the
lower facade are the terra-cotta emblems of the 15th–16thC Florentine

commissioners. In the **Galleria Pittorica** on the second floor is a collection of 14th–17thC Florentine and Sienese pictures by, among others, D. Ghirlandaio and Signorelli; but the museum is worth visiting if only for Rosso Fiorentino's vivid, whirling *Deposition* ☆ (1521). Climb the tower for stunning views.

Quadrivio dei Buomparenti

The intersection of Via Roma with Via Ricciarelli and Buomparenti is the most picturesque corner of the medieval town. The 13thC tower-houses of the Buomparenti are remarkably intact.

San Francesco †

The **Cappella della Croce di Giorno** is entirely covered with frescoes of the *Legend of the True Cross* (1410) by Cenni di Francesco Cenni.

H **Nazionale**
Via dei Marchesi 2, 56048 Volterra, Pisa ☎ *(0588) 86284* ▮□
▱ *34* ▭ *34* ▱ ≈

"The hotel is simple and somewhat rough, but quite friendly, pleasant in its haphazard way." D. H. Lawrence's description of 1927 still fits.
⬍

R **Da Beppino** (*Via delle Prigioni 15/19* ☎ *(0588) 86051* ▮□ *closed Wed*) is the locals' favorite, which also serves the best food. **Etruria** (*Piazza dei Priori 8* ☎ *(0588) 86064* ▮□ *to* ▮▮□ *closed Sat, Nov*) is on the main square; another simple, reliable restaurant is **Porcellino** (*Canto delle Prigioni* ☎ *(0588) 86392* ▮□ *closed Tues, Oct–Mar*).

Shopping

There are dozens of shops selling objects made of alabaster. The central outlet and information center is the **Cooperativa Artieri Alabastro** (*Piazza dei Priori 2* ☎ *(0588) 87590*).

Walks

Walk 1/Etruscan and Roman Volterra

Just to the w of Piazza Martiri della Libertà is the **Arco Etrusco**, the s entrance to the Etruscan city. The uprights and bases on the inner side are Etruscan; the archivolt was rebuilt by the Romans who reincorporated the three Etruscan heads. Via Porto dell'Arco lies on the cardinal axis of the Etruscan-Roman city, which continues with Via Matteotti, lined with medieval tower-houses, and into Via Guarnacci, the site of part of the Roman Forum. Turn left into Via Lungo le Mura del Mandorlo, which overlooks the **Roman Theater** (1stC BC) and **Baths** (3rdC BC). Beyond the Porta Fiorentina, the pretty Via Diana leads to the Porta Diana, the N Etruscan gate of which only fragments survive. Beyond is the site of the **Necropoli del Portone**. The empty underground tombs are mostly unmarked, but some, in the middle of a farm, are signposted *Ipogei dei Marmini*.

Walk 2/To the Balze

Start at the church of San Francesco; the *Balze* are 2km (1¼ miles) by foot from Porta S. Francesco. Taking Borgo S. Stefano, turn left under Vicolo della Penera, then make a sharp right behind the handrails and you will find a path running along the base of the stretch of the **Etruscan walls** known as the Mura Etrusche di S. Chiara, which in summer are festooned with flowering capers, to the **Balze**, the cliffs formed by repeated landslides. The views to the w are superb, and on a peaceful summer midday when the scent of broom is sweet and strong, one may wonder at Augustus Hare's description of the **Balze** as "an arid and ghastly desert." But if you go just before sunset you could share his vertiginous apprehension "that the flowery surface on which you are standing may be hurled into destruction tomorrow."

Biographies

A personal selection of major 13th–17thC Tuscan artists.

Alberti, Leon Battista *(1404–72)*
Influential Renaissance architect, theoretician and scholar.

Ammannati, Bartolomeo *(1511–92)*
Florentine sculptor and architect influenced by **Michelangelo**.

Andrea del Sarto *(1486–1531)*
Flawless painter of the early Florentine High Renaissance.

Angelico, Fra Giovanni *(active c.1418–55)*
Dominican monk and Renaissance painter.

Arnolfo di Cambio *(before 1245–c.1302)*
Gothic architect and sculptor, a pupil of **Nicola Pisano**.

Baccio d'Agnolo *(1462–1543)*
Florentine Renaissance architect and woodcarver. His son,
Giuliano (1491–1555) was a fine Mannerist architect.

Baldovinetti, Alesso *(c.1426–99)*
Florentine Renaissance painter and mosaicist.

Bartolommeo della Porta, Fra *(1472/5–1517)*
A leading painter of the Florentine High Renaissance.

Beccafumi, Domenico *(c.1486–1551)*
The outstanding Sienese Mannerist painter and sculptor.

Botticelli, Sandro *(1445–1510)*
The greatest linear painter of the Florentine Renaissance.

Bronzino (Agnolo Allori) *(1503–72)*
Florentine Mannerist painter, a polished portraitist.

Brunelleschi, Filippo *(1377–1446)*
The creator of Florentine Renaissance architecture.

Buontalenti, Bernardo *(1531–1608)*
Florentine Mannerist architect to the Medici grand dukes.

Castagno, Andrea del *(active c.1442–died 1457)*
Renaissance painter strongly influenced by **Donatello**.

Cellini, Benvenuto *(1500–71)*
Florentine sculptor, goldsmith and autobiographer.

Cimabue, Giovanni *(c.1240–?1302)*
Florentine painter and mosaicist who may have taught **Giotto**.

Civitali, Matteo *(1436–1501)*
The most important Renaissance sculptor of Lucca.

Cronaca (Simone del Pollaiuolo) *(1457–1508)*
Florentine architect and stonemason.

Daddi, Bernardo *(c.1290–c.1348)*
Florentine painter influenced by Giotto and the **Lorenzetti**.

Della Robbia, Luca *(1400–82)*
One of the greatest Florentine Renaissance sculptors; the
inventor of a method of applying vitreous glazes to terra-cotta.
His nephew **Andrea** (1424–1525) and sons **Giovanni**
(1464–after 1529) and **Girolamo** (1488–1556) continued the
family workshop.

Desiderio da Settignano *(1428–64)*
Renaissance sculptor of delicate reliefs and portrait busts.

Donatello *(1386–1466)*
The greatest Italian sculptor of the early Renaissance.

Duccio di Buoninsegna *(documented from 1278, died 1318/19)*
The greatest and most influential of early Sienese painters.

Ferri, Ciro *(1620/34–89)*
Baroque painter, **Pietro da Cortona's** most important pupil.

Francesco di Giorgio Martini *(1439–1502)*
Sienese architect, military engineer, sculptor and painter.

Gaddi, Agnolo *(active c.1370–died 1396)*
Florentine painter, son of **Taddeo**.

Biographies

Gaddi, Taddeo (active c.1325–died 1366)
Giotto's most important disciple.

Ghibertti, Lorenzo (1378–1455)
Florentine early Renaissance bronze sculptor.

Ghirlandaio, Domenico (1449–94)
Florentine Renaissance painter, a teacher of **Michelangelo**, and master of a large studio run with his brother **Davide** (1452–1525) and son **Ridolfo** (1483–1561).

Giambologna (Jean Boulogne) (1524–1608)
Flemish-born court sculptor to the Medici.

Giotto di Bondone (1267/77–1337)
The first great innovatory genius of Florentine painting.

Giovanni da San Giovanni (1592–1636)
Tuscan Baroque painter of frescoes in Florence and Rome.

Giovanni di Paolo (1403–82/3)
A leading 15thC Sienese painter working in 14thC style.

Gozzoli, Benozzo (c.1421–97)
Florentine narrative painter, a pupil of **Angelico**.

Guido da Siena (active mid-13thC)
Founder of the Sienese school of painting.

Leonardo da Vinci (1452–1519)
One of the greatest figures in the history of Western art, with an apparently limitless power and range of intellect. Engineer, anatomist, sculptor, architect and creator, with **Michelangelo** and Raphael, of the High Renaissance style of painting.

Lippi, Filippino (1457–1504)
Son of Filippo and distinguished quasi-Mannerist painter.

Lippi, Fra Filippo (active c.1432–died 1469)
Florentine Renaissance painter; disciple of **Masaccio**.

Lorenzetti, Ambrogio (active 1319–47) and *Pietro* (active 1320–45)
The Sienese Lorenzetti brothers worked in a style which synthesized the prevailing Florentine and Sienese schools.

Maiano, Benedetto da (1442–97)
Florentine Renaissance sculptor especially of fine reliefs. His brother **Giuliano** (1432–90) was an architect.

Margaritone d'Arezzo (active mid-13thC)
One of the earliest Italian painters to sign his work.

Martini, Simone (active c.1315–died 1344)
The leading Sienese exponent of International Gothic painting.

Masaccio (1401–c.1428)
The great founder of Florentine Renaissance painting.

Michelangelo Buonarroti (1475–1564)
Painter, architect, poet and sculptor of deeply expressive human figures.

Michelozzo di Bartolomeo (1396–1472)
Cosimo de' Medici's favorite architect.

Mino da Fiesole (1429–84)
Florentine Renaissance sculptor in marble.

Nanni di Banco (c.1384–1421)
Late Gothic–early Renaissance Florentine sculptor.

Orcagna, Andrea (Andrea di Cione) (active c.1343–died 1368)
The greatest mid-14thC Florentine painter, sculptor and architect.

Piero della Francesca (1410/20–92)
One of the outstanding Tuscan painters and theorists.

Piero di Cosimo (1462–1521)
Idiosyncratic Florentine painter of mythological subjects.

Pietro da Cortona (1596–1669)
Painter and architect: a founder of Roman High Baroque.

Pisano, Andrea (c.1290–1348)
Sculptor known for the bronze s doors of Florence Baptistry.
Pisano, Giovanni (c.1245–c.1315) and Nicola (c.1223–c.1284)
Nicola and his son Giovanni created modern figure sculpture.
Poccetti, Bernardino (before 1548–1612)
Florentine painter, the leading master of *sgraffiti*.
Pollaiuolo, Antonio (c.1432–98) and Piero (c.1441–96)
Florentine painters, sculptors, engravers and goldsmiths.
Antonio, one of the great draftsmen of the Renaissance, is
considered the more talented of the brothers.
Pontormo, Jacopo Carucci (1494–1556)
Deeply religious painter and one of the creators of Mannerism.
Quercia, Jacopo della (1374–1438)
The greatest Sienese sculptor of the early Renaissance.
Rossellino, Antonio (1427–79) and Bernardo (1409–64)
Brothers whose sculpture exemplifies the 'sweet style' of the
Florentine Renaissance. **Bernardo** worked also as an architect.
Rosso Fiorentino (1495–1540)
A founder of Mannerism; important religious painter.
Salviati, Francesco (or Cecchino) (1510–63)
Florentine Mannerist painter and friend of **Vasari**.
Sangallo
Florentine family of architects. **Giuliano** (c.1443–1516), a
follower of **Brunelleschi**, was Lorenzo the Magnificent's
favorite architect. His brother **Antonio the Elder**
(c.1453–1534) introduced the Roman High Renaissance style
to provincial Tuscany. Both were military architects as was
their nephew **Antonio the Younger** (1483–1546).
Sansovino, Andrea (c.1460–1529)
High Renaissance sculptor in terra-cotta and marble.
Sansovino, Jacopo (1486–1570)
Andrea's pupil and namesake and city architect of Venice.
Sassetta (Stefano di Giovanni) (c.1423–50)
The most important early 15thC Sienese painter.
Signorelli, Luca (c.1441/50–1523)
Tuscan painter; an influence on **Michelangelo**.
Silvani, Gherardo (1579–1675)
One of the best High Baroque architects outside Rome.
Sodoma (1477–1549)
Interpreter to Siena of **Leonardo's** style of painting.
Spinello Aretino (active 1373–died 1410/11)
Narrative painter in the style of **Giotto**.
Starnina, Gherardo (c.1354–before 1413)
Florentine painter, a modest anticipator of **Uccello**.
Tacca, Pietro (1577–1640)
Sculptor to the Medici grand dukes after **Giambologna**.
Tino di Camaino (c.1285–1337)
Sienese sculptor who also worked in Pisa, Florence and Naples.
Tribolo (1500–50)
Florentine sculptor and designer of gardens.
Uccello, Paolo (1387–1475)
Florentine Renaissance painter famous as a perspectivist.
Vasari, Giorgio (1511–74)
Architect, painter and author of the first history of art.
Vecchietta (1412–80)
Sienese sculptor, painter and architect.
Verrocchio, Andrea del (1435–88)
Painter, goldsmith and the leading bronze sculptor of his day.
Volterrano (1611–89)
Tuscan Baroque painter influenced by **Pietro da Cortona**.

Tuscan wines

Wine has been an element of Tuscan life for ages. We know that the Etruscans made wine three millennia ago. The Romans followed suit, and though vine cultivation lapsed during the Dark Ages, wine was back in prominence through the Renaissance, flourishing as nutrient of body and soul and as a source of inspiration for who knows how many works of art or grandiose ideas.

Tuscans in their time have contributed notably to the development of wine making as art and science, to techniques of bottling and shipping wine and establishing the rituals that have grown around its service and consumption. Today more than 100,000 Tuscans are involved in the production and sale of wine, the mainstay of the region's agricultural economy.

I believe that there is much happiness in people who are born where good wines are found.

Leonardo da Vinci

Tuscany's hills, with their range of temperate micro-climates, are especially renowned for red wines, which have a similarly broad range of character. Chianti, Italy's most abundant wine of controlled name and origin, classified DOC (*Denominazione di Origine Controllata*), is grown in seven delimited zones covering much of the region, from N of Florence to S of Chiusi and from Pisa inland to Arezzo. It is usually served in the famous rounded flask, but some of the best Chianti, labeled *riserva*, is aged for several years in wood and then put into straight Bordeaux-style bottles.

Strictly outside the Chianti, Brunello di Montalcino, from S of Siena, is among the world's most prized and expensive wines when at its best. This and Vino Nobile di Montepulciano, from SE of Siena, are the two Tuscan wines among the four designated for Italy's highest classification, the government guaranteed DOCG.

All Tuscan DOC red wines are based on the versatile Sangiovese grape, sometimes used alone (as in Brunello and Morellino di Scansano), sometimes mixed with other varieties (as in Carmignano, Chianti, Elba Rosso, Montescudaio Rosso, Parrina Rosso, Rosso delle Colline Lucchesi and Vino Nobile). Not all the fine reds are DOC, however: Tignanello, Monte Antico, Rosso di Cercatoia and Le Pergole Torte are but a few of the Sangiovese-based wines sold under individual names. There is also a trend to introduce foreign vines, such as Cabernet and Merlot. Sassicaia, a Cabernet Sauvignon produced since 1968 from near Livorno, is considered by some to be Tuscany's finest modern wine.

Tuscan whites have gained stature as new wine making methods have improved quality. Among DOC whites, Vernaccia di San Gimignano, from the vine of that name, and Montecarlo, which mixes the native Trebbiano with French varieties, stand out. The other DOC whites are gradually reaching markets beyond the region.

Among a great many unclassified whites produced in Chianti zones, two names are emerging to prominence: Galestro, a light wine produced only by large-scale wineries with the most modern equipment; and Bianco della Lega, made in traditional ways by individual estates in Chianti Classico. Almost every Tuscan vineyard, large or small, makes a special white, though style and quality vary markedly. The introduction of outside grape varieties, such as the Pinots, Chardonnay, Riesling, Traminer and Tocai Friulano, have added fruitiness and fragrance to the rather bland native Trebbiano, which is planted to excess in Tuscany.

Among sweet dessert or aperitif wines, Vin Santo, made from semi-dried grapes and well aged in small sealed barrels, is beloved by Tuscans, but, alas, production is painstaking and there is little of this true 'holy wine' to be found. Another lightly sweet white, Moscadello di Montalcino, is coming back into favor after a long decline, and is appreciated for its refreshingly light Muscat aroma. There are, as well, a great many curiosities, experiments, and esoteric wines to be found here and there around the region.

Everywhere local wine of the latest vintage is served by the flask as the natural accompaniment to the local food. Perhaps because Tuscans take so intuitively to wine, the idea of formal wine tourism has never been exploited. Still, even the most spontaneous sort of wine tour can be rewarding. The authorities of a wine zone, or even an individual estate (*fattoria*), sometimes offer the added attraction of an *enoteca*, or wine library, where the wines can be bought. For those who like to combine the enjoyment of art and history with the pleasures of food and wine, few regions offer such exciting possibilities. All major wine zones are within easy reach of Florence.

Chianti Classico
For all the violent history that transpired in this buffer zone between Florence and Siena, Chianti Classico, the most important of the seven Chianti zones, is today one of the most peacefully handsome of all places where wine is made. Follow the Via Chiantigiana (SS222) s from Florence through Strada, Greve, Panzano and Castellina to Siena, through wooded hills where vines and olive groves, cypresses and pines surround medieval castles, villas and stone farmhouses. The complete Chiantigiana route includes a detour through the domain of the original Chianti League, founded in the 13thC by the feudal barons of Castellina, Gaiole and Radda. This can be extended to take in the Castello di Brolio near San Regolo, where modern Chianti was 'invented' in the last century by Baron Bettino Ricasoli, and the villages of Castagnoli, Villa a Sesta, San Gusme, Castelnuovo Berardenga and Vagliagli.

Most Chianti Classico estates welcome visitors, though to assure a reception it would be wise to arrange a tour with the Chianti Classico *consorzio* (*Via de' Serragli 146 in Florence* ☎(055) 229351/2/3). Two of the most historically important estates, Castello di Brolio (☎ *(055) 263681*) and Marchesi Antinori (☎ *(055) 282202/3*), are not in the *consorzio*, but both welcome visitors by appointment. Antinori's wines are served at the Cantinetta Antinori in the center of Florence (see *Florence/Restaurants*).

A complete selection of Chianti Classico is sold at the Enoteca del Gallo Nero in Greve, the hub of Chianti and the setting of an annual wine fair in early Sept. Other stores with a good selection include the Bottega del Chianti Classico at Greve, the Enoteca del Chianti Classico at Panzano and the Bottega del Chianti Classico at Castellina. Several estates have a *trattoria* or *osteria* on the premises, and noteworthy examples include: the Trattoria di Montagliari near Panzano; the Badia a Coltibuono near Gaiole; the Taverna del Solimano of the Fortilizio Il

Colombaio estate near Quercegrossa; and the Tavernetta
Serristori 'Albergaccio' (where Niccolò Machiavelli spent much
of his exile from Florence) at S. Andrea in Percussina.

Siena/Montalcino/Montepulciano/San Gimignano

Siena is sometimes called the capital of Italian wine, partly
because it is the center of Tuscany's most important production
zones and also because the **Enoteca Italica Permanente**, the
public national wine library, is located in its Medici fortress.
Though the *enoteca* is open only by appointment
(☎ *(0577) 288497*), select wines can be tasted at a bar which is
open daily. The city makes a convenient headquarters for
traveling oenophiles – in Siena's province are the original sector
of Chianti Classico, the Chianti Colli Senesi zone, the vineyards
of the exceptional Brunello di Montalcino and Vino Nobile di
Montepulciano, and the superb white Vernaccia di San
Gimignano.

Montalcino, a hill town 45km (28 miles) S of Siena, is the
home of the fabled red Brunello and the even older but
currently less renowned Moscadello di Montalcino. The Medici
fortress in the center of town houses a museum of Brunello.
Outside Montalcino, visits to one of the leading producers and
what ranks as Italy's most famous wine estate, Il Greppo of
Biondi-Santi, can be made by appointment (☎ *(0577) 47136*),
and the Fattoria dei Barbi has an *osteria* on the estate, where its
several wines are served with good country food
(☎ *0577) 848087*). Other wine estates which welcome visitors
are: Casale del Bosco, Castiglion del Bosco, Col d'Orcia, Poggio
alle Mura, and the immense new conglomeration Poggio d'Oro
of Villa Banfi.

The lovely Renaissance town of Montepulciano, 37km (23
miles) farther E, is surrounded by the vineyards of Vino Nobile,
known for centuries as 'King of Wines.' Visits can be arranged
to the Cantine Contucci (☎ *(0578) 77006*), and the Vecchia
Cantina cooperative (☎ *(0578) 77692/3*). In nearby Pienza, the
Enoteca Regionale of Sandro Morriconi sells good wines from
the area.

San Gimignano, with its many towers jutting over a
landscape of vines and olives, may be the most charming of all
Tuscan wine towns. Many producers of the vigorous white
Vernaccia sell bottles in individual shops in the town.
Vineyards open to visitors include the following: Fattoria di
Cusona, Raccianello, and Pietrafitta. The Ponte a Rondolino
vineyard serves its Vernaccia at its own trattoria situated
outside the town.

Florence/Rufina/Carmignano

Florence is itself a wine town, center of the Colli Fiorentini
Chianti zone and headquarters of many important Tuscan
wineries. Outstanding arrays of Italian wine are available at the
Enoteca Nazionale of Giorgio Pinchiorri (*Via Ghibellina 87*
☎ *(055) 263653*), and the Enoteca Internazionale De Rham
(*Piazza SS Annunziata 4* ☎ *(055) 298849*).

Rufina, a small DOC zone 20km (13 miles) E of Florence,
makes some of the finest Chianti. Within its limits are some of
Tuscany's best-known wine houses: Ruffino and Melini at
Pontassieve; the Pomino and Nipozzano estates of Marchesi de'
Frescobaldi; and Spalletti, in the villa of Poggio Reale, designed
by Michelangelo, at Rufina. All welcome visitors.

Carmignano, a zone some 25km (16 miles) W of Florence,

produces very little of a red wine that insiders consider Tuscany's most consistently impressive DOC. There are only about a dozen producers, and their wine can be sold as Carmignano only if approved by experts in a rigorous annual blind tasting. Carmignano's wines are displayed at a small *enoteca* in the center of town. The Fattoria di Artimino, in the Medici villa of the 'Hundred Chimneys,' is open to visitors, and serves its wines in its own restaurant.

Other itineraries

The Chianti Putto *consorzio* (*Lungarno Corsini 4, Florence* ☎ *(055) 270168*) can help arrange visits to estates in the other six Chianti zones: Colli Aretini, Colli Fiorentini, Colline Pisane, Colli Senesi, Montalbano and Rufina.

Nearly every center of interest to tourists has a wine area nearby. Pisa has Bianco di San Torpe to the SE. Lucca has two DOC zones, Rosso delle Colline Lucchesi, to the N, and Montecarlo, a white wine produced around the village of that name. From farther E, near Montecatini Terme, comes Bianco della Valdinievole. In Arezzo province, the broad Chiana valley between Cortona and Montepulciano is the home of Bianco Vergine della Valdichiana.

The Tuscan coastal strip also produces good wines. Not far from Viareggio and the Tuscan Riviera is the new DOC zone of Candia dei Colli, with red, white and Vin Santo, and the island of Elba, with red and white DOC wines and a sweet red Aleatico di Portoferraio, which Napoleon supposedly liked. In the Maremma hills of Grosseto province there are three DOCs: Morellino di Scansano, Bianco di Pitigliano and, adjacent to the Argentario peninsula, Parrina.

Vintage chart

The chart gives a general idea of recent vintages for five wines. As a general rule, Vernaccia di San Gimignano should be drunk young (1–3yr). Regular Chianti should be drunk from 1–5yr, *riserva* from 5–10yr, or from good vintages even older. Carmignano and Vino Nobile di Montepulciano age similarly to Chianti *riserva*. Brunello di Montalcino needs at least 6yr to mature; from great vintages it can last for decades.

	1970	1971	1972	1973	1974	1975	1976	1977	1978	1979	1980	1981
Brunello di Montalcino	●	◐	○	◐	○	●	○	●	●	●	◐	●
Carmignano	●	●	○	●	◐	●	○	●	●	●	◐	●
Chianti	●	●	○	◐	○	●	○	●	●	●	◐	◐
Vino Nobile di Montepulciano	●	○	○	●	◐	●	○	●	●	●	○	◐
Vernaccia di San Gimignano										●	●	◐

Key: ● above average to outstanding   ◐ average
○ acceptable

Sports, leisure, ideas for children

There is plenty to do in Tuscany besides sightseeing, as families traveling with small children may be relieved to learn, and foreigners can usually buy temporary membership in private sports clubs and organizations.

Bicycling
Bicycles and tandems can easily be rented by the hour or week. *Federazione Ciclistica Italiana*, P. Stazione 2, 50123 Firenze ☎(055) 283926, is the organization for serious cyclists.

Camping
A list of campsites and booking forms is obtainable from the *Centro Internazionale di Prenotazioni Campeggio*, Casella Postale 649, I-50100, Firenze. The *Touring Club Italiano* runs camping sites equipped with tents and restaurants. Information from *TCI*, Corso Italia 10, 20122 Milano.

Mountain huts can be rented from the *Club Alpino Italiano*, Via Ugo Foscolo 3, 20121 Milano ☎(02) 802554.

Fishing
The clear waters off the rocky southern coast are excellent for snorkling, and spearfishing is allowed anywhere except in harbors. Oxygen bottles for aqualungs are available in the main resorts. For fishing in most lakes and rivers, an inexpensive license is required, as is membership in the *Federazione Italiana della Pesca Sportiva*, Via De' Neri 6, 50122 Firenze ☎(055) 214073.

Gardens
Many great Tuscan gardens are still privately owned, but those not normally open to the public can occasionally be visited. Lists of gardens are published by local tourist offices.

Golf
18-hole courses open all year are at: *Ugolino*, Strada Chiantigiana 3, 50023 Impruneta ☎(055) 2051009; and at *Punta Ala* ☎(0564) 922121.

Horse racing and trotting
There are two racecourses in the Cascine in Florence, with trotting races in summer and racing in winter. There are also racecourses at San Rossore, Montecatini and Punta Ala, and trotting races near Follonica.

Hunting
A hunting reserve is open to foreigners near Capalbio.

Italian
Since the purest Italian is spoken in Tuscany, it is an ideal place to learn the language. Most of the schools will help enrolled students find accommodations.
British Institute Palazzo Lanfredini, Lungarno Guicciardini 9, 50123 Firenze ☎(055) 284031
Centro Linguistico Italiano Dante Alighieri PO Box 194, Via de' Bardi 12, 50125 Firenze ☎(055) 284955
The University of Siena's *Scuola Lingua e Cultura per Stranieri*, Banchi di Sotto 55 ☎(0577) 280695, organizes summer courses for foreigners in Siena; and the University of Pisa offers two three-week summer courses in Viareggio. Information from *Corsi per Stranieri*, Istituto di Glottologia dell'Università, Via S. Maria SC, 56100 Pisa ☎(050) 24773.

Music
Florence is one of the musical capitals of Italy; and the *Accademia Musicale Chigiana* at Siena is among the most distinguished Italian music academies. Lucca and Prato are

musically active too, and there are summer festivals at Barga, Batignano, Cortona, Gargonza, Montepulciano, S. Gimignano and Torre del Lago Puccini.

Nature parks and reserves

Some of the reserves can be entered only with permission, usually obtainable from the communal government offices nearest the site. The Maremma is well-supplied: see *Ansedonia, Monte Argentario* and, especially, *Monti dell'Uccellina*. Other reserves are at Bolgheri, Cavriglia, Migliarino (near Pisa), Montecristo and Orechiella (Garfagnana). See also *Zoos* below.

Riding

Riding is popular in Tuscany. The *Associazione Nazionale per il Turismo Equestre* organizes trekking holidays. Information is available from the *Federazione Italiana Sport Equestri*, Via Paoletti 54, 50134 Firenze ☎(055) 480039.

Sailing

There are tourist harbors at Cala Galera, Castiglione della Pescaia, Elba, Giannutri, Giglio, Port'Ercole, Punta Ala, Talamone and Viareggio. Report to the *Capitaneria di Porto* (Harbor Master).

Federazione Italiana Vela Cas post 49, 54036 Marina di Carrara ☎(0585) 57323, for information

Federazione Italiana Motonautica Via Goldora 16, 55044 Marina de Pietrasanta ☎(0584) 20963, for all boats

A useful guidebook is *The Tyrrhenian Sea* by H.M. Denham (John Murray).

Skiing

The best skiing is in the Apennines, at Abetone, Cutigliano and S. Marcello Pistoiese. Nearer to Florence, in the Pratomagno hills, there are winter sports facilities at Consuma, Stia and Vallombrosa. Monte Amiata has some 20km (12 miles) of piste; its principle resort is Abbadia S. Salvatore.

Information from the *Federazione Italiana Sports Invernali*, Viale Matteotti 15, 50121 Firenze ☎(055) 576987.

Swimming

Beaches vary from superb to squalid. The best sandy beaches are shown in the orientation map in *Planning*. Below Livorno and on Elba the coast is mostly rocky with small sandy bays. Although there are some free beaches, those which provide facilities are fairly expensive. Most inland towns have well-maintained public pools: in Florence, the *Piscine Bellariva*, Lungarno Colombo; *Piscine Costoli*, Viale Paoli; *Piscine Pavoniere*, Viale degli Olmi; and at the *Circolo del Tennis*, Via Visarno 1, a private club in the Cascine open to foreigners.

Tennis

Public courts and tennis clubs are widespread; the best in Florence are in the Cascine at Viale Visarno 1.

Walking

All Tuscan cities and villages are best seen on foot. Near Florence there is pleasant country walking in the Fiesolan hills and around Arcetri. There are marked trails through the protected forests at Abetone, Camaldoli, La Verna and Vallombrosa. Maps showing footpaths are obtainable from *Istituto Geografico Militare*, Viale Strozzi 14, Firenze. Information about mountain walking from *Club Alpino Italiano*, Via Proconsolo 10, 50123 Firenze ☎(055) 216580.

Zoos

There are zoos at Pistoia, Poppi, at Tirrenia near Pisa, and a small one in Florence.

WORDS AND PHRASES

A guide to Italian

This glossary covers the basic language needs of the traveler: for for pronunciation, essential vocabulary and simple conversation, finding accommodations, visiting the bank, shopping and using public transport or a car. There is also a special menu decoder, explaining all the most common descriptions of food terms.

Pronunciation

Most Italian words are pronounced exactly as they are written, with each syllable clearly enunciated. Some letters change their individual sounds, however, when grouped together, as shown below. Double consonants, such as in cappello, are strongly pronounced. The letter 'r' is rolled. Stress in Italian nearly always falls on the penultimate syllable. An accent is used when the stress is final (e.g. with città, caffè), but accentuation in any word is always strong.

Vowels

a	as the <u>a</u> in father; e.g. and<u>a</u>re
e	as the <u>e</u> in pet; e.g. p<u>e</u>zzo, or as the <u>a</u> in may; e.g. part<u>e</u>
i	as the <u>i</u> in machine; e.g. pr<u>i</u>mo, or, when followed by another vowel, as the <u>y</u> in you; e.g. p<u>i</u>ù, p<u>i</u>ove
o	as the <u>o</u> in pot; e.g. n<u>o</u>tte, or as in v<u>o</u>te; e.g. R<u>o</u>ma
u	as the <u>u</u> in prune; e.g. <u>u</u>scita, or, when followed by another vowel, as the letter <u>w</u>; e.g. <u>u</u>omo, g<u>u</u>ida

Consonants/letter groups

c,g	before e,i	soft, as the <u>ch</u> in <u>ch</u>urch and the <u>g</u> in <u>g</u>ent; e.g. ba<u>c</u>io, <u>G</u>ino
c,g	before a,o,u	hard, as the <u>k</u> in king and the <u>g</u> in get; e.g. <u>c</u>amera, <u>c</u>osa, <u>g</u>atto, <u>g</u>uida
ch,gh	before e,i	hard, as the c or the g above; e.g. <u>ch</u>iesa, al<u>gh</u>erghi
cc	before e,i	soft, as the <u>ch</u> in <u>ch</u>urch; e.g. fa<u>cc</u>io, salsi<u>cc</u>e
gg	before e,i	soft, as the <u>dg</u> in do<u>dg</u>e; e.g. o<u>gg</u>etto, o<u>gg</u>i
gli		as the <u>ll</u> in million; e.g. fi<u>gli</u>o
gn		pronounced nasally, as the <u>n</u> in new; e.g. ba<u>gn</u>o
qu		as in s<u>qu</u>are; e.g. <u>qu</u>esto
s	between vowels	soft, as the <u>z</u> in gaze; e.g. ri<u>s</u>o, ca<u>s</u>a
sc	before e,i	as the <u>sh</u> in shift; e.g. <u>sc</u>ena, <u>sc</u>iopero
z		as the <u>ts</u> in cats; e.g. gra<u>z</u>ie, or as the <u>ds</u> in birds; e.g. me<u>zz</u>o

N.B. Gender

Gender has been indicated, where necessary, when not apparent from the regular masculine (-o, pl. -i) and feminine (-a, pl. -e) endings.

Reference words

Monday	lunedì	Friday	venerdì
Tuesday	martedì	Saturday	sabato
Wednesday	mercoledì	Sunday	domenica
Thursday	giovedì		

January	gennaio	July	luglio
February	febbraio	August	agosto
March	marzo	September	settembre
April	aprile	October	ottobre
May	maggio	November	novembre
June	giugno	December	dicembre

1	uno	11	undici	21	ventuno
2	due	12	dodici	22	ventidue
3	tre	13	tredici	30	trenta
4	quattro	14	quattordici	40	quaranta
5	cinque	15	quindici	50	cinquanta
6	sei	16	sedici	60	sessanta
7	sette	17	diciassette	70	settanta
8	otto	18	diciotto	80	ottanta
9	nove	19	diciannove	90	novanta
10	dieci	20	venti	100	cento

First	primo, -a	Quarter–past . . . . e un quarto
Second	secondo, -a	
Third	terzo, -a	Half–past . . . . e mezzo
Fourth	quarto, -a	Quarter to . . . . meno un quarto
One o'clock	l'una	
Six o'clock	le sei	

Mr	signor(e)	Ladies	signore, donne
Mrs	signora	Men/gentlemen	signori, uomini
Miss	signorina		

Basic communication

Yes	sì	Hot	caldo, -a
No	no	Cold	freddo, -a
Please	per favore/per piacere	Good	buono, -a
Thank you	grazie	Bad	cattivo, -a
I'm very sorry	mi dispiace molto/mi scusi	Beautiful	bello, -a
		Well	bene
Excuse me	senta! (to attract attention), permesso! (on bus, train, etc.), mi scusi	Badly	male
		With	con
		And	e, ed
Not at all/you're welcome	prego	But	ma
Hello	ciao (familiar), pronto (on telephone)	Very	molto
		All	tutto, -a
Good morning	buon giorno	Open	aperto
Good afternoon	buona sera	Closed	chiuso
Good evening	buona sera	Entrance	entrata
Good night	buona notte	Exit	uscita
Goodbye	ciao (familiar), arrivederci, addio (final or familiar)	Free	libero
		On the left	a sinistra
		On the right	a destra
Morning	mattino	Straight on	diritto
Afternoon	pomeriggio	Near	vicino
Evening	sera	Far	lontano
Night	notte (f)	Up	su
Yesterday	ieri	Down	giù
Today	oggi	Early	presto
Tomorrow	domani	Late	tardi
Next week	la settimana prossima	Quickly	presto
Last week	la settimana scorsa	Pleased to meet you.	Molto lieto/piacere.
. . . . days ago	. . . . giorni fa	
Month	mese (m)	How are you?	Come sta?
Year	anno	Very well, thank you.	Benissimo, grazie.
Here	qui	
There	lì	Do you speak English?	Parla inglese?
Big	grande	
Small	piccolo, -a	I don't understand.	Non capisco.

Words and phrases

I don't know. Non lo so.	When? Quando?
Please explain. Può spiegare per favore.	How much? Quanto?
	That's too much. È troppo caro.
Please speak more slowly. Parli più lentamente per favore.	Expensive caro
	Cheap a buon mercato
My name is .... Mi chiamo	I would like .... Vorrei ....
I am American/English. Sono inglese/americano, -a.	Do you have ....? Avete ....?
	Just a minute. Un momento.
Where is/are ....? Dov'e/dove si trova/dove sono ....?	That's fine/OK. Va bene/benissimo/OK
Is there a ....? C'è un, una ....?	What time is it? Che ore sono?
	I don't feel well. Non mi sento bene/sto male.
What? Cosa?	

Accommodations

Making a reservation by letter

> Dear Sir/Madam,
> *Egregio Signore/Signora,*
> I would like to reserve one double room (with bathroom) –
> *Vorrei prenotare una camera doppia (con bagno) –*
> – a twin-bedded room, and one single room (with shower)
> *– una camera con due letti, e una camera singola (con doccia)*
> for 7 nights from 12 August. We would like bed and breakfast/half board/full board
> *per 7 notti dal 12 agosto. Vorremmo una camera con colazione/mezza pensione/pensione completa*
> and would prefer rooms with a sea view.
> *e possibilmente camere con vista sul mare.*
> Please send me details of your terms with the confirmation.
> *Sarei lieto di ricevere dettagli del prezzo e la conferma.*
> Yours sincerely,
> *Cordi ali saluti,*

Arriving at the hotel

I have a reservation. My name is ....
Ho già prenotato. Sono il signor/la signora ....
A quiet room with bath/shower/toilet/wash basin
Una camera tranquilla con bagno/doccia/WC/làvandino
.... overlooking the sea/park/street/the back.
.... con vista sul mare/sul parco/sulla strada/sul retro.
Does the price include breakfast/tax/service?
E' tutto compreso – colazione/tasse/servizio?
This room is too large/small/cold/hot/noisy.
Questa camera è troppo grande/piccola/fredda/calda/rumorosa.
That's too expensive. Have you anything cheaper?
Costa troppo. Avete qualcosa meno caro?

Floor/story piano
Dining room/restaurant sala da pranzo/ristorante (m)
Manager direttore, -trice
Porter portiere
Have you got a room? Avete una camera?
What time is breakfast/dinner? A che ora è la prima colazione/la cena?
Is there a laundry service? C'è il servizio lavanderia?
What time does the hotel close? A che ora chiude l'albergo?
Will I need a key? Avrò bisogno della chiave?
Is there a night porter? C'è un portiere di notte?
I'll be leaving tomorrow morning. Parto domani mattina.
Please give me a call at .... Mi può chiamare alle ....
Come in! Avanti!

Shopping   La Spesa

Where is the nearest/a good ....? Dov'è il più vicino/la più vicina ....? Dov'è un buon/una buona ....?
Can you help me/show me ....? Mi può aiutare/Può mostrarmi ....?
I'm just looking. Sto soltanto guardando.
Do you accept credit cards/travelers cheques? Accettate carte di credito/travelers cheques?

Can you deliver to ....? Può consegnare a ....?
I'll take it. Lo prendo.
I'll leave it. Lo lascio.
Can I have it tax-free for export? Posso averlo senza tasse per l'esportazione?
This is faulty. Can I have a replacement/refund? C'è difetto. Me lo potrebbe cambiare/rimborsare?
I don't want to spend more than .... Non voglio spendere più di ....
Can I have a stamp for ....? Vorrei un francobollo per ....

Shops

Antique shop negozio di antiquariato	Jeweler gioielleria
Art gallery galleria d'arte	Market mercato
Bakery panificio, forno	Newsstand giornalaio, edicola
Bank banca	Optician ottico
Beauty salon istituto di bellezza	Pastry shop pasticceria
Bookshop libreria	Perfumery profumeria
Butcher macelleria	Pharmacy farmacia
Clothes shop negozio di abbigliamento, di confezioni	Photographic shop negozio fotografico
Dairy latteria	Post office ufficio postale
Delicatessen salumeria, pizzicheria	Shoe shop negozio di calzature
Fish store pescheria	Stationer cartoleria
Florist fioraio	Supermarket supermercato
Greengrocer ortolano, erbivendolo, fruttivendolo	Tailor sarto
Grocer drogheria	Tobacconist tabaccheria (also sells stamps)
Haberdasher merciaio	Tourist office ente del turismo
Hairdresser parrucchiere, -a	Toy shop negozio di giocattoli
	Travel agent agenzia di viaggio

At the bank

I would like to change some dollars/pounds/travelers cheques
Vorrei cambiare delle sterline/dei dollari/dei travellers cheques
What is the exchange rate?
Com'è il cambio?
Can you cash a personal check?
Può cambiare un assegno?
Can I obtain cash with this credit card?
Posso avere soldi in contanti con questa carta di credito?
Do you need to see my passport?
Ha bisogno del mio passaporto?

Some useful goods

Antiseptic cream crema antisettica	Shaving cream crema da barba
Aspirin aspirina	Soap sapone (m)
Bandages fasciature	Sticking plaster cerotto
Cotton cotone idrofilo	Sunburn cream crema antisolare
Diarrhea/upset-stomach pills pillole anti-coliche	Sunglasses occhiali da sole
Indigestion tablets pillole per l'indigestione	Suntan cream/oil crema/olio solare
Insect repellant insettifugo	Tampons tamponi
Laxative lassativo	Tissues fazzoletti di carta
Sanitary napkins assorbenti igienici	Toothbrush spazzolino da denti
Shampoo shampoo	Toothpaste dentifricio
	Travel sickness pills pillole contro il mal di viaggio

Bra reggiseno	Shirt camicia
Coat cappotto	Shoes scarpe
Dress vestito	Skirt gonna
Jacket giacca	Stockings/tights calze/collants
Pants mutande	Swimsuit costume da bagno (m)
Pullover maglione (m)	Trousers pantaloni

Film pellicola	Postcard cartolina
Letter lettera	Stamp francobollo
Money order vaglia	Telegram telegramma (m)

207

Words and phrases

Driving

Service station stazione di rifornimento (f), distributore (m)
Fill it up. Faccia il pieno, per favore.
Give me . . . . lire worth. Mi dia . . . . lire.
I would like . . . . liters of gasoline. Vorrei . . . . litri di benzina.
Can you check the . . . . ? Può controllare . . . . ?
There is something wrong with the . . . . C'e un difetto nel/nella . . . .

Accelerator acceleratore (m)	Lights fanali, fari, luci
Axle l'asse (m)	Oil olio
Battery batteria	Spares i pezzi di ricambio
Brakes freni	Sparking plugs le candele
Exhaust lo scarico, scappamento	Tires gomme
Fan belt la cinghia del ventilatore	Water acqua
Gear box la scatola del cambio	Windscreen parabrezza (m)

My car won't start. La mia macchina non s'accende.
My car has broken down/I have a flat tire. La macchina è guasta/la gomma è forata.
The engine is overheating. Il motore si scalda.
How long will it take to repair? Quanto tempo ci vorrà per la riparazione?
I need it as soon as possible. Ne ho bisogno il più presto possibile.

Car rental

Where can I rent a car? Dove posso noleggiare una macchina?
Is full/comprehensive insurance included? E' completamente assicurata?
Is it insured for another driver? E' assicurata per un altro guidatore?
Does the price include mileage? Il kilometraggio è compreso?
Unlimited mileage kilometraggio illimitato
Deposit deposito
By what time must I return it? A che ora devo consegnarla?
Can I return it to another depot? Posso riportarla ad un altro deposito?
Is the gas tank full? E' il serbatoio pieno?

Road signs

Accendere le luci in galleria lights on in tunnel	Divieto di sosta no stopping
Autostrada highway	Lavori in corso road repairs ahead
Caduta di massi falling stones	Passaggio a livello level crossing
Casello tollgate	Pedaggio toll road
Dare la precedenza give way	Raccordo anulare ring road
Divieto di accesso, senso vietato no entry	Rallentare slow down
Divieto di parcheggio no parking	Senso unico one-way street
Divieto di sorpasso no overtaking	Tangenziale bypass
	Tenersi in corsia keep in lane
	Uscita autocarri exit (for trucks)

Other methods of transport

Aircraft aeroplano	Train treno
Airport aeroporto	Ticket biglietto
Bus autobus (m)	Ticket office biglietteria
Bus stop fermata	Single andata
Coach corriera	Round trip andata e ritorno
Ferry/boat traghetto	Half fare metà prezzo
Ferry port porto	First/second/economy prima
Hovercraft aliscafo	classe/seconda classe/turistico
Station stazione (f)	Sleeper/couchette cuccetta

When is the next . . . . for . . . . ? Quando parte il prossimo . . . . per . . . . ?
What time does it arrive? A che ora arriva?
What time does the last . . . . for . . . . leave? Quando parte l'ultimo . . . . per . . . . ?
Which platform/pier/gate? Quale binario/molo/uscita?
Is this the . . . . for . . . . ? E' questo il . . . . per . . . . ?
Is it direct? Where does it stop? E' diretto? Dove si ferma?
Do I need to change anywhere? Devo cambiare?
Please tell me where to get off. Mi può dire dove devo scendere.
Take me to . . . . Mi vuol portare a . . . .
Is there a buffet car? C'è un vagone ristorante?

Food and drink

Have you a table for . . . . ? Avete un tavolo per . . . . ?
I want to reserve a table for . . . . at . . . . Vorrei prenotare un tavolo
per . . . . alle . . . .
A quiet table. Un tavolo tranquillo.
A table near the window. Un tavolo vicino alla finestra.
Could we have another table? Potremmo spostarci?
I did not order this. Non ho ordinato questo.
Breakfast/lunch/dinner prima colazione/pranzo/cena
Bring me another . . . . Un altro . . . . per favore.
The bill please. Il conto per favore.
Is service included? Il servizio è incluso?

Hot caldo
Cold freddo
Glass bicchiere (m)
Bottle bottiglia
Half-bottle mezza bottiglia
Beer/lager (draft) birra (alla spina)
Fruit juice succo di frutta
Mineral water acqua minerale
Orangeade/lemonade aranciata/limonata
Carbonated/noncarbonated gassata/non gassata
Red wine vino rosso, vino nero
White wine vino bianco
Rosé wine vino rosé
Vintage di annata
Dry secco

Sweet dolce, amabile
Salt sale (m)
Pepper pepe (m)
Oil olio
Vinegar aceto
Mustard senape (f)
Bread pane (m)
Butter burro
Cheese formaggio
Milk latte (m)
Coffee caffè (m)
Tea tè (m)
Chocolate cioccolato
Sugar zucchero
Steak bistecca
  well-done ben cotto
  medium medio
  rare al sangue

Menu decoder

Abbacchio baby lamb
Acciughe anchovies
Acqua cotta thick bread and vegetable soup with egg
Affettati sliced cold meats
Affumicato smoked
Aglio garlic
Agnello lamb
Agnolotti pasta envelopes
Agro sour
Albicocche apricots
Amaro bitter
Ananas pineapple
Anatra/anitra duck
Anguilla eel
Animelle sweetbreads
Antipasto hors d'oeuvre
Aragosta *langouste*, lobster
Arancia orange
Aringa herring
Arrosto roast meat
Arselle baby clams
Asparagi asparagus
Astaco river crayfish, lobster
Baccalà dried salt cod
Basilico basil
Bianchetti whitebait
Bianco plain, boiled
Bietola Swiss chard
Biscottini di Prato small, hard almond biscuits
Bistecca alla fiorentina grilled T-bone steak
Bollito misto boiled meats
Brace (alla) charcoal-grilled
Braciola chop

Branzino sea bass
Bresaola dried salt beef
Brodetto fish soup
Brodo consommé
Bruschetta garlic bread
Burrida fish stew
Burro (al) (cooked in) butter
Busecca tripe soup
Cacciagione game
Cacciucco fish stew
Calamaretti baby squid
Calamari squid
Calzone half-moon-shaped pizza
Cannelloni stuffed pasta tubes
Capitone large conger eel
Cappelletti stuffed pasta hats
Cappe sante scallops
Capperi capers
Carciofi alla giudia artichokes fried in oil and lemon juice
Carne meat
Carote carrots
Carpa carp
Carpaccio raw lean beef fillet
Carrello (al) from the trolley
Casa (della) of the restaurant
Casalingo, -a homemade
Castagnaccio chestnut cake
Castagne chestnuts
Castrato mutton
Cavolfiore cauliflower
Cavolini di Bruxelles sprouts
Cavolo cabbage
Ceche young eels
Ceci chick peas
Cèfalo gray mullet

Words and phrases

Cenci   fried pastry twists
Cervella   brains
Cervo   venison
Cetriolo   cucumber
Cicoria   chicory
Ciliege   cherries
Cima   cold stuffed veal
Cinghiale   wild boar
Cipolle   onions
Cocomero   watermelon
Coda di bue   oxtail
Coniglio   rabbit
Contorno   vegetable side dish
Controfiletto   sirloin steak
Coppa   cooked pressed neck of
   pork or an ice cream
   sundae
Cosciotto di agnello   leg of lamb
Costata di bue   entrecôte steak
Costolette   cutlets
Cotto   cooked
Cozze   mussels
Crema   custard, cream soup
Crespolini   savory pancakes
Crostacei   shellfish
Crostini   small savory toasts
Crudo   raw
Dentice   species of fish like
   sea bream
Diavola (alla)   in a spicy sauce
Dolci   desserts, sweets
Espresso   small black coffee
Fagiano   pheasant
Fagioli all'uccelletto   beans with
   tomatoes and garlic
Fagiolini   French beans
Faraona   guinea hen
Farcito   stuffed
Fatto in casa   homemade
Fave   fava beans
Fegatini   chicken livers
Fegato   liver
Ferri (ai)   grilled
Fesa di vitello   leg of veal
Fettina   slice
Fettuccine   thin flat pasta
Fettunta   garlic bread
Fichi   figs
Filetto   fillet
Finocchio   fennel
Finocchiona   fennel-flavored
   salami
Focaccia   dimpled savory
   bread
Formaggio   cheese
Forno (al)   cooked in the oven
Fragole   strawberries
Fresco   fresh
Frittata   omelet
Frittelle   fritters
Fritto   fried
Frutta   fruit
Frutti di mare   shellfish
Fungi   mushrooms
Gamberetti   shrimps
Gamberi   big prawns
Gelato   ice cream
Giorno (del)   of the day
Girarrosto (al)   spit-roasted

Girello   rump of beef
Gnocchi   small pasta dumplings
Grana   Parmesan cheese
Granchio   crab
Granita   water ice
Graticola (alla)   grilled
Griglia (alla)   grilled
Indivia   endive
Insalata   salad
Involtini   skewered veal and ham
Lamponi   raspberries
Lampreda   lamprey
Lasagne   baked flat pasta
Lenticchie   lentils
Lepre   hare
Lesso   boiled (meat)
Limone   lemon
Lingua di bue   ox tongue
Lombata. -ina   loin, loin chop
Lonza   cured fillet of pork
Luccio   pike
Lumache   snails
Macedonia di frutta   fruit salad
Magro   lean
Maiale   pork
Mandorle   almonds
Manzo   beef
Marmellata   jam
Medaglioni   rounds of meat
Mela   apple
Melagrana   pomegranate
Melanzane   eggplants
Melone   melon
Merlano   whiting
Merluzzo   cod
Miele   honey
Minestra   soup
Minestrone   vegetable soup
Misto   mixed
Mostarda   pickle
Muscolo alla fiorentina   beef
   casserole with beans
Nasello   hake
Naturale (al)   plain
Nocciole   hazelnuts
Noce di vitello   veal top round
Noci   nuts
Nodino di vitello   veal chop
Nostrale, nostrano   local
Oca   goose
Ombrina   black umber
Orata   gilthead bream
Osso buco   veal knuckle
Ostriche   oysters
Paglia e fieno   green and white
   tagliatelle
Paillard   thin grilled steak
Palombo   dogfish
Panforte di Siena   hard cake with
   honey, fruit and almonds
Panino imbottito   roll
Panna   cream
Panzanella   salad of soaked bread
   and fresh vegetables
Pappa al pomodoro   thick
   tomato-and-bread soup
Pappardelle   long flat pasta
Parmigiano-Reggiano   Parmesan
Passato   purée

210

Words and phrases

Pasta e fagioli bean-and-pasta soup
Pasticcio layered pasta pie
Pasto meal
Patate potatoes
Pecorino hard ewe's-milk cheese
Penne all'arrabbiata short pasta tubes with a fiery sauce
Peperoni sweet peppers
Pera pear
Pernice partridge
Pesca peach
Pesce fish
Pesce persico perch
Pesce San Pietro John Dory
Pesce spada swordfish
Pesciolini small fry
Pesto green basil sauce
Petto di pollo chicken breast
Pezzo piece
Piacere according to taste
Piatto del giorno today's dish
Piccante spicy, piquant
Piccata thin scallop
Piccione pigeon
Pinzimonio oily vegetable dip
Piselli peas
Polenta corn pudding
Pollame poultry
Pollo chicken
Polpette meat balls
Polpettone meat loaf
Polpo octopus
Pomodoro tomato
Pompelmo grapefruit
Porchetta roast suckling pig
Prezzemolo parsley
Primizie spring vegetables
Prosciutto ham
Prugne plums
Quaglie quails
Radicchio red bitter lettuce
Ragù meat-and-tomato sauce
Rane frogs
Ravanelli radishes
Ravioli stuffed pasta squares
Razza skate
Ribollita thick vegetable soup
Ricci sea urchins
Ricciarelli almond biscuits
Ricotta cheese – similar to cottage cheese
Rigatoni ridged pasta tubes
Ripieno stuffed
Risi e bisi pea-and-rice soup
Riso rice
Risotto savory rice dish
Rognoni kidneys
Rombo liscio brill
Rombo maggiore turbot
Rosmarino rosemary
Rospo angler
Salsa (verde) (green) sauce
Salsiccia sausage
Saltimbocca alla romana veal scallops with ham and sage
Salvia sage
Sarde sardines

Scaloppine scallops
Scampi Dublin bay prawns
Scelta (a) of your choice
Schiacciata alla fiorentina vanilla sponge cake
Scottadito grilled lamb cutlets
Selvaggina game, venison
Semifreddo frozen dessert
Semplice plain
Seppie cuttlefish
Sgombro mackerel
Sogliola sole
Sottaceti pickled vegetables
Spaghetti
  all'amatriciana spaghetti with bacon, tomatoes
  alla bolognese with ragù
  alla carbonara with bacon, eggs
  alla napoletana with tomato
Spezzatino meat stew
Spiedini skewers, kebabs
Spiedo (allo) on the spit
Spigola sea bass
Spinaci spinach
Squadro monkfish
Stagionato hung, well-aged
Stagione (di) in season
Stoccafisso stockfish
Stracciatella clear egg soup
Stracotto beef in red wine
Stufato braised, stew(ed)
Sugo sauce
Supplì rice croquettes
Susina plum
Tacchino turkey
Tagliatelle thin flat pasta
Tartufi truffles
Tegame (al) fried or baked
Telline cockles
Timballo savory pasta pie
Tinca tench
Tonno tuna
Tordi thrushes
Torta flan, tart
Tortellini small stuffed pasta
Tost toasted sandwich
Totano squid
Tramezzino sandwich
Trancia slice
Trenette flat, thinnish pasta
Trifolato fried in garlic
Triglia red mullet
Trippa tripe
Trota trout
Uccelletti grilled beef on skewers
Umido (in) stewed
Uova eggs
Uva grapes
Verdure green vegetables
Vitello veal
Vongole clams
Zabaglione egg-yolks-and-Marsala whip
Zucca marrow
Zuccotto ice cream liqueur cake
Zuppa soup
Zuppa inglese trifle

211

GLOSSARY

Glossary of art and architecture

Aedicule Niche framed by columns

Ambo Early form of pulpit

Architrave A supporting beam above a column

Archivolt Continuous moulding around a door or window

Atrium Central room or court of pre-Christian house; forecourt of early Christian church

Baldacchino Canopy, usually over altar, throne, etc.

Basilica Rectangular Roman civic hall; early Christian church of similar structure

Bottega An artist's workshop

Campanile Bell tower

Camposanto Cemetery

Caryatid Carved female figure used as column

Chiaroscuro (Heightened) light and shade effects in painting

Ciborium Altar canopy; casket for the Host

Crossing Space in church at intersection of chancel, nave and transepts

Diptych Work of art on two hinged panels

Ex-voto Work of art offered in fulfilment of a vow

Fresco Technique of painting onto wet plaster on a wall

Herm Sculpted male nude or bust on tapered pillar

Intarsia Inlay of wood

Loggia Gallery or balcony open on at least one side

Lunette Semicircular surface or panel, often painted or carved

Misericord Ledge or bracket projecting from pew or stall

Ogival Of a double-curved line, both concave and convex

Piano nobile Main floor of house, usually raised

Pietà Representation of the Virgin lamenting over the dead Christ

Pietradura Mosaic of semiprecious stone

Predella One or more small paintings attached to the bottom of an altarpiece

Putto The plump, naked child, often winged, in works of art

Scagliola Plaster-work polished to resemble marble

Sgraffiti Designs scratched into glaze to reveal base colour

Sinopia Preparatory drawing made beneath a fresco

Stucco Light, reinforced plaster

Tondo Circular painting or sculpture

Transept Transverse arms of a cruciform church

Tribune Raised area of gallery in a church; the apse of a basilica

Triptych Work of art on three hinged panels

Clothing sizes

When shops give clothing sizes in centimetres, use the following conversion scale to determine the correct size

12 in	16	20	24	28	32	36	40	44	48
30 cm	40	50	60	70	80	90	100	110	120

When standardized codes are used, although these may be found to vary considerably, the following provides a useful guide.

Women's clothing sizes

UK/US sizes	8/6	10/8	12/10	14/12	16/14	18/16
Italian sizes	36	38	40	42	44	46
Bust in/cm	31/80	32/81	34/86	36/91	38/97	40/102

Men's clothing sizes

European code (suits)	44	46	48	50	52	54	56
Chest in/cm	34/86	36/91	38/97	40/102	42/107	44/112	46/117
Collar in/cm	13½/34	14/36	14½/37	15/38	15½/39	16/41	16½/42
Waist in/cm	28/71	30/76	32/81	34/86	36/91	38/97	40/102
Inside leg in/cm	28/71	29/74	30/76	31/79	32/81	33/84	34/86

Men's and women's shoe sizes

UK/US sizes	3/4½	4/5½	5/6½	6/7½	7/8½	8/9½	9/10½	10/11½	11/12½
European	36	37	38	39	40	41	42	43	44

Index and gazetteer

The Florence index contains only items particular to Florence, arranged by category. Other categories, such as artists' names, are in the general index, as are all places outside Florence. Sights or places of interest are indexed individually in the general index, rather than under the town or city where they are found, because entries in the text are themselves arranged alphabetically by town. Hotels, restaurants, etc. are not indexed because they too are easily located within A – Z entries.

Page numbers in bold indicate the main entry.

Florence index

Florence gazetteer

Museums

Anthropological, 47, Map 5C5
Antica Casa Fiorentina, 54, Map 4D3
Archeological, 47–8, Map 3B–C5
Argenti, 65, 67, Map 4F2
Bardini, 49, Map 5F5
Bargello, 45, 49–51, 52, 63, Map 5C–D5
Botanical, 52, Map 3B4
Casa Buonarroti, 61, 77, 98, Map 5C5
Castagno, 71–2, Map 3B4
Cathedral, 55, 56, 57–8, Map 5C5
Coach, 68, Map 4F2
Davanzati, 54, Map 4D3
Firenze com'era, 58, 64, Map 5C5
Fra Angelico, 79–80, Map 3B4
Horne, 59, Map 5D5
Michelangelo, 61, 77, 98, Map 5C5
Opera del Duomo, 55, 56, 57–8, 87, Map 5C5
Opificio delle Pietredure, 78, Map 5A5
Pitti, 67, Map 4F2
Porcelain, 52, Map 4F3
S. Croce, 63, 75, Map 5D6
S. Marco, 79–80, Map 3B4
Science, 87–8, Map 3D4
La Specola, 99, Map 4F2
Stibbert, 92, Map 7C4
Strozzi, 92, Map 7D5
Topographical, 58, 64, Map 5C5
Zoological, 99, Map 4F2

Palaces

Altoviti, 103
Antella, 73
Antinori, 101, Map 4C3
Arte della Lana, 63
Barbolani di Montauto, 102
Bartolini-Salimbeni, 86, 101
Castellani, 87
Corsi, Map 4C3
Corsini, 81, Map 4C2
Coverelli, 101
Davanzati, 54, 101, Map 4D3
Giugni, 102
Gondi, 76, 89, 103, Map 5D4
Grifoni, 70, 102
Guadagni, 59, 85, Map 4E2
Guicciardini, 76, Map 4D2
Horne (Corsi), 59, 73, Map 4C3
Lanfredini, 101
Matteucci Ramirez di Montalvo, 103
Medici Riccardi, 24, 60–1, 64, 89, 90, 95, 102, Map 5B4
Niccolini, 70, 102
Nonfinito, 47, 103
Oddo Altoviti, 72
Pandolfini, 86, 102
Parte Guelfa, 100, Map 4D3
Pitti, 52, 60, 62, 64–8, 75, 89, 99, Map 4F2
Podestà, 50

Pucci, 70, 102, Map 5B4
Riccardi Manelli, 70
Rosselli del Turco, 72
Rucellai, 24, 69, 101, 160, 185, Map 4C2
Serristori-Cocchi, 73, Map 5F6
Signoria, 23, 51, 60, 64, 83, 87, 88–91, Map 5D4
Strozzi, 92, 101, Map 4C3
Taddei, 102
Torrigiani, 99, Map 5E4
Uguccioni, 89, 91
Vecchio, *see* Signoria
Vitali, 103

Refectories

Ognissanti, 62, 80
S. Apollonia, 71, 72
S. Salvi, 84, 85, 87, 98
S. Spirito, 85

Towers

Castegna, 100
Gallo, 47, 64
Montauto, 51
S. Niccolò, 64, 84
Petraia, 64
Signoria, 49, 88, 89, 90

Villas

Bellosguardo, 51
Belvedere al Saracino, 51
La Gallina, 47
Il Gioiello, 47
Ombrellino, 51
La Pietra, 92
Stibbert, 92

Florence gazetteer of street names

A

Lung. Acciaioli, Map 2D3
V.d. Acqua, Map 5D5
V.d. Agli, Map 4C3
V.d. Agnolo, Map 2C–D5
V. S. Agostino, Map 4E1
Borgo d. Albizi, Map 4D5
V. Aleardo Aleardi, Map 2D2
V.d. Alfani, 78, Map 4A–B5
V.d. Alloro, Map 4B3
Lung. Amerigo Vespucci, Map 3C1–2
V.d. Amorino, Map 4B3
V.d. Anguillara, Map 5D5
V.d. Anselmi, Map 4C3
V. Antonio Gramsci, Map 3C6
Arcetri, 47, 164, Map 7E4

Lung. Archibusieri, Map 4D3–4
V.d. Ardiglione, 104, Map 2D2
V.d. Ariento, Map 4A3
Arno, 12, 62, 64, 68, 85, 86, 93, 99
V. Arte d. Lana, 62, 63, Map 4D3
V.d. Artisti, Map 2B5–6
V.d. Avelli, Map 4B2

B

V.d. Banchi, Map 4B2–3
V.d. Barbadori, Map 4E3
V.d. Bardi, 84, Map 5E4
V.d. Bartolomeo, Map 3A5
V.d. Bellosguardo, Map 2D1–2

V. Belfiore, Map 2B2
V.d. Belle Donne, Map 4B2–3
Bellosguardo, 51, 76, Map 6F3
V.d. Belvedere, Map 3E4
V.d. Benci, 59, Map 5D–E5
V. Benedetta, Map 4B1
V. Benedetto Marcello, Map 2B1
V.d. Bentaccordi, Map 5D5
V. Bolognese, 92, Map 7C4
Borgognissanti, Map 4C1
V.d. Brache, Map 5D5
Pza. Brunelleschi, Map 4C3
V. Bufalini, Map 55
V.d. Burella, Map 5D5

Florence gazetteer

General index

General index

General index

220

General index

General index

FLORENCE AND TUSCANY

1

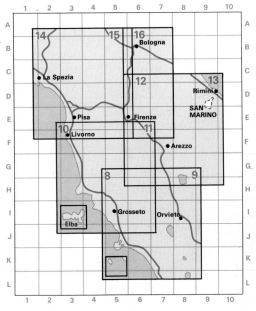

LEGEND

Area Maps

0   5   10   15   20 Km

=O= Superhighway (with access point)
=== Main Road-Four Lane Highway
Other Main Road
Secondary Road
Minor Road
Scenic Route
SS73 Road Number
--- Ferry
Railway
✈ Airport
✛ Airfield
International Boundary
Province Boundary
⌂ Abbey, monastery
⁙ Ancient site, ruin
♜ Castle
⚓ Good Beach
12 Adjoining Page No.

City Maps

Major Place of Interest
Other Important Building
Built-up Area
Park
†† Cemetery
† † Named church, church
✡ Synagogue
✚ Hospital
i Information Office
⊠ Post Office
✋ Police Station
🕳 Parking Lot
→ One Way Street

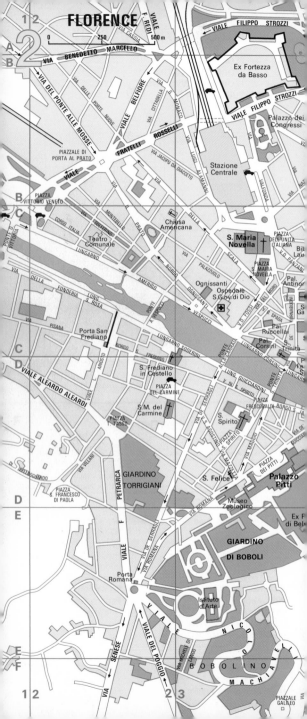

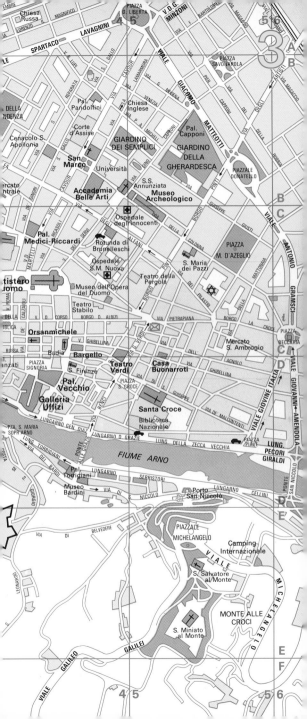

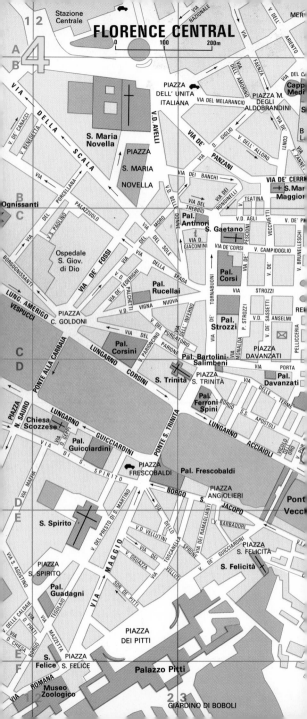

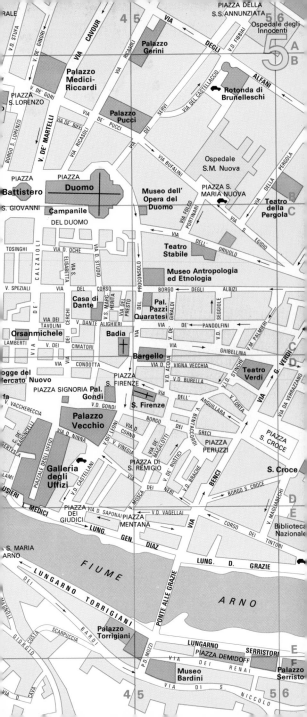

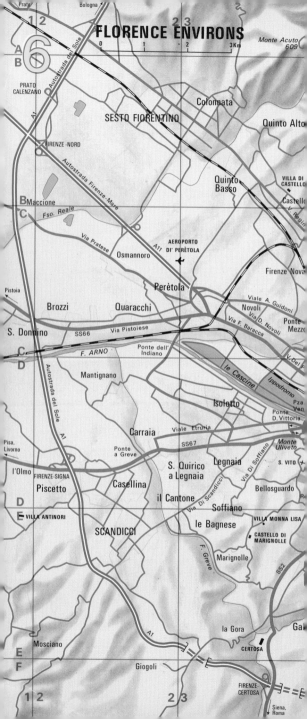

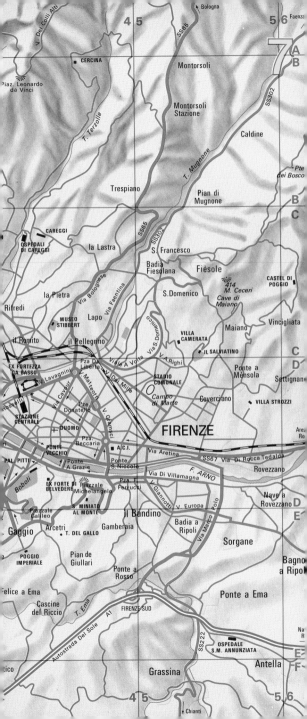

TOSCANA

Le Cornate
1060
Chiusdino
11
S. GALGANO
Murlo
AB. DI
M. OLIVE
MAGGIO
Montieri
Monticiano
Buoncon

M. Quoio
647
M. Arsenti
561

SS13
Casale
di Pari
Montalcino
S. Quiri
d' Orci

Massa
Marittima
Roccastrada
Ba
Vig

10
Civitella
Marittima
S. ANTIMO

Gavorano

SS1
Batignano
Campagnatico
Castel
del Piano

NECROPOLI
ETRUSCA
Arcidosso
Pia

Tirli
Cinigiano

Vetulonia
ROVINE DI
ROSELLE
M. Labbro
1193

Roselle
Roccalbegna

GROSSETO
Istia d' Ombrone
SS322
SS323

Marina di
Grosseto
Semproniano

Principina
a Mare
M. Bottigli
319
Scansano
ROVINE
ETRUSCHE
Pitig

Alberese
Saturnia

M. Cornuto
246

S. RABANO
Magliano
in Toscana
Montemerano
SS322

10
Fonteblanda
S. BRUZIO
Manciano

Talamone
SS74
M. Cavallo
234

Porto
S. Stefano
Capalbio
PONTE DELLA
ABBADIA

Orbetello

Monte
Argentario
COSA
RUDERI
Ansedonia
TAGLIATA ETRUSCA
VULC

Port' Ercole
L. di Burano
Montalto
di Castro

I. DEL GIGLIO

MARE

4 5
J
K

Campese
Giglio Castello
K
Giglio Porto

I. del Giglio

TIRRENO

I. GIANNUTRI

I. di Giannutri
Villa
Romana
CLE

4 5

6

SARDIN

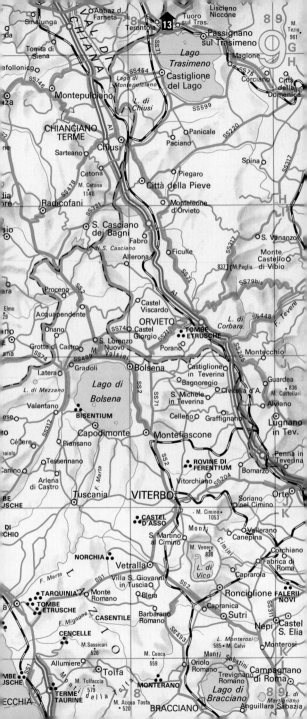

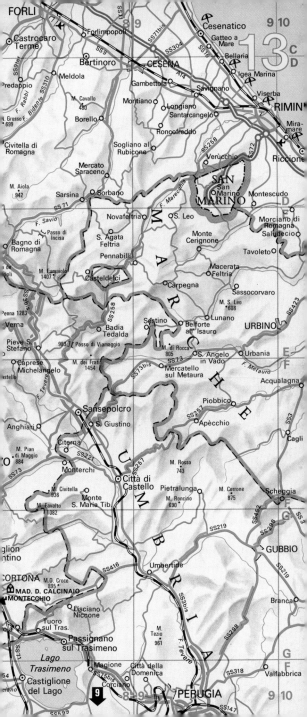

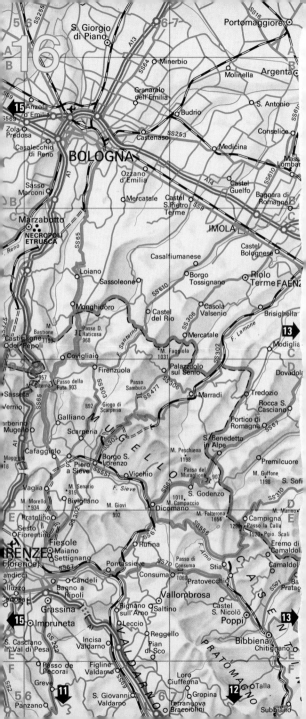